JEROME HAMER, O.P.

# karl barth

*Translated by Dominic M. Maruca, S.J.*

THE NEWMAN PRESS · WESTMINSTER, MARYLAND
1962

This translation was made from *Karl Barth, L'Occasionalisme théologique de Karl Barth,* published by Desclée de Brouwer, Paris, France, in 1949.

*Imprimi Potest:* WILLIAM J. MALONEY

*Nihil Obstat:*    EDWARD A. CERNY, S.S., S.T.D.
               *Censor Librorum*

*Imprimatur:*    LAWRENCE J. SHEHAN, D.D.
               *Archbishop of Baltimore*

April 21, 1962

The *nihil obstat* and *imprimatur* are official declarations that a book or pamphlet is free of doctrinal and moral error. No implication is contained therein that those who have granted the *nihil obstat* and *imprimatur* agree with the opinions expressed.

# foreword

I F THE influence of Karl Barth seems to have declined somewhat in Protestant Germany since the last war, the interest shown in him among French circles has definitely increased.

Practically unknown in France until 1933, today his thought distinctly characterizes a group of Protestant thinkers of ever-increasing importance. In some measure he even attracts the attention of Catholic thinkers. And yet, no one familiar with dialectical theology can fail to notice the superficiality of the information on a subject that arouses such keen interest. Diametrically opposed theories are blandly combined under Karl Barth's name. Such confusion and lack of precision can be attributed both to the rarity of works on Karl Barth and to the difficulty of his language, style, and manner of exposition.

A comprehensive work on Karl Barth, therefore, will fill a real need. We have limited ourselves, however, to his dogmatic method, because we are of the opinion that therein lies the key to his entire system. Up to the present, his method has received only partial treatment. There is need for a treatment which will approach the question in its entire scope and make use of the Swiss theologian's latest works.—Among the monographs devoted to particular aspects of the subject, we may mention the works of Père L. Malevez, and the excellent theses of J. Fehr and J. C. Groot, both devoted to the problem of revelation.[1] In our opinion, from the Catholic viewpoint, few other works can be compared with these.

[1] We must add to this list the name of G. Rabeau, whose bulletins on contemporary Protestant theology contain excellent studies on the works of Karl Barth. We are equally indebted to Père H. U. von Balthasar for several critical analyses of major Barthian themes.

We have followed a method of exposition which is simultaneously critical and historical. We have never separated the critique from the exposition itself. The exposition has been developed so as to elucidate both the merits and the insufficiencies of the system under consideration. Furthermore, a theologian such as Karl Barth can be understood only from within an entire context. As a Protestant theologian, Karl Barth still retains some connection with the reformers, with whose thought he constantly compares his own. As a contemporary thinker, he is directly or indirectly dependent on the currents of thought which have permeated German culture since the time of Kant. To comprehend a doctrine so different from our own, it seemed advisable to compare Barth's thought with the systems upon which it depends, and with those against which it is reacting.

If someone were to request a brief definition of Barth's method, we would characterize it as a *theological occasionalism*. Perhaps some will be astonished to see us summarize his basic orientation by this formula. Does not this term pertain more to sacramentology than to supernatural knowledge? Since revelation, according to Barth, is rather a force than an enrichment of the intelligence, it seems to us that *theological occasionalism* expresses adequately a theory which reduces Scripture, limited in its claim to contain divine truth, to a simple appeal to the intervention of that mysterious energy which Barth designates by the expression *Word of God*.

*Le Sarte-Huy, May 10, 1949*

# contents

PART ONE

*The Divine Criterion of Dogmatics:*
*The Word of God*

PART TWO

*The Human and Provisional Criterion of*
*Dogmatics: The Bible*

# List of Abbreviations

## THE WRITINGS OF KARL BARTH

CD ........ *Die Lehre vom Worte Gottes. Prolegomena zur christlichen Dogmatik, 1927.*

DG ....... *Dogmatik im Grundriss, 1947.*

GG ....... *Gotteserkenntnis und Gottesdienst, 1938.*

KD ....... *Kirchliche Dogmatik, 1932 ff.*

KK ....... *Die Kirche und die Kirchen, 1935.*

PD ........ *Parole de Dieu et parole humaine, 1933.*

RB(1919) .. *Römerbrief, First Edition, 1919.*

RB ........ *Römerbrief, Seventh reprinting of revised edition, 1940.*

SK ........ *Die Schrift und die Kirche, 1947.*

TK ....... *Die Theologie und die Kirche, 1928.*

## PERIODICALS

ChW ...... *Christliche Welt.*

ETL ...... *Ephemerides Theologicae Louvanienses.*

RHPR .... *Revue d'histoire et de philosophie religieuses.*

RSPT ..... *Revue des sciences philosophiques et théologiques.*

RSR ...... *Recherches de science religieuse.*

RTP ...... *Revue de théologie et de philosophie.*

ThLZ ..... *Theologische Literaturzeitung.*

## USEFUL REFERENCE WORKS

CR ........ *Corpus reformatorum*

DTC ...... *Dictionnaire de théologie catholique*

EA ........ M. LUTHER, *Exegetica opera latina.*

————, *Sämtliche Werke.*

ONE ...... *Origine et nature de l'Église.*

PRE ...... *Realencyclopädie f. protestantische Theologie.*

R ........ W. RUTTENBECK, *Soeren Kierkegaard.*

RGG ...... *Die Religion in Geschichte u. Gegenwart.*

SW ....... G. W. F. HEGEL, *Sämtliche Werke.*

WA ....... M. LUTHER, *Werke* (Weimar edit.).

# introduction
## to the american edition

*A Reflective Glance and Precisions*

Towards a Program of "Coherent Christology."

T HIS WORK is the translation of a study of the dogmatic method of Karl Barth first published in 1949. We have thought it wise that nothing be added to or excised from the original text. Only the introduction is new, but we accord it great importance. I must here warmly thank the group of Jesuit scholastics who have devoted their talents and leisure to translate this work and this new introduction.

I have been informed that no one reads introductions nowadays. This is unfortunate for this introduction is absolutely *indispensable* in reading this book. It is the key to the understanding of this work. A busy reader can eventually skip other parts of the book, but not this section.

This study was published in 1949. But it was already completed in March of 1948. During the thirteen years since its first appearance, many events have occurred. The situation is not the same. First, Karl Barth has continued to teach and to write; during this interval he has published many important works. Further, Catholic theologians have prepared critical studies of value about this author. I will mention only three of these: von Balthasar, Bouillard, and Küng. Finally, I myself have been able to benefit from critical reviews and many comments on my work. Also, after thirteen years, I can see things with more objectivity and in a broader perspective. The reader of this English translation has a right to know how I react to all this at the time when, at the insistence of an American friend, I consent to this publication. Let us first consider the works of the Catholic theologians whom I just cited.

## Presentation and Interpretation of the Theology of Barth by H. U. von Balthasar.

A prolonged contact with the work of Barth and a diligent personal acquaintance with Karl Barth have permitted Hans Urs von Balthasar to write an interesting work.[1] The accord which Karl Barth himself manifested to him shows that the author could give to this complex thought an expression acceptable to the man who is its originator.[2] We do not find ourselves in the presence of an introduction to the thought of the Protestant theologian under the form of a résumé of his principal positions. It is a broad confrontation of the Barthian synthesis and of Catholic doctrine on certain essential points. The author makes analogy and Christology the center of this comparative study.[3] In the present pages our only objective will be to summarize certain important sections of the author's book. What are the stages in the development of Karl Barth's thought? Those who know the thought of Karl Barth only superficially could be tempted to define his thought as the categorical rejection of analogy. Nothing is less true. Von Balthasar shows us the reality which is quite the contrary of this general and too hasty impression. In his eyes, the work of Karl Barth is a slow evolution towards a complete idea of analogy. In this progress we must discern three principal stages: a period of dialectic which is that of the first two editions of *Römerbrief* (1919 and 1922); *The Orientation Towards Analogy,* whose progress one can follow in *Die christliche Dogmatik in Entwurf* (1927); and finally,

---

[1] *Karl Barth, Darstellung und Deutung seiner Theologie* (Olten and Cologne: Editions Jakob Hegner, 1951).
[2] Kirchliche Dogmatik, vol. IV, book I, p. 858.
[3] *Karl Barth, Darstellung und Deutung,* etc., pp. 52–54.

*Vollgestalt der Analogie,* which we find expressed in a more and more precise fashion in the different volumes of *Kirchliche Dogmatik* (first volume, 1932). The dialectic of the first period has a triple function: it plays a corrective role with respect to an already existing thought; it indicates the way to follow beyond itself, and finally it protects the Word of God against the enterprises of a human thought which attempt to treat God as a pure object. Nevertheless, dialectic cannot be the whole of a theology. We cannot confuse method and content. This triple role which manifests a very pure intention can be exercised only at the price of introducing a new denser element: analogy.[4]

The substitution of analogy for the principle of dialectic does not occur abruptly. It cannot be grasped in a determined text; it is realized progressively and insensibly in the first volumes of the *Kirchliche Dogmatik,* and can be considered as finished in the third volume (*Die Lehre von Gott,* 1940) and in the works which are its contemporaries (*Credo,* 1935; *Gotteserkenntnis und Gottesdienst,* 1938). The second volume (1938) examines its principles without taking the occasion to develop them. The doctrine of analogy will unfold in an ever more manifest fashion from volume to volume in such a way as to become the central theme of the treatises devoted to creation (1945), to man (1948), and to predestination (1950). Whoever does not take this development into account will search in vain in the first volume of *Kirchliche Dogmatik* (1932) for a precise formulation of this doctrine.[5]

The ever more exigent recourse to analogy is only the corresponding member of a parallel movement of Christology. Analogy and Christology are intimately linked in the work of Karl Barth. It is no surprise, then, that we will see the Christological development correspond with the stages of the development of analogy. Christology is henceforth the organizing principle of the thought of Barth in *Kirchliche Dogmatik.* The second volume (1938) is his first undertaking in the still provisory exposition of the doctrine of Christ, true God and true Man. Beginning with the third volume (1940), it unfolds systematically in the ensemble of his thought.[6]

If, therefore, analogy finally evinces dialectic only in order to

---

4 *Ibid.,* pp. 79–93.
5 *Ibid.,* pp. 116–117.
6 *Ibid.,* pp. 124–125.

safeguard its profound intention, it is because, on the other hand, Christology replaces the Word of God as the axis of theology. In the *Kirchliche Dogmatik* there is progressively, though imperceptibly, effected the substitution of the idea of Jesus Christ, God and Man, for the concept of the Word of God. The expression *Wort Gottes* can designate only one of the aspects of the nature and content of revelation. " 'Word' is only one of the names of the Son. The single adequate term is precisely that of 'Son.' It is in him that God decided to gather up all reality into heaven as upon earth." [7]

The miracle of the Incarnation is thus the foundation and justification of analogy. As Christ is the measure of all things, there can therefore no longer be any opposition between God and the world. The reconciliation is effected in the person of Jesus Christ in the existence of two natures in one person. Every incompatibility is resolved in this profound and mysterious compatibility of the created and uncreated.[8]

What are the results of this confrontation? The very importance of the book of H. von Balthasar forces us to follow its conclusions step by step.[9] We will permit ourselves simply in summing them up to enumerate them in a continuous fashion for the convenience of our readers.

1. At the end of an inquiry, whose unique concern was the questions concerning nature and grace, von Balthasar thinks that there is a real movement of convergence between the positions of Karl Barth and those of an important group of Catholic theologians. Although real, the differences which remain are not of such a nature as to justify a rupture on the ecclesiastical level. They are no more important than those which separate Barth from Emil Brunner in the bosom of Protestantism, or those which opposing schools of Catholic theology hold on different points on the doctrine of grace and Christology.

2. This conclusion, whose significance readily can be perceived, is valid only for the questions considered in the section on *De Deo Creante, Elevante, Redemente*. It does not apply to the motives

---

[7] *Ibid.*, p. 124.
[8] *Ibid.*, p. 124.
[9] For the general conclusions, see *ibid.*, pp. 389–393.

for separation which can be found in a second section, that on *De Ecclesia* and *De Sacramentis.*

3. In situating these fundamental choices in the treatises of the first division, Karl Barth has reversed the movement of the Reformation which, starting out from the concrete life of the Church and its sacramental practice, first of all elaborated a theology of the Church and of the sacraments, whose echoes resounded only later in the treatises which occupy the first place in Karl Barth. Barth, from this point on, sees himself obliged to resume the respective positions of Protestantism and Catholicism in the context of a relationship between nature and grace. Whence the antinomic opposition of *analogia entis* and *analogia fidei.* Is this opposition real? Von Balthasar does not think so. It was possible only at the price of an unjust simplification of the Catholic position. Was not his adversary, whom Barth attacks with such vigor, previously and completely constructed by Barth himself? This intuition will be developed by Henri Bouillard, as we shall see below.

The analogy of faith in which Karl Barth condenses his Christocentrism implicitly contains an analogy of being. On the other hand the Christocentrism of many Catholic theologians envisages the analogy of being in the exclusive framework of the analogy of faith. If the points of departure are different, the convergence is no less real.

4. The exigencies of the Church are in fact reconcilable with the principle lines of the thought of Karl Barth in the circumscribed domains stated above. In the eyes of the Church, what is essential is the existence of an order of nature and reason whose authenticity and relative independence with respect to the order of grace are assured, as well as the relative priority of the first order over the second. These exigencies are satisfied by the Catholic theologians who hold that grace is the motive and the end of creation, for they affirm at the same time that reason maintains its proper structure and keeps its own laws. The fact that the second Adam is the end and motive of the first does not prevent the latter from having a determined nature.

This twofold fundamental aspect of a unique concrete problem permits us, on the one hand, to envisage the exercise of apologetics and the *praeambula fidei,* and on the other hand, to admit that

xvi                                          *Introduction to the*

reason is reason only in the economy of faith. The apologetic movement towards faith is possible in fact only within the order of grace in the economy of the given revelation. Let us sum up this theological position in the following way: Absolute priority of grace and revelation, relative priority of nature and its possibilities. Are we very far from what Barth understands in his own theological vocabulary by external and internal motive?

Von Balthasar felt necessitated to make precise his general conclusions upon what concerns the Church: [10]

5. As the ecclesiology of Karl Barth is principally founded on the positions that we have summed up, and as, moreover, the latter are no longer of such a nature as to justify a rupture on the level of ecclesiological communion, it appears clearly that the Barthian doctrine of the Church can today no longer remain what it was in the decade from 1920 to 1930. At that time his ecclesiology was conditioned by the rejection of all continuity of every permanent conditioning. At this stage, it corresponded, moreover, very exactly to a doctrine of the event identified with the vertical eruption of the Word of God. Today this form of actualism is abandoned by Karl Barth for whom, henceforth, the Incarnation is the event par excellence. As Christology and Ecclesiology correspond, the horizontal continuity which the Incarnation postulates must have its echo in a new Ecclesiology.

6. In the eyes of Karl Barth, Catholic doctrine is essentially a position of synthesis realizing once and for all the unity of divine nature and created nature. The human, considered as the complement of the divine, would thus have in itself its own consistence and could, henceforth, claim the right of putting itself in the service of the divine and even of taking the initiative in this service. All of this is what Karl Barth groups under the general rubric of *analogia entis:* synthesis of the divine and human realized by the power and the initiative of the creature.

But nothing is less exact. Is it not the contrary which happens? It is not the divine which happens in the human. On the contrary, the created order is assumed by the free Will of God who disposes of it according to His wishes. Nature and its limitations are claimed by the free initiative of Christ. The way in which grace

[10] *Ibid.,* pp. 393–397, which concerns the Church.

is accorded to nature is one of the clearest manifestations of this doctrine. Never is nature, no matter how perfect it may be, the measure of grace (Rom. XII:3). The seed of nature becomes fruitful in grace only after passing through the cross and through death. In the order of grace, there is no fruitfulness which would simply be the outgrowth of an activity or of a perfection of nature. It is only when it has entered into the vine that the branch becomes fruitful.

Here in this introduction we are not *ex professo* engaging in dialogue with von Balthasar. The pages that follow will permit us to establish indirectly our degree of accord and our points of divergence with certain of the suggestive theses advanced by the author. The important book of Henri Bouillard owes much to the work of von Balthasar; in commenting on it, and in giving our personal appreciation of it, we will often touch on points that have already been proposed a first time by the Swiss theologian.

One word, however, before going further. In 1949 von Balthasar wrote that the Ecclesiology of Barth would have to take another direction in the years to come in order to be faithful to the new Christological orientation of his whole thought. Twelve years have gone by. Nothing permits us to suppose that Karl Barth has profoundly modified his Ecclesiology. Certainly there is in Barth a reestablishment of the primacy of the Christian community. This is a very precise reaction against Protestant individualism. This reaction is even of such a nature as to surprise certain Catholic readers. The 'event-happening (*évènementiel*) character' of the Church remains entire. If Barth rejects all the constitutions of the Church in order to keep only its congregationalist structure, it is because the organization of the Christian community has density only in immediate and exclusive dependence upon an event. But this thesis of Barth is not independent of the ensemble of his thought; *it is an immediate consequence of his theological anthropology.*

## The Theses of Henri Bouillard on Karl Barth.

The presentation of the doctorate to Fr. Henri Bouillard, S.J., was a notable intellectual event. At the Sorbonne on Saturday,

June 16, 1956, the Quinet Auditorium was filled. Catholics, Protestants, and unbelievers were assembled there. In the first row Karl Barth assisted as an interested but mute witness to a great debate which centered upon him. The jury of this unusual defense comprised Jean Wahl, Henri Gouhier, Oscar Cullmann, Paul Vignaux, and Henri Marrou.

According to the norms of the Sorbonne, Henri Bouillard presented two theses. The secondary thesis bore the title, *Karl Barth. Genesis and Evolution of Dialectical Theology.* The principal thesis was entitled, *Karl Barth. Word of God and Human Existence.*[11] A well-informed, consummate historian, an attentive critic and a benevolent examiner, Henri Bouillard offers us a book of religious philosophy which does honor to Catholic science, an indispensable instrument of our study.

Despite its interest, we will not consider the secondary thesis. Let us simply point out that it retraces the story of Karl Barth, and that of a small number of friends gathered around him in the first years. In the progressive affirmation of the personal thought of Barth, Henri Bouillard discerns three periods: the theology of crisis, the theology of the Word of God, and coherent Christology.[12]

In the principal thesis, in the form of a dialogue with the thought of Barth, Bouillard takes up the main problems which concern the relationship of nature and of grace. Barth is here the partner in an examination in common of the major problems situated within the confines of theology and philosophy. His radical thought "obliges us to a radical reflection." [13]

In Jesus Christ, God challenges man. One volume is devoted to the work of God. The doctrines of the Reconciliation and Predestination of creation and of man are successively considered. In this

[11] These two theses appeared in Paris, in 1957, in the series entitled *Théologie.* In this series they are numbered 38 and 39 respectively. The supplementary thesis is offered as the introduction to the principal thesis, which was published in two volumes. In these pages the volumes will be cited as follows: vol. I indicates the first study; vol. III refers to the second volume of the principal study.

[12] A decisive moment in Barth's development was the publication in 1931 of his commentary on the *Proslogion* of St. Anselm, *Fides quaerens intellectum. La preuve de l'existence de Dieu chez Anselme, en liaison avec son programme théologique.* It marks Barth's desire to free the theology of the Word from any justification which is borrowed from an autonomous philosophy of existence. Cf. *Theologie,* vol. I, p. 260.

[13] *Ibid.,* vol. II, p. 11.

ensemble the chapter on Predestination will particularly hold attention. The twofold Calvinistic predestination is rejected in
favor of collective election in Jesus Christ. Predestination, such
as Karl Barth conceives it, is the decision by which God in Jesus
Christ "turns toward man, founds, maintains, and governs His
alliance with him." [14] Predestination, alliance, and Christology are
closely related. Jesus is at once God who elects and the elected
Man in whom all men are touched by the election. He is also the
reproved. There is reprobation only in Jesus Christ. God has
taken our place. Henceforth reprobation is no longer our job. The
election of men is included in that of Christ: that of the community at first, then that of individuals. Barth separates himself
from Orthodox Protestantism which is entirely concentrated on
the relationship between God and the individual. The object of
Predestination is certainly the individual, but insofar as he stands
before God, insofar as he is the object of grace in Jesus Christ.
"That comes down to saying that the election 'denies' his isolated
individuality." [15]

Perplexed, Fr. Bouillard sets out first of all to underline all that
appears to him an opportune development of the scriptural datum.
"The mystery of Predestination in St. Paul has no other content
than the mystery of the Redemption. . . . In Jesus Christ, God first
of all elects His people, then individuals, insofar as they are gathered into this people. Predestination is Christological and eccle-
sial." [16] This was recognized as a positive contribution, but Fr.
Bouillard cannot defend himself against the discomfort provoked
by too abrupt a systematization. Barth's doctrine on reprobation
manifests a fundamental ambiguity. The bond which ought to
unite divine grace and human decision is not perceptible. The
general scheme reveals "the appearance of a system in which everything is given at the outset," in which sin is reduced to "a defect
completely necessary and without gravity." [17] Calvinist predestination and Origenist *apocatastase* are two stumbling blocks which
Barth wishes to avoid. But the aspect of human cooperation "prevents him from attributing to human decision an active part in

14 *Ibid.*, vol. II, p. 126.
15 *Ibid.*, vol. II, p. 135.
16 *Ibid.*, vol. II, p. 146.
17 *Ibid.*, vol. II, p. 163.

salvation." [18] How then to incorporate in the synthesis the single corrective capable of retaining the lapse into a new form of *apocatastase?* After this has been noted, the merit of Barth is to have shown that "the Christological interpretation is here the only legitimate one and that it suppresses false problems." [19]

*The response of man.* Before God what is the attitude of man? Can man know God? The insistence upon the cognitive character of faith is truly remarkable.[20] This precise affirmation immediately poses the problem of analogy. The words *redemption, wisdom, mercy,* can be applied to God and to the creature. Certainly there is no equivalence of meaning, but neither is there absolute non-equivalence. The concept of analogy is wronged by the usage that natural theology has made of it, Barth thinks. But how to get around it? Let us then attempt to adopt it while at the same time purifying it.

Assuredly our intuitions, our concepts, and our words can be applied of themselves only to the creature. But when God gives us the permission and the order to apply them to Himself, He claims for them a meaning which already belongs to them originally and properly. For creatures, their adequate object is *His* creation. Our thought and our language in their adaptation to this object are also *His* creation. Consequently the truth of our adequate knowledge of this object is also *His* creation, *His* truth.[21]

This sentence of Fr. Bouillard resumes quite well the thought of Barth. God has the right of being the object of our concepts and of our words, but we are not able to claim any right for them and for ourselves. Our terms *can,* therefore, be found in analogy with the Divine Being. This power becomes reality when God disposes of it and causes our words to be truthful. *Analogy is not, it becomes,* "it is conceived in a dynamic, not a static fashion." [22] Never can the gift be transformed into a static fact.

In the eyes of Barth, the *analogia entis* of Catholic theologians "would consist of admitting that there is a supreme concept (*Oberbegriff*), a common denominator, a genus "being" (*Sein*), embrac-

18 *Ibid.,* vol. II, p. 164.
19 *Ibid.,* vol. II, p. 164.
20 *Ibid.,* vol. III, p. 30.
21 *Ibid.,* vol. III, p. 192.
22 *Ibid.,* vol. III, p. 193.

ing at once God and His creature; that both, despite their dissimilarity, would have this being in common; that this analogy would be transparent and could be grasped synthetically from a speculative point of view." [23] In rejecting this notion, Barth does not touch the Thomistic doctrine of analogy at all. Moreover, this is not the real problem as Fr. Bouillard has shown. In substituting his *analogia fidei* for the *analogia entis,* Barth leaves the domain of the classical problematique. His objective is not to replace a deficient notion by a philosophical elaboration more valuable than analogy. "He abandons the field of structure or of meaning for that of event." [24] Against a tendency of thought, which in the study of the problem of God neglected to explicitate the hidden reference to faith, Barth had the merit of recalling the import of this event. But, instead of articulating the perspective of the event with that of the structure, Barth has neglected this structure and left intact the classical problem of analogy. He believes that he is affirming analogy "by stating this twofold thesis: our intuitions, our concepts, and our terms *qua* ours are totally inapt to grasp and to express what God is; they receive this aptitude, they become truthful through the grace of revelation. One would be tempted to say that the author superimposes upon a natural equivocity a univocity lent by grace." [25] Fr. Bouillard has remarkably put his finger upon the epistemological fault of Barth's theology. We must take this fact into account in order to judge the ensemble of Barth's affirmations on the knowledge of faith. We must read them in the framework of this *analogia fidei* in order to attribute to them their exact import *without risk of exaggeration.* With Barth every Christian will admit that "we know God through God upon the foundation of revelation and in faith. But we must also admit that it is *we* who know Him." [26] Without the intimate association of event and structure in analogy, there is no human language possible concerning the mystery of God and the plan of salvation.

In the last pages of his third volume the author summarizes his conclusions. The first concerns the doctrine of Christ. It is normal to judge, especially from this point of view, a work which desires

23 *Ibid.,* vol. III, p. 205.
24 *Ibid.,* vol. III, p. 208.
25 *Ibid.,* vol. III, p. 210.
26 *Ibid.,* vol. III, p. 217.

to be uniquely and exclusively Christological. After once more recognizing the value of Barth's enterprise, Fr. Bouillard, whose procedure is prudent and whose terms are measured, does not hesitate before the formula: "Christological dream projected upon a Platonic heaven." [27] The judgment is severe, but it appears just to me. In a vigorous reaction against liberalism, Barth takes up the dogma of the two natures defined in Chalcedon. But does he understand it in the same way? According to him the *union* of the two natures is transformed into an *exchange* and *permutation*. In the reconciliation God puts Himself in the place of man and man is put in the place of God.[28] The action of Christ is, as it were, absorbed in that of God. "The human conduct of Jesus appears to be no more than, as it were, the veil of the unique divine action." [29] In Christology the Barthian thought does not recognize any true density in the instrumentality of human action.

What is the origin of Barth's thought? The second conclusion answers this question. Fr. Bouillard wishes to discourage all seekers of dependence or relationship: the originality of his thought is irreducible. "One can truly situate it only with respect to the Reformers whose principles it has accepted with the desire of making them fructify in a more coherent fashion in the bosom of a new mental universe." [30] If we had directly interrogated Karl Barth, he would have given no other reply. Certainly in his work we can discover borrowings from almost all the currents of German philosophy after Kant. But we should look elsewhere for its sources properly so-called. Kant, Hegel, Kierkegaard, Jaspers, Heidegger, and even Sartre furnish more or less important contributions, but only in the order of conceptualization and expression and never in that of doctrine.

Barth is categorical. He wishes to reinstate the reformers and the Bible while he subordinates confessional attitude to Biblical attitude. Is he not the victim of a retrospective illusion? The scrupulous analyses of Fr. Bouillard furnish sufficient elements for us to respect his conclusion on Barth's sources. He studied this

27 *Ibid.*, vol. III, p. 291.
28 *Ibid.*, vol. II, p. 116.
29 *Ibid.*, vol. II, p. 118.
30 *Ibid.*, vol. III, p. 299.

thought step by step in the progressive elaboration of a synthesis; he followed closely not only the extension of theological options to ever new realms, but also the different reprisals of these options themselves. After this research, which is a model of method, he arrives at the absolutely convincing conclusion of the perfect homogeniety of the Barthian thought: a single "fundamental intention," a single "object" from the first edition of the *Römerbrief* down to the last volume of the *Dogmatique*. But in the first stage of his work, Barth did not hesitate for an instant to recognize the profound influence exercised on his thought by a certain number of great thinkers.[31] Since, moreover, it is impossible to attribute to the Holy Spirit or to the reformers the responsibility for a radicalism which characterizes the work from its beginnings, we must admit the striking role of doctrinal contributions of which Barth is no longer conscious today.[32]

We can consider as a third and final conclusion the general judgment which terminates the work of Father Bouillard: "By a massive and unilateral reaction against the acceptance of philosophy, of psychology, and of historical criticism within the bosom of Liberal Theology, Barth has adopted an ultra-dogmatic position which does not appear to reserve their normal place for the human criteria of the truth of a human statement: philosophical reflection and historical analysis." This results clearly from all of the research that has been brought to light in these two theses and will win the adherence of all those who have followed thus far the course of the author. We will now interrupt our commentary on

---

[31] Among the sources of the theology of crisis, Fr. Bouillard examines Overbeck and Nietzsche, Plato and Kant, Dostoievsky, Kierkegaard. It is generally known that Barth clearly and repeatedly has shown the influence exerted on him by the Danish theologian. This influence, however, does not exclude that of the others. On the contrary, these different thinkers all point in the same direction.

[32] For instance, I find it difficult to assert that the thought of Barth presses the choices of the Reformers to their logical conclusions. Thus, his thought is faithful to the spirit of their choices, without the limitation of literalness. Since such an affirmation will always be challenged by historians of the Reformation, it is best to present the problem in another way and inquire under what influences Barth has interpreted the doctrine of Luther and Calvin. As an example of this, an examination of *locus I. De theologia naturali et revelata* in Heinrich Heppe's *Die Dogmatik der evangelisch-reformierten Kirche* would be enough to demonstrate how much the categorical refusal of any natural knowledge of God is at discord with the spirit of the Reformed tradition.

the work of Henri Bouillard and take it up again in the last section of this introduction where it will permit us, at the same time, to make a precision on a personal position.

## The Barthian Doctrine of Justification Presented and Discussed by Hans Küng.

We will pass more rapidly over the book of Hans Küng.[33] It is only indirectly connected with our purpose. This work has caused a great deal of stir. There exists a fundamental agreement between the Barthian doctrine of justification and Catholic theology. Such is the thesis advanced and vigorously defended by the author. On both sides justification is considered as a declaration of justice. But equally on both sides in this declaration there is recognized the whole force of the Word of God which does not remain without effect and effects in man what it pronounces. The decree is efficacious in its term. It renders just the man whom it absolves.

Has Hans Küng given a complete account of the thought of the reformed theologian? To this question Barth himself replies in a letter inserted at the beginning of the work: "Let your readers know that you have me say what I said, and I think just as you have me say it." Is the position of Küng entirely faithful to Catholic teaching? Here the reply is given by Father Guy de Broglie, professor at the Gregorian University of Rome and member of the jury for the author's doctorate: "No serious and well-informed mind will question the full Catholic orthodoxy of the thought proposed and defended by Doctor Küng." [34] This double approbation cannot be underestimated.

The coherent Christocentricism of Küng is, "Catholic, not in the sense that everything it affirms is covered by the Magisterium of the Church and imposed under this title on every believer, but in the sense that what he says can be held by a Catholic theologian without the existence of any reason to suspect his orthodoxy." This remark of Charles Boungartner in a *Bulletin de theologie dogmatique* permits us to situate the position of Küng within

---

[33] *Rechtfertigung. Die Lehre Karl Barths und eine katholische Besinnung* (Einsiedeln, 1957).
[34] This statement is reproduced on the inside cover of the book.

Catholic theology without involving the Magisterium in each of his affirmations.[35]

On the Barthian interpretation of justification presented by Küng, agreement is far from unanimous and that despite the full approbation given by Barth himself. There are texts of the *Kirchliche Dogmatik* which do not easily enter into the perspective traced by the author. Barth recognizes the ontological reality of justification, but is this in the same sense as Catholic theology? It can be doubted. For my part I would concur willingly with the opinion of Henri Bouillard:

According to Barth faith, insofar as it is an act of man, changes nothing. It only lets us know and attests a change which has already taken place: the change of the human situation which was effected in the Death and Resurrection of Christ. Doubtless, it also has a creative character in virtue of the action of Christ which is its foundation (through the Holy Spirit): in it the Christian is a new creature. But this newness consists simply in the fact that he is constituted a *witness* of the change of the human situation which was brought about in Jesus Christ.[36]

Even to suppose that one can share the optimism of Hans Küng, who, moreover, remains perfectly conscious of the dangerous tendencies inseparable from the Barthian theology in general, is to remain no less certain that agreement touches only a limited point cut off by his method from the whole ensemble into which it is inserted and without a direct consideration of its consequences. The author proceeds by analysis and separation. He cuts the Barthian theology of justification from the bonds which attach it to questions on the Church (her tradition, authority, and sacraments), on Christology (and its consequences in Mariology), and on the knowledge of faith (with the rejection of a natural knowledge of God). Finally the result of an exclusive analysis does not substantially modify the conditions of the theological dialogue with Karl Barth. Yves Congar has very justly insisted upon the importance of a global understanding in the inter-confessional dialogue for an exact appreciation of the respective positions: "Where objective statements are in their materiality unanimously

[35] *Recherches de science religieuse*, XLVII (1959), p. 137.
[36] *Theologie*, vol. II, p. 103.

held, differences arise concerning their *meaning* and their *value*. The present great divisions are decisions *in the Christian consciousness;* they come to bear upon the overall *interpretation* of that very thing which we have in common." [37]

## Karl Barth, Yesterday and Today. The Humanity of God.

After this examination we can answer two questions: 1. Has the thought of Karl Barth substantially evolved? 2. Does this evolution challenge the position that we adopted in 1948?

Yes, the thought of Karl Barth has undergone an evolution. Certainly those who have studied this problem do not always situate the landmarks of a development in the same places. Barth, moreover, is the first to confirm them in their conviction. At the beginning of chapter 7 of our work, we related the lecture which Barth gave in 1920, at Aarau, in the presence of Harnack. In the exposition of the young Barth there was not a single idea that the old titan of liberalism could accept.

On September 25, 1956, Karl Barth was invited to speak in the same place before the assembly of the Swiss Pastoral Society. The place invited comparisons as well as the consideration of the time that had elapsed. This time Barth is judging himself and measuring the progress made in thirty-six years of theological work. It is of the *humanity* of God that Barth wanted to speak in 1956.[38] "I would certainly have been in an embarrassing situation if I had been asked to speak about the humanity of God in 1920, the year when I resisted in this very room my famous master, Adolph von Harnack. We would have suspected many reservations under this title. At any rate the subject did not occupy us at that time." [39]

What occupied Barth during the years 1915 to 1920, the Barth of the "theology of crisis," was the divinity of God: "We were struck by what is absolutely unique in God in His relation to man and the world, by the insurmountable height, the distance, and the difference before which man finds himself situated when he

[37] *Regards et réflexions sur la christologie de Luther,* in *Das Konzil von Chalkedon,* vol. III (Würzburg, 1954), p. 458.
[38] Karl Barth, *L'humanité de Dieu,* in *Cahiers du renouveau,* 14 (Geneva, 1956).
[39] *L'humanité,* etc., p. 7.

pronounces the name of God, and when God touches him." [40]
God, *entirely other,* He who hides Himself at the very instant
when He unveils Himself, the majesty of the cross—such were the
major themes of the period.

In 1920, the theology of Barth set itself up in a rather inhuman
grandeur. Today it is clothed with indulgence and mercy. We are
no longer in the period of "crisis," but in that of "coherent Christology"—to use the felicitous phrase of Henri Bouillard. As von
Balthasar has well shown, Barth was working at that time almost
uniquely with the notion of *"diastasis."* Today he accords an important place to analogy in his thought.[41] The word, *diastasis,*
evokes distance, division, discord. This term is well suited to a
theology comprised of jutting angles: after a break the edges remain sharp. Analogy on the contrary looks to a unity beyond all
*diastasis.* It is Christ Who is the humanity of God; it is in Him
that analogy is realized.

Was Barth right or wrong? His reply in 1956 is categorical:

Certainly we were right: there could have been no question at the
time of simply continuing in the same direction that Wobbermin,
Schaeder, and Otto had just tried to take; a radical about-face such as
this was absolutely necessary. The vessel threatened to founder. . . .
This reconstruction could not be questioned. It is a question today of
a retraction. But this word does not precisely involve the cancellation
of what preceded; it signifies that one is going to try by a new effort to
say better what has already been said, to say it in a way that will be
in the final analysis more just.[42]

It is a question then of going beyond what was said before, of a
transposition into a new situation. But the fundamental movement remains the same. At the present stage of Christological concentration we are assisting first of all at the abandonment, or
better still, at the forgetting of terminology that will henceforth
be obsolete. Barth no longer talks about the *entirely other* who
descends vertically, of the mathematical point, of the infinite
qualitative difference between God and man, of the tangential

---

[40] *L'humanité,* etc., p. 6.
[41] *L'humanité,* etc., p. 17.
[42] *L'humanité,* etc., p. 13.

action which does no more than skim lightly over the earth. More
noticeable is the recuperation of certain themes that had formerly
been scorned: "The problem of ethics appeared to us to rejoin the
mortal illness of man." [43] It is in a positive way that Barth today
takes up the problem of culture. What is characteristic above all
of the present stage is the fullness of the vision. Stated more precisely and better formulated in the course of many years of reflection, teaching, and living dialogue, the basic intuitions have found
numerous points of impact in this richness of subjects that Barth
is led to consider one by one in the development of his monu-
mental work, *Kirchliche Dogmatik.* The daily confrontation with
the complexity of the theological datum has not failed to enrich
the professor himself, and to force him to add many nuances to
his positions. It is this Christological concentration which gives
this vast literary activity its profound unity. The three Catholic
theologians we have just discussed have shown quite well how this
approach to the theological problem permitted Karl Barth to rediscover for the benefit of Protestantism a considerable part of the
traditional Christian patrimony. This is his historical role acquired
from the present. We do not have to insist upon it at this point.

At the different stages of development everything is accomplished in the unity of a sane fundamental objective. Certainly
upon reading the first works of Karl Barth, it was impossible to
foresee his future orientations. But the theologian remained faithful to himself. A single intention animated all his writings. It is
not sufficient however to disengage this unity of intention; it is
necessary to recognize once more the moment at which the unity
of a sane body of doctrine is affirmed. It appears to me incontest-
able that Barth is in sure possession of his principles as early as the
book on Saint Anselm (1931). These principles are then developed
in homogeneous fashion according to a very regular plan beginning with the first volume of the *Kirchliche Dogmatik* (1932).
Since that time we have been assisting at the methodical construction of a vast edifice, stages are added to stages, one wing is begun
after the other. The style scarcely changes. The material remains
practically the same. The thought is explicitated, is completed;

[43] *L'humanité,* etc., p. 15.

the interest is shifted. *But no major position is revoked.* The Christological orientation is present from the point of departure.

When this orientation is assured, and this unity of a single body of doctrine recognized in the overall picture of the *Kirchliche Dogmatik,* we can wonder whether the evolution of Barth has finally led him to cross this threshold which would give to the fundamental options of his thought the right to be cited within Catholic theology wherein the plurality of *schools* of theology (in the unity of the same faith) is an expression of the freedom of theological research and reflection. Call to mind, for example, the different explanations of the efficacy of grace, in complete common conformity to the teaching of the Council of Trent: the different methods of presenting sacramental causality. . . .

If to this question it is necessary, I think, to give a negative reply, it is not because the program of Barth is illegitimate. On the contrary, it is because he did not carry it through to the end. So the true question is the following: How is it that Barth could not realize his plan of coherent Christology; how could he not execute the task that the had assigned himself: to recognize in all the humanity of God? This will bring me to present under another form and in a different context the appreciation which I had brought forward in 1948. In my turn I would like "to say better what has already been said," while remaining within the realm of Christology. With more nuance I should like to take up again at this point what I proposed at that time in the abrupt and determined language of a young theological student on the eve of his doctorate.

Can one treat of the humanity of God without its full dimension to the humanity of man? This is the whole problem. In Christology the instrumentality of the human action is stripped of all true density. We stated this above when we were discussing Henri Bouillard. The manner in which Barth treats of the history of salvation and of temporality is particularly typical. "In this theology of event and of history perhaps nothing can happen, because everything has already happened in eternity," writes von Balthasar.[44] The history of salvation is transported outside of concrete

[44] *Karl Barth, Darstellung,* etc., p. 380.

human existence. Our justice is there; our sin is past, but the passage is real only in Jesus Christ, in no way in our existence. Barth does not know a history of salvation in the strict sense, which would pass into the humanity of man. One has the impression that everything is reduced to projections of the unique, salvific event upon several temporal levels.

The theology of the Incarnation is not, therefore, fully developed. Can it be in the Barthian perspective? I do not think so: the defect is in the principle. If Christ assumed a human nature, He must have assumed the historicity proper to every human nature. Time is at once the form and condition of human existence. But a curious ambiguity weighs upon the Barthian theology of the temporality of Christ. The time of Jesus becomes an "eternal time," removed in one way or another from common temporality.[45] The truth of the Incarnation is thus compromised. As Henri Bouillard remarks quite justly: "The time of Jesus in His terrestrial reality is not the 'eternal time' of God, but the human time of an existence in which the eternal life of God is manifested." [46]

Barth finishes by extenuating the human notion of time—that which is evident from common experience—in order to reconstruct it entirely, beginning with the time of Christ. This manifests the necessary limit of the Barthian thought. Never does he analyze humanity as such. Never does he consider in themselves these realities of terrestrial human existence which Christ assumed in the measure in which they concurred with His plan of mercy, the salvation of humanity. To speak of the humanity of God in such a way as to be understood, it is necessary to know the humanity of man. Without that, one contents oneself with *fashioning* for God a completely human aspect. It is necessary to proclaim the alliance

[45] Barth discusses temporality in *Kirchliche Dogmatik*, vol. III, book II. The exact references can be found in Bouillard, *Theologie*, vol. II, pp. 268–279. In his treatment of the time of Christ, Barth says plainly: "Thus human time is equally and simultaneously (*zugleich*) the time of God, eternal time." (Cf. *Kirchliche Dogmatik*, vol. III, book II, p. 557.) Bouillard very opportunely remarks on this point: "Just as humanity and divinity do not blend in a mixed term, neither do time and eternity blend in an eternal time. Is there not a risk of inducing the mind to effect this fusion, when it is stated that the time of the man Jesus, although it is still the duration of his life, assumes the character of eternity, in which past, present and future are contained in each other?" (*Theologie*, vol. II, p. 271.)

[46] *Ibid.*, vol. II, p. 272.

of God with man, says Barth, in his lecture of 1956; then he adds: "This is what we have to proclaim to man, in function of the *humanity* of God, and without any reference to *their* humanism more or less dense in its incredulity." [47] Certainly Barth can be deceived by the successive "humanisms" encountered in the history of philosophy. But the theologian cannot be content with this conclusion. He must put himself to the task. It pertains to him, then, to scrutinize as a *philosopher* what a true humanism can be. Without that, what he will say about the humanity of God will escape the grasp of the demanding mind. Barth has succumbed to this temptation of such an "overflight" which plagues every theologian.[48]

## The Human Element in the Theological Process.

It remains for us to verify all of this with regard to theological method, the proper object of the present work. Barth will tell us: It is the task of the theologian to place himself in God's point of view in order to contemplate his work from there. This is in reality the wish of every theologian. Where then is the "overflight"? Before answering this question, which involves the whole problematique of a theological dialogue with Barth and also, it seems, that of the nature of theology, we would like to sketch in broad outline what could be the structure of a dialogue that begins with the doctrine of faith considered in its absolute supernaturality, in order to find out whether a theologian who places himself at God's point of view must necessarily come to the conclusions which the Protestant dogmatist proposes to us. The outline proposed here pursues the precision of a personal position. Analyzing the French edition of my book, Fr. H. Davis is a bit surprised at the recourse which I made to the Thomistic theology of faith, a very natural platform for a fruitful encounter with dialectic thought.[49] There was a lacuna. A previous elaboration of the biblical theology of faith *as illumination* and as *gift of God*, in the tradition of the Augustinian School, the entire heritage of which Thomism has

---

[47] *L'humanité*, etc., p. 47.
[48] The expression is that of Fr. Bouillard, *Theologie*, vol. III, p. 300.
[49] *The Downside Review*, LXVI (1950), pp. 140–141.

made more valuable, seems to me today the indispensable condition for a rigorous and efficacious doctrinal exchange with Barth.

Faith depends entirely upon God. The internal action of the
Holy Spirit assures the gratuitous and supernatural character of
the first act of faith. Saint Augustine showed this in the controversy against Semi-Pelagianism. The *initium fidei*, the act in which
conversion consists, is a work of grace. But there is more. Faith is
not only supernatural, as the first step in Christian life, as a salutary act of submission to God; it is also and above all supernatural,
insofar as it is knowledge. In his *Treatises on the Gospel of John*,
Saint Augustine shows that faith is the attraction of truth and the
illumination of the intellect:

> If you show a green branch to a sheep, you attract it; if you show
> nuts to a child, you attract it. . . . If it is true that a man lets himself
> be drawn towards an object whose delights and pleasures solicit his
> affection . . . , would the Father, in causing him to know Christ, exer-
> cise no attraction? *Quid enim fortius desiderat anima quam veritatem?*
> Why should the soul desire its interior palace to be rather healthy in
> order to discern the true? Is it not in order to eat and drink wisdom,
> justice, truth, eternity? [50]

Further on St. Augustine will again say of Christ: "The Light
then gives testimony of itself: it opens the eyes that are healthy,
and it is for itself its own witness to make itself known." [51] Without the teaching of the interior Master, preaching is only an empty
sound:

> *Sonus verborum nostrorum aures percutit, magister intus est.* . . . We
> can by the sound of our voices address lessons to you; but if God is not
> in your heart to instruct you, it is useless for us to make you listen. . . .
> Outside there are found masters, helps, lessons; but in heaven is the
> pulpit of Him who instructs interiorly. Thus the Savior Himself said
> in the Gospel: Prevent yourselves from calling masters on earth anyone
> from among yourselves, for your one Master is Christ.[52]

In the middle ages Saint Thomas will synthesize all the richness
of this biblical and Augustinian patrimony in the formula: "It is

[50] *Tract. in Joan.*, 26, 5, PL 35. 1609. *Commentary on John 6:66:* "No one can come
to me, unless he is enabled to do so by my Father."
[51] *Tract. in Joan.*, 35, 4, PL 35. 1659. *Commentary on John 8:13:* "I bear witness to
myself, my witness is true."
[52] *In Epist. Joan. ad Parthos*, 3, 13, PL 35. 2004. *Commentary on I John 2:27:* "His
anointing teaches you concerning all things."

upon the medium of divine truth that faith rests." [53] Since, moreover, God alone can give us God, He alone is also the *propria causa fidei.*[54]

It is in the heart of the supernaturality of the act of faith that the human moment must find its value. But this will be first of all subordinate to a contemplation of the mystery. The communication by God of a truth that is hidden but certain will inspire "the desire to penetrate its content and to give its full meaning to the *crede ut intellegas.*" [55] The concrete existence of faith in which the adherence of the Spirit is inseparable from the purification of the heart transforms human thought. This *understanding*, the recompense of faith, is not natural reason pure and simple. Faith and *understanding* in Augustine do not yet pose the modern problem of the relation between faith and reason. In search of a knowledge which will blossom fully in eternal life, the summit of contemplation, faith seeks from the present time a transition between belief and the face to face vision. God accords this *intellectus* to our prayers: "Pray with strength and fidelity so that God might give you *understanding*." [56] *Fides quaerit, intellectus invenit,*[57] this other formula of Saint Augustine, introduces us without difficulty to the *fides quaerens intellectum* of Saint Anselm. Anselm will begin the work of a more independent rational knowledge, but will remain in the same context of contemplation. The prayer which opens the *Proslogion* dispels all equivocation: "Famished I beg You, Lord; I have begun to seek You, do not let me go away hungry. . . . Teach me to seek You and show Yourself to him who seeks." [58] Anselm does not turn toward the exterior. He is a monk who addresses himself to monks.

Never does one leave the soil and the roof of the Church. It is a point on which Barth insists willingly in his Commentary on the *Proslogion*. This interpretation expresses his personal concept of theology. It is under this title that it interests us above all. Bouillard writes:

---

[53] *Summa Theol.*, IIa–IIae, q. 1, a. 1.
[54] *Ibid.*, IIa–IIae, q. 6, a. 1.
[55] Etienne Glison, *Introduction à l'étude de saint Augustine*, 2e éd. (Paris, 1943), p. 36.
[56] *Epist. 120*, III, 14, PL 33. 459.
[57] *De Trinitate*, XV, 2, 2, PL 42. 1058.
[58] Chap. I, Schmidtt edition, pp. 99–100.

Theology is a meditation upon the faith of the Church such as it is expressed and imposed upon us in the Sacred Scripture, the Creeds, the Conciliar definitions, and the writings of the Fathers. It does not seek to found its object, but to understand it precisely in its incomprehensibility. It is human knowledge, imperfect and susceptible to progress. It is developed in obedience, and its success depends on divine grace which the theologian ought to implore in prayer.[59]

We know that Karl Barth thought that he recognized this method in the ensemble of the religious work of St. Anselm, and that he is convinced that the so-called ontological proof is only one example among others of the deepening of faith by reason, a simple realization of the internal coherence of the revealed doctrine. God exists and nothing can be conceived greater than He. It is Revelation which teaches this to us. In presenting a *ratio necessaria,* Anselm does not have in view a rational demonstration accessible to the unbeliever, but a simple theological analysis within the sphere of faith. Father Bouillard has shown that Barth did not grasp the singular character of this theology. Ignorant of the distinction which will only appear later, Anselm "thinks he can prove *sola ratione* all the truths of faith including the Trinity, the Incarnation, and the Redemption." [60] But for all that, he is not a Rationalist. The levels are not confused. Dialectic, to which the unbeliever has access, shows the necessity of a faith which goes beyond it. "It is situated at an inferior level and it is from below, so to speak, that it is referred to faith." [61] Upon this point Father Bouillard adopts the penetrating conclusion of an investigation of Father Vignaux on the *Monologion.* When a position appears as necessary, "one must consider this necessity not as absolute, *omnino necessarium,* but only as a provisory, *interim necessarium,* so long as this same conclusion is not at all confirmed by a *major auctoritas.*" [62] A necessity of the rational order yields to a higher necessity, that of Scripture and tradition.

Beyond this problem of the interpretation of a major text of the history of theology, it remains no less true that Barth has admira-

---

59 *Theologie,* vol. I, p. 145.
60 *Ibid.,* vol. III, p. 154.
61 *Ibid.,* vol. III, p. 154.
62 P. Vignaux, *"Structure et sens du Monologion,"* in *Revue des sciences philosophiques et théologiques,* XXXI (1947), p. 197.

bly grasped that which is and remains the principal function of theology. In the two centuries which separate the *Proslogion* from the *Summa Theologica,* a recantation is going to be effected. Theologians are going to distinguish carefully among the Christian truths those which they can demonstrate and those which will always escape their proofs properly so called: they will reduce the section reserved for the *rationes necessariae* in order to give a large part to the *rationes probabiles.* But it remains that, for a St. Thomas, the theological procedure, of which he made the widest use, is that of a *manifestation* of a mystery through recourse to *rationes persuasoriae* with the purpose of uncovering the internal harmony of the datum of faith.[63] In acting in this way St. Thomas knows to what tradition he subscribes. More than once he claims for himself the example and the authority of St. Augustine, as this appears in the *De Trinitate.*[64]

Nevertheless, the contemplative intention of a St. Augustine continues to preside over the ensemble of theological effort and not merely over one of its functions. In requisitioning new forces, Anselm does not turn his back on his master. In analyzing with care the different services that reason can render to the understanding of faith, St. Thomas also remains in the pure line of the *Crede ut intelligas.* Barth, on the contrary, seems fixed in a pre-Anselmian Augustinianism. Where we see the historical unfolding of an interior dynamism, he would doubtless see only infidelity to the original intuition. Certainly the merit of a St. Thomas is to have determined carefully the sector accessible to reason in the domain of Revelation: *ea quae per rationem cognosci possunt;* [65]

---

[63] We are discussing here the deductive process which starts from the articles of faith. In the present dialogue with Barth, this process is beyond the limit of the debate.

[64] *Ratio persuasoria* is the opposite of *ratio demonstrativa* in *In Boeth. De Trin.,* p. 2, a. 1, ad 5. "Inducitur ratio non quae sufficienter probet radicem; sed radici jam positae ostendat congruere consequentes effectus" (*Summa Theol.,* I, q. 32, a. 1, ad 2). "Rationes quae inducuntur a sanctis ad probandum ea quae sunt fidei, non sunt demonstrativae, sed persuasiones quaedam manifestantes non esse impossibile quod in fide proponitur" (*S.T.,* IIa–IIae, q. 1, a. 5, ad 2). "Ad notificandum per aliquas similitudines ea quae sunt fidei, sicut *Augustinus* utitur multis similitudinibus . . . ad manifestandam Trinitatem" (*In Boeth. De Trin.,* q. 2, a. 3). "*Augustinus* vero procedit ad manifestandam Trinitatem personarum ex processione verbi et amoris in mente nostra: *quam viam supra secuti sumus*" (*S.T.,* I, q. 32, a. 1, obj. 2).

[65] *S.T.,* IIa–IIae, q. 2, a. 4, c.

but this is in no way to eliminate in these matters the necessity of the Word of God. On the level of the divine collective economy, which considers the ensemble of collective humanity in the ensemble of the concrete conditions which can be those of its members, the revelation of natural truths is indispensable, even if it is superfluous for particular individuals in favorable circumstances. Thus the *sacra doctrina* maintains the entire extent of Revelation such as it has been historically delivered: it is without restriction *doctrina secundum revelationem divinam;* [66] it is not limited to the knowledge of the *articuli fidei,* of the mystery, properly so-called. The presence in it of arguments of strictly rational making does not transform it into an artificial arrangement of philosophical and theological fragments. The speculative penetration which ought to bear upon the entire revealed datum will sometimes take the form of a demonstration, properly so-called; sometimes that of a manifestation by reasons of convenience; sometimes that of a process of explicitation by way of deduction. At the end of a demonstrative reasoning process, the evidence of the conclusion will vitiate faith. But it does not remain less true that this argumentation, insofar as it is a speculative penetration of the revealed datum, constitutes for St. Thomas an authentic theological process. It is under this title that the *quinque viae* for proving the existence of God appear simply as a breakthrough of evidence, as a success in the contemplative effort.

Barth cannot recognize this reason, frankly utilized in the *intellectus fidei* in fashioning a superior logic *as bearing upon a metaphysic.* Nevertheless, it is the same reason which, on the one hand, is the instrument of a search into the heart of the mystery, and, on the other hand, can set itself up as proof and constitute itself as knowledge because it has its own laws and autonomy. The continuity between the two usages is well marked when the proof comes to light within the very bosom of the *sacra doctrina.* In history the realization of the virtualities of reason is not accomplished in a continuous fashion. Abelard, utilizing dialectic methods in the sacred domain, will already encounter the resistance of those "for whom reason and its methods have no valid consistency in the

[66] *S.T.,* I, q. 1, a. 1, c.

divine vocation of the spirit." [67] But soon a new zone is disengaged in which reason does not furnish merely *procedures* but *objects*, as Father Chenu has well shown:

It is no longer a question simply of referring to God by a dialectic or symbolical way the created realities whose supreme finality would devaluate their terrestrial content, makeup, and usage. There is an autonomous knowledge of this world and of man, valid in its own order and truly efficacious in the realm of speculation and of action, which is transferable to theological science. . . . In St. Thomas we will have a complete anthropology in his theological treatise of man, and in his treatise on divine government a complete vision of the universe; it will be a mortal sin to eliminate them from his theology under the pretext that both are philosophical matter.[68]

Karl Barth would not recognize himself easily in the Abelardian idea of theology. Nevertheless, his method remains related to it under a certain aspect.

But it is the second zone that Barth resolutely refuses to cross. It would appear inconceivable to him to integrate in his *Dogmatik* an anthropology that is valid in its own order and independent, in its structure, of an ontological reference to the Word of God.[69]

Before the lack of a theology of the Word of God in Jesus Christ which does not manage to find contact with man, Father Bouillard makes his own the echo of both the discomfort of the philosopher and the uneasiness of the apologist. In the face of an attempt at a pure position which goes absolutely to the end of transcendence, he makes valid all that constitutes in man the "transcendental condition of faith." [70] The theologian would desire still more: a doctrinal dialogue carried directly to the very heart of faith. From the time that God addresses Himself to man, there is an introduction of God's point of view into theology. This eruption into the universe of nature and of history poses problems for a certain autonomy of man. But in order to go to the heart of the debate, the

[67] M.-D. Chenu, *La théologie au douzième siècle* (Paris, 1957), p. 314.
[68] *Ibid.*, pp. 314–315.
[69] I had the occasion to treat certain aspects of Barth's Christological anthropology in *"Le chrétien et la société selon le protestantisme contemporain"* in *Istina*, III (1956), pp. 99–124.
[70] See Chapters II and III of volume III, especially pp. 100–112.

theologian ought to grasp the *human moment in the very act of faith,* according to the example of St. Augustine and of his disciples. In the instant at which the knowledge of God becomes faith, there is mediation of a created intelligence. Entirely at the service of the divine dimension but in the perspective of a unique providential economy which encircles Creation and Redemption, this understanding remains itself, preserves its own consistency, its own proper laws, and the possibility of developing its virtualities in the realms of metaphysics and of history. A theology of the absolute supernaturality of the act of faith reveals how the Word of God, far from compromising, on the contrary, safeguards human integrity.

We are in no way, therefore, enclosed in a dilemma. With Barth we shall say that the task of the theologian is to place himself at God's point of view and not at the point of view of man.[71] Theology departs from on high; its movement is descending, but to reach man in his concrete situation, to avoid gliding in this "overflight," which Father Bouillard has so correctly described, humanity, unfolded in all its legitimate dimensions, must be present to the theological elaboration. This is another consequence of a "coherent Christology," of a theology of the Incarnation drawn out to its very end.

[71] "Fit nobis in statu viae quaedam illius cognitionis participatio (St. Thomas is referring here to the vision of God) et assimilatio ad cognitionem divinam, in quantum per fidem nobis infusam inhaeremus ipsi primae veritati propter se ipsam" (*In Boeth. De Trin.,* q. 2, a. 2, c).

# karl barth

# 1

# statement
# of the problem

I T IS impossible to approach Barth's dogmatics directly if we are ignorant of his vocabulary. Moreover, to avoid losing our way on countless crossroads, we must know the main purposes of the author. This first chapter, therefore, has a twofold aim: to present certain notions in Barth's theological vocabulary, and to define the limits within which he conducts his investigation. Once we have taken stock of the questions we are entitled to ask the theologian of Basle, we shall be able to see the line of development our exposition must follow.

## A. The Place of Dogmatics in Theology.

What is dogmatics? Barth, who is rather free in his use of words, attributes to this term a meaning with which we are not familiar. Let us begin with a definition which is quite general: dogmatics is a part of theology.[1] This leads us to a further inquiry: what meaning does he give to theology? We will follow Barth's own explanation of this term, and comment on it in passing.

The word *theologia* in its etymological sense, is translated in German by *Rede von Gott*. [The closest English translation would be "Word of God" or "Word concerning God." But we cannot use either of these expressions, for then we would be unable to distinguish between *Rede von Gott* and *Wort Gottes*, which have a different extension and technical sense in Barth's writings, though they are connected.] Therefore, we will translate *theologia* as "discourse pertaining to God," retaining for this expression sufficient amplitude to designate both those discourses which have God as their object and those which have God as their origin.[2]

This cannot be done, however, without some disadvantages. *Discourse* in English can be construed only with difficulty to signify something other than speech. The same is not true of *Rede,* at least in Barth's theological vocabulary. This term can designate any manner of self-expression, whether it be with the aid of words, or through the medium of certain activities. At the risk of distorting the meaning of words somewhat, we will allow *discourse* the same amplitude as *Rede.*[3] Well then, these "discourses pertaining to God," which we designate by the collective term *theology,* are not any discourses whatsoever concerning God, but only those which are pronounced and effected within the brotherhood of that society which has as its mission to speak of God, namely, the Church. In other words, all the activities of the Church pertain to theology; they are all "discourses pertaining to God."[4]

Once this has been granted, it is quite legitimate for Barth to distinguish between three main categories of theology: the activity of the faithful in the Church; the diverse functions of the Church considered as a collectivity; and, finally, the science of theology itself. The first two categories can thus include such diverse activities as divine worship, works of social solidarity, teaching catechism to youth, preaching, and conferring the sacraments. All these activities, however, are not of the same rank. Preaching and conferring the sacraments, for example, constitute the very nucleus of the Church's work.[5] The other activities are merely consequences, and therefore occupy a secondary place in the Church's sphere of activity.

The third category, the science of theology, can also assume various forms. In fact, it is subdivided into biblical theology, practical theology, and dogmatics. Though it would be superfluous to dwell on the proper character of practical theology—which is equivalent to our pastoral theology [6]—it is of utmost importance to note carefully the division between biblical theology and dogmatics. The former has as its sole aim the organization of biblical testimony and its presentation as an organic whole. Dogmatics, on the other hand, has as its essential concern the task of presenting these "discourses pertaining to God" to our contemporary world. Whereas biblical theology organizes the disparate elements of the preaching of the apostolic era, dogmatics has as its mission the construction of a framework for today's preaching. Its role is to transpose the Word of Christ and of His apostles into a modern key. Dogmatics, therefore, presupposes the testimony of Scripture presented systematically by biblical theology; but it adds to that testimony contemporary considerations. We might say that biblical theology gives us the first historical expression of dogmatics; the history of the Church and its teaching fills in for us all the intervening stages.[7]

This brings us to the consideration of the content of dogmatics. The principal activity of the Church, one which was commanded by an explicit order of God, constitutes the matter of this science: the *Verkündigung* (which includes the Sacrament). Since it is a question of present-day preaching, the "dogmatician" must see to it that the preaching is adapted to our contemporary mentality; consequently, he must correct yesterday's preaching in terms of today's demands.[8]

Such a correction, however, is possible only if the "dogmatician" has at his disposal a norm. Adaptation to our contemporary mentality is restricted solely to the *form* of the preaching; it may not be extended to the *content*. The Liberal School has understood this adaptation as a reduction of the substance of preaching into the philosophical and cultural thought of today. Such a position ignores the fact that only the *Word of God* can claim the right of being judge and criterion of all preaching. We are no longer dealing with the general term "discourses pertaining to God" (*Reden von Gott*), but with one of these discourses, namely, that which God Himself pronounced (*Wort Gottes, Gottes Selbstwort*). Preaching has value only inasmuch as it is accepted and appropriated by the Word of God.[9]

To summarize what we have set forth thus far, we can say that

dogmatics, the foremost of the theological sciences, has as its func-
tion the comparison of yesterday's preaching with the Word of
God, so that it may prepare the Christian message which the
Church must proclaim tomorrow.[10]

Must dogmatics be distinguished from moral theology ? In other
words, is there a Christian ethic distinct from a Christian dogmatics? [11] Though the contemporary Catholic theologian is accustomed to distinguish "dogma" from "moral," he does not do so
in terms of two theologies, two different sciences. Theology in
itself is one; it has only one formal object. But within the limits
of this one science it is possible to distinguish several disciplines,
just as it is possible to differentiate between various treatises.[12]
Barth, likewise, insisted on emphasizing quite clearly the unity of
theology (which he calls dogmatics). He foresees—and he is probably not mistaken—that if he admits two different sciences, one
called Christian dogmatics, the other Christian ethics, the former
will claim as its exclusive prerogative the right of being the science of revelation and Scripture; while the latter will sink to the
level of a pure morality of the natural law—an element foreign
to the realm of theology. These two sciences no longer would have
—to use a scholastic term—the same formal object. The first would
proceed from faith; the second, purely and simply from natural
reason. For this reason, Barth considers moral as an essential and
inseparable part of dogmatics.[13]

## B. Dogmatics as "Knowledge."

The characteristic which distinguishes the different forms of
theology from the other legitimate activities of the Church is
their scientific status. We have accepted the word *science* thus far
uncritically. Now we must examine the meanings which Barth
assigns to it. He had a choice between two types of science: one
derived from Aristotle; the other developed by the modern experimental sciences. Science in the Aristotelian sense is the science
of evidence and demonstration.[14] To this class belong the philosophical and mathematical sciences. The other type of science
intends only "empirical verification," and the formulation of laws

which correlate established observations. "In this way we know that heat expands metals and that ruminants have a cleft hoof." The experimental type of science is inferior to the Aristotelian because it never attains to essences in themselves and reaches merely "essences which are concealed." [15]

Both types of science have been applied to theology. "St. Thomas was the first who knew how—and had the courage!—to propose clearly the principle of an integral application of scientific technique and procedures to revealed data. In this way, he established an organic discipline in which Scripture, the article of faith, is no longer the very material and subject of scientific research, as was the *sacra doctrina* of the twelfth century; rather, it became the source, previously known, which serves as a point of departure. From this source, one proceeds in accordance with all the demands and laws of the Aristotelian *demonstratio.*" [16] As a consequence, St. Thomas gave to theology a status which was recognized throughout all of Christian theology, even within the domain of Protestant theology. This status prevailed as long as, and wherever, orthodoxy prevailed.[17] In the modern period, an attempt has been made to bring theology into the category of the empirical sciences. Where this has been done, theology has become the study of religious phenomena and their laws. In brief, under the influence of these tendencies Christian theology has become a chapter in the treatises of religious psychology and the history of religions.[18]

Barth meets face to face this second type of theology, which has been well defined by Georg Wobbermin: "A study of observable reality as complete and as precise as possible." [19] There is no difficulty in showing that such a theology would be a poor one, for the "observable reality" of which Wobbermin speaks is purely and simply a religious phenomenon. Such a study would in no way proceed from faith. Another definition of science, evidently inspired by Aristotle's notion, is presented by Heinrich Scholz.[20] Barth rejects this definition also. According to Barth, at the basis of Scholz's concept of science is found the postulate of evidence. The idea of truth, therefore, would be the center of such a theology; but the entire Barthian dogmatics is grounded on the idea of

obedience. For, though the sole norm of truth is the Word of
God, this Word ever eludes human research. Neither truth nor
(a fortiori) evidence pertains to dogmatics; the Aristotelian category of science, consequently, must be rejected without appeal.

Barthian theology, therefore, refuses to accept any concept of
science elaborated outside its own sphere. Nevertheless, it feels no
obligation to propose its own definition of science which could
include all other human activities of the same name. While accepting his complete isolation, Barth still retains the word *science*
to designate his dogmatics.[21] Since no one has a monopoly on the
word, he feels free to accommodate the meaning to his personal
usage. Within the term *science* he includes three ideas: 1. science
is a human enterprise concerning an object of knowledge; 2. it
follows a predetermined method; 3. it can justify its method.[22]
We would say with more exactness that dogmatics, as conceived
by Barth, is no longer a science; rather, it is an ordered reflection
on a determined subject. In this case, we consider it more precise
to designate it simply as a "body of knowledge," granting to it a
definite value as knowledge, but denying to it any claim to a
properly scientific status.[23]

## C. Organized Dogmatics and a Theological System.

It now remains for us to determine the structure which Barth
intends to give to his dogmatics. There are, in fact, two principal
branches of dogmatics. The first, owing to its academic character,
aims above all at being complete. Its scope includes all theological
themes: the whole of biblical testimony, the whole of ecclesiastical
definitions, minute details of possible difficulties, and it justifies
its own method. This is organized dogmatics.

Accompanying this—and prior to it—necessity created a dogmatics which has in view neither teaching nor a systematic synthesis; moreover, it makes no pretense at constantly rendering an
account of its own method. This type of dogmatics, of its very
essence occasional and composed of writings improvised to meet
particular circumstances, is irregular. The writings of the Fathers,
for the most part, are to be included in this category. The same is
true of Luther's writings. *The Institution of Christian Religion,*

on the contrary, is one of the best examples of organized dogmatics in the Protestant tradition.

Calvin has had countless imitators among orthodox theologians
and religious philosophers of the nineteenth century. Schleiermacher, Ritschl, and Troeltsch have left us complete and detailed
treatises. In an age when Protestant theology has rather abused
occasional writings, prophetic declarations, and aphorisms, it is
good to reflect a little on a mode of acquiring knowledge which
can also serve as an instrument of instruction. Barth's dogmatics,
then, will be an organized one.[24]

Although organized dogmatics is synonymous with a theological
system in contemporary language, this equivalation is not legitimate with regard to Barth's synthesis. For him the word *system*
evoked the idea of a complete and closed construction. Consequently, only that theology could be considered *"systematic"*
which is completely self-contained; and it could be completely
self-contained only if it had sifted through the screen of its critique all future preaching of the Word. There can be no system
except where there is possession of total truth, without the possibility of a new critique, evolution, or further explicitation. The
theology which comes closest to this notion, according to Barth,
is Catholic theology. But even Catholic theology departs from the
ideal to the extent that it admits an evolution of dogma.[25]

## D. Justification of the Plan of Our Exposition.

At the conclusion of this initial survey, it is possible to draw
the principal lines of thought which must be followed in our exposition. Barth, as a dogmatic theologian, focuses all his attention
on two elements: the Church's preaching (the material of dogmatics), and the Word of God (the criterion of dogmatics). His mission consists in appraising each of these elements in terms of the
other. The Word of God, the real and ultimate criterion of dogmatics, however, remains inaccessible, inasmuch as human intelligence must rest content with a provisional criterion: the Bible.
Within this tripartite division, it will be possible to set forth
Barth's theological methodology. A fourth part, moreover, will
be dedicated to Barth's principles. We will give a brief evaluation

of those principles, inquire into their origin, and compare them with corresponding principles of Catholic theology. Our exposition, therefore, will be presented in the following order:

I. The divine criterion of dogmatics: the Word of God.

II. The human and provisional criterion: the Bible

III. The Church's proclamation: the material of dogmatics.

IV. The value of Barth's principles and their immediate origin.

# notes
## to chapter one

1 Cf. KD, vol. I, 1, p. 1.

2 Translation of J.-L. Leuba in his *Résumé analytique de la Dogmatique ecclésiastique de Karl Barth*, p. 19.

3 Barth expounds his position on this matter in KD, vol. I, 1, pp. 48–57. We can summarize in the following brief table the different meanings which Barth accords to the collective expression, "discourse relative to God," Rede von Gott:
1. Gottes Selbstwort = das Wort Gottes,
2. Die religiöse Rede von Gott = die menschliche Rede von Gott = die in der Kirche stattfindende Rede von Gott:
   a. Der Gottesdienst,
   b. Die Solidarität,
   c. Der Jugendunterricht,
   d. Die Theologie,
   e. Die Verkündigung:
      aa. Die Predigt,
      bb. Das Sakrament.

4 Cf. KD, vol. I, 1, p. 2.

5 Cf. KD, vol. I, 1, pp. 57–58. This is what Barth calls: "Die im kirchlichen *Gottesdienst* stattfindende Rede von Gott" (KD, vol. I, 1, p. 49). As we shall see later, cult is in fact the place in which God normally intervenes. Cf. SK, p. 37.

6 See, for example, KD, vol. I, 1, pp. 82–83.

7 Cf. KD, vol. I, 1, p. 3. Chapter VII in its entirety will be devoted to this problem.

8 Since this is nothing but an anticipation of the exposition presented in Chapter X, the reader is referred to that chapter for references.

9 A constant teaching of Barth, which is found on almost every page of the first volume. One entire chapter, entitled *Reine Lehre als Problem der Dogmatik*, develops this doctrine. Cf. KD, vol. I, 2, pp. 848–874.

10 Here are several definitions of dogmatics: "Die Theologie als Frage nach dem Inhalt der der Kirche eigentümlichen Rede" (KD, vol. I, 1, p. 3). "Die Selbstprüfung der christlichen Kirche hinsichtlich des Inhalts der ihr eigentümlichen Rede von Gott" (*ibid.*, p. 10). "Die Wissenschaft vom Dogma" (*ibid.*, p. 14). With reference to this last definition, it must be noted that in this context dogma signifies a *Beziehungsbegriff*, a type of relation between today's proclamation and

11

the Word of God. Cf. KD, vol. I, 1, pp. 289–290. Accordingly, dogma (not dogmas) can be defined: "Die kirchliche Verkündigung, sofern sie mit der Bibel als dem Worte Gottes wirklich übereinstimmt" (KD, vol. I, 1, p. 283).

11 Barth proposes the question clearly: "Gibt es neben der kirchlichen Dogmatik eine besondere und selbständige kirchliche Ethik" (KD, vol. I, 2, p. 875). On this point all the reformers are not of one mind: "Die Theologie der Reformatoren, jedenfalls Luthers und Calvins, ist typisch für die Aufassung, nach der eine selbständige Ethik voraussetzungsmässig unmöglich ist" (*ibid.*, p. 876). If Melanchthon in his youth held the same opinion, we must bear in mind that he is also the author of the *Epitome philosophiae moralis* (1538) and of the *Elementa doctrinae ethicae* (1550). Aristotle, rejected by Luther, was reinstated (cf. *ibid.*, p. 877). A study of the ensemble of Protestant theology led Barth to the following conclusion: "Mann kann im Blick auf die Geschichte des Problems gewiss nicht sagen, dass die vereinigte Behandlung von Dogmatik und Ethik schon als solche notwendig die Übereinstimmung mit der reformatorischen Erkenntnis bedeute; man kann aber sagen, dass man sich mit ihrer Trennung notwendig von der reformatorischen Erkenntnis entfernt" (KD, vol. I, 1, p. 880). This is how Barth finally resolves the problem: "Die Frage der Dogmatik ist die Frage nach der Reinheit der Lehre. Das Wort Gottes, das der in der dogmatischen Dialektik intendierte Ursprungs-, Beziehungs- und Zielpunkt ist, ist aber das von Gott an den Menschen gerichtete und also das vom Menschen gehörte Wort. Der Mensch ist aber der existierende, d.h. der nicht bloss denkende, sondern, indem er denkt, lebende, handelnde und leidende, der in der Tat seines Daseins begriffene Mensch. Nur der Täter des Wortes ist sein wirklicher Hörer" (*ibid.*, p. 886). "Die ethische Frage, d.h. die Frage nach dem richtigen Handeln, ist die menschliche Existenzfrage" (*ibid.*, p. 887). These considerations remain as yet quite theoretical. The question arises as to how, from such principles, a person can derive a concrete morality which will give precise precepts for daily life. In short, the entire problem of the relations between nature and grace are broached at this point.

12 "Theology is one; the divisions commonly made between dogmatic, moral, ascetical, etc., are due to the practical needs of teaching, not to a scientific necessity" (G. Rabeau, *Introduction à l'étude de la théologie,* p. 231). Cf. also M. J. Congar, in DTC, vol. XV, col. 494.

13 If we refuse, with Barth, to distinguish two sciences, this refusal in no way implies that we agree with his manner of conceiving the ethical problem properly so-called. As note 11 above may have led you to suspect, Barth's system contains a contempt for nature which we cannot admit.

14 Der "moderne Begriff des Wissens und der Wissenchaft deckt sich nicht mit dem aristotelischen. Im weitesten Sinne des Wortes kann man zwar unter 'Wissen' jede Erkenntnis irgendwelcher Art, die gewisse wie die wahrscheinliche, verstehen. Im engsten und eigentlichen Sinne schliesst aber nach aristotelisch-thomistischer Terminologie das wissenschaftliche Erkennen, die *épistêmê,* nicht nur die unvollkommenen Erkenntnisweisen der Meinung (*opinio, doxa*) und des Glaubens aus, sondern ist ausserdem innerhalb des evidenten Erkennens auf das apodiktische oder beweisende Schliessen beschränkt, das nach Aristoteles nichts anderes ist als ein sicheres Erkennen der Dinge aus ihren Gründen" (Paul Wyster, *Die Theologie als Wissenschaft,* p. 65).

15 J. Maritain, *Les degrés du savoir,* p. 67.

16 M. D. Chenu, *La théologie comme science au XIII^e siècle,* in *Archives hist. doct.*

*litt. du m.a.*, 1927, vol. II, p. 33. In the second edition of this work (separate edition, Paris, 1943), Père Chenu makes a greater allowance for the preparatory steps taken by various authors prior to St. Thomas. Cf. p. 10: "Die theologische Erkenntnis ist nach Thomas von Aquin in der Tat eine wissenschaftliche Erkenntnis nicht deshalb, weil sie die Glaubenswahrheit vor der Profanwissenschaft rechtfertigen, rationell 'begründen' möchte, sondern weil sie aus der unmittelbar gegebenen Glaubenswahrheit, ihrem ureigensten Erkenntnisgebiete, schlussfolgernd neue, darin *virtuell enthaltene Wahrheiten ableitet*. Sie ist also ein Beweiswissen im eigentlichen Sinne und darum gleich jedem anderen, wenn auch auf der höheren Ebene des übernatürlichen Glaubens, wissenschaftliches Erkennen in der strengen, aristotelischen Bedeutung des Wortes" (P. Wyser, *Die Theologie als Wissenschaft*, p. 13).

[17] J. Wolleb (1626), while recognizing the complex character of the "theological *habitus*," nonetheless states clearly that theology is a science. "Quaeritur autem, si theologia ut habitus intellectus consideretur, quod ei genus ex habitibus intellectus assignandum foret? Sane nullum est, quod solum ac seorsim sumptum definito non sit angustius; cum enim *intelligentia* principia apprehendens, *scientia conclusiones ex principiis demonstrans . . .* , *prudentia* vero et *ars* sit, theologia partim in contemplatione partim in actione consistit" (*Christianae theologiae compendium*, paragraph 1, canon II, ed. Bizer, p. 1).

[18] Cf. H. Stephan, in RGG, vol. V, col. 1119–1121.

[19] *Richtlinien evangelischer Theologie*, 1929, p. 29, cited by Barth in KD, vol. I, 1, p. 7.

[20] *Wie ist eine evangelische Theologie als Wissenschaft möglich?* in *Zwischen den Zeiten*, 1931, vol. IX, pp. 8–53, cited in KD, vol. I, 1, p. 7.

[21] In 1927 Barth explained the necessary isolation of dogmatics in the following manner: "Nicht eine *splendid isolation* der Theologie unter den Wissenschaften und in der Kultur ist unser Anliegen, aber dass sie es wieder lerne, im eigenen Haus eigene Ordnung zu halten, dass ihr Haus aufhöre ein Allerweltshaus zu sein. Solange uns aber keine Garantie gegeben ist zur Sauberkeit in dieser Beziehung, solange die Belehrung durch eine allgemeine Wissenschaftslehre eitel Störung und Zerstörung der uns notwendigen eigenen Sachlichkeit bedeutet, solange der Historiker, der Psychologe, der Logiker, der Pädagoge usf. seine Grenzen und unsere Grenzen so wenig kennt, dass wir keinen Augenblick vor allen möglichen Kuckuckseiern sicher sind, solange danken wir für alle Wissenschaftslehre, solange ziehen wir die *splendid isolation* einer *universitas litterarum*, in der wir unseren eigenen eigentümlichen Platz nich wahren können, vor" (CD, p. 117). See what is said on this subject by Th. Siegfried in *Das Wort und die Existenz*, I, p. 7.

[22] Cf. KD, vol. I, 1, p. 6. In the same volume, pp. 296–301, the reader can see in what the *Wissenschaftlichkeit* of Barthian dogmatics consists. Still further developments on theology as a science can be found on p. 86.

[23] Père Wyser expresses this neatly: "Die energische Rückkehr der gegenwärtig wohl bedeutendsten theologischen Richtung innerhalb des Protestantismus, der dialektischen Theologie, zu einer Theologie des Wortes Gottes, das heisst zu einer Glaubenstheologie, bedeutet im Grunde genommen eine derart übertriebene irrationale Auffassung der theologischen Erkenntnis, dass jeder Anspruch auf eine hochschulmässige Wissenschaftlichkeit derselben ohne Zögern fallen gelassen wird" (*Die Theologie als Wissenschaft*, p. 11).

14

24 Cf. KD, vol. I, 1, pp. 293–296.

25 "Unter *System* ist im Sinne aller derjenigen, die etwas Derartiges geschaffen haben, zu verstehen: ein unter Voraussetzung einer bestimmten Grundanschauung mit Benützung bestimmter Erkenntnisquellen und bestimmter Axiome aufgebauter, in sich *abgeschlossener und vollständiger Zusammenhang von Grundsätzen und Folgesätzen*" (KD, vol. I, 2, p. 963). Cf. KD, vol. I, 1, p. 80. In CD, pp. 449–450, one can see what Barth thought, as early as 1927, of dogmatics as a system of theology.

# PART ONE

*The Divine Criterion of Dogmatics:*

*The Word of God*

# 2

# the WORD of God
# in protestant tradition

THE FUNDAMENTAL characteristic of Barth's theology is the disjunction made between the Word of God and Sacred Scripture.
Without becoming totally different realities irrelevant to each
other, the Word of God and the Bible no longer are perfectly co-
incidental; while still preserving certain common points, they are
no longer interchangeable notions. The relation between the two
will be established according to an original method. Protestant
theology of the past provides no precedent for this method.

A. Identification of the Word of God and of Scripture
   According to Luther.

Protestant orthodoxy has made of this identification, denied by
Karl Barth, its fundamental dogma. An attempt to separate the
Word of God from the sacred text (be it ever so slight a separation)
is the worst of heresies and the open door to all sorts of excesses.
But this was not always the Protestant position. Luther in certain passages declared himself in favor of greater liberty and considered the bonds between the Word and the sacred text as rather
flexible. All the Bible, in his view, was not the Word of God—far
from it! One had to make a choice. He had to know how to dis-
criminate, to distinguish what goes back to Christ and what has
its origin in man. Faith must intervene at this point, and faith
will enable Luther to determine the canon of authentic books.

17

Faith can do more than that. All canonical books do not possess the same degree of authenticity. There is a complete scale of tones and semi-tones, a continuous gradation of shades and hues. Some books are more Christian than others and possess greater value. Luther states his principle in the preface to his translation of the New Testament (1522):

> All the authentic books of Sacred Scripture have this in common: they treat of Christ and preach Christ. It is this which serves as a touchstone in evaluating each of the books. . . . Anything which does not teach Christ is not apostolic, even if St. Peter or St. Paul taught it. On the other hand, anything which preaches Christ is apostolic, even if it should be Judas, Anna, Pilate, or Herod who has instructed us. . . . By this principle, you may conclude and know which are the best (among the sacred books). . . . Thus the Gospel according to St. John is the principal Gospel. It is affectionate and righteous. It must be ranked far above the others. In the same way, the Epistles of St. Peter and of St. Paul far surpass the writings of Matthew, Luke, and Mark. In a word, the Gospel according to St. John, his First Epistle, the Epistles of St. Paul (especially those to the Romans, to the Galatians, and to the Ephesians), the First Epistle of St. Peter—these are the books which teach you to know Christ and all that you must know in order to be holy. *It will not be of any use for you to know any other sacred book* or teaching. In comparison with the books I have mentioned, the Epistle of St. James is truly a straw letter, because it exhibits no evangelical character.[1]

Relying on this principle, Luther reconstructed the New Testament. The number of books was reduced from twenty-seven to twenty-three. The Epistle to the Hebrews, the Epistles of James and of Jude, as well as the Apocalypse, " . . . works which formerly possessed a rather great prestige," are demoted to the rank of deuterocanonical books.[2]

At first sight, this principle enuntiated by Luther should apply to everyone. Each person's faith should enjoy the same liberty. In its full rigor, this principle seems incompatible with the verbal inspiration of Scripture. How can we still speak of the inspired character of each word, when every reader is permitted to determine what is truly central in a text and to weigh for himself the Christian import of each book? Would Luther be opposed to verbal inspiration of Scripture? Not in the least. He is firmly bound to the letter. Harnack puts forward the theory that Luther reverted to verbal inspiration as a consequence of the excesses of the Anabaptists.[3] This theory, however, has little likelihood. Although the first appearance of the sect did not occur until 1522, Luther clearly expressed himself in favor of verbal inspiration seven years prior to that date.[4]

He will continue to teach this same doctrine throughout his entire lifetime. It is this doctrine, moreover, which will enable him to adopt a definite position in the controversy with Zwingli. Must we admit that Jesus Christ is present in the Sacrament of the altar? Should not this dogma be cast out along with the rest of Roman ecclesiastical pomp? Why not adopt the Swiss reformer's thesis? Why should Holy Communion be more than a pure symbol? Luther certainly would have liked to see in the Eucharist nothing but a bit of bread and a few drops of wine. "I writhed and struggled," we hear him say; "I saw that I could strike at papism the most crucial blow of all. But what could I do? I was *imprisoned;* I could not get out of the difficulty; the *text* was too powerful; nothing could uproot it from my soul." [5] The Word of God contained in the text describing the institution of the Eucharist demanded the retention of the real presence. Luther simply shared the viewpoint of most theologians of his time. Is not God, the author of the Bible, often represented under the image of one who dictates to a secretary the text which he has determined in His own mind?

Was Luther inconstant to such a degree? Could he pass from one thesis to another without perceiving the contradictions which set them off against each other? Such a contradiction exists only on the theoretical level. In Luther's psychology, everything was reconciled in a marvelous unity. Luther's faith had made a division among the sacred texts. Once this division had been made, he recognized in the chosen texts the Word of God. Those texts which he had selected because they were "Christian" are verbally inspired. The reformer of Wittenberg does not deny the liberty of faith to others; but it was difficult for him to believe that their liberty could lead them to conclusions other than his own. His entire system is based upon the rather naïve conviction that his religious experience represents the normal religious experience, that every Christian freed from the Roman yoke must necessarily undergo a religious experience in the same manner in order to achieve the same results. The famous "incident of the tower," in which Luther discovered his theory of justification by faith alone, is, in Luther's eyes, more a decisive event for all Christianity than for Martin Luther alone. His successors do not confide in a subtle dialectic. The variegated difficulties which an unregulated liberty presented simply impelled them to allow half of Luther's legacy to sink into oblivion, in order that they might retain the identification of the Word of God with the text of Sacred Scripture.[6]

## B. The Spiritualist Attack.

From the beginning of the reform, an attitude diametrically opposed to that of complete identification developed among the Anabaptists. Less than five years after he posted his ninety-five theses on indulgences upon the principal door of the Wittenberg castle chapel, Luther was obliged to abandon his refuge at Wartburg (where he had taken cover from the consequences of the Edict of Worms) so that he might restore order in Wittenberg. What had happened? The Reform seemed endangered. A group of illuminati—among whom was Thomas Münzer—had just arrived from Zwickau in Saxony. They claimed that they were favored with special heavenly revelations, and they preached a renewal of baptism. This was the first appearance of Anabaptism, elements of a doctrine destined to be embraced by a vast apocalyptic movement. The sect, against which Luther would have to struggle so vigourously, was preaching the establishment of Christ's Kingdom on earth in a kind of community of "religious," among whom there would be no private ownership. Laws and authority would be superfluous, since each Christian would live in conformity with the new law inscribed on his conscience. In this amalgam, the principal element, to be sure, was the suppression of Scripture, so that the Spirit alone might rule.[7]

Each member of the sect was, as a matter of fact, a prophet and doctor. Not only did he have the power to teach, but the obligation to do so each time that the Spirit's urging made him conscious of a revelation from on high. Some enlightenments of this kind were not always perfectly in accord with Scripture. That need be no obstacle! Has not Scripture, in the form in which it has come down to us, been falsified and corrupted? Subjectivism is given free rein. No longer is there any restraining bit, not even the words of Scripture. Christianity is entirely released from any historical bond. Why continue adhering to professional preachers appointed to expound, after study of the text, the content of the Scriptures? They are superfluous and even detrimental. The criticism which Lutherans leveled at Catholics was now turned against them. They had reproached priests for preaching exclusively the teaching of the Church; now they heard it said that they themselves were sacrificing the living Spirit for the dead letter. "Luther stated boldly that anyone convinced of the doctrine which he was teaching, to such an extent that he could fearlessly curse any opinion opposed to his own, would have given, by that very fearlessness, proof for the doctrine he put forward." [8] Following this line of reasoning, the Anabaptists should surpass by far all their contemporaries. The feeling of being possessed by the Spirit must have inspired them with an unshakeable confidence, since it required no confirmation other than their own interior inspirations.

## C. The Reaction of the Reformers: Scripture Is Identified with the Spirit.

Some counterplan was expedient. On the political level, this took the form of a bloody repression of the Peasant Revolt. On the religious level, this provided an occasion to bring the reformer's doctrine into focus. Contradiction forced the system to submit to self-scrutiny. Up to the present, we have seen how Sacred Scripture was identified with the Word of God and thus became the means placed at our disposal for obtaining a knowledge of God and of the supernatural order. But would the Spirit be restricted to Scripture? Would He be unable to operate beyond these limits? Or could there be some element of truth in the Anabaptist position? Could the affirmation of the Spirit's independence be preserved with the respect to the written word? Since the Spirit breathes where He will, can we impose prescribed limits on Him?

Luther's reply took the form of a demurrer. The Spirit acts through Scripture and the sacraments; He resorts to no other means for conferring grace on us. Moreover, sacraments cannot be considered independently of the Word; for they are simply a reflected image of the Word. They do not possess an immediate bond with divine causality, as they do in the Catholic doctrine of *ex opere operato;* they serve only as a visual expression of the Word of God contained in Scripture, whose oral counterpart is preaching. A sacrament is a *"pictura verbi."* The *Augsburg Confession,* the first official declaration of Lutheranism, states this formally.[9]

In 1537, the Articles of Smalkald were forced to re-emphasize this same position:

> In matters pertaining to the external, spoken Word, we must adhere to the following principle: God gives no one His Spirit or grace except by means of the Word and together with the external Word, which must precede (*nisi per verbum et cum verbo externo et praecedente*). This principle is our protection against the *illuminati* or spiritualists (*enthusiastas*), who boast of having received the Spirit without and before the Word and who, as a consequence, judge, interpret, and falsify Scripture or the oral Word according to their fantasy. This is what Münzer did, and it is what is being done today by many, who, wishing to set themselves up as judges, distinguish between the Spirit and the letter, though they know not what they are saying or doing.[10]

Sacred Scripture, then, is not the sole means whereby we can know God, but also the only means which God uses to reach us through His grace. The Holy Spirit operates only through Scripture. There is an identification between the activity of the Holy Spirit and the written Word.

Though it introduces more subtle overtones, the Calvinist tradition is in perfect harmony with Lutheranism on these various points. There is not a single discordant note. One text from the *Confessio Helvetica Posterior* of 1562 might appear ambiguous at first sight. It states that God " . . . *can* enlighten whomsoever He wishes whenever He wishes, even without the assistance of an external minister, since He is all-powerful." This annotation, however, has the limited value of a correction: it appears at the end of a lengthy paragraph which has established the practical necessity of the preaching of Scripture. It is, nonetheless, quite characteristic of Calvinist thought. The Genevan reformer himself said that God is able to act by means other than the Word, and that He sometimes does so act.[11] The divine sovereignty, indeed, cannot be bound by any form external to itself. Nevertheless—and this fact is essential—such a mode of action is not God's habitual manner of proceeding, nor is it in accord with the divine precept. No one may act on the authority of God's freedom as a justification for the belief that he has been favored by the Spirit through extraordinary channels. The *Confessio Helvetica Posterior* seems to present evidence that God wills to refrain from direct intervention. God could have " . . . justified Cornelius the Centurion either through His Holy Spirit, or through the ministry of an angel, without the assistance of Peter; He chose neither of these courses, and sent Cornelius to Peter." The same text goes on to state: "Since the Word of God is being announced in the Church today by preachers legitimately designated for that function, we believe that the Word of God is being declared, that this same word is being received by the faithful, and that, therefore, we must not devise any other Word or expect one from heaven." And the paragraph concludes: "We are speaking of the ordinary manner in which God deals with men, as well as of the command and example which He gave unto us." [12] In brief, the Word of God, the rightful sovereign, for all practical purposes is identified with preaching in conformity with the sacred text.[13]

At the very source of the Reformation, then, we discover two divergent and apparently irreconcilable mainstreams of thought dealing with revelation, the central problem of Christianity. In one direction the orthodox current, which identifies the Word of God with the Bible ever more closely, will evolve with increasing precision a theory of verbal inspiration, already found in the writings of Luther. It will go as far as to maintain that the entire Hebrew text of the Bible is inspired: the consonants, vowels, and very punctuation.[14]

In another direction a spiritualist current takes as its starting point a depreciation of the letter, so that it might flow exclusively from the Spirit. This revolutionary movement has found its proponents in every age. The Anabaptists were the first to appear.

Later, the Quakers resume the same theme with slight variations: the Spirit visits His elect, in a moment which He Himself determines, by means of an interior enlightenment of some sort. The Labadists (who derive their name from Jean de Labadie, an itinerant French Congregationalist preacher) prefer to place their trust in God speaking to them today, rather than in the pen of some writer. The Protestant sects inspired by similar tendencies are innumerable.

*

*  *

Barth had to choose between a literal and a spiritualist Protestantism; between the letter which imprisons the spirit, and the spirit which no longer wishes to recognize the letter. He chose neither: he seeks an intermediate solution. Either extreme is distasteful to him; he would like to avoid both. In opposition to the presumptions of the letter, he extolls the liberty of the Word of God and the Spirit's sovereignty. To an unbridled spiritualism, he recalls the fact that God has restricted Himself by providing a witness to His Word in the sacred text. Henceforth, we will perceive how arduous and delicate a task it is for Barth to adopt a position between assent and denial. The remainder of this study will point out whether he has truly succeeded in realizing the impossible.

# notes
## to chapter two

1 Kidd, *Documents Illustrative of the Continental Reformation*, pp. 104–105, cited by L. Cristiani in DTC, vol. XIII, col. 2042.

2 Cf. H. von Soden, RGG, vol. I, col. 986. According to this principle of Luther, the entire Bible does not comprise the Word of God, but only a part of this Word. A question arises: does the written word exhaust the Word of God? Léonhard Hutter, one of the most faithful disciples of the reformer and defender of his heritage against the influence of Melanchthonism, was of the opinion that the Bible is only a summary of the Word of God. "Verbum Dei est doctrina de salute hominis divinitus patefacta in Scriptura Sacra *comprehensa.*" (Cited by H. Auer, RGG, vol. V, col. 2019.) The Word of God, then, is more extensive than Scripture, but it expresses itself only through Scripture.

3 Cf. A. von Harnack, *Lehrbuch der Dogmengeschichte*, vol. III, p. 878.

4 "Omne verbum vocale (scil. praedicationis), per quemcumque dicatur, velut Domino ipso dicente, suscipiamus, credamus, cedamus et humiliter subjiciamus nostrum sensum. Sic enim justificabimur et non aliter" (*Vorlesung über den Römerbrief*, 1515–1516, ad III, 22, ed. Ficker, *Anfänge*, vol. I, 2, pp. 89–90). Elsewhere Luther says further: "Fides enim consistit in invisibili, aut ergo tota est et omnia credenda credit aut nulla, si unum non credit." (*See* the same text, *op. et ed. cit.*, p. 86.)

5 EA, vol. LIII, p. 364, trans. by L. Febvre, *Un destin. Martin Luther*, p. 262.

6 Harnack does not hesitate to say that Luther effected only a semi-reform. Because of his inconsistency, in defending at one and the same time two contrary theses, he permitted the thesis which Catholicism had always sustained to prevail. Moreover, he subjugated religious thought once more to a canon of ecclesiastical origin. Luther owes the restoration and complete development of his principle of liberty to modern Protestantism. Cf. *Lehrbuch der Dogmengeschichte*, vol. III, p. 879.

7 J. A. Möhler, *Symbolik*, pp. 459–461 and 474–477.

8 J. A. Möhler, *Symbolik*, p. 477.

9 "Ut . . . fidem consequamur, institutum est ministerium docendi evangelii et porrigendi sacramenta. Nam per verbum et sacramenta tamquam per instrumenta donatur Spiritus Sanctus, qui fidem efficit, ubi et quando visum est Deo, *in iis, qui audiunt evangelium.* . . . Damnant Anabaptistas et alios, *qui sentiunt*

*Spiritum Sanctum contingere sine verbo externo* per ipsorum preparationem et opera" (*Conf. Aug.*, art. 5, ed. J. T. Müller, *Die symbolischen Bücher* . . . , pp. 39–40).

10 *Articuli Smalcaldici,* pars III, art. 8, J. T. Müller, *Die symbolischen Bücher* . . . , p. 321. Philip Melanchthon says further: "Cum Deo non potest agi, Deus non potest apprehendi nisi per Verbum. Ideo justificatio fit per verbum" (*Apologia Confessionis Augustanae,* art. 4, 67, J. T. Müller, *Die symbolischen Bücher* . . . , p. 98). There can be no doubt as to the position taken on this subject by primitive Lutheranism. Elsewhere Luther also says: "Solum verbum est vehiculum gratiae" (WA, vol. II, p. 509). Cf. on this subject the study of R. Seeberg, PRE, vol. XXI, p. 497.

11 Cf. *Inst. chrét.,* IV, 16, 19, Cr, vol. IV, col. 954.

12 "Agnoscimus interim Deum illuminare *posse* homines etiam sine externo ministerio, quos et quando velit: id quod ejus potentiae est. . . . Equidem potuisset per Spiritum suum Sanctum, aut per ministerium angeli, absque ministerio sancti Petri instituisse Cornelium in *Actis* Deus, caeterum rejicit hunc nihilominus ad Petrum: de quo angelus loquens, Hic, inquit, dicet tibi quid oportet te facere. . . . Cum hodie hoc Dei verbum per praedicatores legitime vocatos annunciatur in ecclesia, credimus ipsum Deum annunciari, et a fidelibus recipi, neque aliud Dei verbum vel fingendum vel coelitus esse expectandum. . . . Nos autem loquimur de usitata ratione instituendi homines, et praecepto et exemplo tradita nobis a Deo." Art. I, E. F. K. Müller, *Die Bekenntnisschriften* . . . , p. 171.

13 The following text is an excellent summary of what has become the classical Calvinist position: "Modus vocationis opposite consideratus in externum et internum distinguitur. Ille foris per verbi et sacramentorum administrationem, hic intus per operationem Spiritus sancti peragitur. Non semper Deus utrumque vocationis modum ad hominum conversionem sibi possibilem adhibet, sed quosdam interno tantum Spiritus Sancti lumine ac numine *absque externo verbi sui ministerio* ad se vocat. Qui vocationis modus per se quidem est ad salutem sufficiens, *sed rarus admodum, extraordinarius, nobisque incognitus* (*Syn. pur. Theol.,* Leiden, 1624, disp. 30, 32, 33, cited in KD, vol. I, 1, p. 54).

14 Cf. *Helvetische Konsensus-Formel von 1675,* can. 2, ed. E. F. K. Müller, *Die Bekenntnisschriften* . . . , p. 862.

# 3

# the nature of the word
# of god: barth's personalism

As the name indicates, the Word of God as discourse (*Rede*) belongs to an intellectual domain and is connected with all that appertains to the sphere of thought. Therefore, declares Barth, we must avoid seeing in it the symbol of a power, an image for manifesting a motivating force. It is for a definite reason that the Scripture, when it treats of the Word of God, calls it *Pneuma* or *Logos*. It is, indeed, an event of the rational order, a phenomenon linked primarily with the Divine Intelligence. If the Word were simply an original name to indicate the almightiness of God, why would Scripture say that God *speaks,* or why would it ask man to listen, to understand, to obey? No doubt the Word is also an act of God, but above all exegesis and all comparison, it is the Truth of God, it is Revelation.[1] Such are the premises. Did Barth remain faithful to them? Is the Word of God truly an enlightening of the intelligence? We must answer this question before proceeding further.

## A. The Point of Departure.

This is not particularly new, and Barth dwells on it only long enough to indicate in passing the dangers of a certain anti-spiritualistic realism, a current affliction. His truly new contribution consists in a series of elements which do not admit of easy unification at first glance. The words *creation, event, decision, act of*

*God, contemporaneity,* clash without our perceiving their relationship. On first meeting them, one is confused, and the uninitiated believes that he has been transported into a deep mystery. The thought of Barth is, nevertheless, quite coherent and worthy of the best logicians. The essential task is to discover his point of departure, a rather narrow basis upon which his entire system rests like an inverted pyramid. In my opinion, one must start with the exegesis which Barth makes of the Prologue of St. John. It is here that we find the nucleus of his entire doctrine. "In the beginning was the Word, and the Word was with God, and the Word was God" (John 1:1). In place of the term "Word" let us substitute the "Word of God," and we will have crossed the threshold into Barth's theological system; for his system is founded upon the strict equivalence between God, the Word, and the Word of God. The last mentioned, understood in its full sense, is God. There is revelation only where there is God. In other words, the Word of God is a person and a Divine Person: It is Christ (John 1:18). This is also what the Apocalypse says: "Then I saw Heaven thrown open and there appeared a white horse. His rider was called Faithful and True, and he judges and wages war in uprightness. His eyes blazed like fire. There were many diadems on his head, and there was a name written on him which no one knew but himself. The garment he wore was spattered with blood, and his name was the Word of God" (Apoc. 19:11–13). The *Logos tou Theou,* represented here as the image of a rider in a role of an avenger, is then truly a person.[2]

In the following chapters, the immediate consequences of this position will appear. By reason of its identification with the Being of God, the Word is identified also with the Divine Act, and is, therefore, almighty and creative. It shares, likewise, the principal attribute of God, and is, therefore, completely free. Finally, it is inseparable from the person of Christ, and must, therefore, be contemporaneous.

## B. The Word of God is Almighty And Creative.

The tragedy of human utterance consists in its own impotence, in the abyss which exists between it and reality. The human word can only *speak;* it can sometimes order, but it can never *realize,* never *create.* No doubt, this is the reason for the atmosphere of distrust which surrounds all words, even the most eloquent. Sooner or later, acts are required. Is it for this reason, to protect himself in a certain way against a weakness, which he knows too well, that the speaker, by vocal intonations, through facial expressions and his gestures, tries to bolster his argument? Is this the reason why he speaks mainly about acts already accomplished or to be accomplished? These false expedients do not succeed in hiding the defect of all human utterance. It is nothing more than words, that is, an expression of a personal thought. In order to be an act, it should be in itself a modification of the encompassing milieu. A word changes nothing; acts make history. *"Ipse dixit et facta sunt"* (Ps. 33:9). Word and act become synonymous when God is concerned. God speaks; something happens; a change is produced. The word of God is creative: "God said, 'Let there be light,' and there was light" (Gen. 1:3). It raised the dead: *"Talitha koum"* (Mark 5:41). It heals: "Arise and take up thy pallet and walk" (Mark 2:9). It punishes (Apoc. 19:12–13). It pardons, etc. . . . Nothing resists it.

The Word of God cannot be otherwise than efficacious. The very nature of this Word is the underlying cause of its efficacy: it is a Divine Person; therefore, God Himself. The word of a human person fails, because it comes into opposition with everything which is not itself: the inertia of matter, other wills, not to speak of its own indigence. When God speaks, it is the Lord, the Master of history, who is intervening, the unlimited Being, who needs no assistance to make His word triumph, who has no obstacle to overcome since He alone *is.* The Word of God, therefore, is act.[3]

If the Word of God is act, we say equivalently that the Word of God is creative. It *realizes* what it *says.* All the Christian concepts of revelation, separation, election, new birth are not invitations of the moral order, limiting themselves to exterior actions on our wills; rather they are truly realizations of the *hic et nunc.* When God calls us forth, we are created; we are His. By His Word we are His property and no longer belong to ourselves.

The human word could not have this physical efficacy.[4] It acts through persuasion, is able to present the best aspects of a thing, and thus arouse a desire for it. In unveiling other aspects, it is able to provoke repulsion. But it does not act immediately on the very principle of individual action: it is only able to arouse, excite, and invite. This is true even when it commands. It then appeals to the moral sentiments of the individual to whom the command is given, but this appeal limits in no way the area of liberty and self-determination of the person concerned. He can obey or disobey; the order given cannot do violence to his will. The Divine Word, on the contrary, is not a mere wish, nor a mere promise, nor even a command. It places man in a new state. The man to whom God speaks, by this very fact, becomes a "Christian" in the full sense of the word. By demanding, it effects what it demands. It is *Inanspruchnahme,* the requisition of man by God.[5]

This power of the Word must not be considered as one of the powers of God. It is not one of the attributes of power; it is the omnipotence of God. There is no other way by which God acts. The Holy Spirit Himself must not be considered as a parallel power. He is not of another order, nor does He act independently of this power; rather, He is the power of life which acts in and through the Word. Consequently, nothing is beyond the reach of the Word of God; Its power is as universal as the divine power. "Everything was made by it, and without it nothing was made of that which was made" (John 1:3).[6]

## C. The Word of God is Free.

The Word of God is identified with the act of God; It is *God-Who-acts.* Consequently, it enjoys all the prerogatives of the divine personality—primarily, that of liberty. This divine attribute is, according to Barth, the principal attribute which sums up and conditions all the others. The Word of God is free; for this reason, it is called a decision. God is free with a total but pledged liberty. The concept of liberty applies to God in two ways: one negative, the other positive. Both one and the other are indispensable and complement each other. The action of God acknowledges no obstacles, no limits, no conditions. But again, this does not express

completely what the liberty of the God of Christians is. To express
this concept fully, we must add that God is His own principle;
that He finds in Himself the source of His liberty; in a word, that
He is *a Se*.

*Aseitas* is the essential element of Divine liberty.[7] It goes back
even to the writings of the Fathers. God Himself is Being, Life,
and Goodness. Soon, however, men wished to consider only the
negative aspect and believed themselves justified in identifying
*aseitas* with independence. Such an identification reveals a very
limited appreciation of God's Being; for it reduces God's Being
to that which separates His will from all created wills. When
Yahveh gave His name in the Old Testament, He gave a positive element: "I am Who am" (Exod. 3:14). When we say God is
independent, we do not say what He is, but only what He is not.
We remain on a philosophical level.

If Barth insists so much on this aspect of the question, it is because he fears reuniting the Christian notion of God with a neoplatonic, philosophical notion. The neoplatonic God is pure transcendence, a separated being, the "existing beyond." He is not a
person, a subject; He is much more the object arrived at by a
negation of our terrestrial experience. In brief, it is not God, but
rather a new way of expressing our limitations. It is the "Unre-
stricted," the "Infinite," the "Absolute." The God of the Bible is
free with regard to His own liberty. His subjective liberty is not
the same as His transcendent liberty. His transcendence would
confine Him outside the world and bar Him from any interest in
it. Personal liberty frees Him from a transcendence which would
separate Him excessively from the world. God is not *necessarily*
separated from the world to such a degree that He is not able to
intervene directly. True, God is not conditioned by the world;
but this form of liberty cannot transform itself into a new form
of restriction. God intervenes in the world. He calls the world to
Him, makes promises to humanity, and is faithful to those promises. These interventions in the world and fulfilled promises in no
way oppose true liberty.[8] Consequently, there is a twofold aspect
to God's liberty: the first frees this liberty from all created limitations; the second frees this liberty from all false transcendence.

God is free, but His freedom is a utilized freedom, which commits itself, determines itself, and chooses. His liberty is decision (*Entscheidung*).[9]

If then the Word of God is decision—that is to say, totally unlimited divine intervention—it cannot be identified with an historical fact (*Geschehen*); for historical fact is limited by nature. Everything which appertains to history is bound to a continuity from which it cannot detach itself. Every fact depends upon some cause and is itself associated with the entire unfolding of history, which serves as its frame. This is true not only in the order of nature but equally in the order of history and humanity. So we must not think that man's liberty is an exception; it, too, is inserted into history. Without falling into the error of absolute determinism, we must admit, says Barth, that practical realities limit man's choice to certain possibilities, and that man, when facing a decision, does not have an unlimited scale of choices. He is limited, first of all, by his capacities; moreover, his choice must rely upon what has gone before and consider the future as somehow continuous with the past. It is not possible for him to say, *"Ecce nova facio omnia."* On the other hand, there is no possibility of complete coincidence between an historical fact and a divine decision. The Word of God is not enclosed within the continuity of history; though it intervenes in history, it never allows itself to be absorbed by it. Sometimes, it will be *in* history, without ever being a part *of* it. If the Word of God were able in some way or another to identify itself with definite occurrences enclosed within the succession of human events, it would no longer be the Word of God; for it could no longer claim identity with the Uncreated Act.

Such, too, would be the teaching of Scripture. For the prophets, as well as for all the Jews of the Old Testament, the Word of God appeared as an event which was to be awaited from God alone. It would be the object of our prayer, but in no way has it become immanent.[10] Is it not for this reason that the Eternal Word becomes rare in certain periods (1 Sam. 3:1)? "Behold the days are coming," saith the Lord, the Eternal One, "when I will send famine upon the land; not a famine of bread, not a thirst for water, but for hearing the word of the Lord. And they shall wander from sea to sea and run from north to east, to seek the word of the Lord; but shall not find it!" (Amos 8:11–12). "Therefore, it shall be night for you without vision, and darkness for you without divination. For the sun shall set upon the prophets, and the day shall become dark over them . . . , because there is no answer from God" (Micah 3:6–7). Barth maintains that the same teaching is to be found in the New Testament, but he is hard put to find the conclusive texts to support his assertion. So it is not surprising that he has recourse to the favorite text of spiritualists, "The wind blows where it will" (John 3:8).[11]

## D. The Word of God Is Contemporary.

Barth's personalism, moreover, is inclined toward spiritualism. If the Word of God is a person, it exists only where that person intervenes. The Word exists only as long as God speaks and man hears; when the Divine Voice ceases, the Word ceases. The actualism of the Word of God distinguishes it—more than the characteristics already mentioned—from the mere human word.

The human word is indeed actual at the moment when it is pronounced, but something of its actuality remains: its content persists after it has been spoken. It is, therefore, possible to repeat it again. We can repeat today the words of Roosevelt. Those collections of words which we find in his notes or on phonograph records are truly the words of the president. The human word is like the word of an artisan; as soon as it is pronounced, it has, in itself, its own value, independent of the person who pronounced it. In human speech, therefore, we can distinguish the form and the content of the word. By form, I mean the very act of speaking: the work of the mind and the movements of the vocal apparatus. The content is the unity of ideas expressed by the words and arranged in phrases, which the act of speaking exteriorizes and delivers to the world. When a man ceases speaking, his word remains, and we have an authentic testimony of what he has said. His word has its own existence.

In God, it is impossible to distinguish these two aspects of the Word: form and content are identical. The Word of God is addressed to man, but not entrusted to him. As soon as God stops speaking, the Word disappears entirely; no authentic image of it remains. The Word is personal as well in its form as in its content. Jesus Christ *is* His message as well as the act of teaching: what Christ speaks is Himself. Therefore, it is impossible to conceive of a depersonalized Word, which would be introduced into history and continually reverberate, as an echo, the Word once spoken. Unless there be a face to face encounter between Christ and the Christian, an actual contact between two persons, one of whom speaks and the other listens, there can be no authentic Word of God.[12]

In slightly modified form, such is also the content of the theme of contemporaneity (*Gleichzeitigkeit*) which plays so large a part in the theology of Kierkegaard and in that of Barth. Through preaching and the Bible, we are placed in the presence of God. We do not find God by return to the past, by a *"repristination"* of Biblical times, by recourse to history; rather, we do so by transcending history and affecting an immediate reference to God. More precisely, through the accomplishment of the Word, we are grasped by God, elevated to His level, put in His presence. In brief, we are His contemporaries.[13]

The actualism of Barth is opposed to any kind of immanence which would be real and continued. Christian life is nothing but the outcome of an act or series of acts on the part of God. In itself, it has no continuous endurance. It is not, as is the grace and revelation of Catholic theology, a gift formerly granted by God and maintained in existence by His constant support. No, it is nothing more than a succession of moments, a line formed by a juxtaposition of events, the intervention of the Word of God. One of the most enthusiastic admirers of Barth's theology states quite simply:

One point on which it is difficult to agree with Barth is exaggerated actualism. By this, I mean a constant tendency to insist on what could be called the dynamic aspects of faith and Christian life to the detriment of the static aspects. The idea of a state of being appears almost offensive to Barth. His usual way of conceiving creation, consequently, is to think of it as a *creatio continua,* a constantly renewed call into existence of the finite universe. In his opinion, created beings do not remain such, but at every moment fall back into nothingness. Their existence must be continually renewed. This idea was familiar to the theology of the past, but whenever it reached such a predominance as to exclude all qualification, it never won the sympathy of the better Christian thinkers. No careful reader of the prophets and the apostles will deny that the idea of perpetual creation is truly a part of biblical teaching. But he never goes so far as to exclude the fact of a divine, once-and-forever creation of the world. If the Bible is really our guide, we must provide for two complementary aspects: God has created the world; He has established it in a created state by the instrumentality of His omnipotent Word; but within this Word, He continues to create.[14]

\*

\*  \*

The idea of conservation is unknown to the theology of Barth. He is then unable to admit the perduring existence of a created effect. Grace and revelation are not *existing* realities; rather they are in a constant *state of becoming*.

Who will deny then that reference to God, even today, is an actual and, consequently, an atemporal relation? But it is also evident that this reference cannot occur without some temporal mediation. Whether such mediation be effected by the Bible or the Church, it is beyond doubt—at least if we wish to avoid pure spiritualism—that revelation needs an instrument or a support, an element of history. Within the Barthian synthesis, the entire difficulty arises from the fact that the action of God never produces an *effect;* rather it is conceived as an uncreated force, which is *applied* momentarily to beings and given situations, but which is never *given*. The personalism of Barth is thus responsible for such consequences.

# notes
## to chapter three

1 In the name of the rationality of the Word of God, Barth is opposed to the "irrational" of Rudolf Otto. As is well known, the specifically religious element for Otto, the experience of the divine, is radically distinct from any intellectual expression which could be given to it. Not only the religious experience (which Otto calls "Numenal"), but also the cause of that religious experience (the "Numen"), is irrational, because it is inexpressible in terms of conceptual thought. Otto, however, comes to no conclusion regarding the nature of the "Numen" in itself, and his method by no means excludes the possibility that it is a spirit. Consequently, the question arises whether the criticism which Barth levels at Otto might not be turned back upon its author. The Bible, preaching, and theology belong to the rational order; but, as we shall see, Barth refuses to grant them the least degree of equivalence with the Word of God taken strictly as such. Barth's God is as irrational as the "Numen" (cf. Rudolf Otto, *Le Sacré*, pp. 16–19 and 92–96). "Irrational" can have several meanings. For Barth it is a force of nature (as opposed to "spirit"); for Otto it is all that can be perceived through a mode of knowledge irreducible to conceptual perception. The former operates on the metaphysical level, while the latter remains on an epistemological plane. Cf. KD, vol. I, 1, p. 140.

2 Among others, see KD, vol. I, 1, pp. 141–142. "Revelation is God himself" (*Révélation . . .* , p. 17).

3 Cf. KD, vol. I, 1, pp. 148–149.

4 "Es gibt kein Wort Gottes ohne physisches Geschehen" (KD, vol. I, 1, 138).

5 Barth is opposed to any purely forensic justification.

6 KD, vol. I, 1, pp. 155–158. Cf. also vol. III, 1, pp. 122–123.

7 Von Balthasar has clearly defined this aspect of Barthian thought: "The image of God which Barth delineates is evidently based on a model whose dominant element is voluntaristic, or rather, personalistic. The *Aseitas*, which seemed essential to theology as that which is properly divine in God, is called 'liberty' in Barth's writings (KD, vol. II, 1, p. 340) and this is, in its term, the name of the spirit and the person (KD, vol. II, 1, p. 611). . . . This implies that there is no intellectual restriction at the basis of divine liberty" (RSR, 1948, vol. XXXV, p. 104).

8 Cf. KD, vol. II, 1, pp. 338–342.

9 Cf. KD, vol. I, 1, p. 163.

10 Père L. Malevez expresses this well: "The Christian fact is nothing but an event, in the strictest sense of the term. The Word which echoes in Christ comes from above into the uninterrupted design of universal life; it does not advance the historical evolution of the species any more than it advances thought or religious sentiment; it is absolutely other; nothing human either prefigures or foreshadows it, and no reality other than itself is a sign of its proximate approach or actual presence in our lives" (RSR, 1938, vol. XXVIII, p. 411). But must we perceive an opposition between the terms 'event' and 'decision'? "Such is the aggregate of ideas and viewpoints which the word 'event' must connote when applied to the Incarnation. As a matter of fact, after having used the term, *Barth deletes it from his theological vocabulary.* The precise reason for this lies in the fact that his notion of event is based upon facts of nature and of history; consequently, an *event* includes the idea of a *relation of dependence with reference to the entire temporal unit of which it forms a part.* The eternal Word can contract no such relation. It is far better to speak of an action and a decision: the Incarnation is an act of free decision" (*ibid.*, p. 415; emphasis added). This can give rise to confusion. I do not believe that Barth has manifested any disaffection whatsoever for the term *event,* neither theoretically nor in practice. Moreover, we must note that though there may be opposition between the concepts of *Entscheidung* and *Ereignis* on the one hand, and those of *Geschehen* and *Geschichte* on the other hand (inasmuch as the former pertain to the vertical plane, while the latter refer to the horizontal), there is no opposition between *Entscheidung* and *Ereignis* (decision and event). The fact that "event" can also be a translation for *Geschehen* is probably at the root of this misunderstanding. The word "event," which throughout the work of Père Malevez translates *Ereignis,* corresponds on page 415 to *Geschehen.* To avoid all ambiguity, we will reserve the word "event" for *Ereignis,* and translate *Geschehen* by "historical fact." In KD, vol. III, 1, pp. 84–85, Barth makes a further distinction between *Historie* and *Geschichte.* The latter then becomes *Heilsgeschichte,* a succession of events pertaining to salvation, while the former remains an immanent history, as we have just explained. This does not at all affect (from God's viewpoint) the identification between *Ereignis* and *Entscheidung.*

11 Cf. KD, vol. I, 1, p. 164.

12 "Was Gott redet, das ist nie und nirgends abstrahiert von Gott selbst bekannt und wahr. Es wird bekannt und wahr dadurch und darin, dass er selbst es sagt, dass er in Person *in und mit* dem von ihm Gesagten gegenwärtig ist" (KD, vol. I, 1, p. 141). "Nicht irgend etwas, nicht ein *Theion,* sondern er selbst kommt zu uns in seinem Wort. Gerade in seinem Wort is Gott Person" (*ibid.,* p. 143).

13 Cf. KD, vol. I, 1, pp. 150–155.

14 H. R. Mackintosh, *Types of Modern Theology,* pp. 314–315. We cite this as a confirmation of what has preceded. We are dealing with supernatural creation. Although different points can be applied to creation in general, at this point we are not considering the question of the creation of nature. On this latter subject Regin Prenter, professor of theology at Aarhus (Denmark) and a former pupil of Barth, has written an excellent monograph entitled: *Die Einheit von Schöpfung und Erlösung. Zur Schöpfungslehre Karl Barths,* in *Theologische Zeitschrift,* 1946, vol. II, pp. 161–182.

# 4

# the present state
# of the word of god

THE PRECEDING chapter was principally concerned with God as emanating from God Himself and as identified with Him. We must pass on now to a new consideration and study just how this Word is received in the created world. One fact dominates this whole question: namely, sin. The nature into which the Word descends is no longer the nature which came from the hands of God, but a corrupted nature, which has become unsuited for the elevated role to which God has nevertheless destined it.

## A. The Doctrine of the *Welthaftigkeit*.

There is no more surprising doctrine in Barth's system than that of the *Welthaftigkeit*.[1] With this word "which is applied to all that is imprisoned in this world," Barth defines the essential character of revelation in our present condition.[2] God reveals Himself without dissipating our darkness. He is nonetheless present and it is by this presence (at least under the form of actual events) in complete darkness that God gives Himself to us. Ultimately this veil which covers the whole of revelation becomes its vehicle. Here we are faced with a paradox.

When God speaks to man, this fact is in no way distinguished from any other fact, with the result that it can easily be interpreted as an element of our habitual structure. The Church is ontally a sociological spectacle, identical with all others of the same genre, as much by

her historical past as by her present structure. Proclamation is likewise a discussion. The Bible can be envisaged as an historical document, dealing with a Middle Eastern tribal religion and its Hellenistic
prolongation. In history, Jesus Christ . . . does not appear as specifically different from other founders of religions . . . He is a rather com-
monplace rabbi from Nazareth. Nor can we overlook the fact that
theology, which must necessarily make use of human language, is also
a philosophy, or rather, an amalgamation of variegated philosophies.
The miracles themselves are confined within the limits of the *Welthaftigkeit:* from the very moment they occurred, men have been able
to interpret them as something other than proofs of the Word of God.
A veil covers everything. We possess the Word of God only in the
mystery of His *Welthaftigkeit.*[3]

## B. The Christological Unknown.

This *Welthaftigkeit,* consequently, applies to all the created
forms of the Word of God. Among them, however, there is one of
an altogether special type: the humanity of Christ. We are referring here to a personal, hence constant and intimate, union of the
Word of God with a created form. God does not associate Himself with the humanity of Christ only through successive manifestations, as in the case of the rest of creation, but in an abiding
manner. The study of this form of the Word of God, therefore,
is of major concern, and its conclusions a fortiori are of value for
all other forms of the Word of God. If the humanity of Christ is
not illumined by His divinity, the Bible and the Church could
not be a reflection of it.

Barth clearly poses the problem. Is the humanity of Christ
revelation? Is there something in this humanity which sets it apart
and thus renders perceptible the presence of the divine? Barth's
reply is negative. Christ's nature hides His divinity. How otherwise can it be explained that, of all those who knew Christ, so few
perceived the revelation? One of them even went so far as to be-
tray Him. Besides, Christ's death is an unquestionable manifestation of the limits of His humanity.[4]

This is absolutely opaque. All the systems which place the human nature of Christ in a separate category are therefore to be
rejected. Christ is not the "good Lord" of mysticism, nor the

"Saviour" of pietism, nor the teacher of wisdom and the philanthropist of the *Aufklärung*. Jesus is not the apex of elevated human nature, as conceived by Schleiermacher; nor Hegel's Jesus, the incarnation of the idea of religion. He is not even the religious personality of Carlyle. Christ did not appear to the Jews of His own time as a hero or a saint. All of these systems in the end only cause the divinity to be depreciated. It is undoubtedly present in Christ's humanity, but this immanence does not compromise its transcendency.[5] Revelation consists in *God* acting through Christ's humanity. And yet, this role of intermediary in no way transfigures that humanity. God hides Himself even when He reveals Himself. *Deus revelatus* remains *Deus absconditus*.[6]

Barth feels obliged to accept this extreme position by the logic of revelation and redemption. In order to reveal Himself and to save us, Christ must descend to our level, become what we are. That is what the Scripture means when it says: "The Word was made flesh." He has taken on our status. He has assumed human nature with all its properties, but also with all its limitations. Christ, then, is of the same nature, of the same physical structure, as we are. He has entered into an historical framework and so is subject to that contingency which confines all men within the bounds of birth and death. But this is still not a picture of the whole man. Human nature is not morally neutral. Can man be completely a man without knowing sin, or at least without encountering the inclination to evil and the interior struggle it supposes?

The thought of the Church is quite clear on this point. A letter of Pope Honorius I declares that Christ assumed human nature such as it was before the Fall. The *Verbum Dei* had no contact whatsoever with fallen nature.[7] This excludes not only sin, but equally as well that interior weakness, consequent upon Adam's sin, which caused evil to appear under tempting guises. This ancient tradition was accepted by the Reformers just as it was. For Luther, Christ's human nature was perfect even from the physical point of view: Jesus had a healthy body, the purest flesh, and was conceived without sin.[8] Calvin held that nothing of the scandal associated with the Incarnation or the cross should be extenuated. But for him it did not suffice that Jesus was man. He insisted that in the days of his earthly ministry, Jesus was a man whose external appearance was contemptible. He even says "abject" and "ignoble." "Being at the time vested with the form of a servant, he was contemptible because of the abjection and lowliness of his flesh" (John 8:14). "Christ . . . had nothing about his bearing which was not contemptible" (Luke: 23:11).[9] Despite this typically Calvinistic insistence—intended to reveal the absoluteness of God's Holiness and the absoluteness of human perdition—it never would have entered the mind of the Reformer of Geneva to suppose that the humanity of Christ, like our own, could have a proclivity for sin. In connection with the prologue of Saint John, he states: "The word 'flesh' ought not to be understood here to mean corrupted nature, but signify mortal man, as Paul was wont to use it." [10] It is not befitting that the Son of Man be united to a nature which is subject to the attractions of sin.

This cannot satisfy Karl Barth. Is not our present nature a corrupt nature? For once the theologian of Basle finds better understanding among the Liberals; [11] for in their camp, there is no dearth of theologians disposed to affirm that Christ was no exception in this matter.[12] Besides, all other explanations merely weaken Saint Paul's vigorous affirmation: "From this curse invoked by the law Christ has ransomed us, by himself becoming, for our sakes, an accursed thing" (Gal. 3:13). "Christ never knew sin, and God made Him into sin for us, so that in Him we might be turned into the holiness of God" (2 Cor. 5:21). Is it necessary to point out that these two texts, taken in any sense, cannot lead to Barth's conclusion? Two possibilities present themselves: either we must conclude that Christ is simply the representative of sin, the object of the curse, one Who took upon Himself the consequences of the crime and so was punished in the name of others; or we must go so far as to say that Christ has been a sinner.[13] No intermediate solution can find any foundation in these texts.

Christ has not sinned. Barth naturally admits that. The teaching of the Church on this point is among the clearest of its teaching.[14] But then how can this exception in Christ's assimilation of our condition be explained? Barth recalls at this point, and quite appropriately, that the man-Jesus is also God; that consequently, there is in him a sanctification of humanity by the divinity, a sort of reflection from which the human nature benefits. How then can we imagine that Christ was a sinner? This would be tantamount to admitting conflict in God Himself. In sinning, God would revolt against Himself. We understand Barth's conclusion without the least difficulty, and we are in wholehearted agreement. But the reasoning which leads to it remains rather confused. Is all of it perfectly conformed to the absolute principle enunciated above? For the authenticity of revelation and redemption, Christ had to become what we are. But man is not only prone to evil; he succumbs to it. Strictly speaking then, we must conclude that Christ is a sinner like us. Such a conclusion is inadmissible. Is not this proof that the principle, itself, is the cause and that its absolute value is unreliable? If the present conclusion is unwarranted, it is possible that others based on the same principle would likewise be unwarranted. Is it, then, still certain that Christ was inclined to evil, that His nature was a corrupt nature?

The authentic Christian doctrine, which the Reformers still echoed on this point, has a more refined vocabulary. Two facts are considered: the hypostatic union, and the end of the Incarnation. The humanity of Christ remains united to the Divinity; consequently, it is truly a transfigured humanity. Because of this proximity, it occupies the summit of created goodness.[15] From this flows a series of prerogatives which transforms the humanity of Christ: first of all, the beatific vision which fixes Christ's will on the good; next, the entire hierarchy of moral virtues which suppress all proclivity towards evil.[16] This transformation ought to be extended to the whole of Christ's humanity and make of it a totally glorified humanity. The end of the Incarnation, however, forbids such an extension beyond certain limits. Christ has thus accepted the assumption of certain limitations and imperfections proper to our nature, inasmuch as this was necessary to bring about the realization of His salvific mission.[17] In order to satisfy for sin, to attest to the reality of His Incarnation before the eyes of the world, and to serve as an example for us, it was necessary that Christ submit, among other things, to suffering, both corporal and spiritual, and to death itself. Barth's principle is basically a sound one: Christ has taken our place. But he was wrong to see in that a purely material substitution; thus he lost sight of God's holiness and the finality proper to the Incarnation.[18] Barth's dualism is often extended at the expense of substantial unity; certain aspects of his thought come close to an unconscious Nestorianism.

Despite His innocence, Christ's situation, such as Barth described it, is, therefore, interiorly and exteriorly that of a human sinner. His obedience was the result of an interior struggle. He had taken upon Himself the inclination to evil and had to struggle against it. The temptation in the desert actually corresponded to a moral drama, which was not unreal because Christ triumphed in it.[19] To the Jews, Christ did not pass for an ideal of the moral life: "Here is a glutton; he loves wine; he is a friend of the publicans and sinners" (Matt. 11:19). His neighbors did not hesitate to say: "He must be mad," and the Scribes added: "He is possessed by Beelzebub" (Mark 3:21–22). He is accused of deliberately misleading the people (John 7:12), of blaspheming (Matt. 9:3). Did not Christ, before these prejudices arose, give grounds for them by receiving the baptism of repentance from John the Baptist? (cf. Matt. 3:15). Barth thus traces for us a picture of Christ where only that which is common to all men is placed in relief; nothing of what renders that humanity transparent and permits sight of the divinity is noticeable. Neither the miracles, nor the Transfiguration of Christ on Thabor, nor His Resurrection are to be brought up here. Christ apparently is present to the eyes of His contemporaries like any other man; His true worth completely unrecognizable. His humanity is not a theophany. In no way and at no moment does it disengage itself from the *Welthaftigkeit* into which it has been totally absorbed.[20]

This conclusion is significant for the ensemble of created forms into which the Word of God has penetrated. What is said of the humanity is equally true of the Church, the Bible, and proclamation. Above all else, God in all of these is the hidden God. This abnormal state is not what God wanted, but what man has provoked. The world in which the Word is found today is that of sinful humanity. Human nature no longer presents itself as an integral nature, "which, as such, would immediately stand out against everything alien surrounding it." [21] Nothing, not a reflection, not a vibration, reveals today the presence of the Word.

## C. The Image of God and Sin.

Man has been most heavily wounded by the consequences of sin. To the extent that his faculties have been weakened, the presence of God in the material creation and even in the humanity of Christ has become that much less perceptible.[22] The subsidiary question must then be asked: In his actual state, is man still able to hear the Word of God? Has he not, because of sin, lost not only all contact with God, but also all possibility of contact? Has he not lost the ability to hear God? On these different aspects of one and the same question, Barth and Brunner had already exchanged frequent volleys, when, in 1934, after having clearly stated their respective positions, Brunner wrote his manifesto, *Natur Und Gnade.* Before expounding his own point of view, Brunner summarized in six theses Barth's principal positions. Up till this time, Barth was still considered the head of a school of dialectical theology. Of the six theses, only the first and the fifth are of interest to us. They read as follows:

Neither an intellectual nature, nor the disposition for culture, nor anything else whatsoever pertaining to the human side of man—howsoever human they may be—can in any fashion be considered as traces or remnants of a likeness to God which was lost by sin. For the same reason, one cannot admit in man a 'point of insertion' (*Anknüpfungspunkt*) for the salvific action of God. Such an admission would contradict the thesis of the exclusive action of Christ's grace, the central thesis of the Reformers' Scriptural theology.[28]

Primitive nature, therefore, is totally corrupted by sin and, as such, has no more relationship with grace. Man no longer can hear the Word of God.

Brunner could not share these views. A denial of the existence of a 'point of insertion' for grace can be due only to a misunderstanding. God speaks to man, not only to Adam and Eve in their earthly paradise but to the sinner equally. On the other hand, God speaks to man alone. Neither animals nor inanimate creatures engage in conversation with God. Can this be a proof that there is something in man which renders him capable of hearing the Word of God and that this 'something' has remained with man after the Fall? This 'something' is also proper to man since he alone in the entire realm of creation possesses it.[24]

What is this 'remnant' which persists in man after the Fall and which renders him capable of hearing the Word of God? It is simply his intellectual activity and his conscience; in other words, his personality.[25] Luther declares:

> If the natural law had not been given by God and engraved by Him upon the heart, it would be necessary to preach for a long time before consciences would be touched. Were one to preach to an ass, a horse, a steer, or a cow, for a thousand years in order to make them obey the law, it would be labor lost. Although they have ears, eyes, and a heart like man, they understand nothing; the Word of God does not penetrate into their hearts. Why? What is it they lack? *Their hearts have not been formed and created to receive the Word.* Man, on the contrary, when the law is presented to him, gives heed to it immediately. It is indeed so; he cannot deny it. *He could not be convinced so easily if the Natural Law were not engraved upon his heart. But because it happens to be already in him,* even though faintly and nearly extinct, the Word can give new life to everything.[26]

Man remains man and, as such, he can reenter into conversation with God. This element which remains in man is a remnant of God's image as God first created it. This element is the formal, indestructible, and constant constituent of that image. Nevertheless, God's image is no longer what it was in the earthly paradise: another element (material) has entirely disappeared because of sin.[27] This element is original justice. It does not suffice that man be a person; his entire life must be the life of a person. The harmony of the human person requires a life immersed in God's love, a constant dependence upon His Word, a personal subordination to God at the very heart of a creation subject to divine decisions. In brief, the normal state of the person is that of a continual exchange with God, an incessant conversation in which God speaks while man listens and responds. Sin has completely destroyed this state of friendship; nothing of the material element of God's image remains. Therefore, after a fault has been committed, a person lives in a violent state; he leads an existence not at all conformed to his nature. Yet, in this situation the human person still retains the dignity that God gave him in the beginning,

and this *cor incurvatum* has not lost the possibility of hearing
anew the Word of God, when It makes Itself known to him. In
other words, God, in order to reveal Himself, will not have to
make a new creature capable of hearing Him; it will suffice to
restore the fallen creature. He will not have to create a faculty
since it already exists. His revelation and grace will simply have
to heal it.

In opposition to Barth, Brunner affirms vigorously man's ability to hear the Word of God again. Undoubtedly, it is not necessary to hear the Word in the manner prescribed by the liberals,
who draw the Word of God from the well of their own being in
a religious experience of some sort, plumbing the depths of their
own interior. The Word of God can be heard in and by faith
alone. This theologian, therefore, in no way endangers Luther's
doctrine of *sola gratia*.[28] Faith comes from God and from Him
alone. It is a gratuitous gift that human nature cannot claim for
itself. Yet, this faith does not hover over a void; human nature
provides a solid basis upon which it can be established.

Brunner's initial proof has no cogency in the eyes of Barth.
Would intelligence and conscience be the 'point of insertion' of
grace because man alone enjoys the favor of revelation? Is this
exclusive favoritism so certain? God reveals Himself to the angels.
What is more, can one exclude a priori the existence of unknown
natures, also capable of hearing the Word of God? Finally, have
we anything more than a presumption upon the non-revelation
of God to non-rational creatures? Does Scripture tell us anything
on this point? [29] What conclusion must be drawn? The possibility
of other 'points of insertion'? But where would that lead us? Is
it not proof that, from the fact of God's revelation to a given being,
one cannot conclude to the preexistence in him of a natural disposition to hear the Word? Before the actual coming of the Word
of God, man is as foreign to It as is a stone.

Barth cannot see in man's intellectual activity, which places
the person in relation with creatures like himself, an adequate
aptitude for entering into contact with God. Because man speaks
and hears and is endowed with a responsible conscience, he is an
apt subject for life in society and he can enter into relationships
with other beings endowed with similar capacities. Because he is

a person, he can enter into contact with other persons. Brunner
concludes from this that man can also enter into contact with
God. Barth bridles at such an inference. By what right can one
place the divine personality on a level with human personalities?
The human person might very easily remain deaf, mute, and
powerless before God. And that, despite the integrity of his personal being, despite the activity of his intelligence, and despite
his conscientious sense of responsibility. Have we not proof of
this *a contrario* from the fact that Christ died equally for those
who were not endowed with intellectual or volitional activity?
Redemption, likewise, extends to the newborn and the mentally
deficient. Now, from all this evidence, there can be no question
here of the *Anknüpfungspunkt* of Brunner's theology.[30]

This allows us finally to state Barth's position with precision.
Two ways were open to him: either to deny human integrity in
affirming that sin has basically impaired humanity; or to deny all
relationship between an integral humanity and revelation. Barth
has chosen this latter solution. Before, as well as after sin, man
remains man; he has become neither turtle nor cat.[31] But from
this fact, one cannot draw any conclusion with regard to the Word
of God. Barth freely admits that a human creature is endowed
with intelligence, that this intelligence enables him to engage in
personal contact with others of his kind, and that he has a sense of
responsibility. This is self-evident, for it is a matter of everyday
experience. Barth did not need Professor Brunner's work to enlighten him. But why see precisely in this a 'point of insertion'
for grace? [32] One could just as easily say the same of the instinct
of animals or the gravity of a stone. Human nature has no value
in the face of revelation.[33]

Barth does not seek to justify his position at length. It suffices
for him to know that man is a sinner by all that he is (*"durch und
durch Sünder"*), that he owes everything, therefore, to grace and
Scripture alone. He will owe everything to them, even the faculty
of knowing God. Besides, such a thesis would be fundamentally
Protestant, for in accordance with it human intelligence would
be just as blind to the presence of divine truth as the will is powerless to realize what is just in God's eyes. Any sort of connection be-

tween the human intelligence and knowledge of the true God must be denied, just as the least cooperation of the human will in accomplishing or carrying out the Commandments.[34] There is no reason for believing that the intelligence has been preserved intact when sin has rendered the will incapable of all that is truly good.

However, such is not the attitude of the Reformers. They do not share Barth's pessimistic views on human intelligence. A reading of the first four chapters of *l'Institution de la religion chrétienne* suffices to convince us of this. It contains a theory of the knowledge of God, undoubtedly 'diminished' and 'corrupted' by sin, but which, nevertheless, plays a great role in the preparation for faith. The "feeling for God" remains in all of us, even after our sinful revolt.[35] How are we to explain this difference of opinion? In order to understand a situation which might appear paradoxical, it is necessary, according to Barth, to place the Reformer's statements into their historical context.[36] At a time when they stood in such clear opposition to Catholic theology, they did not have before them the synthetic thought of a Saint Thomas, summed up in the phrase: *Gratia non tollit sed praesupponit et perficit naturam;* rather, they were confronted with a form of Pelagian nominalism. And so, the adversary of the day was the one they attacked. Reacting against a Catholic Neo-Pelagianism, Protestantism accentuated all that concerns the will. The theologian became interested in all that referred to justification without the concursus of works—redemption through Christ's intervention alone. Everything else became secondary, even the problems dealing with revelation. These latter, however, were not neglected; the Scriptural principle was proposed vigorously in opposition to tradition, but this antithesis was not exploited to its limits; all the implicit conclusions which it contained were not brought out. Does not the final condemnation of Catholic tradition carry with it in seed the affirmation of the nothingness of human intelligence before Scriptural revelation? It is certain that the Reformers fought against an intellectual competence in the domain of revelation, but their criticism was not extensive enough. It lacked the same fullness and acuteness that characterized their depreciation

of volitional acts. This default was due to a very definite historical situation which they had not been able to control. Since that
time the theology of Saint Thomas has emerged anew, and a
'secularized Thomism' has infiltrated Protestant theology since
the time of Schleiermacher. Against this complex background,
which appears as a knotty synthesis of the problem of the natural
and the supernatural viewed in all its fullest and far reaching
consequences, it is impossible to take up the doctrinal affirmations of the sixteenth century in a material sense. To remain
faithful to the Reform, it is necessary to go beyond the Reformers
and grasp their fundamental attitude rather than this or that
point of doctrine.[37]

Neither Luther nor Calvin has gone so far as to pretend that
God's image was entirely destroyed: a remnant persists. This
'remnant' undoubtedly is not a notable thing—Luther calls it
the *larva Dei*—but it is nonetheless real.[38] For Barth, all has been
annihilated; nothing remains.[39] For this reason he is opposed not
only to Emil Brunner's thesis, but also to Catholic theology.[40]
The *Anknüpfungspunkt* resides, according to the theologian of
Zurich, in human *activity*. *Acts* of the intellect and the will—warped
by sin—become the fulcrum for supernatural renovation.[41] The
search for God is renewed, a search which had gone astray in pursuit of foolish fancies, but which now will serve as the foundation
for the true God's revelation. This point of view, conditioned by
Fichte's philosophy [42] (which can conceive of the ego only as an
ever-present reality and never as a substantial reality), seems to
lack internal coherence.[43] These acts are either partially or totally
disorientated. If only partially, they are, therefore, also partially
orientated and can, consequently, lead to a certain notion of the
true God without the help of revelation. This would be contrary
to the basis of all of Brunner's theology: natural knowledge is
possible only in conjunction with revelation. If these acts are
totally disorientated, far from being able to prepare the way for
the supernatural, they can only oppose it. Therefore, the Catholic
theologian does not seek to find in them the 'point of insertion'
for grace.[44] It is human nature as such which is the *Anknüpfungspunkt;* not human nature as the principle of activity, but as the

principle of passivity, for, insofar as it is a potency, it is open to the supernatural. It is well known that on this point, even within the sphere of Catholic theology, there are opposing theses. Some wish to see in the relationship between the natural and supernatural only an expression of obediential potency common to every creature: the entire created universe depends upon its Author. God can transform it at His liking; of stone He can make bread. Others—and it seems that Saint Thomas truly belongs to this group—base man's aptitude for grace upon an obediential potency proper to a rational creature, upon a natural capacity of the being endowed with intelligence and a will with regard to its adequate object: God.[45] Whichever thesis he may prefer, however, the Catholic theologian still affirms that *man* himself is elevated to the supernatural state, and that grace does not create in him new powers, but perfects his intelligence and will. The supernatural descends into these two preexistent faculties.

For Barth these distinctions are irrelevant: *it is the human faculties as such which he condemns.* The intellect and will are radically incapable of having any relationship whatsoever, even a purely passive one, with the gift of God. It is true that certain Catholic theologians could see between the natural and supernatural simply non-contradiction, but it would never occur to anyone to affirm that humanity as such has become *useless.* Therein lies the conclusion which is evolved from Karl Barth's premises. Having become totally profane through sin, human nature is of no account in God's eyes.

\*

\* \*

The effect of sin, therefore, is radical: the blackout is complete. Not only has the *Welthaftigkeit* totally dissimulated God's presence under created forms, but the secularization of the human intellect has deprived it of its means of attaining the supernatural. Can man recognize revelation? At this point in our exposition, we can only give a partial reply: After the Fall man has become a total stranger to the Word of God; nothing any longer binds him to It; he no longer has an ear for the divine. One would even be tempted to go further and draw another conclusion: All knowledge of God is impossible; all quest for it, vain; all hope of obtaining it, illusory: man's status before God is one of total agnosticism. But such a conclusion is premature, because Barth claims that, *despite all that has been said,* there is an authentic knowledge of the Word of God, though it be a purely indirect knowledge. We must suspend judgment, then, until we have examined the other aspects of his epistemology.

# notes

# to chapter four

1 J. L. Leuba translates *Welthaftigkeit des Wortes Gottes* by "secular character of the Word of God." Cf. *Résumé analytique* . . . , p. 46.

2 Jean Rilliet, *Notion de révélation* . . . , RTP, 1944, vol. XXXII, p. 129.

3 Cf. KD, vol. I, 1, p. 171.

4 Cf. KD, vol. I, 2, p. 341. Barth is rather embarrassed when it comes to explaining the fact of the Resurrection and the miracle of the Virgin Birth from this perspective. Cf. KD, vol. I, 2, p. 161.

5 The immanence of this divine transcendence is and remains an event. "Die Gottheit ist der Menschheit Christi nicht so immanent, dass sie ihr nicht auch transzendent bliebe, nicht so, dass ihre Immanenz aufhörte, ein *Ereignis* ganz im Sinne des Alten Testamentes: immer wieder ein Neues, ein von Gott her in bestimmten Begebenheiten wirklich Werdendes zu sein" (KD, vol. I, 1, p. 341). Barth most certainly does not wish to deny the Christological dogma. It is the action of divinity through humanity which he characterizes as "event," not the union of divinity and humanity.

6 Cf. KD, vol. I, 1, p. 338.

7 "A divinitate assumpta est nostra natura, non culpa; illa profecto, *quae ante peccatum creata,* non quae post praevaricationem vitiata. Christus enim sine peccato conceptus de Spiritu Sancto, etiam sine peccato est partus de sancta et immaculata Virgine Dei genitrice, *nullum experiens contagium vitiatae naturae*" (*Denz.,* 251). Even though the conclusion that Pope Honorius I drew from this principle is doubtful, at least in its formulation (but a single will in Christ), and even though it ought to be understood according to its restatement by his successor John IV (*Denz.,* 253) and according to the censures of the Sixth Ecumenical Council (Constantinople), the principle itself is universally admitted. Cf. E. Amann, DTC, vol. VII, col. 93–132.—The impeccability of Christ is a truth which, although not defined, is *proxima fidei.* Some authors consider it as defined, on the score that it is contained in the condemnation of a proposition of Theodore of Mopsuestia by the Second Council of Constantinople (533): "Christum post resurrectionem immutabilem cogitationibus et impeccabilem omnino factum fuisse" (*Denz.,* 224).

8 *Enarr, 53 cap. Iesaiae,* 1544, EA, *ex. op. lat.,* vol. XXIII, 2, p. 457 (cited in KD, vol. I, 2, p. 168).

9 Cf. M. Dominicé, *L'humanité de Jésus d'après Calvin,* p. 123.

10 CR, vol. XLVII, p. 13 (cited in KD, vol. I, 2, p. 166).

11 Barth's argument is far from new; Cyril of Alexander referred to it long before him: "Stolidi vero ac dementes prorsus sunt, qui ipsum etiam Christum, nescio quo pacto, peccare potuisse affirmant, eam ob causam, quod in forma nobis simili per incarnationem sit factus . . ." (*Adversus Anthropomorphitas,* c. XXIII, PG, vol. LXXVI, c. 1119–1120).

12 Cf. KD, vol. I, 2, pp. 168–169.

13 M. J. Lagrange, *Épître aux Galates,* pp. 71–72; E. B. Allo, *Seconde Épître aux Corinthiens,* pp. 171–172. Cf. also F. Ceuppens, *Theologia biblica,* vol. III, part I: *De Incarnatione,* pp. 158–164.

14 Cf. John 8: 46; 14: 30; I John 3: 5; I Pet. 2: 22–25; Hebr. 7: 26.

15 St. Thomas, *Summa Theologica,* III, q. 7, a. 9.

16 Cf. III, q. 9, a. 2; q. 15, a. 2 and 10. St. Thomas gives us an additional argument drawn from seminal transmission. The inclination to evil, designated as concupiscence or *fomes peccati,* is the material element of original sin (cf. III, q. 82, a. 3). Since Christ was born of a virgin, he could not have contracted original sin (cf. III, q. 15, a. 1, ad 2).

17 III, q. 14, a. 1; q. 15, a. 1 and 2.

18 To those who think that only a Christ inclined by nature to sin could be a convincing example for sinners, St. Thomas replies: "Fortitudo spiritus aliqualis ostenditur ex hoc quod resistit concupiscentiae carnis sibi contrariantis: sed major fortitudo spiritus ostenditur si per ejus virtutem totaliter comprimatur, ne contra spiritum concupiscere possit" (III, q. 15, a. 2, ad 3).

19 KD, vol. I, 2, p. 173. On this point once again Barth is closer to the liberals than to Calvin. After citing the reformer of Geneva, M. Dominicé, a theologian of liberal tendencies, concludes: "That is a strange way to remove all value from the struggle of temptation! We regret that Calvin has pursued the argument to extremes" (*L'humanité du Christ d'après Calvin,* p. 181). What a wretched appearance the scene of temptation assumes, if it is reduced to a sort of moral test! The temptation of Christ, such as narrated by the Evangelists, is entirely different from the temptation which St. Thomas Aquinas endured when imprisoned in the castle tower. It is an undisguised attempt on the part of Satan to resolve a perplexing problem: is this man, so extraordinary in some respects and yet so human in others, truly the Son of God announced by the prophets? This is how tradition, which St. Thomas draws upon, has understood this pericope: "Sicut Augustinus dicit, in *IX de Civ. Dei,* Christus tantum innotuit daemonibus quantum voluit: non per id quod est vita aeterna, sed per quaedam temporalia suae virtutis effecta, ex quibus quandam conjecturam habebant Christum esse Filium Dei. Sed quia rursus in eo quaedam signa humanae infirmitatis videbant, non pro certo cognoscebant eum esse Filium Dei. Et ideo eum tentare voluit. Et hoc significatur *Matth. IV,* ubi dicitur quod, postquam esuriit, accessit tentator ad eum: quia, ut Hilarius dicit, tentare Christum diabolus non esset ausus, nisi in eo, per esuritionis infirmitatem, quae sunt hominis recognosceret. Et hoc etiam patet ex ipso modo tentandi, cum dixit: si Filius Dei es. Quod exponens Gregorius dicit: Quid vult talis sermonis exorsus, nisi quia cognoverat Dei Filium esse venturum, sed venisse per infirmitatem corporis non putabat?" (III, q. 41, a. 1, ad 1).

20 Cf. CD, p. 222. Cf. J. Fehr, *Das Offenbarungsproblem* . . . , pp. 44–45.

21 Cf. KD, vol. I, 1, p. 172.

22 Barth puts up a poor defense against the charge levelled against his failure to distinguish adequately between creature and sin. Does not one frequently receive the impression that the metaphysical antithesis, which separates the Creator from His creature, is identified with the moral antithesis, which contrasts the holy God with the sinner? This problem has been treated by G. Wingren in an illuminating, well-documented article: *Gott und Mensch bei K. Barth* in *Studia Theologica*, 1947, vol. 1, pp. 27–53.

23 *Natur und Gnade*, pp. 7–8.

24 *Natur und Gnade*, p. 18.

25 The constitutive characteristic of personality is expressed by Brunner through the concepts of *Ansprechbarkeit (Wortmächtigkeit)* and *Verantwortlichkeit*. In *Offenbarung und Vernunft*, Brunner comes back to this point: "Der Mensch is immer, auch als Sünder, etwas anderes als die übrigen Kreaturen. Er ist es darum, weil er immer, durch die ursprüngliche Offenbarung, verantwortliches Wesen ist. Die Verantwortlichkeit ist der Kern des Menschseins, der Personalität" (p. 55).

26 Luther, WA, vol. XVI, p. 447 (cited by Brunner, *Der Mensch im Widersprucht*, p. 549).

27 A distinction proposed in *Natur und Gnade* (pp. 9–11) and resumed at length in *Der Mensch im Widersprucht* (pp. 541–553). In this latter work the author no longer employs the same terminology (matter and form). This is due not to a change in his position, but solely to avoid a vocabulary which some consider as "inclined to Catholicism." Cf. *Der Mensch im Widersprucht*, p. 530. We are presenting an exposition of Brunner's thought only to the extent that it will aid us to a better comprehension of Barth's doctrine on the particular point under consideration. We wish to indicate, however, the importance of the above-mentioned distinction for the method of theology. The recognized fact of the survival in the order of nature of the image created by God at the beginning of the world, despite the catastrophe of sin in the order of nature, permits Brunner to envision a natural ethic: that is to say, a morality based on the study of social institutions. Consequently, the theologian has a twofold source of knowledge: the Word of God and creation. Knowledge of creation, however, is possible only in conjunction with the Word of God. In fact, outside the realm of grace, the knowledge of nature is totally falsified and vitiated. It regains its clearsightedness and equilibrium only in Jesus Christ. This is the problem of natural theology so severely indicted by Barth. We must note, however, that Brunner always took a precaution: he qualified *theologia naturalis* with *christliche* or *rechte*. The natural theology of which he speaks exists only in the economy of faith (if we may so speak). Cf. *Der Mensch im Widerspruch*, pp. 540–641. Barth's thought on natural theology *in general* can be found in GG, pp. 41–49. For a Catholic critique of Brunner's position, cf. the article of G. Söhngen, *Natürliche Theologie und Heilgeschichte*, in *Catholica*, 1935, vol. IV, pp. 97–115. Without a doubt the most complete critique of Brunner's system is the remarkable work of L. Volken, *Der Glaube bei Emil Brunner*. Cf. also J. Fehr, *Das Offenbarungsproblem* . . . , pp. 19–41; cf. an excellent article by Père L. Malevez, *La Pensée d'E. Brunner sur L'homme et le péché*, in RSR, 1947, vol. XXXIV, pp. 407–453.

28 A. Hoffmann, *Zur Lehr von der Gottebenbildlichkeit des Menschen* . . . , dans *Divus Thomas*, 1941, vol. XIX, p. 19.

29 K. Barth, *Nein. Antwort an Emil Brunner,* p. 25. Barth's refutation of Brunner seems rather poor. The recourse to imaginary creatures is not a very solid argument.

30 *Nein,* p. 25. It is noteworthy that on this latter point, Barth's argument is valid solely because Brunner conceives man's dispositions confronted by revelation as active: revelation's fulcrum consists in acts of the intellect and will. It cannot exist for the mentally deficient or newborn. If Brunner had conceived his *Anknüpfungspunkt* in a potential order, Barth's argument would have been irrelevant.

31 "Der Mensch ist auch als Sünder der Mensch und keine Schildkröte" *(Nein,* p. 16. Cf. also p. 25). When we recall Luther's constant refusal to admit even the least degree of free will in man, we can easily perceive the divergence between the thought of the Reformers and Barth's affirmation of man's integrity after the Fall. How can we reconcile such an absolute negation with the *Verantwortlichkeit* which Barth, following Brunner, acknowledges so willingly in man?

32 Brunner has not allowed this objection to pass unanswered. Human nature carries with it a responsibility, and by that very fact, it places man before God. "Hat diese Humanität etwas mit der Gottesbildlichkeit zu tun? Das ist zu bejahen, weil Menschsein die Verantwortlichkeit einschliesst, also das Vor-Gott-sein voraussetzt" *(Offenbarung und Vernunft,* p. 55).

33 "Ein theologisch irrelevanter Tatbestand." This is how Brunner defines Barth's position on the question *(Der Mensch im Widerspruch,* p. 531).

34 *Nein,* p. 34.

35 "We consider it unquestionable that man has within him a sense of divinity, even a natural tendency" *(Inst. chrét.,* I, 3, 1, CR, vol. III, c. 46). "Among men of sound judgment, the existence in the human spirit of a sense of divinity so profound that it is ineffaceable is a closed question. . . . I go so far as to say that no matter how much hard-hearted callousness, which the wicked absorb and gather with utmost effort to contemn God, may stagnate and corrupt their hearts, nevertheless, *the feeling which they have of God's majesty* and which they desire to extinguish as much as possible, *always prevails.* From this fact I conclude that God's majesty is not merely a doctrine which we begin to learn only in school; rather it is a truth which each person must have mastered and taught himself from his mother's womb" (I, 3, 3, CR, vol. III, c. 50–51). In speaking of sinners who attempt to expel God from their thoughts, Calvin adds still further: "Finally, they entangle themselves in such a web of errors that the obscurity of their malice smothers and then quenches the sparks which shone to give them light that they might perceive God's glory. Nevertheless, *there remains that seed* which cannot be uprooted totally; namely, that there is some divinity. But the seed, which was good at its origin has become so corrupt that it produces nothing but rotten fruit" (I, 3, 4, CR, vol. III, c. 58).

36 The purpose of the explanation which follows is to justify the attitude of the Reformers as a whole. The interpretation of the texts cited in the preceding note is presented in *Nein,* pp. 41–45. The exegesis which Barth there proposes is not very convincing.

37 *Nein,* pp. 37–38.

[38] We may often cite an additional text of Calvin, chosen at random: "Wherefore, however much we may confess that God's image has not been totally annihilated and effaced in him, it has been so thoroughly corrupted that the remnant is a frightful deformity" (*Inst. chrét.*, I, 15, 4, Cr, vol. III, c. 222).

[39] Cf. KD, vol. I, 1, p. 251.

[40] Cf. *Nein*, p. 19.

[41] *Der Mensch im Widerspruch*, p. 550.

[42] Cf. A. Hoffmann, *art. cit.*, p. 19.

[43] Barth points this out in *Nein*, pp. 16–17.

[44] We cannot enter into details here. Our end is not to present a parallel exposition of Barthian and Catholic positions. On the doctrine of St. Thomas: A. Gardeil, *La structure de l'âme et l'expérience mystique*, vol. II, pp. 268–349, and L. Charlier, *Puissance passive et désir naturel*, ETL, 1930, vol. VII, pp. 5–28.

[45] The Aristotelian notion of potency often fails to impress a mentality formed exclusively by modern thought. "Potency" indicates a purely passive principle capable of receiving a perfection; in no sense does it mean concentrated energy. This confusion is at the root of numerous misunderstandings between Catholics and Protestants.

# contact with the word of god in faith

WE HAVE chosen the title of this chapter with a definite end in view. It might have been called 'Knowledge of the Word of God'; but, though we shall treat various aspects of the problem of knowledge in these pages, our findings will not let us speak of 'knowledge' in its proper sense without risk of ambiguity. 'Contact' is a more precise rendering of the idea intended by Karl Barth than is knowledge. (Barth's thought is couched in a somewhat loose vocabulary.) The central topic of this chapter will be the problem of faith; all related questions will group themselves about this. We shall therefore take up the following problems simultaneously: religious knowledge through experience, the *analogia fidei,* and the response of man in the faith.

## A. Is Knowledge of God Possible?

The arguments of the last chapter led us almost inevitably to question whether or not man can know the Word of God. We had to suspend our judgment so that we could again listen to Barth, for he states without the least hesitation that knowledge of the Word of God is an undeniable fact. It is so evident that one cannot demonstrate it; it is presupposed in our whole Christian life. Barth rests this assertion on the fact that the Church preaches. God has given Himself to us in the form of the Word. If there is no certain means of knowing and understanding the Word, the gift loses its significance. The Church, itself, would be a source of delusion and its preaching would have no purpose. Is not the fact that God speaks sufficient proof that man can understand God? It is not necessary that the human race as such should hear God—nor even that any given individual should hear Him; but at least some few men should. If these few cannot hear Him always and everywhere, they ought to have the ability at least in certain determined circumstances. The Word would not be a word if it could not be known.

Barth does not wish to determine a priori exactly what knowledge of the Word is. It will be the work of this chapter to examine his idea of knowledge more closely. At the outset he gives a concept of knowledge which is sufficiently broad so that he can, as his work proceeds, add all the necessary restrictions, clarifications, and modifications. Knowledge is for him the state of an object which, true in itself in both its essence and its existence, becomes equally true, with a certain measure of distinctness and certitude, for the knowing subject. This definition contains two elements: the object is true in itself, and it is true for me. The intrinsic truth of the object certainly enjoys a primacy in Barth's thought. It is there that our own knowledge begins. God is true in Himself; His Word is true in relation to its own norm. That the object be equally true for us means that, by knowledge, we are henceforth bound to the object; that we cannot think of ourselves without reference to it; or better, that we are determined by it.[1]

Although this formulation is intentionally vague and is to find a more exact expression in the theology of faith, we feel that we should here point out an ambiguity which it implies. Barth vigorously affirms that the expression 'Word of God' connotes as its necessary counterpart the possibility of knowing God. This is evident; but it presupposes a precise concept of knowledge. Barth is, nevertheless, not precise. Keeping his reader in suspense, he puts off a more exact definition of his terms until later in his work. His theory thus loses much of its value, and we are forced to doubt it until he gives us a definition of knowledge which is compatible with that element of apprehension contained in every word. There is here a fault in method which can vitiate his whole doctrine.

## B. Knowledge of the Word of God since Schleiermacher.

A clearly formulated definition never hampers thought. It would be difficult to think of a more inexact definition than Barth's. Could it perhaps have been formulated to include experience within its extension? Would experience be a legitimate form of knowledge of the Word of God? A priori there is nothing to obviate this conclusion. We are indeed aware that, since the beginning of the nineteeth century, such has been the chief religious epistemology of Protestantism. It is reflection on the knowing subject's experience of himself that enables him to reach God. This is undoubtedly to put aside the traditional concept of the 'Word of God,' which lends itself poorly to the test of experience, and to replace it with the more easily handled concept of 'revelation.' Practically, however, both ideas amount to the same thing. The concept of revelation has the simple advantage of referring less to the liberty and initiative of God than does the 'Word of God.' We can find a type of revelation in ourselves more easily than we can find the Word of God. "Word of God" connotes too strongly an immediate encounter with a being exterior to ourselves.

The fundamental principle of Barth's system—perhaps its only principle—is its unreserved condemnation of this alleged manner of knowing God. In Barth's eyes, two postulates characterize all theology since the time of Schleiermacher: 1) the encounter of man with God must be seen as a manifest religious experience, i.e., it must be subject to investigation by history as well as by psychology; 2) such experience is the actualization of a religious 'faculty' inserted in the very nature of man.[2] The second is the more important of these two postulates, and it clearly marks the theological revolution which put religious psychology in the place of traditional dogma.

Schleiermacher stands at the source of this stream of thought. His primary intention was to reestablish in the esteem of the cultivated minds of his time, minds thoroughly imbued with romanticism, a religion which they had rejected, as they had rejected all of the past. He wanted to create a theological epistemology rooted in the same philosophical substrata as literary romanticism. We are in the presence of a 'well adapted' theology; not only does the theologian conform his language to the needs of his audience, but he goes so far as to conform his doctrine to their wishes. It was a hazardous endeavor as Schleiermacher realized.

I know that the only domestic gods in your tastefully regulated homes are the maxims of the wise and the songs of the poets. I know that mankind and fatherland, art and science—for you think you can entirely comprehend all these—have taken such complete control of your spirit that nothing remains for the eternal and holy Being Who is, according to you, outside the universe. I know that you have no feelings either for Him or against Him. You have tried to make life in this world an existence so rich and varied that you no longer need eternity; you believe that, once you have created a universe for yourselves, you will no longer have to think of Him Who created you.[3]

To adapt Christianity to the needs of such a mentality was to paganize it. Schleiermacher did not shrink before such a prospect, and his work provides us with the spectacle of an almost complete secularization of Christian revelation.

Schleiermacher's work is not lacking in originality. It is the first attempt ever made to disengage religion from the philosophical implications which had compromised it. Contemporary thought had built on religion a superstructure of morality or of metaphysics.[4] It became necessary to restore religion to itself. Thus Schleiermacher wrote: "Piety is neither knowledge nor action. It is rather a conviction of the feeling or immediate consciousness of oneself." [5] In this manner religion will regain its proper characteristics: "The practical belongs to the domain of art; the speculative, to that of science; religion is the taste and touch of the infinite." [6] Schleiermacher maintains that the positive religions have gone astray on this point, but that their error is understandable. The fact that morality, metaphysics, and religion all have the same object explains their confusion. Their common object is "the universe, and man's relations with the universe." Each of them must approach this common goal by a different path, and thus must clearly limit itself in relation to the others. Schleiermacher here manifests his diffidence towards all philosophical speculation. Metaphysics, a discipline of the mind, which analyzes the universe by ascending to first causes and attempts to demonstrate the real, follows a path totally different from that of religion; and the mode of knowledge of metaphysics is subordinate to that of religion. Yet the theologian of romanticism is no less opposed to the moral metaphysics of Kant. Morality, legitimate and autonomous in itself, need not entangle itself in a domain which surpasses it. It cannot raise itself to the level of religion. As I. J. Rouge well remarked: "Thus to decree the existence of God and, as a consequence, to establish religion on the basis of a logical deduction seemed completely arbitrary, dangerous, and, therefore, to be condemned for a romanticist who conceived such a reality only as something demanded and established by an immediate feeling, directly perceived by intuition." [7]

Feeling has thus returned to religion its independence. We may now propose a positive definition: "That which is common to the most varied expressions of piety is that man is conscious of being totally dependent, in a word, of being in relation with God." [8] The feeling that is most properly religious is that of total dependence. It is distinguished from other feelings of dependence, as the absolute is distinguished from the relative. The religious feeling of dependence is not what puts a man on the level of other beings; it is rather that which affects him at the same time as it does other finite beings. It is the relation of all that is not God to the Divinity itself. This feeling of dependence is, moreover, the formal act of religion, and the faculty from which it emanates is the proper organ of religion within man. This point is particularly important. Religion depends not on intelligence but on feeling (*sentiment, Gefühl*). All knowledge must, then, have its beginnings here; it is here that knowledge is to find its norms and its laws. Schleiermacher has put religious emotion in the place of intellectual perception and of all that could belong, whether legitimately or illegitimately, to the essence of religion. Religious knowledge thus becomes an experience.

Any other form of religious knowledge is excluded; faith is no longer an operation of the human intellect. Orthodox Protestantism is thus rejected in company with metaphysical philosophy. If, then, the intellect retains no part in religious perception, properly so-called, are we to conclude that it has absolutely no function in the whole field of religion? Schleiermacher stops short of such an extreme conclusion, for the truth is much too clear.

He has to explain the intellectual element present in all religion. The role of the intellect is to be, if secondary, absolutely indispensable; it is to attire the various states of religious sentiment in the garb of spoken language.[9] It can describe religious feeling and insure its propagation. The intellect does not replace feeling, but it can take the activity of feeling as its object. By reflection on itself, it can fix within the categories of thought the necessarily fluid state of a religious emotion. Thought thus allows us to record the data of experience, to crystallize an emotion in its proper setting, and to guarantee its repetition under the same conditions. Unexpressed thought does not, however, provide us with a sufficiently precise definition of religious feeling. Though less fluid than emotion, unexpressed thought runs the risk of being so fluid that it simply becomes confused. Thought is clear and precise only when it is expressed in words. It then becomes highly intelligible, and the experience which it represents becomes correspondingly precise.[10] It is not until the end of this interior process that the intellect can fulfill its protective function in a fitting manner.

This role, in no wise negligible, is but the first of the services which the intellect can render to feeling. In the very act of affirming the stability of feeling, the intellect gives it a social value. Indeed, different religious experiences which have found the same intellectual expression can be grouped into confessions. Intellectual expression, moreover, will assure the propagation of religious experience. This is not to say that one can deduce what religious experience is from its intellectual formulation; it is rather that the latter plays the role of an external stimulus for religious feeling; it awakens, it stirs to spontaneous action.[11] All of this, however, must not let us lose sight of the fact that the work of the intellect does not belong to religion itself—that the intellect works rather at the periphery of religion. Only experience totally exhausts the concept of religion.

The proper act of religious knowledge is, then, the experience of total dependence. The faculty from which it flows is feeling, a faculty which all men possess.[12] Such, in short, is the position of Schleiermacher. In the previous chapter we saw Barth's answer to any system that gives nature a function in the perception of the supernatural. What is there said, concerning the total destruction of the image of God within man, holds for our other faculties as well as the intellect. Feeling is not spared in this universal ruin. It is just as blind as any other faculty; sin has rendered it insensitive to the supernatural. We can sum up Barth's first criticism in a phrase he never tires of repeating: *Peccator non capax verbi divini.*

Along with this first answer, which is based on the present state of the Word and of man, there is another based on the nature of the Word Itself. If man can find the Word of God in his reflections on himself, if a choice made on his own initiative suffices for him to find the Word within his own consciousness, what happens to the sovereignty, liberty, and reality of the Word of God? [13] Man would no longer be subject to God; God would be subject to man. We find ourselves faced with a synthesis of God and man in which man would be the principal element. God could no longer give Himself or withdraw Himself as He saw fit. He would be subject to man's good pleasure and subordinate to his religious emotions. Protestantism, reasoning in this fashion, forgets the distance separating man from God, a distance that Barth sums up in the expression, *Finitum non capax infiniti.* Sin, which has shut man off from God, as well as the personal element in the Word of God, is basically opposed to Schleiermacher's position and excludes all possibility of a compromise.

But this is a compromise which modern theology has tried to effect.[14] Contemporary theology has yielded much to Barth. To be sure, the Word of God must take the initiative. Man cannot, of himself, have any religious faculty whose object would be God; of himself, he has no faculty that can attain to the divine. All this, however, is perfectly in harmony with the fact that *some* men possess the faculty of knowing God—but for this they depend on a gift. The liberality of God will bestow on Christians a faculty which in no way belongs to their complement of natural faculties, but which will be added to them much in the same manner as musical talent can enrich the human nature common to all.[15] A man who has been sanctified will be able to know God. Sanctification will come from God, but it will be received in man. It will then be permissible "for the believer to discover by a simple reflection on himself, on the holiness he has acquired, on the experiences he has accumulated, the needs, the meaning, the very nature of the Word, and for him to build up his religious self according to the norms he perceives in the divine truth." [16] In this system, the Word of God is no longer the unique center of our knowledge of God; it has become an ellipse with man at one of its focal points.[17] The Word of God is no longer a person; it has become a thing with which man may deal as he pleases. God has allowed man to take over.

Barth's judgment also looks to those who are outside the pretorium. It is not only the liberal Protestant who is condemned here; it is every attempt to set up a theory of knowledge of God which begins with man. Barth rejects all philosophical anthropology as a starting point in a theory of revelation. Knowledge of man sheds no light on the knowledge of God; rather we must ask God to teach us what man is. If an anthropology is at all legitimate it is not that of the philosophers, but that of the Word of God.

## C. In Faith God Knows Man.

We have now advanced far enough to take up the heart of our problem. How does knowledge of the Word of God come about? Barth answers that it comes through faith. What is faith? Barth declares solemnly: the historical manifestation of the Word of God. We have at last a reply that allows us to clear up all ambiguity. This is the heart of the problem: knowledge of God is identified with the historical manifestation of the Word of God.[18] What we have previously stated about the nature of that manifestation and its present state now permits us to set forth our opinion more clearly and distinctly.

The Word of God is free and permanent in its being; it is not distinct from the very act of God; it is a Divine Person. There can thus be no prolongation on the human plane which corresponds to it.[19] But there is more. This Word which intervenes in the plane of creation becomes completely unrecognizable because of the opacity of the world of sin.[20] The light of revelation is absorbed in the darkness of sin, even though it is present under the veil of that darkness. We conclude, then, that the historical manifestation of the Word, real in itself, passes unperceived. The historical event of faith, which is identified with the Word, is beyond all human perception.[21]

We can say, in brief, that what we have here is simply not knowledge of the Word of God. What Barth tells us of the possibility of such knowledge is a delusion. Man does not know and can not know the Word of God. This conclusion, which Barth does not reach explicitly, is not exactly a consequence of his theory; but it is definitely contained in other words in his system. Where there is no human perception of an object—whether this be by means of an innate or a superadded faculty, by intelligence or by experience—there is simply no knowledge.[22]

Whence the ambiguity? It results simply from this: Barth does not set up a sufficiently clear distinction between man as an object and man as a subject. Man does not truly know, until he is the subject of knowledge. Knowledge is a vital operation of the knowing subject. But, in the event of faith, man is simply the object, the term of God's action. In other words, in faith man does not know God; God simply knows man. The knowledge of faith is a knowledge of man by God in which the intellectual activity of man has no part; God is an object that escapes him.

Moreover, Barth realizes all this. One need but read his commentary on the text of Saint Paul: "Formerly you had no knowledge of God; you lived as the slaves of deities who were in truth no deities at all. But you have recognized the true God, or rather, the true God has recognized you. How is it that you are going back to those old schoolroom tasks of yours, so abject, so ineffectual . . . ?" (Gal. 4:8–9).[23] Barth sees in this text a reversal of the problem of the knowledge of God. He thinks he can deduce from these two verses a theory that we can sum up in the following manner: because God knows man, one can say that man knows God. Here we have complete ambiguity. Barth is not using words in their proper meanings. We have here a vacillation and a lack of focus that are inadmissible in a matter where the greatest precision is necessary. It is not because God knows man that we

can say that man knows God. Such reasoning is completely illegitimate. We have only to transplant these conclusions to the plane
of ordinary human knowledge to show the strange consequences
resulting from such a principle.

Thus it was that J. Fehr, in an article published in 1937, had
come to the conclusion that a knowledge of God by man is impossible within the framework of Barthian theology.[24] He did not
hesitate to add: "Revelation is, then, for all practical purposes, a
non-revelation." His conclusion seems to be solidly based on his
sources. Nevertheless, Père Malevez could not agree completely
with it:

> We recognize that here and there Barth's thought does point in
> that direction; but it does not commit itself irrevocably. To say that
> it did would be to say that Barth's doctrine is rooted in the unthink-
> able. If God alone comprehends His own Word, what meaning can we
> give to the words 'revelation' and 'faith'? Belief would in reality indi-
> cate only a negation of thought, but Barth does not quite go to that
> extreme. Whether he wishes to do so or not, he is forced to admit
> that the believer himself hears God. This hearing is so much our own
> that we can speak of it as we would speak of an experience we have
> of the Word.[25]

The writer of these lines has let himself be swayed by certain
of Barth's statements and has been tempted to take them literally.
We must not lose sight of the fact that, for Barth, 'faith,' 'revelation,' and 'experience' lose their ordinary meanings and take on
completely new meanings, which are thoroughly conformed to
the system which uses them. Père Malevez maintains that for Barth
there is a true experience of the Word of God. This seems to us
to be inexact.[26] There is no experience of the Word of God itself;
there is rather a real experience *of another object,* totally distinct
from the Word of God. Since Barth speaks now of one experience,
now of the other, without adverting to the difference, he causes
much misunderstanding. Other theologians of note have fallen
into this trap; and not a few Protestants have rejoiced to see that
Barth, who in his original works showed nothing but disgust
for any claim of experience of the Word of God, more recently
has given experience an important place in his dogmatic system.[27]

## D. *Analogia fidei* replaces *analogia entis*.

The rejection of all human perception of the Word of God becomes still more apparent in Barth's refusal to admit the *analogia entis,* and in the fact that he replaces it with his own notion: the *analogia fidei*. We are familiar with Barth's idea that the *analogia entis* is the fundamental principle not only of Catholic theology, but also of Protestant liberalism. In the preface to the first volume of his dogmatic tract, he does not hesitate to state that the *analogia entis* is an invention of the Antichrist, and that any other reason for not becoming a Catholic is meaningless.[28] It is thus in the idea of analogy that he sees an attempt to bring about the impossible synthesis of God and man. His position amounts to a complete denial of analogy as a means of attaining knowledge of God. However—and Barth ought to admit this himself—the notion of analogy was presupposed by orthodox Protestant theology. Quenstedt, the great systematizer of the seventeenth century, gave an explicit formulation to this presupposition.[29] For his part, Emil Brunner brings back analogy, not as a theological law proper to the thought of a single religious confession, but simply as an indispensable tool for any theology. "The *analogia entis* is not a peculiarly Catholic idea. It is at the basis of all theology, whether Christian or pagan." [30] Barth must feel extremely sure of himself to reject analogy in opposition to the thought of all other theologians.

Confusion can result from the use of the term *analogia entis*.[31] Applied to the knowledge of God, it normally designates nothing more than a method used in the philosophy of God, a law of theodicy. For Barth the expression has a wider meaning; it refers to all knowledge of God, whether natural or supernatural. In the following pages we must, therefore, when we speak of the *analogia entis,* give it the broader meaning of Barth. In other respects the method is the same. Both positions use human words to designate divine realities. The problem is to fix precisely the intellectual value of such language.

Barth has formulated the problem clearly. "Is there a simple equivalence of content and meaning when I apply a word now to a creature and now to God? We know, or rather we think we know, the meanings of being, spirit, sovereignty, creation, redemption, justice, wisdom, goodness—when these concepts refer to creatures. Do they have exactly the same meaning when we apply them to God?" [32] The answer is evident: As long as God is God and man is man, it is impossible to see an identity or an equality between realities even though they are designated by the same terms. That would mean either that God has become a creature or that the creature has become God. The other extreme is equally unacceptable. One cannot say that the human words we apply to God have no relation to Him. God and human words designating God are not totally dissimilar; they have something in common. To affirm the contrary would be to deny the gift of God. [33]

Barth is disposed to see between complete equivalence and complete dissimilarity an intermediate state which he calls 'analogy,' for he does not in any way deny analogy as such. In spite of his difficulties, the term has retained his favor in that he calls his theory the *analogia fidei*. [34] But what does he mean by analogy? At first glance his definition seems to be thoroughly acceptable: *Ähnlichkeit, teilweise Entsprechung und Übereinstimmung*. [35] Analogy is thus "similarity or partial correspondence" of realities designated by the same words. If a casual reader were to stop his reading here, he would think Barth a thorough-going Thomist. He would be deceived indeed! Barth first owes us an explanation of his definition. When he has given us that explanation, we will be far from the Thomist notion of analogy.

There are two elements in the Barthian definition of analogy: 1) there is a correspondence; 2) that correspondence is partial. The correspondence consists in the fact that the words we use can denote, even by way of complete equivalence, the divine reality. [36] (We shall see later that this type of equivalence is in no way opposed to the second part of the definition.) When, taking our cue from inspired texts, we say that God is Father, Son, and Spirit, the words we use can denote perfectly the reality of God; that is to say, God can *requisition* these human words to express his own thought. [37] In the historical manifestation of His Word, God can make these words the adequate expression of a reality which is incommunicable to the human intellect. We thus find ourselves in the strange situation in which God uses words to designate a reality that is completely different from that which we designate by the same words.[38] What God understands by 'Father' has, in itself, *nothing* in common with the human being whom we denote by that term. All human words are empty shells which God fills with a content that we cannot even guess. There is thus in the event of revelation a perfect identity between human words and the Word of God.

This equivalence is nevertheless one-sided. It is *von Gott her nicht vom Menschen her*. This is why, in the final analysis, Barth sees no more than a partial correspondence. It is partial, because it *totally* escapes man. There is no line going up from man to God which is complementary to the line coming from God to man. God sees His own thought in human language; but, in the same language, man expresses a completely different reality. On one side, the correspondence is perfect; on the other, it is non-existent. The result is expressed by a sort of compromise—a partial agreement, which Barth calls the *analogia fidei*.[39]

Such, for Barth, is analogy.[40] It leaves man to himself. But does it not actually do more than this? Does it not accentuate the tragedy of our human plight, which lets created intelligence take an illusion for reality? Is it necessary to point out that this destroys our whole concept of revelation? [41] If God speaks to us in the Scriptures, He would be using words whose true meanings would be hidden from us; yet He would let us believe that we are to understand them in a sense which is connatural to us. Are we not here dealing with a sort of trickery on God's part, in that He allows us to think we can know something about Him even though He always conceals Himself, never lifting us out of our complete ignorance? This unilateral equivalence takes us far indeed from the *analogia entis* [42]—a human manner of knowing God by means of terms that give us an imperfect, but nevertheless real, representation.[43] We have to purify these concepts of all that is created, so that we may see in them an expression of the divine reality. Barth's theology, far from being an application of traditional analogy, bears only the appearance of equivocation. Our way of speaking about God is stripped of all intellectual value. In the *analogia entis* a very imperfect knowledge of God was possible; in the *analogia fidei* God knows us, but we do not know God.

## E. Human Initiative and Faith—Indirect Knowledge and *fiducia*.

Barth's theology does not, however, slight man to the extent of neglecting him entirely. The *analogia fidei* uses human words.[44] Since God employs words to communicate a revelation, which He alone understands, they are not superfluous. Words play a role here—they give God a chance to intervene. In the final analysis, Barthianism, therefore, does have a theory of the response of man in the presence of faith. God makes use of human knowledge without extending it, without making it productive in its own order; but He does use it. Human understanding does not grow in its knowledge of God; yet it has value in the act of faith. In short, the exercise of our faculties serves merely as a *vehicle* for an intervention of the Divine Word. "For Karl Barth, it is a principle of religious knowledge that *the chosen means of communication does not correspond to the thing He wishes to communicate; it rather contradicts than corresponds.* To defend the freedom of revelation, Barth thinks that the wrappings of revelation cannot establish the value of their content." [45]

Barth calls this indirect knowledge. He even claims to find it in the text of Saint Paul: "At present, we are looking at a confused reflection in a mirror; then, we shall see face to face . . ." (1 Cor. 13:12). We have here knowledge which is doubly indirect: God reveals Himself in a mirror, and the mirror itself is an enigma. We do not have even an imperfect and dim knowledge; we have a non-knowledge. There is nothing here which in any way resembles the indirect knowledge of Catholic theology, for which the darkness does not extinguish the light but always admits of a partial clarity. According to Barth, God gives Himself without showing Himself. The only object which He presents to our human faculties is the veil which covers everything; the knowledge of this veil is the indirect knowledge of the Word of God.

Although he attributes such a paradoxical role to knowledge, Barth does not feel that he is forced to rule out our human faculties entirely. All the faculties which take part in the cognitive process have their role here—intellect, will, consciousness, and emotions work together.[46] Man's cognitive activity, with no subtle distinctions, with no prejudice either intellectualist or anti-intellectualist, is the stage where divine intervention can occur.

It would be unfair not to mention here a point which we shall treat at greater length in Part Two of this work. Even though all of man's cognitive powers are brought into play, we must still admit that there remains a choice of objects. If there were no determined limits to intellectual activity, we would be in the presence of a veritable theological anarchy. A human knowledge which petitions the favor of the event of faith must, says Barth, submit to a discipline. The divine commandments will set certain limits on it.[47] It is not just any exercise of our knowledge that can hope for an intervention of the Word; it is only a certain kind of knowledge: that which is willing to limit itself to an object which has been precisely and clearly set before it. It is by submitting itself to these conditions, and only thus, that human knowledge can legitimately hope for the grace of revelation.

The response of a human being in the presence of the event of faith is, then, an attitude of prayer and patient waiting, joined with a real uncertainty. Will I be the object of a divine revelation? I hope so; I do not know. This is not the attitude preached by the religion of the Reformers. For them the idea of confidence and the idea of faith are closely connected. Certitude about one's personal salvation is precisely the act of faith. Moreover, at the basis of this certitude is the divine revelation which one has received—whose purpose one has understood. Barth rejects any position which will not fit within the framework of his system. The *fiducia* of the reformers is not true *fiducia*. A short study of this problem is necessary here in order that we may understand Barth's concept of the response of a Christian, as contrasted with the Reformers' concept of that response.

## F. *Fiducia* in Barth and in Luther.

The Protestant theology of faith has been worked out less as a direct reaction against the Catholic notion of faith than as a protest against a doctrine of justification, which Protestants consider pagan. This protest makes use of a new elaboration of the idea of faith. In this new theory all the weight of Christianity rests on faith; works count for nothing. Catholic justification is something legal, forensic. When Luther speaks in this manner, he is not speaking of the moral law, the law of the Commandments; he speaks rather of a complex of practices which have come to take the place of the law. Preachers, if we are to believe Luther, interest themselves solely with such vain and puerile works as the celebration of feasts, numerous fasts, membership in pious confraternities, pilgrimages, devotion to the saints, recitation of the rosary, entrance into the religious state, etc.[48] All these practices make the Christian life extremely complicated, but they bring no peace. This is the starting point of the Lutheran reaction. The great fault, which the Reformer finds in this allegedly Catholic system, is that it gives no consolation, no security, but rather turns the anxieties of otherwise well-disposed souls into a permanent disposition.[49] Luther's personal experience plays an important role in all this. He frequently remarked that, despite all his strivings, he could not realize the ideal of perfection which the rule of his order held up to him. He extended the controversy by stating without reserve that works can never give peace to a soul. Works can perhaps drive a man into the desert, but they will only plague him, even there, with the very unrest which drove him from the world.

Men are saved by trusting God, by abandoning themselves to Him. They must learn from their faith that Christ, by dying on the Cross, has saved them and has remitted their sins. That should be enough. Since the time of Luther, Christian faith has been understood as *fiducia,* a firm trust. The Heidelberg Catechism, a witness to the Calvinist tradition, defines this principal element of faith as "a deep trust which the Holy Spirit infuses in me by means of the Gospel, convincing me that the remission of sins has been won for others, and even for myself, and that God has given me justification and eternal life by means of a pure grace, solely through the merits of Jesus Christ." [50] It is *fiducia* that justifies and saves. A faith which is not complemented by trust is worthless.

We must remember that the Reformers are not preaching a blind faith. Trust does not replace the intellectual element of faith; it perfects it. Faith does not mean merely a knowledge of the histroy of Christ, His miracles, and His doctrine. It means, above all, the result of that history—trust. If faith is crowned by trust, the role of knowledge, the *historiae notitia,* is in nowise excluded; it is presupposed.[51] This is what gave rise to the distinction between *fides historica* and *fides salvifica. Fides historica* regards knowledge of the gospel history, of the objects of our faith. Since the work of J. Gerhard it has been called *fides quae creditur,* or objective faith.[52] This faith is worthless of itself, since even the impious and the devil himself can have it. In order that it may be rendered salvific, we must accept it by reason of our trust in the promises of Our Lord; it must be subjective. Scholastic Protestantism calls such faith the *fides qua.* Theology has made a more detailed analysis by distinguishing two elements in *fides quae,* or historical faith: *notitia,* or a simple intellectual grasp of the objects of our faith without any definite attitude toward their truth value; and *consensus,* or an intellectual assent which recognizes that these objects of faith are true. We find, therefore, in the completed scheme of orthodox Protestant theology a trilogy: *notitia, consensus, fiducia.* Although the post-Lutheran and post-Calvinist theological systems have worked together in seeking the exact meaning of the *fides quae,* we must not overlook the fact that *fiducia (fides qua)* is for them the only important element. A faith which is merely knowledge would be meaningless.[53] This is the reason for the Protestant rejection of the Catholic notion of faith, a notion which all the Reformers consider to be no more than a historical faith, existing only in the intellect, belonging neither to the will nor to the heart.[54]

The faith of the reformers is thus primarily the antithesis of justification by works; whereas the latter causes nothing but anxiety, the former brings peace of conscience. It is in this way that the word *fiducia* is to be understood. The English word 'trust' is only a rough translation of its Latin equivalent, *fiducia;* it conveys only partially the idea which the Reformers understand by *fiducia*—the peaceful assurance, the certitude of the Christian that he has been redeemed by Christ.[55] A believing Christian cannot doubt his salvation. The slightest hesitation would be an insult to Christ's grace and His redemptive death. It would be to stop short at the thought that our sins are too many and too evil, that their weight is more than can be counterbalanced by the sacrifice of

Calvary.[56] The faith of the Reformers is a prophetic possession of personal salvation. By my faith I know that Christ has undoubtedly saved the world; but, even more, I know that He has saved me personally.[57]

Such a certitude fits poorly into Barth's system. Thus, without discarding the word *fiducia,* he seeks a meaning which is more in conformity with his own opinions. He finds here that legal parlance can help him. Barth prefers the notion of 'hope' to that of 'certitude'—the notion of 'expectation' to that of 'possession.' The *fiducia* of the jurists can get him out of his difficulty, and he adopts it readily. This demands a somewhat technical explanation. Suppose a man wishes to favor someone in his will without giving this person the right to appeal directly to the will. This could happen for any number of reasons: legal considerations, convenience, or simple decency. One easy solution to the difficulty is to will the property in question to a third party with the tacit condition that this person will transmit the legacy to the intended beneficiary in a proper fashion when he sees fit. Such a contract has absolutely no legal value; the beneficiary has no legal means of establishing a claim. The testator has relied entirely on the good faith of the intermediary, and it is upon this good faith that the solidity of the contract rests. The sentiment which binds the beneficiary of the will to the third person does not depend on a juridically established relation of creditor and debtor, but only on *fiducia.* The word of the intermediary is the beneficiary's only guarantee; he has no recourse to any legal claim. The intermediary can freely determine the time, place, and manner in which he will acquit himself of his obligations; he is bound only by his conscience. The *fiducia* of the beneficiary will be simply an attitude of submission, prayer, and hope.

It is in this juridical sense that Barth understands *fiducia.* It is a relation between a man and someone who surpasses him, whose final decision he awaits. It directs man to the Word of God, gives direction to his expectations, orients him to a future event of a divine intervention. Barth is, therefore, far from the religion of the Reformers. Their certitude is cast aside. Their *fiducia* was a confirmation of a gift from God to men. I have trust because God has spoken to me. My *fiducia* is the term of what might be a long and difficult process; it is, however, the end. When one has

experienced *fiducia,* he has finished the process. He can say with
full certitude, "God is with me." Though he retains the formulas
of the Reformers, Barth changes their meanings. He frequently
changes meanings in this manner and can easily confuse the un-
wary reader. His fidelity to the sixteenth century is often to be
found more in his words than in his thought. The *fiducia* of Luther is robbed of its proper meaning, and Barth puts his own ideas
into the completely empty form that remains. Instead of the *tran-
quilla possessio,* which is the term of an interior struggle, we have
nothing more than the empty hands of the Christian who awaits
all in some future event. The certitude of Luther rests entirely
on a divine decree which has been already manifested, a decree
sealed by faith. Barth puts all his hope in the expectation of an
event which has yet to take place.[58]

The element of certitude, which is so characteristic of Luther's
faith, has totally disappeared.[59] Barth has chosen its direct opposite;
he has not just appealed to a lower form of certitude. He is not
content, for example, with simple probability. He has not reduced
the degree of certitude; he has totally suppressed all certitude.
A Christian cannot even say, "It seems that I have faith." The
accomplishment of the Word of God is totally veiled when it
happens to us; we cannot recognize it with certitude; we cannot
even suspect its presence. We have no ability to pierce its obscurity, not even a momentary and extraordinary illumination of the
intellect by God.[60] Nevertheless, if by 'faith' we understand that
*fiducia* which directs us toward God, the legitimate attitude of a
man in hopeful expectation, we can say that we have faith. Such
faith is not, however, true faith. True faith consists in God's giving
Himself to us in the miracle of revelation. Revelation surpasses
all our perceptive abilities. Barth makes his own the statement
of Paul Althaus, who sums up the mystery of the Word of God
and the corresponding human attitude thus: "I know not *whether*
I believe, but I know *in whom* I believe." [61]

This first section has had as its object the criterion of dogmatics.
Now that we have finished our survey, we can summarize its principal conclusions:

1. By reason of his creaturehood, man is opposed to the substantial
   Divinity of the Word, and to His identity with the Act and very
   Being of God. Moreover, as a consequence of sin, which affects the

whole man, which "secularizes" him with all his faculties, the Word of God becomes for him a mystery without the least ray of light.

2. From this it follows immediately that man cannot know God.

3. If, then, Barth gives a definition of the knowledge of God which is intentionally vague, it is not in order to include experience. It is simply to be able to call the knowledge of God something which is, in fact, nothing more than the knowledge of man by God.

4. True faith is the accomplishment of the Word of God, or, what comes to the same thing, knowledge of man by God. Since, moreover, the human intellect can have no perception of this accomplishment, one is never sure that he has faith.

5. The response of a human being placed in these conditions comprises two elements:

   a. An element of knowledge. Superfluous of itself, this is imposed by the command of God. The intellect must apply itself to attaining a knowledge of this veil, which hides the divine reality. Barth calls this the indirect knowledge of the Word of God.

   b. A psychological element, *fiducia*. Man knows that he neither possesses nor has the ability to possess the Word of God. He will thus live in expectation of an event which depends completely on the divine initiative.

We thus come to the deceptive conclusion that the only real and true criterion of dogmatics is completely inaccessible. A criterion that cannot be known is a strange criterion indeed. Theology would be absolutely impossible if Barth had not given us another criterion. It is the Bible, the object of that paradoxical indirect knowledge which we have discussed above. We shall devote the next section of this book to a study of the properties of this criterion.

# notes
## to chapter five

1 Cf. KD, vol. I, 1, pp. 194–198.

2 Cf. KD, vol. I, 1, p. 200.

3 *Discourse on Religion,* first discourse, trans. by I. J. Rouge, p. 119.

4 We understand the word "religion" in the wide sense it has assumed in modern usage. Compared with the Thomistic classification, it includes not only the moral virtue of religion, but also the three theological virtues. Religious knowledge, therefore, is the knowledge of faith.

5 "Die Frömmigkeit, welche die Basis aller kirchlichen Gemeinschaften ausmacht, ist, rein für sich betrachtet, weder ein Wissen noch ein Tun, sondern eine Bestimmtheit des Gefühles oder des unmittelbaren Selbstbewusstseins" (*Der christliche Glaube,* 3, Berlin edition, vol. I (1830), p. 7).

6 *Discourse on Religion,* second discourse, trans. by I. J. Rouge, p. 152.

7 I. J. Rouge, Preface to his translation of *Discours sur la religion,* p. 35. In the early editions of his apology, Schleiermacher had coupled the word "intuition" with that of "feeling." Later, he dropped "intuition," and no element of intellectual apprehension comes to be mingled with "feeling."

8 "Das Gemeinsame aller noch so verschiedenen Äusserungen der Frömmigkeit . . . ist dieses, dass wir uns unserer selbst als schlechthin abhängig, oder, was dasselbe sagen will, als in Beziehung mit Gott bewusst sind" (*Der christliche Glaube,* 4, Berlin edition, vol. I (1830), p. 16).

9 "Christliche Glaubenssätze sind Auffassungen der christlich frommen Gemütszustände in der Rede dargestellt" (*ibid.,* 15, p. 108).

10 Cf. *Der christliche Glaube,* 16, ed. cit., p. 111.

11 R. Otto is, therefore, in perfect accord with his master, Schleiermacher, on this point; but he parts company with him on his irrationalism. Conceptual language cannot, from his viewpoint, provide an adequate expression for the religious emotion; for Schleiermacher, on the contrary, a religious emotion is the ambition of a well-conceived dogma. Schleiermacher considers a concept the intellectual equivalent of the religious emotion. Cf. *Le Sacré,* pp. 16, 19, and 22–23.

12 Schleiermacher does not make use of the word "experience." In his terminology, *Gefühl* signifies the act, *Gemüt,* the faculty.

13 "Es kommt für die Bündigkeit dessen, was wir hier behaupten und verneinen, alles darauf an, dass wir als Redende und als Hörende bei der Sache sind. Aber dass wir bei der Sache sind, das kommt ganz und gar nicht auf uns, sondern auf die Sache an. Und zwar gerade darum, *weil diese Sache, das Wort Gottes, keine Sache, sondern der lebendige persönliche und freie Gott ist*" (KD, vol. I, 1, p. 206).

14 Barth attributes this position especially to the two German theologians, Wobbermin and Schaeder. Cf. KD, vol. I, 1, p. 223.

15 KD, vol. I, 1, p. 219.

16 L. Malevez, RSR, 1938, vol. XXVII, p. 397.

17 KD, vol. I, 1, p. 222.

18 "In diesem Ereignis des Glaubens vollzieht sich auch die Erkenntnis Gottes" (KD, vol. II, 1, p. 11). "Die Möglichkeit der Erkenntnis des Wortes Gottes liegt im Worte Gottes und nirgends sonst. Dass sie wirklich wird, das kann schlechterdings nur *geschehen* und zwar als Wunder vor den Augen jedes Menschen, des profanen und des frommen, des Griechen und des Juden. Dieses Wunder ist der Glaube" (KD, vol. I, 1, p. 234).

19 Cf. ch. II.

20 Cf. ch. III.

21 "Die Öffnung von oben, die sich im Ereignis des wirklichen Glaubens vollzieht, bleibt uns so verborgen, wie dieses Ereignis selbst und wie Gott selbst" (KD, vol. I, 1, p. 256). "Es gibt keinen Beweis dieses Beieinanderseins des Wortes und eines Menschen" (*ibid.*, p. 254). "Der auferstandene Christus geht durch verschlossene Türen" (*ibid.*, p. 261).

22 Barth's repeated affirmation that God grants a purely transitory disposition for understanding the Word of God does not alter the question in the least. "Er wird ja im Glauben, indem er das Wort Gottes wirklich vernimmt, dazu geeignet, es zu vernehmen" (KD, vol. I, 1, p. 251). "Keine ihm eigene, sondern eine ihm im Glauben geliehene und keine zu betrachtende, sondern nur eine im Glauben zu gebrauchende (Eignung)" (*ibid.*, p. 251). "Die Versöhnung des Menschen mit Gott in Christus schliesst auch das in sich oder fängt schon damit an, dass der verlorene *Anknüpfungspunkt* neu gesetzt wird" (*ibid.*, p. 251). The reason is simple: this disposition does not adapt man for a reception of God's Word; it is not *received* within man, and, moreover, is indistinguishable from the event itself.

23 "Das menschliche Erkennen Gottes wird umgekehrt in ein Erkanntwerden des Menschen durch Gott. . . . Er erkennt indem er von Gott erkannt ist" (KD, vol. I, 1, p. 257). The exact same position is found in KD, vol. II, 1, p. 46.

24 *Die Offenbarung als Wort Gottes bei Karl Barth und Thomas von Aquin*, in *Divus Thomas*, Fribourg, 1937, vol. XV, pp. 55–64, especially pp. 58 and 61. This article has been republished in another work by the same author: *Das Offenbarungsproblem* . . . , pp. 69–86.

25 L. Malevez, RSR, 1938, vol. XXVIII, pp. 298–399.

26 Cf. KD, vol. I, 1, p. 218.

27 H. R. Mackintosh presents a discriminating evaluation of Barth's position in general. "This is an attractive position, yet one with difficulties of its own; for we are led to ask how "the once-for-allness" of the event of the revelation in Jesus-Christ is to be harmonised with the contention that revelation as complete, *includes man's believing acknowledgement of its reality.* Is the "givenness" of the revelation in Christ quite real and unconditioned if after all, to be fully realised, *it must be apprehended* by man, even if that apprehension is wrought by the spirit?" (*Types of Modern Theology*, p. 281). Mackintosh feels obliged to formulate this question, solely because he thinks that divine intervention and human experience are in the same line and encounter one another. The apprehension under discussion is not an apprehension of the Word of God given *hic et nunc.*—Consider what Mackintosh adds later on: "Students of Barth will not miss the striking change of tone he here displays with regard to the character of faith as an experience. Earlier he had expressed a deep distaste *for any accentuation of the experimental realization* of the Divine truth, as though content alone mattered, not inward form" (pp. 283–284).

28 Cf. KD, vol. I, 1, pp. viii–ix.

29 Cf. KD, vol. II, 1, pp. 267–269.

30 *Natur und Gnade*, p. 41.

31 Barth came into contact with this notion, which is new to him, due to the work of Père Erich Przywara. Cf. H. U. von Balthasar, *Divus Thomas* (Fribourg), 1944, vol. XXII, p. 171.

32 KD, vol. I, 1, p. 253.

33 Nevertheless, as we shall see later, this is not a rejection of *equivocation* as the term is understood in Thomistic theology.

34 Cf. KD, vol. I, 1, p. 257 and pp. 459–460. ("Es gibt keine *analogia entis,* es gibt nur eine *analogia fidei.*")

35 Cf. KD, vol. II, 1, p. 254.

36 Cf. KD, vol. II, 1, pp. 256–257, 265.

37 Cf. KD, vol. II, 1, p. 259. In this reference, nevertheless, Barth defends himself against the charge of evolving an "as if" theology.

38 "Was wir tun in unserem in Anschauungen, Begriffen und Worten zu vollziehenden Erkennen seiner Schöpfung, das hat *seine uns verborgene Wahrheit* in ihm als ihrem und unserem Schöpfer" (KD, vol. II, 1, p. 258). "Wir haben mit unseren Anschauungen, Begriffen und Worten keinen Anspruch darauf, dass er ihr Gegenstand sein müsse" (*ibid.*). "Unsere Worte sind nicht unser, sondern sein Eigentum" (KD, vol. II, 1, p. 259).

39 Cf. KD, vol. II, 1, pp. 263–266. This partial agreement cannot be conceived in terms of quantitative analysis. On the one hand there is all; on the other, none.

40 It goes without saying that in the *analogia fidei* there can be no question of an arbitrary imagining of God. The meaning which it imposes on our concepts is their true and original meaning (Cf. KD, vol. II, 1, p. 257). The acceptation which we accord our words, on the contrary, is a shaded and falsified meaning, which no longer has anything in common with the meaning accorded to the words by the Divine Intelligence. "Der Vater und der Sohn ist, *uns unbegreiflich*

*und verborgen,* aber in der unbestreitbaren Priorität des Schöpfers vor dem Geschöpf, Gott selber. Wenden wir diese Worte auf Gott an, dann entziehen wir ihnen also nicht ihren eigentlichen Sinn, wir reden dann nicht *als ob,* wir reden vielmehr gerade dann in der ursprünglichen Wahrheit dieser Worte" *(ibid.,* p. 259).

41 We are in complete agreement with E. Brunner, who is severely critical of Barth on this point. "Das ist ein unerhörter theologischer Nominalismus, gegenüber dem auch der Occams harmlos erscheint. Denn das würde ja heissen: Dass wir Gott 'Vater,' 'Sohn,' 'Geist' nennen, dass wir Gottes Wort sprechen usw., liegt nich darin, dass Gott eher mit einem Vater als mit irgend etwas sonst Ähnlichkeit hat, sondern einfach darin, dass Gott es in der Schrift so sagt. Gott sagt es nicht darum, weil es—durch seine Schöpfung, von seiner Schöpfung her—schon so ist, sondern es wird erst durch Gottes Schriftwort" *(Natur und Gnade,* p. 39).

42 "Es ist also nicht an dem, dass wir mittels einer Klärung des Sinnes und Verständnisses unserer Worte als solcher zu einem Vorsinn und Vorverständnis ihres Gebrauches im Verhältnis zu Gott vorzustossen vermöchten" (KD, vol. II, 1, p. 260).

43 "Hujusmodi quidem nomina significant substantiam divinam, et praedicantur de Deo substantialiter, sed deficiunt a repraesentatione ejus" *(Summa theol.,* I, q. 13, a. 2, c).

44 It utilizes a human activity, but not the receptivity of nature. This is an additional proof that the notion of "potency" eludes Barth, as it does the majority of his contemporaries. Cf. KD, vol. I, 1, p. 209.

45 J. Rilliet, RTP, 1944, vol. XXXII, p. 129.—"Seine Gestalt ist nicht ein geeignetes, sondern ein ungeeignetes Mittel der Selbstdarbietung Gottes. Sie entspricht der Sache nicht, sondern sie widerspricht ihr. Sie enthüllt sie nicht, sondern sie verhüllt sie" (KD, vol. I, 1, p. 172).

46 KD, vol. I, 1, pp. 210–212.

47 "Dadurch und nur dadurch bekommt das menschliche Wort von Gott konkreten Inhalt und konkrete Form, dadurch und nur dadurch wird es fähig, etwas zu sagen: dass es auf Gottes Erlaubnis und Befehl hin ausgesprochen ist" (KD, vol. II, 1, p. 261).

48 "De quibus rebus olim parum docebant concionatores, tantum puerilia et non necessaria opera urgebant ut certas ferias, certa jejunia, fraternitates, peregrinationes, cultus sanctorum, rosaria, monachatum et similia." Nevertheless, at the very moment when Luther was approving the articles of the Confession (1530), preachers had already evolved a better doctrine: "Haec adversarii nostri nunc dediscunt nec perinde praedicant haec inutilia opera ut olim. Praeterea incipiunt fidei mentionem facere, de qua olim mirum erat silentium. Docent nos non tantum operibus justificari, sed conjungunt fidem et opera, et dicunt nos fide et operibus justificari. *Quae doctrina tolerabilior est priore, et plus afferre potest consolationis* quam vetus ipsorum doctrina" *(Conf. Aug.,* art. 20, J. T. Müller, *Die symbolischen Bücher* . . . , p. 44).

49 "Olim vexabantur conscientiae doctrina operum, non audiebant ex evangelio consolationem. Quosdam conscientia expulit in desertum, in monasteria, sperantes ibi se gratiam merituros esse per vitam monasticam. Alii alia excogitaverunt opera ad promerendam gratiam et satisfaciendum pro peccatis. Ideo magnopere fuit opus hanc doctrinam de fide in Christum tradere et renovare, ne deesset con-

solatio pavidis conscientiis, sed scirent fide in Christum apprehendi gratiam et remissionem peccatorum et justificationem" (*Conf. Aug., loc. cit.,* p. 45).

50 *Cat. de Heidelberg*, p. 21, ed. E. F. K. Müller, *Die Bekenntnisschriften . . . ,* p. 687.—In 1521, at the very outset of Lutheranism, Melanchthon was already stating in his *Loci:* "Fides non est aliud nisi fiducia misericordiae" (cited by H. Auer, RGG, vol. II, col. 1209).

51 "Admonentur etiam homines quod hic nomen fidei non significat tantum historiae notitiam, qualis est impiis et diabolo, sed significet fidem, quae credit non tantum historiam, sed etiam effectum historiae, videlicet hunc articulum: remissionem peccatorum. . . . Augustinus etiam de fidei nomine admonet lectorem, et docet in scripturis nomen fidei accipi non pro notitia qualis est in impiis, sed pro fiducia, quae consolatur et erigit perterrefactas mentes" (*Conf. Aug.,* art. 20, J. T. Müller, *Die symbolischen Bücher . . . ,* pp. 45–46). See also the beginning of the reply to question twenty-one of the Heidelberg catechism, the conclusion of which has been quoted above. "Was ist warer glaub? Es ist nicht allein ein gewisse erkandtnuss, da durch ich alles für war halte, was uns Gott in seinem wort hat offenbaret; sondern auch ein hertzliches vertrauen, welcher der heilige Geist durch Evangelium in mir würcket . . ." (E. F. K. Müller, *Die Bekenntnisschriften . . . ,* p. 687).

52 Cf. KD, vol. I, 1, p. 248. J. Gerhard, a seventeenth-century Lutheran systematizer, used the formula *"fides quae, fides qua,"* which he borrowed from St. Augustine (*De Trin.,* XIII, ch. II, 5).

53 "Forma fidei, docendi causa, tribus partibus describi solet, notitia, assensu et fiducia. *Notitia* est eorum cognitio, quae ad salutem necessaria sunt. *Assensus* est, quo firmiter creditur vera esse, quae verbo Dei traduntur. *Fiducia* est, qua quisque fidelium sibi promissiones evangelicas applicat. Notitia et assensus fidei historicae cum salvifica communis est, fiducia huic propria existit. . . . Fiduciae autem nomine vel apprehensio et applicatio Christi cum ejus beneficiis vel pacatio conscientiae intelligitur. . . ." Nevertheless, faith cannot exist without knowledge; it is not a simple surrender. That is the reason why the implicit faith of the Roman Church is rejected: "Implicita igitur fides, qua caeco assensu creditur quod Romana Ecclesia credit, nulla est. Fides sine notitia esse nequit. 1. Quia ex auditu est; auditus autem per verbum Dei. 2. Quia Sapientia est, qua Deus cognoscitur." Likewise, a faith which would be solely knowledge would be of no value. "Nec melior est quam historica fides quae cum firma fiducia non est conjuncta. Papani fidem tantum in intellectu esse docent, in voluntate et corde non item. Scriptura vero aperte contrarium statuit" (J. Wollebius, *Christianae theologiae compendium,* 1, I, ch. XXIX, canons VII–X, ed. Bizer, p. 115).

54 Catholic theology in no way denies the necessity of trust. Far from it! Faith is perfect only when joined to the other theological virtues; it can, therefore, be the instrument of justification only inasmuch as it is united with hope. But is not hope Christian trust in the fidelity of God? Nonetheless, we must avoid identifying the trust of Catholic theology with the *fiducia* of Protestantism: these two notions do not coincide perfectly. Melanchthon drew attention to this in his *Apologia confessionis:* Dicimus spei objectum proprie esse eventum futurum, fidem autem de rebus futuris et praesentibus esse et *accipere in praesentia remissionem peccatorum* exhibita in promissione" (art. III, § 191, J. T. Müller, *Die symbolischen Bücher . . . ,* p. 140). More exactly, that which distinguishes *fiducia* and trust is a question of certitude or lack of certitude. The Protestant is certain of the actual and complete remission of his sins. The hope of Catholic theology, under its human aspect, remains uncertain. Though the Christian may have pre-

sumptions concerning the actual state of his soul, he has no certitude as to his predestination and final perseverance. Cf. *Denzinger,* 826.

55 "In der innigsten Verbindung mit der Lehre vom Glauben steht im protestant- ischen Lehrgebäude die Ansicht, der Gläubige müsse von seiner Rechtfertigung vor Gott und künftigen Seligkeit vollkommen überzeugt sein, so zwar, dass Melanch- ton von den Scholastikern, die dies leugneten, sagt, man sehe schon allein daraus, dass kein Geist in dieser Art von Menschen sei" (J. A. Möhler, *Symbolik,* p. 191).

56 "Sola fides, quae intuetur in promissionem et sentit ideo *certo* statuendum esse, quod Deus ignoscat, quia Christus non sit frustra mortuus, etc ..., vincit terrores peccati et mortis. Si quis dubitat, utrum remittantur sibi peccata, contumelia afficit Christum, quum peccatum suum indicat majus aut efficacius esse, quam mortem et promissionem Christi; quum Paulus dicit (Rom. 5: 20) gratiam exuberare supra peccatum, hoc est, misericordiam ampliorem esse quam pecca- tum" (*Apol. conf.,* art. III, § 27, J. T. Müller, *Die symbolischen Bücher . . . ,* p. 113).

57 "Faith is essentially a trust, a complete trust of the heart with regard to Christ, trust in the mercy which has been granted us because of Christ; through this trust, we maintain as certain that our sins have been forgiven because of the Son of God, Victim and Mediator. But this trust does not remain in the realm of generality. Luther insisted emphatically that the *believer apply the object of his faith to himself: I believe that God is favorable to me, that He pardons me.* This condition, according to Luther, renders adhesion to this article of God's pardon particularly difficult. With faith of this type, I believe and I am certain that God is my own personal God, because He speaks to me individually and forgives my sins" (Julius Köstlin, *Luthers Theologie,* vol. II, p. 180, cited by J. Paquier, DTC, vol. IX, col. 1231).

58 Cf. KD, vol. I, 1, pp. 246–248.

59 Among numerous texts, cf. KD, vol. I, 1, p. 486. Our knowledge of God is stamped with *Ungewissheit:* KD, vol. II, 1, pp. 6–8. "Nicht so, dass man sie (die Wirklich- keit des Wortes), diesen Menschen betrachtend, irgendwo in oder an ihm ent- decken oder ablesen könnte" (KD, vol. I, 1, p. 249).

60 "Es ist nicht an dem, als ob Gottes Offenbarung etwa auch nur zuguterletzt in ihrer Spitze identisch würde mit einer Erleuchtung der Vernunft" (CD, p. 138).

61 P. Althaus, *Grundriss der Dogmatik,* 1929, p. 19, cited in KD, vol. I, 1, p. 249.

# part two

*The Human and Provisional Criterion*

*of Dogmatics: The Bible*

# scripture, testimony of the word of god

A s we said at the end of the preceding chapter, the Bible is not theology's true criterion; it is nothing but a substitute criterion, a makeshift criterion. To arrive at such a poor conclusion is certainly disappointing. We must now examine if and how such a criterion can be of any use, and how its authority can be established. The conclusions to which an objective analysis will lead us, will be, alas, still more disappointing and will do nothing but confirm our apprehensions.

## A. Human Utterance.

Christian tradition has always insisted on the preparation of the soul before it approaches the Scriptures. To understand their deep meaning, a person must approach them with the supernatural dispositions of the one who recorded them. If, imbued with rational prejudices, anyone believes that he can deeply penetrate the meaning of the inspired text, he is mistaken. He will find in them only a reflection of his own thought; the true meaning of the Scriptures will certainly escape him. In the same way that a poetic work will remain completely foreign to him in whom poetic sentiment has never flourished, so the Bible will remain a partially closed book to him who does not share the hagiographer's faith. For faith corrects and strengthens the work of reason in its own order. The believer will make a better rational exegesis than the non-believer, because through faith he is already sympathetic towards it and in close contact with the object of his knowledge.

Faith is still more necessary when it is a question of strictly theological knowledge. The science that has God for its object is based solely on the testimony of God. The articles of faith, of which we have had perhaps a rational certitude through the study of exegesis, are taken now as theology's starting point and enjoy a certitude of a superior order. It is no longer a matter of personal conviction but of God's testimony. The motive of our faith is divine authority, itself. Without faith, theological knowledge is inconceivable.

If Luther had been content with recalling this principle to mind, subsequent tradition would have been grateful to him. Certainly we have no difficulty in conceding that the light of the Holy Spirit is necessary to enter the specific domain of the Scriptures; God's actual presence in the soul of the reader is necessary. In this sense the formula: *"Duae res sunt, Deus et Scriptura Dei, non minus quam duae res sunt, Creator et creatura Dei,"* has an authentically traditional sound.[1] What spoiled this valid intuition was Luther's insistence on opposing illumination by the Holy Spirit to the authentic interpretation of the Church's teaching authority. Here Luther goes beyond his premises. Certainly the magisterium of the Church does not replace the faith of the members; it cannot give an appreciation of the Scriptures to one who has no faith. But it can and must guide the individual's faith and help him to discern what really comes from the Spirit and what is nothing but imaginary fantasy. The role of the Church is simply to disentangle what springs from authentic faith and what is wild overgrowth in the complex mechanism of human psychology.[2]

Faithful to his basic principles, which we have already presented, Karl Barth goes further. Luther and Catholic tradition agree in declaring that, to understand the true content of the Scriptures, illumination by the Holy Spirit is necessary in the spirit of faith. These supernatural illuminations do not give a new meaning to the text, but enable one to fathom the proper sense intended by the author. Barth cannot go so far. If there is any relation in his system between the Spirit and the Scripture text, it is much looser. The text of Scripture is totally opaque to revelation; faith cannot constitute a deeper insight into its meaning. The Spirit will not throw light on the text; the text is nothing but the *occasion* of the Spirit's intervention.

This doctrine, implicitly contained in the substitution of the analogy of faith for the analogy of being, must be explained at greater length. It can be summarized in two words: Scripture is, at one and the same time, human and divine utterance. The human-divine character of Scripture is also firmly defended by Catholic tradition and has found its most satisfactory and precise expression in the theory of instrumental causality applied to inspiration. God is the principal author of the inspired texts, and the hagiographer is the instrumental author. The text is simultaneously God and man's work; it is for this reason that there is no contradiction in the fact that the same page may contain God's eternal and supratemporal thought in a framework of human thought, conditioned by all the limitations of a determined time, place, and culture. Thus the thought of the hagiographer is not foreign to God's thought but is its nearest human image. In Barth's system this continuity disappears: the divine word and the human word are juxtaposed in Scripture.

We harbor no resentment against Karl Barth when he says that it would be ridiculous to "suppose that the contact with revelation would have bestowed upon the apostles and prophets a sort of 'Solomon-like' or even divine knowledge, of truly encyclopedic range, encompassing all beings of heaven and earth, nature, history, and humanity. Such powers would have made them the representatives of an ideal, supratemporal culture and would have rendered them capable of proclaiming all truth. In fact, it was not so. Each of them, in a certain measure and in their own peculiar way, participated in the culture of his time and milieu. Henceforth, the form and content of this specific culture may, quite naturally, appear questionable to any other age or set of circumstances." [3]

But Barth does not stop here. His liberal formation, against which he so vehemently reacted, has left a deep imprint on his mind. When it is a question of judging the religious and theological values of the sacred writings, he is not far from adopting purely and simply the most radical positions of the liberals. In that heap of writings, dedicated to the study of the history of religions, Christian documents are barely discernible. They are neither better nor worse than the others. In the eyes of reason and from the viewpoint of purely historical and comparative investigation, the Bible appears stripped of all revelational value, since so much of its contents has parallels in similar writings. Moreover, none of the sacred authors took the trouble to present his doctrine in a complete and systematic way, with the result that subsequent efforts to order their scattered affirmations are based to a great extent on conjecture. More serious still is the complete absence of concordance among the writings that claim to be the testimony of a unique revelation. It is not a question of differences in points of detail but quite often of contradictions in the most fundamental doctrines. Consider all the countervailing texts in the law and the prophets, St. John and the Synoptics, St. Paul and St. James. Nothing, moreover, can solve these contradictions; nowhere can you find the key to them. Some exegetes have undoubtedly done their utmost to solve these difficulties by adopting the viewpoint of one or several writings and endeavoring to judge the others according to this criterion. Such a choice remains, nevertheless, purely arbitrary and cannot solve the question in a way that will satisfy an exacting logic. The Scriptures, even in their purely religious and theological affirmations, cannot pretend to escape in any way the curse that necessarily affects every human enterprise.[4]

## B. Theory of Inspiration.

If the Bible, which is human utterance, is at the same time— although in a mysterious way—the Word of God, we must now consider the Barthian theory of inspiration.[5] Barth claims to find his theory in two Pauline texts which the exegetes do not generally apply to this matter.[6] The first of these texts (2 Cor. 3:4–18) is a fragment of a long apology where St. Paul appeals to his mission as an apostle. It could not be summarized better than by quoting verses 5 and 6 of the passage: "All our ability comes from God, since it is he who has enabled us to promulgate this new law to men. It is a spiritual, not a written law; the written law inflicts death, whereas the spiritual law brings life." What follows goes on to develop this antithesis. Despite this brief excerpt, the written law as such must not be considered something bad leading to death and condemnation. As Barth correctly points out, St. Paul is not here belittling Scripture. With good reason might one recall St. Matthew's text (5:17): "Do not think that I have come to set aside the law and the prophets; I have not come to set them aside but to bring them to perfection." All the a fortiori argumentation of verses 7 to 11 is based on the value of the Old Testament. It is because the sentence of death, engraved in writing upon a stone, was promulgated in a dazzling cloud that St. Paul thinks he is authorized to affirm that the promulgation of the spiritual law, which he represents, must be much more dazzling. If, however, Paul does not hesitate to say that the written law inflicts death, that it is a proclamation of our guilt and condemnation (vv. 7 and 9), this is so because it no longer has its proper lustre. A veil separates it from the understanding of the Jews. "To this day, I say, when the law of Moses is read out, a veil hangs over their hearts." The written law, nevertheless, is not condemned to remain hidden and unappreciated; St. Paul says so in verse 16, which is the key to his interpretation of the old covenant: "There must be a turning to the Lord first, and then the veil will be taken away." The rest of the text treats of the presence of Christ's Spirit and the Gospel's liberty in relation to this conversion to the Lord.

This antithesis between the letter and the Spirit is reduced in fact to the opposition between unbelieving Jews and Judaizers, who can understand only a dead letter, and the Christians, who have the Spirit of Christ, who are capable of comprehending the spirit underlying the letter. They alone understand the profound sense of the texts whose meaning escapes the veiled hearts of the Jews.[7] If Karl Barth wishes to say nothing more, if for him this passage simply teaches us that the Old Testament, to be fully understood, must be seen in the light of the New (that is, must be enlightened by the Spirit of Christ), we would be in complete accord with him. Before considering Barth's conclusions, we must examine another passage which he considers of great importance as a complement to the first.

The text (1 Cor. 2:6–16) contains also one of those emphatic antitheses so dear to St. Paul. He contrasts the wisdom of religious persons with that of "men" (vv. 5 and 13). In the verses that precede this passage, St. Paul has severely reproved the "wisdom" of his adversaries. However, he is not opposed to wisdom as such, because there is another wisdom, mysterious and hidden, which comes from God. It contains those things "no eye has seen, no ear has heard, no human heart conceived" (v. 9). In a word it consists "in the knowledge of Christ and of Him Crucified" (2:2). "Time, the present age, and the universe in its visible course," [8] which St. Paul designates by "the world," cannot grasp such a wisdom; nor, moreover, can "the rulers of this world" (v. 8), "the human merchants of wisdom who guide men not subjected to the Gospel along the paths of their own reasoning." [9] Is not the most evident proof of this the fact that they crucified Him Who was the very object of that mysterious wisdom (v. 8)? "For mere man with his natural gifts," real wisdom is nothing but folly (v. 14). But God in his mercy has prepared for those who love Him (v. 9) a revelation of the mysterious wisdom, and He has communicated it to us through His Spirit. For this reason St. Paul calls those who have been favored with His lights "men who have *spiritual* gifts" (v. 15) or "those who are fully grounded" (v. 6). The Spirit that is bestowed on them is not the spirit of worldly wisdom, but the Spirit that comes from God Himself (v. 12). As the spirit of man scrutinizes the most hidden secrets of man, so the Spirit of God penetrates the mysteries of God (v. 11); thus to him who has the Spirit of God the mysteries of God's gifts to us are revealed (v. 12). St. Paul does not fear to say: "Christ's mind is ours ($\nu o\hat{\upsilon}\nu$ $\chi\rho\iota\sigma\tau o\hat{\upsilon}$ $\check{\epsilon}\chi o\mu\epsilon\nu$)." And this privilege gives extraordinary rights to the man who has spiritual gifts, for he "can scrutinize everything, without being subject himself to any man's scrutiny" (v. 15).

Is this all that Karl Barth affirms in support of his theory of inspiration? It should be noted immediately that the problem of inspiration is not dealt with in the texts just quoted; the only point with which St. Paul is concerned is to prove the independence of his message, in relation to both the written law of the Old Testament and the body of human wisdom. It is a question of a strong affirmation of the liberty of the Spirit in the face of certain human constraints: on the one hand of texts in which they refuse to see Christ, and on the other, against a pseudo-wisdom in which the mystery of Christ is nothing but folly. We can admit, however, that the problem is dealt with from afar and *in obliquo.* Under these circumstances what can we deduce from all this? Simply the necessity of the Spirit's gift in order to understand the message of the Old Testament and to "understand God's gift to us" (1 Cor. 2:12).

The Barthian theory of inspiration sees even more. It is not a new doctrine; it is a new name for "the historical manifestation of the Word of God." We find ourselves on familiar ground. "When we speak of the Word of God, we speak of a reality and an event beyond the reach of human dispositions and human expectations." [10] The word of God is *Ereignis,* it is a miracle.[11] Inspiration for Barth is the momentary and mysterious intervention of the Word, that gives itself and withdraws without human consciousness becoming aware of it. For him, the Word ever remains a mystery.[12] He does not withdraw anything that he had vigorously affirmed in his denial of analogy as a means to supernatural knowledge.

How far we are from St. Paul's categorical affirmations! The veil that covers the Old Testament is removed when hearts turn to the Lord (2 Cor. 3:16). The glory of the letter is apparent to those who have the Spirit of the Lord. Karl Barth's doctrine, moreover, does not fit a strict interpretation of the second text. To be faithful to the main lines of his thought, one would have to deny that the man who has spiritual gifts can perceive divine wisdom. Such an interpretation finds no support in the text and deprives the antithesis of all meaning. Christ Crucified is revealed, and the divine wisdom is bestowed upon him who has the Spirit of God. It may be of value to point out that St. Paul did not hesitate to declare that a person can *receive* the Spirit of God, just as he can *have* the mind (νοῦς) of the Saviour (1 Cor. 2:12, 16). Elsewhere, St. Paul assuredly says that this knowledge is manifested only *in speculo et in aenigmate* (1 Cor. 13:12), i.e., given only partially; but that does not deny the fact that divine wisdom is given in this life. It is no longer then a mystery screened from our eyes as Barth contends.

This already indicates clearly—and we shall have to return to it again—that Karl Barth's exegesis is weak and governed by certain a priori premises whose origins we shall later consider. A refusal to admit that the mystery of God is partially granted to human minds here on earth is contrary to the Scripture; it leads to the elaboration of an artificially constructed system.

If we wish to understand what Karl Barth means by inspiration we must keep two facts in mind: the temporal and spatial limitations of inspiration. The prophets and the apostles were inspired; they were assisted by the light of the Holy Spirit in the composition of their works. But such inspiration is a gift granted to a person at a given moment. The work that results from this inspiration is not inspired as such. *Per se,* it is dead. It can, however, again become inspired if the Holy Spirit intervenes. Yet, we must not imagine that the intervention of the Holy Spirit will take the Holy Writings in their entirety and grant them that human-divine authority which distinguishes inspired works. Far from it. Inspiration does not exist outside the use that is made of the Scriptures. It cannot occur unless someone is actually reading, preaching, or listening to the message of the Bible. Here we must not think that the text is inspired every time we come in contact with the Bible. It is not and cannot be inspired unless God decides so in an absolutely free act. Inspiration occurs at the intersection of two perpendicular lines: one horizontal, representing the Bible; the other vertical, representing the actual and unconditioned intervention on the part of God. The horizontal line might be prolonged indefinitely, but it would never be the bearer of inspiration unless the vertical line intersects it at some point.

Barthian inspiration is elusive. One can never say: it is here or it is there. It is nowhere and can be everywhere. At the turn of the century Protestant authors and a number of modernists attempted to exclude from the influence of inspiration some work or other or some part of a work; they restricted inspiration to a particular type of affirmation; they even falsified the concept of inspiration. But never has such a radical position been upheld. How far removed is Barth's theory of inspiration from the Catholic doctrine on this point, in which each and every canonical book is inspired, and particularly from the Thomistic school that does not hesitate to defend inspiration *usque ad verba*.[13] Barth's basic error consists in confusing the inspiration of Scripture with the gift of faith. Can we say that the sacred writers have been inspired without admitting that they were inspired so that their work might benefit from this charism? What would be the meaning of a private inspiration that would not pass to the works for which it has been granted? The books are inspired; the texts are inspired; but that does not deny the necessity of faith to penetrate them in all their depth. Faith is not a private inspiration parallel to the inspiration of the prophets and the apostles. It only gives a *better* understanding of that which the inspired text already contains.

Here again discussion is difficult, because we have seen that, for Barth, faith is a divine intervention that bypasses the human faculties of intellect and will.[14] If God uses for a moment a certain text, that does not alter its human structure in the least. We saw above the consequences to the value of the Bible's truth. The inerrancy of the Bible—certainly the consequence of inspiration most precious to Christians—is a concept without meaning in Barth's system.[15] It matters little for me to know that God cannot err if I cannot participate in His inerrancy. Is not this the role of inspiration?

## C. The Signs of Inspiration and the Authority of the Bible.

At the end of Chapter II, we said that Barth had to choose between a literal Protestantism and a spiritualistic Protestantism, between the letter that imprisons the Spirit and the Spirit that no longer recognizes the letter. He chose neither; he took a middle-of-the-road position. Our findings to this point place his theology nearer spiritualistic Protestantism. One sometimes wonders what value and role are reserved for the written text in Barth's system. Can such a corrupted text still be of any use? Would it not be better to align oneself purely and simply with the spiritualists and reject writings which private revelations would advantageously replace? Such is not Barth's choice. After he strips Scripture of all traditional prerogatives, he turns around and grants it a major role in his synthesis. We must study this other aspect of the Barthian paradox and try to understand how the downtrodden

Scriptures can still have authority in the eyes of the faithful. Practically the question is this: Are there writings in some way associated with inspiration, and how can we recognize them? What is the sign that enables us to recognize God's intervention? [16]

It is not at all strange that we should now deal with the fact of inspiration after our lengthy exposition on the theory of inspiration. Such procedure is perfectly normal. How can one know if there is an inspiration, if he does not first know in a precise and detailed manner what the word means to a particular author? Such precaution could be superfluous, but not when dealing with Barth, who gives completely new meanings to words of traditional usage. The question we presently face is this: Are there inspired writings and how can they be recognized? In fact, we are treating the question of the Canon of the Scriptures. Is the Canon more than the list or catalogue of inspired writings? How do you establish this catalogue? Catholicism has a very simple answer. The Church preceded the Scriptures; the Scriptures have been entrusted to the Church. It was her privilege then to determine during the first centuries, from a mass of documents—many of which were of doubtful value—those which could and ought to be recognized as inspired by God.

The basic principles of the Reformation prohibit Protestants from recourse to this criterion. For them the Church is subject to the Bible, not vice-versa. They must, therefore, look elsewhere for signs of divine intervention in the composition of certain human works. We have seen above how Luther proceeded.[17] Everything, in his eyes, was dominated by the principle of justification through faith. If a work speaks of Christ and preaches Christ, it is authentically inspired; it matters little whether it was written by Peter, Paul, Pilate, Judas, Anna, or Herod. In referring to the Apocalypse he says: "My soul cannot feel at home with this book, and it is enough for me to see that in it Christ is neither honored nor known, whereas the primary task entrusted by Jesus to the apostles was this: You will be my witnesses. That is why I confine myself to books where Christ is clearly and purely represented." [18]

John Calvin, too, was concerned with the same problem: Why can certain writings be called inspired? The answer to these questions is contained in Chapters VII and VIII of the First Book of the *Institution chrétienne*. As is evident, the adversaries Calvin had in mind were the theologians of the Catholic Church.

As for those who ask us from what source and how are we persuaded that the Scriptures come from God if we do not avail ourselves of the Church's decrees, it is as if someone were to ask how do we learn to distinguish light from darkness, white from black, the sweet from the sour. It is because the Scriptures have something that distinguishes them, a quality as manifest and as striking as that by which white and black things exhibit their color, or bitter and sweet things produce their savor.[19]

Thus, a quality, immanent in Scripture without recourse to an external criterion, enables man to discern that a writing comes from God. It is the Spirit's testimony in the very soul of the reader that bestows upon it an unquestionable authority.[20] This criterion has such an importance that, when it is lacking, any recourse to what could be only a crutch is perfectly useless. "If we do not have this certitude, which is of a higher degree and more firm than any human judgment, in vain will the authority of the Scripture be proved by arguments; in vain will it be established by the consent of the Church or confirmed through other aids. For, if this foundation does not underlie all, the authority of Scripture will always remain doubtful." [21] If, however, everything rests on the intimate agreement that exists among the divine qualities of the book, recognized by certain supernatural dispositions of the reader, does not the danger of confusion exist and do we not run the risk of accepting human complacency for a harmony preestablished by the Spirit?

Calvin retorts:

Truth is exempt from all doubt because without any aid it can hold its own. How properly this power belongs to Scripture is seen from the fact that among human writings there is none, however polished and adorned, that has *such a power to move us*. We may read Demosthenes or Cicero, Plato, Aristotle, or any other of their kind—I confess that they are marvellouly attractive and will delight and move a man to a point of ravishing his spirit. But, if we then turn to the Holy Scriptures, whether we wish it or not, *they will touch us so vividly, they will pierce our hearts so deeply, they will implant themselves so firmly in*

*the very marrow of our bones,* that the power of rhetoricians or philosophers compared to the force of such feeling is but a wisp of smoke.
Thus it is easy to perceive that the Holy Scriptures have a peculiarly
divine quality of inspiring men, insofar as they surpass by far all the
charms of human industry.[22]

The probative value of a work's inspiration lies in its power to
stir up an intimate experience in the Christian. The entire Calvinistic doctrine on canonicity is based on the interior witnessing
of the Spirit.

Everywhere and as long as Calvin's doctrine was kept in its
purity, we find the same assertions. The *Confession de foy de 1559,*
which is at the same time the great French confession and the first
confession of a national church, states: "We recognize these books
as canonical and as the unquestionable rule of our faith, not so
much by the common agreement and consent of the Church, as
*by the testimony and interior persuasion of the Spirit,* which enables us to distinguish them from the other ecclesiastical books,
on which, even if they be useful, you cannot base an article of
faith." [23] The same confession, practically in the same terms, is
found in the *Ecclesiarium belgicarum confessio,* drafted two years
later.[24] This position could not be maintained long in its original
purity. This was soon realized. Little by little, especially in the
seventeenth century, a more refined doctrine was elaborated,
which reintroduced into the Church the theory of canonicity. It
was found principally among the Swiss Calvinists and the Lutherans. Overflowing spiritualism had opened the eyes of Protestant
theologians. "They distinguished two types of criteria. The one,
called internal, was derived from the form and content of Scripture; the other, called external, came from antiquity, the propagation of the Gospel, the faith of the martyrs, the credibility of
biblical writings, the character of the inspired authors, miracles,
prophecies, and finally, above all, from the testimony of the primitive Church." [25]

Karl Barth too takes pleasure in citing the *Confessio Gallicana*
and others of the same viewpoint.[26] If he quotes them, it is to
oppose the Roman Catholic stand, represented by a passage of
Msgr. Bartman's "dogmatic": "The books are canonical *in actu
primo quoad se* because the are inspired; *in actu secundo quoad*

*nos* because the Church has received them as inspired in her canon. A divine act made them suitable to be included in the canon; an act of the Church recognizes this quality already inherent in them." [27] It could not be better expressed. The Church does not bring about inspiration by a decision; rather, she recognizes and proclaims it to the world. Moreover, such is the explicit teaching of the Vatican Council: *"Eos (libros) vero Ecclesia pro sacris et canonicis habet . . . propterea quod Spiritu Sancto inspirante conscripti Deum habent auctorem atque ut tales ipsi Ecclesiae traditi sunt."* [28] This prerogative of the Church is the indispensable complement to the inerrancy of Scripture. It allows her members to base their faith on unshakable foundations. Evidently, Karl Barth can see in this doctrine nothing but a deification of the Church which subordinates the Word of God to the word of man.

Is it not curious, however, that Barth carefully avoids quoting the most formal texts, the most precise and doctrinal passages that have ever been written against the Catholic theology of canonicity? Is it not strange to find in his writings not the least allusion to Chapter VIII of the First Book of the *Institution chrétienne*? It is all the more curious since this part of Calvin's work is the origin of the confessions cited above. Why this omission? The reason is quite simple. The text is too clear, too explicit. It is too directly opposed to Barth's basic principles. The internal testimony of the Spirit is, according to Calvin, the sign of the inspiration of a given book. This testimony is manifested in the fact that certain books "have such a power to move us" that they distinguish themselves by that very power from all profane writings. The Sacred Scriptures "will pierce our hearts so deeply, they will implant themselves so firmly in the very marrow of our bones," that the emotion aroused in us by the non-inspired writings will vanish as smoke. For Calvin, therefore, something authentically divine, perceptible by human intelligence, remains in the sacred text. On the other hand, the psychology of man is not so corrupt as to be unable to react any longer to God's presence in the Scriptures. Scripture remains transparent to the Divine, and the human mind is incapable of detecting the imprint of God. This is the counterpart of the Barthian thesis exposed above, in which man and the world are buried in sin; thus every work produced by the hand of man is totally opaque to anything transcending the human order. Man is as capable of hearing the Word of God as a pebble on the beach is of appreciating the poetry of the sea.[29]

In this case, it is not possible for Barth to accept only the negative part of Calvin's affirmations: it is not for the Church to discern whether or not a writing is inspired. As for the positive part, he is obliged to pass over it in discreet silence. It is always painful for a Reformed theologian to find himself disagreeing with the most theologically-minded of the Reformers. The question of the *authentic* canon is connected, for Barth, with all the other concepts of his system designed to express the intervention of divine transcendence in human immanence. *Grace, revelation, inspiration, canon* are different words, designating one and the same reality: the intermittent and hidden intervention of the sovereign Word in the created sphere. The question of a true canon is, therefore, something that necessarily escapes us.[30]

Our author, however, agrees to use the word 'canon' (ecclesiastical) in a sense close to the habitual one: "The canon (of the New Testament) is the list of biblical books *recognized as normative* by the Church because of their apostolic origin." [31] Let us note, however, that normative does not mean "inspired." We must not lose sight of the fact that the double relativity of a created and sinful being that affects every human creature affects, for the same reason, the Church herself. Karl Barth really attempts to square a circle when he tries to justify a list of normative writings, while stripping them of any solid criterion of discernment. By what right can a writing be normative if it is not inspired? No criterion has sufficient weight to impose itself. Recourse to tradition, to apostolic origin, even to the content of the Bible—all are invalid from the very start.[32] One might say, perhaps, that those writings are normative which were composed by the immediate witnesses to Christ: the apostles. And why? These witnesses were men like us; what they have transmitted to us might well be a fabric of errors. Or else, one might be satisfied by Luther's argument and recognize as normative any writing which tells us something about Christ. This criterion cannot escape the same condemnation. Where the choice of a determined criterion is concerned, a lack of certitude will be a necessary concomitant. Thus, it is not surprising that Karl Barth admits the possibility of re- forming the canon in the sense of lengthening or shortening it.[33]

The Bible is a canon unto itself. Barth does not and could not say more.[34] For in Barth's theory, the Bible is the norm of all Christian activities: preaching, dogmatics, moral, etc. One can see where that can lead. It is useless, then, to ask why the Bible is a law; there is no "why." It is just as impossible to answer this question as to say why we got up this morning on our right foot and not on our left.[35] If you ask a child why among so many women, that particular woman is his mother, only one answer is possible: She *is* my mother. The answer to this question is free from doubt, and, therefore, from any need of proof.[36] The Bible is a fact that is not discussed. It has been accepted and continues to be so; that should be enough for us. One of the most surprising facts of the history of modernism is precisely the retention of the Bible in a preaching otherwise so secularized. Though the testimony of God's Word was no longer officially recognized as a criterion, the use of the Bible in acts of worship recalled the presence of an irreplaceable criterion.[37] If then Barth accepts the Bible as Holy Writings, as the 'place' where God could intervene, he does so by a completely arbitrary choice for which he can give no valid reason. If someone objects that there is no Sacred Scripture, or that it does not consist in the books recognized as such by the ecclesiastical canon but in others, Barth is absolutely incapable of advancing even the shadow of a refutation.

\*

\* \*

At the basis of his system, therefore, is found an irresolvable contradiction. The authority of the Barthian synthesis claims to rest on the sole authority of the Bible; the Bible's authority rests on nothing. It is like a construction without any foundation. As soon as Barth begins to think out his theology, he is obliged to close his eyes to the fact that it is unthinkable; and he must con- ceive everything as if it were possible to build on a cloud. Barth has been reproached for building an *"als ob"* theology, an "as if" theology. Notwithstanding his denials, it is difficult to see how he can escape this accusation.[38] The Protestant theologian has noth-

ing before him but his Bible; this Bible is the only norm of his
Christian activity, the only source of his preaching and doctrine.
In it he must find everything and seek nothing elsewhere. At the
same time he must not lose sight of the fact that this Bible does
not give him what he was commanded to look for, because supernatural truth is necessarily hidden from him. For every question
that his mind and Christian conscience asks, he can find in the
Bible only an answer which might well be purely and simply erroneous. Karl Barth's theology imprisons him within a paradox,
from which no escape is possible.

# notes

## to chapter six

1 "Darum ist die Schrift ein solch Buch, gehört nicht allein das Lesen, sondern der rechte Ausleger und Offenbarer, nämlich der Heilige Geist. Wo der die Schrift nicht öffnet, da bleibt sie wohl unverstanden" (*Pred. ü. Luk.*, XXIV, 13ss., 1534, EA, III, p. 334, cf. KD, vol. I, 2, p. 563).

2 "To derive the fuller meaning of a text, one must penetrate the thought of the author in order to arrive at the full inwardness which is realized through a communion with his operative genius. When it is a question of the Bible, communication with the operative genius of the author consists in nothing other than an intense communication with the thought of God Himself. Exegesis, which commences as a purely literary endeavor, evolves into a theological enterprise. In this way it achieves its supreme accomplishment. Work of this nature can be pursued only in the light of faith, which is the same as saying in the light of the Church, the guardian of that faith. Such exegesis cannot be conducted in an individualistic manner, with each person using his own mind and heart as a touchstone for each text. Rather it must be conducted in perfect union with the apostolic teaching authority; for Christ promised to this *magisterium* the Holy Spirit's aid in attaining to the organic integrity of all truth, and entrusted to it the mission of proclaiming the Word of God at all times and in all places" (F. Braun, *Les études bibliques*, pp. 35–37).

3 KD, vol. I, 2, p. 564.

4 Cf. KD, vol. I, 2, pp. 565–566. Later Barth adds (p. 568): "(Die Bibel ist) auf der ganzen Linie anfechtbares Menschenwort."

5 Cf. KD, vol. I, 2, pp. 571–585.

6 The theological doctrine of inspiration is of biblical origin. It is derived from two texts of the New Testament. In 2 Tim. 3:16, St. Paul says that Scripture is *theopneustos*, a term which the Vulgate renders through two words: *divinitus inspirita*. St. Peter (2 Pet. 1:21) says that the prophets have spoken "carried away by the Holy Spirit," a text which the Vulgate renders in the words *Spiritu Sancto inspirati*. These two texts constitute the scriptural foundation for every theory of inspiration. Cf. E. Mangenot, DTC, vol. VII, col. 2068–2069.

7 E. B. Allo, *Seconde Épître aux Corinthiens*, pp. 107–111.

8 E. B. Allo, *Première Épître aux Corinthiens*, p. 41.

9 *Ibid.*

10 KD, vol. I, 2, p. 585.

11 Cf. KD, vol. I, 2, pp. 585–586.

12 "Wir haben die Gottgeistlichkeit der Bibel als eine als Gottes Werk und Wunder und in seinem Geheimnis fallende, im Glauben und Gehorsam und in treuer Exegese zu bedenkende und zu erwartende ereignishafte Entscheidung verstanden" (KD, vol. I, 2, p. 593).

13 "Post infaustam discessionem a sancti Thomae doctrina altissima de Dei influxu in hominem, saeculo XVI duce Molina, prima apparent tentamina restringentia inspirationem ad veritates, exclusis verbis. Propter necessariam tamen inter veritatem et verba connexionem dixerunt, quoad verba eligenda haberi in hagiographos Spiritus assistentiam seu custodiam ne errarent, quae, ut patet, est assistentia mere negativa" (J. M. Vosté, *De divina inspiratione et veritate Sacrae Scripturae*, p. 102).

14 Cf. ch. IV et chap. V.

15 "Verbalinspiration bedeutet nicht: Unfehlbarkeit des biblischen Wortes in seinem sprachlichen, geschichtlichen, theologischen Charakter als menschliches Wort. Verbalinspiration bedeutet: das fehlbare und fehlende menschliche Wort ist jetzt als solches von Gott in seinem Dienst genommen und *ungeachtet seiner Fehlbarkeit* als solches anzunehmen und zu hören" (KD, vol. I, 2, p. 592).

16 In traditional Protestantism the question of the fact of inspiration does not arise, since it is clearly affirmed in the Scriptures. This does not hold true in Barth's system.

17 Cf. ch. II.

18 *Vorrede auf die Apocalypse,* 1522. Cf. DTC, vol. II, c. 1556.

19 *Inst. Chrét.,* I, 7, 2, CR, vol. III, c. 92.

20 As Calvin himself states in the title to Chapter Seven.

21 *Inst. Chret.,* I, 8, 1, CR, vol. III, c. 98.

22 *Inst. Chret.,* I, 8, 1, CR, vol. III, c. 99.

23 Art. I, 4, W. Niesel, *Bekenntnisschriften* . . . , p. 67.

24 "Hosce omnes libros solos pro sacris et canonicis recipimus, ut ad eos, veluti ad regulam, fides nostra exigatur: iisque tanquam fundamento innitatur, et stabiliatur. Eaque omnia, quae illis continentur, absque omni dubitatione credimus: idque non tam, quod Ecclesia eos pro hujusmodi recipiat et approbet, quam imprimis, quod *Spiritus Sanctus in cordibus nostris testetur a Deo profectos esse, comprobationemque eius in se ipsis habeant*" (Art. 5, W. Niesel, *Bekenntnisschriften* . . . , p. 121). This confession was drawn up in 1561 by the preacher, Guy de Bray, who adhered to the French confession of 1559 faithfully. The initial purpose for the formulation was to provide Calvinism with a systematic structure in its opposition to the Spanish authorities. Soon, however, it became the confession for all the communities of the Netherlands.

25 E. Mangenot, DTC, vol. II, col. 1558. This author's observations have greatly facilitated our research.

26 KD, vol. I, 2, pp. 525–526.

[27] B. Bartmann, *Lehrbuch der Dogmatik,* vol. I, p. 14.

[28] *Const. dogm. de fide cath.,* c. 2, *Denz.,* 1787.

[29] Cf. Chapter IV.

[30] "Wir haben da, wo die Kirche heilige Schrift gefunden zu haben erklärt, heilige Schrift tatsächlich zu erwarten" (KD, vol. I, 2, p. 531).

[31] "Der Kanon der heiligen Schrift, d.h. die Liste der in der Kirche als massgebend, weil als apostolisch erkannten biblischen Bücher" (KD, vol. I, 1, p. 103).

[32] "Diese Antwort ist an sich eine gottliche und also untrügliche und definitive Antwort. Das menschliche Hören dieser Antwort aber, das Hören der Kirche einst und unser eigenes Hören heute ist ein menschliches und also *der Möglichkeit des Irrtums nicht einfach entzogenes,* nicht ein als solches über jede Verbesserung erhabenes Hören. . . . Das gilt auch von unserer Antwort auf die Frage nach dem Kanon" (KD, vol. I, 2, p. 526s.).

[33] "Eine Verengerung oder Erweiterung des Kanons . . . kann auch heute dogmatisch-grundsätzlich betrachtet, nicht als eine Unmöglichkeit bezeichnet werden, nur dass sie, um sinnvoll und legitim zu sein, immer ein Akt der die Offenbarung glaubenden Kirche sein müsste und nicht etwa dem Urteil der historischen Forschung oder gar dem Geschmacksurteil Einzelner überlassen sein könnte" (CD, p. 339).

[34] "Die Bibel macht sich selbst zum Kanon. Sie ist Kanon, weil sie als solcher der Kirche imponiert hat und immer wieder imponiert" (KD, vol. I, 1, p. 110).

[35] Cf. KD, vol. I, 1, p. 279.

[36] Cf. SK, p. 3. See the same place: *"Ein Satz über die Autorität und Bedeutung der Bibel* ist dann gehaltvoll, wenn er als analytischer Satz einen aller Problematik entzogenen Sachverhalt umschreibt und also die Kenntnis dieses Sachverhalts zur Voraussetzung hat."

[37] Cf. KD, vol. I, 1, p. 267.

[38] In the opinion of Erik Peterson, Barth's theology is a mixture of *"Schein und Möglichkeit."* It would be difficult to improve on this characterization. Cf. *Was ist Theologie,* p. 7.

# the approach to this testimony through exegesis

In 1906, Karl Barth attended Harnack's course at Berlin as a most docile student and took part in his seminar in history. Fourteen years later, the same men met again; each had been invited to speak at a discussion held by the students at Aarau. The young pastor was thirty-four years old; Harnack was seventy. The remarkable paper presented by Harnack could contain nothing new; his position was known from his earlier works. The same was not true of Barth's position. Although forewarned, the old historian could not believe his ears: there had not been one phrase, not one idea that he could share. Such a theology made him tremble. "I asked myself," he would later write, "how a man who has charge of souls could speak in such a way." [1]

This simple anecdote demonstrates better than lengthy explanations how diametrically opposed were their respective concepts of Christianity. In 1929, in a letter to Rade, Harnack wrote: "I could never have believed that a new theory would arise to which my mind could not have been attuned." [2] The conflict extended beyond the two men, who stood face to face. In Karl Barth, a new understanding of Scripture and its interpretation was measuring its strength against the rationalistic exegesis which had become the norm in Protestant university circles. This exegesis at the end of the century had perfected a method which it thought definitive. Only the details had yet to be worked out. The task of future generations would be to apply in yet wider areas this precision instrument which the great artisans had fashioned. With no other aid than historical criticism and its auxiliary sciences, they thought they had given to the sacred texts a truth which ecclesiastical dogma or philosophical concordance had too often deformed. A feeling of satisfaction and of self-sufficiency was already taking hold. Liberalism was becoming established. Is not the fact that at this time there appeared liberal professions of faith, modeled along the lines of the ancient confessions of faith, an indication that this movement believed it had reached a summit from which no person nor thing could cause it to tumble? [3] Believing itself definitive, the liberal school was becoming crystallized.

## A. The Theory of the *Römerbrief:* Objective exegesis.

The astonishment, then, was great when Karl Barth, pastor of Safenwil, a small village of Argovie, had the audacity to put on the market a commentary on the Epistle to the Romans which was governed very little, if at all, by the principles of critical exegesis. From the very Introduction, the critical method, without being directly scorned, was carelessly put aside, not ranked among the elements prerequisite for a real exegesis.[4] Karl Barth claimed to present in his commentary on the Epistle to the Romans a profound, real, supratemporal exegesis. Such audacity could not pass without creating a shock wave. Barth was not one of those traditional Protestants, closely bound to the confessions of their Church and to the texts of the Reformers. If one of these latter had ventured to write such a book, no one in liberal circles would have stooped to opening its cover. The pastor of Safenwil had been a convinced liberal. He had been an honor to his masters and even had occupied, under the immediate direction of Martin Rade, a position on the staff of the *Christliche Welt,* the chief organ for the propagation of liberalism in Germany. Now Barth had the temerity to declare that "if he had to choose between critical exegesis of the Bible and the old Protestant theories on inspiration, he would choose the latter without hesitation." [5] This return to the flesh-pots of Egypt was something incomprehensible for those who considered themselves the liberators of Protestant religious thought. Fortunately Barth did not go quite that far.

He immediately corrected himself by adding: "I am glad, however, not to have to make the choice." This admission diminished apprehensions very little. One thing was clear: Barth was withdrawing from the ranks of the liberals. Henceforth, agreement between the established exegesis and the exegetical current issuing from Karl Barth would be difficult. In spite of the reciprocal dealings maintained by R. Bultmann for some years between the *Formgeschichte* and the young Barthians,[6] the bridges were destroyed and remained so.

As soon as his first edition had been published, Barth was summoned to explain himself. The liberal school had delegated one of its best authorized representatives, A. Jülicher, to call Barth to account for his desertion.[7] Karl Barth readily complied and gave us an account of his exegetical method in the Preface to his second edition. From the start he was bent on affirming that he was not an enemy of historical criticism. He criticized it for not having done what it claimed to do: it made no attempt *to understand and explain*. What do the critical exegetes do? Their aim seems simply *to determine what was written*. For them this consists in transcribing the Greek into German, in drawing some light from archeology and philology, and finally, in systematizing into a more or less defensible whole the various scattered elements. They proceed no further. Should they at times pass beyond this limit, their efforts are so timid that they are not worthy of note. But one must go further. Although this preliminary work is clearly necessary, one must still go beyond it.

Barth explains the meaning of *Verstehen und Erklären* from the example of Calvin. The reformer of Geneva, after he established what was written (*Was da steht*), strove to make the texts before his eyes live. By means of arduous reflection, he did his utmost to abolish the distance separating Saint Paul from the reader of his Epistles, to make transparent that thick wall dividing the first century from the sixteenth. This effort had to be extended to the point where the dialogue between the document and the reader was concentrated solely on the object, *auf die Sache*. It is not the mystery of the form which ought to terminate our penetration, but solely the mystery of the object. Karl Barth will go as far as to say that the reader should be able to identify his views with those of the text to the point of forgetting that he is not its author. The text must truly be able to speak in his name.[8]

For Adolf Jülicher, the place of Barth is not among exegetes, but among practical theologians.[9] There, certainly, he would be less obnoxious. Certain liberties with science are granted a practical theologian; no one is disturbed at this. Why had he not done as Niebergall, who was free to choose for himself from those truths taught by Saint Paul whatever he wished to use in his own preaching? Such, in fact, is the role of the practical theologian. But Barth did not allow himself to be led along this path; he claimed that he was doing more and refused to make a choice. Such choices are arbitrary and consist simply in finding in an author the reader's own thought. What is important is to hear all that Saint Paul says. To make a distinction between what was conditioned by the apostle's day and what has eternal value is to introduce subjectivism into an interpretation which ought to remain completely objective.[10] In Saint Paul everything is at one and the same time historical and suprahistorical.

The expression that most adequately describes this stage of Barth's thought is 'objective exegesis.' Since this period, however, the term 'theological exegesis' has gained favor. I believe, nevertheless, that we must be prudent in identifying as 'theological' that kind of exegesis proposed in the Preface to the second edition of the *Römerbrief*. It is above all *a literary process* that Barth declares himself ready to apply to any document whatsoever. It is a law of interpretation that equally applies to Lao-tzu, Saint Paul, or Goethe.[11] A properly Christian element such as faith or *fiducia* does not of itself pertain to this method of hermeneutics. As Barth conceives it, this method would be suitable for reuniting all living thought formulated in the past, whether it be sacred or profane.

The method is perfectly legitimate in itself. That an exegete of such renown as Oscar Cullmann defended it certainly argues in its favor.[12] The philological, psychological, and historical interpretations of a passage cannot be but a preliminary work. They simply explain the place that such a religious idea holds in the life and doctrinal synthesis of an author and the sources through which it has come to him. We must go beyond historical contingencies and study an idea for its own sake. Let us take the example of justification by faith. One could restrict himself to a study of the psychological state of Paul's personality that predisposed him to adopt this religious idea; one could stop at the historical circumstances that favored it. As long as one stops there, he is an archeologist approaching living thought in the manner of a scholar reconstructing a monument of the past. One must penetrate the intrinsic and objective thought not simply with the Apostle, but with this objective truth which presents itself with a particular tonal quality in the author. History ought to be able to do more: it ought to bring to the present the thought of the past, to reproduce and recreate the content of a text. In this way alone will its interpretation be perfect.[13]

The disregard of history, then, would not be a favorable condition for securing a truly objective exegesis. One can reach suprahistorical truth only in its historical form. This form is the shell that one must break open; there exists no other way of getting at the kernel. The content must be sought not beside the *"zeitgeschichtlich bedingt,"* but in it.[14] Biblical affirmations in their temporal context are like the starting-points of lines converging toward a center situated on a supratemporal plane of absolute religious truths. The concrete truth which we read in the sacred texts is but the *transparent material* on which absolute truth is projected. The role of the historian and exegete is to reascend from the transparent material to the source of light and to project this light anew on another screen, namely, that of our time and our setting.

Some have eagerly styled this new exegesis (is it so new?) as an allegorical or pneumatological exegesis. Without doubt one is not wrong in so identifying Karl Barth's exegetical method; one is mistaken, however, if he intends this term to represent his *theory* adequately. Allegorical exegesis and objective exegesis are two clearly different methods, depending upon laws which we must plainly distinguish. For the former, a deeper meaning is hidden behind a secondary one; from this fact, one deduces that there can be several allegorical meanings for one and the same text. For the latter, the sense taken literally is no different from the objective sense; it is simply another form of it. If the sense taken literally seems obscure to us, it is not because the author wanted to "hide" his thought, but because he wanted to present it clearly in a time and setting different from our own. Whereas allegorical exegesis treats a text casually and simply substitutes one *sense* for another, objective exegesis is satisfied with the substitution of a more comprehensible *form* for one less comprehensible. Objective exegesis is aware that its work is purely provisional. It knows that the images it proposes, the expressions it advances, are valid today, but tomorrow will probably be out of date. Its language can always be improved. Allegorical exegesis, however, whose attachment to the letter is more flexible, pretends to do definitive work: it has discovered the hidden treasure.[15]

If in theory the distinction is well established, investigation shows us how delicate the task of objective exegesis is.[15a] In practice it is easy to slip from one form into the other. What must protect the exegete from the freedom of allegory is precisely a thorough acquaintance with the auxiliary sciences of exegesis. Only a patient and minute analysis of texts can avoid those bold deductions which the literal text does not permit. But if it is a delicate task to identify with certitude absolute truth contained in contingent form, it is still more so to find in the language of today the best form to express the truth anew. To discover the truly apt concrete word is often impossible; but to be satisfied with an approximation is betrayal, since this is to falsify the author's thought. It is more prudent in such a case to confine oneself to an abstract description of the truth. The effect produced is less striking doubtless, but closer to the truth. Here one will readily observe how the historian and theologian should ceaselessly effect an exchange of points of view, if one wishes to avoid the risk of doing violence to the texts. Such an exchange, we must recall, is not provided for by Barth. Though his theory of exegesis might be of value, his method is questionable.

## B. The Exegetical Method of the *Römerbrief*.

"The naive mixing of exegesis and contemporary theology is the distinctive trait of principal periods of reform." [16] This expression of Paul Althaus remarkably suits Barth, provided the mixture is so proportioned that contemporary theology is predominant. As a matter of fact, Barth's *Römerbrief* contains little commentary; it is rather the manifesto of a new school of theology. A. Jülicher rightly remarks: "For those who wish to understand the mentality of our day, it is most advantageous to read this work; but those who are interested in the Apostle Paul will find in it nothing new." In a vein of humor, the great liberal exegete, harsh to the end, applies to Barth's work an expression taken from Goethe: *"Mischmasch von Irrtum und Gewalt."* [17]

As far back as the first recensions, Karl Barth was accused of Alexandrianism, Gnosticism, Origenism, and Marcionism. All these ideologies have this in common: their protagonists align themselves with the enlightened who claim that they alone understand Scripture. "The spiritual man judges everything and is judged by no one." Such accusations—which authors as serious as Adolf Harnack and Adolf Jülicher do not hurl lightly—are not unjustified. The role of personal preference is truly excessive in Barth's commentary. One can easily verify this by reading, for example, the exegesis of Chapter VII in the first edition. A mere glance at the titles of the subdivisions makes one feel ill at ease. Verses 7 and 13 are grouped under a rather surprising heading: "The Law and Romanticism." The end of the same chapter is entitled: "The Law and Pietism." These transpositions are too coarse to be accurate. What Barth wants to single out at the beginning of the chapter is the aspect of independent and self-confident human activity, of man's sufficiency before God—an aspect that the many-sided concept of law surely contains. The νόμος for Saint Paul includes all this, and more. Barth, however, did not let nuances delay him. Without hesitation he found contemporary equivalents: religion, the Church, school, Judaism, Christianity, moralism—in a word, all idealisms.[18] Clearly our author has not escaped the reef, but has capsized into allegory. In the transposition of an absolute truth, the substitution of a new form for an old expression is a delicate task, which does not seem to fit the headstrong, pugnacious temperament of a Barth. What he sees in the Pauline concept of law is a very limited aspect of it. Moreover, the identification of this limited aspect with the modern concepts cited above heaps together such a mass of disparate elements that the original concept of law becomes unrecognizable, even to the trained eye. In these circumstances, it is no longer a question of a transposition but of a deformation.

The second edition takes into account the criticisms leveled at the first. The whole study was taken up anew; many immature choices were deleted and new elements introduced. Certain passages were expressed more carefully; the provocative affirmations, whose sole purpose was to shock, have become more rare; the pamphleteering tone has disappeared. In spite of numerous repetitions, the work would appear to have been conceived according to a comprehensive plan. Finally, the long passages of religious lyricism and the "spiritual bouquets," which gave the 1919 edition the appearance of an edifying work, have completely vanished. Though Barth reduced the volume of his voice, he did not change the orientation of his thought. On this point, in a new recension, A. Jülicher draws attention to some characteristic definitions. Flesh, according to Barth's Saint Paul, would be "relativity without limit; nothingness; unintelligibility." Faith could be defined as "respect before the divine unknown"; "assent to the divine 'no' in Christ." Again it would be "the fear which this 'no' includes": "the desire of the void" (*der Wille zum Hohlraum*): "perseverance in negation." To believe, lastly, would consist in "acceptance of this 'no' as if a 'yes' on the part of a man, who is the negation of God." [19] The abuse of paradox shows clearly that Barth is to such a degree full of his own thought that he is imposing it, perhaps unawares, on the Apostle Paul. The Epistle often becomes only the original and brilliant language which Barth makes use of to deliver his own point of view.

If Barth had been satisfied with formulating an exegetical method, such as we find laid down in the Preface to the second edition, and such as Professor Cullmann has so harmoniously developed, if he had not hazarded to illustrate it by such poor examples, I am convinced that he would have arrived at an understanding with several of the critical exegetes of whom he spoke so ill. I see a proof of this in a text of the erudite scholar Hans Lietzmann, who had been ranked by Barth among those who refuse "to understand and explain." [20] In the Preface to one of his last volumes of the *Handbuch zum Neuen Testament,* speaking in his own name and in the name of his collaborators, Hans Lietzmann writes:

> My opinion has always been precisely that the theologian more than anyone else, in the matter of exegesis, is concerned with penetrating to the core through the literary form. For me, however, there is no doubt that the indispensable condition is precisely to understand the biblical text such as it has been determined by language and history. . . . But when, having studied and grasped a text, I arrive at something, then a dialogue replaces the monologue of the biblical author. I begin to speak, breaking in on the conversation with questions and answers, with my doubts and my faith; and *the biblical text ceases to be a discourse belonging to a determined time;* the text becomes a message resounding through history, which must answer the countless questions hurled by a humanity tormented by a growing anguish. It is a message that reaches me and places me in the presence of God.[21]

Let one compare this text with the Preface of 1922, and he will have great difficulty in discovering perceptible differences between the two theologians.

## C. The Theory of the *Kirchliche Dogmatik:* Theological Exegesis.

We refused to define the Barthian exegesis of the *Römerbrief* as theological exegesis. It did not claim to be anything but a purely literary process, applicable to any work, sacred or profane; it did not rise to the level of theology. The same is not true when we approach the exegetical theory set forth in the *Kirchliche Dogmatik* and in the other works which are its contemporaries. Here a properly Christian element arises that could not be found in the interpretation of a writing that did not pertain to a special category. Three elements characterize the exegesis Barth proposes to us: a choice dictated by religious conviction; a way of approaching Scripture in close dependence on a determined Church; and, lastly, clear awareness of the impossibility of interpreting Scripture without a philosophical "prejudice." The first two elements give Barth's exegesis a claim to the title "theological." A study of the second will be saved for a special chapter (10) treating of ecclesiastical tradition. In the course of our treatment of this chapter, we must consider: 1) how this Christian "decision" can influence exegetical methods; 2) what is the legitimate role of philosophy in an exegesis worthy of the name.

We have seen at length how the Bible is and remains human utterance; how nothing in it is an apparent indication or sign of a special divine presence; how one can find in it no apologetic sign that would permit the supposition that it is not only human utterance, but also and especially the Word of God. On the other hand, we have established that, in the synthesis we are studying, the Bible *is* the Word of God. The last assertion, however, does not rest on any objective and controllable element, but on the decision of the believer. This decision *determines* that the Bible, by all that it is, can likewise be the Word of God; that it is the ordinary place of divine intervention. It is useless to point out that this decision is completely gratuitous, a risk that the believer must take. All is based upon an unlimited confidence which can depend on nothing else, and which one is tempted to label as irrational.

The decision, however, will not be without its influence on the interpretation of the Bible. For one who has made this leap into the unknown, one question is especially important: "To what extent is the text a testimony of the Word of God?" [22] For him the Bible above all will be a place of recollection and expectation. In it he will seek the witnesses of the first word spoken to the prophets and the apostles; in it, as well, will he look today for the living Word of God. This decision, as a result, affects appreciably the frame of mind of the one who makes the exegesis. The Barthian will approach the Bible differently from the rationalist who sees only the texts, versions, dictionaries, concordances, and parallels in the history of religion.

It is not our task to point out here all that is common to the Barthian and the critical exegesis. In the *Kirchliche Dogmatik,* Barth explains more fully and clearly than in the *Römerbrief* what he means by literary and historical analysis of a text. On this point, there could no longer be any misunderstanding.[23] For the subject now at hand, it is more important to determine how and why critical and theological exegesis are obliged to follow different paths. In his response, Barth is bent on showing that the conflict is *not necessarily* inevitable, but that it is due to the evident deficiencies of historical science, as it is habitually employed in rationalist circles. Ordinary hermeneutics, that is, one used indiscriminately for all profane texts, is in opposition to theological exegesis, only if it is founded upon too narrow a criterion of truth. It is, as a matter of fact, impossible to approach the study of a past event without having clearly determined, to begin with, what one means by a real event, without having delimited for oneself the realm of the possible. Such a criterion will be derived from either present experience, or the comparative history of religions, or some system of philosophy.[24] One runs a great risk if he limits "what can take place" to the rather narrow circle of purely human historical events. All that is connected with the proximately or remotely "preternatural" or "supernatural" risks being considered suspect and, consequently, unworthy of a science which demands exactness. Briefly, the result is that rationalist exegesis starts from an a priori exclusion, before any investigation of the idea of a God Who would take part in history, whereas theological exegesis springs precisely from this idea. Conflict is *practically* inevitable.[25]

This fact is connected with the distinction established by Barth between *Geschichte* and *Historie*. The two words are not synonymous by any manner or means: *Geschichte* is of itself opposed to *Historie,* and the juxtaposition *historische Geschichte* is simply unthinkable. *Historie* is the history that a man can approach, perceive, view completely—in brief, that he can understand. Its object, on its part, consists in a determined series of created events, similar to every other series of the same kind, with which, moreover, it can always be compared. As for its subject, *Historie* is the faithful representation of the concatenation of created events. As a result, this discipline never in any way leaves the confined circle of created things.[26] *Geschichte,* on the other hand, pertains immediately to God; it is the divine activity: "It is the series of *Ereignisse* in which God makes an alliance with men, seeks the realization of this alliance, and finally, brings to a successful issue in the bosom of creation what He decreed from all eternity." [27] It is always the *salvific* activity of God, the only activity to which Barth seems to pay attention; it is always God's activity in the order of grace, established by a series of intermittent interventions of His Word in the Holy Spirit. There is no difference, then, for Barth between *Geschichte* and *Heilsgeschichte*.[28] The opposition between *Historie* and *Geschichte* contains not only the antithesis of created and uncreated, but also of profane and sacred.

The problem has been especially treated by Barth in connection with his interpretation of the first chapters of *Genesis*. Does the account of creation pertain to *Historie* or *Geschichte?* Barth's answer is clear: the account, not answering to the criteria of *Historie,* cannot pertain to it. These chapters certainly describe real events which took place at a determined moment of time and at a determined point in space; but they took place screened from the observations of the historian. The events which they relate pertain to a sphere of historical events which elude human control. It is in this sense that we must understand Barth's repeated assertion that creation pertains to prehistory.[29] We must not understand the word in the sense in which we ordinarily understand it: all the research that has gone into the attempt to reconstruct the evolution of human races and civilizations before the appearance of writing—an attempt based on the study of the remains of representative primitives of the human species and of the testimonies that their activity has left, namely, habitations, hunting equipment, rudimentary tools, etc. Prehistory, thus understood, then, has not at its disposal means (written documents) specifically suited for knowing the past; it stands in a position of inferiority with respect to history properly so-called. Barth uses the word in a sense which he takes from F. Overbeck.[30] Barthian prehistory refers to events about which we have *no document* of any sort whatsoever. Does this mean to imply that the events narrated took place in an era so far back that it is prior to the first hewn flint or the most rudimentary implement that geological layers have preserved for us? Certainly not; these events belong to prehistory, as he understands it, because they elude human control, because they are imperceptible *ex propria natura* to human intelligence. They belong rather to a "metahistory."

One is tempted, then, to identify this *Geschichte* or prehistory or metahistory with a kind of historical coating of purely metaphysical values. One readily believes he is uncovering there a poetic fiction designed to travesty some of the great eternal and immutable truths. This would be a defect in interpretation. "Metahistory" is not a synonym for metaphysics. When Barth speaks of *Geschichte,* he is concerned not with verities but with events, *"zeitlich und raumlich,"* with moments and instants, and in no way with atemporal references.[31] The events, moreover, intervene in the horizontal unrolling of history, taken in the more narrow sense (in this Barthian *historie*), but they remain there unperceived.

These subtle distinctions become more clear when one compares the literary types to which they are related. The Bible contains, as a matter of fact, some passages pertaining to *Geschichte* and others pertaining to *Historie*. It is clear that the Books of Kings, for example, belong to this latter type. The events they relate are based on the personal verification of hagiographers or, at least, on trustworthy documents. But alongside this literary type, there is another, that of *Sage,* which Barth defines: "Divinatory and poetic reproduction of a concrete fact inserted in time and space, but pertaining to special spheres of prehistory and *Geschichte.*" [32] The qualifying adjective "divinatory" indicates the manner of acquisition of knowledge presupposed for this literary type; not an objective manner reserved to history, but a mysterious and paradoxical intuition on which, moreover, Barth sheds no further light. This kind of intuition expresses itself usually in poetic form. The *Sage,* then, is a fable which refers to a real event.

If it is necessary to mark out clearly the boundaries that separate *Sage* from the classical narration pertaining to history, it is still more important to mark out precisely the difference between *Sage* and myth. The object of the latter is not constituted by a concrete *Geschichte,* whose elements are situated in a determined time and place, but rather by realities and relations belonging to the universal essence of the natural or supernatural universe. Mythology, which is its expression, is only the exterior form of its atemporal content.[33] The absence of a real historical event, then, distinguishes the myth from the *Sage.* The same lack of a basis in the sphere of time and space renders superfluous any recourse to a divinatory mode of knowledge. The stories narrated in myths pertain to pure fiction and, thus, to the imagination of their author. Therefore, if we compare the three literary types: *Historie, Sage* (= *Geschichte*), and myth, we observe that the first refers to a real event controllable by the customary methods of historical science; that the second, likewise, refers to a real event, but a prehistoric one which can be perceived only by 'divination'; and that the third refers to no real event, since it is a pure invention of the human mind. This defines clearly, I believe, the meanings of the three concepts in the system of Barth.

The notions presented so far are too briefly sketched by Barth and at times deliberately transformed.[34] Certain clarifications are necessary. We must determine more precisely what we must understand by myth and *Sage* and, at the same time, touch upon the related notion of allegory. For Barth, outside of *Historie* there are two general types: *Sage* and myth. As subcategories, legends fall under the former type; tales, under the latter. The former is based on real events; the latter, on pure fiction of the imagination. These distinctions, however, are inadmissible. For critical science, likewise, has its own classification of genres: on the one hand, the *sage* with legends and tales; on the other, the myth. Both nevertheless, are a matter of fiction. All these types have this in common, that they explain a certain verifiable reality by recourse to imaginary events.

The supreme type here is the myth whose explanations, as its name indicates, are made up of mythological accounts.[35] Since the gods are not supposed to be interested in trifles, they can provide an explanation only for the great realities of the universe. Cosmogonies, for example, by their accounts of the war between the gods, answer questions that primitive man asked about the origin of the world. Certain anthropological myths seek to account for human nature, the conformation of the body, or the difference between sexes, through an idyl or an intrigue of Olympus. The lesser realities belong to the field of *Sage,* which does not venture so far as to lay claim to such important patronages.[36] The part of mystery that contains human life will be cleared by recourse to stories of ghosts, spirits, or witches. In mountainous country, such and such a conformation of rock surface or peak will be the point of polarization for one or several popular traditions on the races of giants that inhabited the regions. This type offers innumerable varieties and many examples. We can say in conclusion: the fiction that comprises myth and *Sage* presents itself as a final explanation of a tangible and unquestionable reality, but it remains mysterious for the minds of the simple.

Allegory is not the same.[37] This form of style uses a series of metaphors designed to express in a poetic and picturesque manner an event, an enduring reality, or an instruction. Here the figure (fiction, if you wish) is no longer an explanation, but a language. One calls on metaphors, as one would express himself by recourse to another language. Allegory, then, does not imply the idea of an explanatory "untruth," like the myth or *Sage*. Allegory explains nothing; it recounts.

We can observe that Barth was afraid to use a word which the Protestant critic has never held in great favor. The famous *Sage* of Barth's is not a *Sage* properly so-called, but is entirely an allegory whose hidden meaning can be perceived only by certain persons enjoying this double vision, which Barth calls 'divination.' The allegorical type in its most perfected form reflects clearly the teaching which it wants to deliver. When the prophet Nathan tells David the parable of the rich man who did not blush to carry off the only sheep of the poor man in order to feast with his friends, he demonstrates clearly the tie between this fictitious story and the sin of David who exposed Uriah to certain death: "You are this man" (2 Sam. 12:7-13). The link, however, is not always established with such clarity. If the exegete has serious reasons for believing that, despite all, it is a matter of allegory, he will be bound to devote himself with the means at his disposal, to a research for the meaning intended by God. He will study the context and parallel passages.

All literature, as a matter of fact, includes a diversity of types, among which the imaginative element often occupies an important place. Scripture is no exception. It has been written by and for men. It is, then, perfectly normal that it includes the entire range of ways of expression that we find in all other literature. Only one type is excluded and that, because it is unworthy of the Holy Spirit: the type which represents error and untruth as true. Nothing, then, prevents us from *affirming* the presence in the Bible of parables, allegories, and idealizations. On one condition, however: this *affirmation* must be one in the full sense of the word, based on the objective elements of the text, context, or mentality of the hagiographer, and in no way on a purely arbitrary choice of the interpreter. Every affirmation in the Bible is true in the sense in which the sacred writer presents it.[38]

In brief, the reader must be in a position to determine, by the means at his disposal, the literary type to which a text belongs. Such is not the position of Barth. The *Sage* is this impossible in-between: an allegory whose sense the author and his interpreter alone perceive, in no way by virtue of objective elements, but in the light of a subjective conclusion. In this way, Barth seems to justify positions which exceed the most questionable Alexandrian allegorization.

These indispensable clarifications permit us now to provide the Barthian reply to a complementary question: If, by reason of the *fiducia* of the exegete, the conflict with *Historie* is practically inevitable, what is the area in which the two sciences disagree? Certainly there cannot be opposition between them as long as the historical science restricts itself to positively acknowledging the truth of a narration; nor further, claims Barth, when the historian believes himself obliged to classify a passage, or even a book, as *Sage*. This classification would signify nothing more than the problematic nature of the above-mentioned passage with respect to its control by reason, and the fact that human thought, in applying its ordinary criteria, cannot acknowledge the events narrated as real. The theologian's cry of protest is fully justified as soon as the historian makes bold to speak about 'myths.' In acting thus, the historian refuses to limit his judgments to the reality of an event, but goes further and decides on its non-reality. "The notion of myth strikes a blow at the very principle of theology." [39] The initial decision of the Christian has, then, a considerable influence on the use of the ordinary methods of critical exegesis.

Much could be said on this clarification of Barth's position. In the language of the Catholic theologian we would say that an exegesis which does not take into account the possibility of the supernatural and preternatural runs the risk of taking the wrong road. A sound philosophy, aware of its limits, should teach the critic what he must understand by real, and it should show him that, if God is the Author of nature, this does not limit His action to this area alone or prevent His acting beyond natural laws or on a more elevated plane. Faith, then, does not directly intervene in exegetical knowledge, but it is the ever-present witness that testifies to the existence of the preternatural and supernatural, an account of which exegesis must render. Faith does not directly intervene in its work, but it is a constant reminder to be on one's guard against premature conclusions. Its role is to force the exegete ceaselessly to check the degree of certitude of his conclusions with the fundamental laws of his own discipline. It is an invitation to reflect.

We are, then, in full accord with Barth when he says that theology and exegesis will be in conflict when the latter, identifying itself with *Historie* and exceeding its rights, ventures to speak of myths in the Bible.[40] To speak of myth is to speak of pure fiction, and pure fiction is incompatible with the Word of God. The mythological explanations of the Bible are clear cases of exegetical conclusions that have gone beyond the cogency of their premises. We now know what we must think of the *Sage*. It is an allegory without foundation. Allegory, in our eyes, is indistinguishable from pure fiction. Such an exegesis deserves a call to order, as well as one that juggles with myths.

Catholic theology is not hostile to allegory. The Church, in its role as guardian of the very principles of exegesis, does not forbid the acknowledgment, alongside historical narrations, of other passages which pertain to a type in which the imaginary element serves as a vehicle for doctrinal truths.[41] It adds, however, that this decision cannot be taken lightly without sufficient guarantees. Barth does not even seem to be concerned with guarantees when he decides without further ado that the first chapters of *Genesis* contain a *Sage*. His exegesis feels the effects of this and slips into the arbitrary; the divinatory knowledge of Barth permits him to discover, in the narration of creation, the transposition of the *Geschichte* of God's redemptory acts; in the narration of the six days, he sees Jesus Christ.[42] He is not the first to make this discovery; certain Fathers have done it before him. But such a venture is legitimate only in the measure in which one is fully aware that there is in question a secondary sense which depends on a primary sense, the literal sense.[43] This is not the case with Barth: the Christological explanation is the literal and sole meaning of the so-called narration of creation. Theology loses every solid foundation and is consigned to the caprice of an interpretation free from ties and law. We are led, as a result, through a different approach, to the deviations which the exegetical method of the *Römerbrief* had already displayed. Here Barth goes further: he seeks to justify by right these very liberties.

## D.  Exegesis and Philosophy.

"If I could hear only with my own ears and see only with my own eyes, how could I, in order to understand, go beyond my own intellect and use that of another? " In citing this phrase of A. Ritschl, Barth intends to show that the intellect cannot approach its object without preconceived forms.[44] It is not a question of a virgin intellect that begins to operate, but of a mind that already has its categories of thought and does not know how to free itself from them. What is true of all knowledge is true also of exegesis. Whoever wishes to study and explain a text, cannot free himself of a *Mitgebrachtes* which necessarily orients his research in a given direction. Whether aware or unaware of it, he cannot free himself from the constraints imposed on him by his theory of knowledge from a determined logic and ethics, and, finally, from his ideas on the relations between God and man. All this Barth terms philosophy. Since one's philosophy can be either a very elaborate system or an accumulation of trite aphorisms, it is assumed out of simple good sense that no one, either the university exegete or the simple believer, escapes its ascendancy.

Barth enjoys pointing out this dependence on philosophy in the history of exegesis. The Fathers were Platonists; the scholastics were dedicated to Aristotelianism. The Reformers themselves had also been under the influence of philosophy: Luther was Neoplatonic; Zwingli, a pantheist of the Renaissance; and Calvin, an adherent of the ancient system of Plato. Since 1600, orthodox Protestants have returned to the Aristotelianism of Scholasticism. The *Aufklärung* of the eighteenth century and a large part of the exegesis of the nineteenth were clearly under the influence of rationalism. The Tübingen school of F. C. Baur drew its inspiration from Hegelianism. Kierkegaard appeared as an adversary of Hegel; but this was still in the name of philosophy. Ritschl's school gave evidence of an astonishing naïveté in claiming to have discarded all metaphysics and speculation. Even the *Formgeschichte,* for which Barth does not conceal his sympathies, is obviously dependent on the phenomenology of Husserl and Scheler.[45]

It is, indeed, curious to confirm this last declaration of Barth's and to assert a certain relationship between the two schools. With both the one and the other, we have to deal with an *Einklammerung,* with a putting-in-parentheses of a part of what is given. The method of phenomenology is based on a separation of all that is existence, as well as of all that is interpretation.[46] One of the theses of the *Formgeschichte* is that the first elements of tradition (*Kleinlitteratur, Kleineinheiten*), artificially put together by the Evangelists, provide us only with the faith of the first community, which elaborated the tradition for its own practical needs.[47] All interest in research is centered, then, on the primitive pericopes. We can know what the community related about Jesus; we can no longer know what Jesus really said or did.[48] The historical events, handed down amidst these elements of popular literature, are put in parentheses. In the most favorable cases, one asserts of them neither 'yes' nor 'no.'

The relationship is certainly striking. It can be, however, entirely fortuitous; it is not necessary to exaggerate a dependence that Barth alone, I believe, maintains. Rather than a direct dependence, there is here doubtlessly the influence of some ideas which 'are in the air' at a given moment and which are, for the majority of men, a means of participating in the thought of their time. Even more clear, as Fr. Benoit has judiciously remarked, is the influence of Hegelian rationalism which makes itself clearly felt in Dibelius and Bultmann, the principal representatives of the *formgeschichtliche Methode.* [49]

Can an exegete be found who is capable of freeing himself from this yoke? No, says Barth. It is impossible to approach Scripture without a 'key.' This 'key' must be provided by ourselves.

In every age, we have seen the absurd spectacle of theologians and exegetes contemptuously pointing out with scorn those who have prostituted themselves to philosophy. They themselves, they were convinced, could be content with the real and trust solely in their own two eyes. This is to forget, Barth tells us, that our sight must be adjusted to reality. Without corrective lenses, we must resign ourselves to seeing nothing.[50] The use of philosophy is not only inevitable, but obligatory. In Scripture we are ordered to approach, read, understand, and explain it in our preaching. It is a duty from which we cannot excuse ourselves: this would be to deny the Incarnation. The use of philiosophy, then, becomes indispensable and legitimate.

Though the use of philosophy is legitimate, not every use of it is. There are conditions governing this legitimacy. Barth points out five:

1. From the start, the exegete must be perfectly aware of what he is doing in employing a 'predetermined scheme of thought' to explain Scripture. He should know that every form of human thought is necessarily different from the content itself of the text: our philosophy is not that of Scripture.

2. The adaptation of a philosophical 'preconception' to the Bible can never claim to be more than an hypothesis, a testing, a risk which we must take in obedience. This adaptation, then, is essentially provisional and can be improved.

3. The use of philosophy can never become an end; it must remain subordinated to the Word. It is not even an adequate means; still less is it a matter of two absolutes confronting each other. Every heresy began with this *curiositas,* springing up from a philosophy which, having set itself on the same plane as the testimony of the Word, became vain deception.[51]

4. With reference to the Bible, every philosophy has merit; no system has more value than another. We must simply choose the explanation more suitable *hic et nunc* for the text under study. Never, then, must one tie himself to a single system. The synthesis of thought, which has furnished me an excellent explanation for this particular verse of Scripture, would lead me, perhaps, to a deplorable interpretation if I apply it to the following one. It would be better in these circumstances to have recourse

to another philosophy, even if it be diametrically opposed to the first.

5. The philosophical explanation will always be chosen in dependence on the text; one could almost say, chosen *by the text*. The testimony of the Word of God will never become, as a result, the object of our criticism, but the subject of a higher criticism. The sacred text is not judged by philosophy, but it, itself, passes final judgment on philosophy.[52]

In an excellent article on Barth's attitude towards philosophy, J. L. Leuba affirms that the theologian of Basel "wants to give full liberty to Scripture, sovereignty to the Word of God to which Scripture bears witness, a specific function to the theologian. . . . In other words, Barth does for the theologian what men of science have done for science: he liberates Scripture and grants it sovereignty, just as men of science in all ages and in various ways have continually liberated science." [53] Certainly the Protestant theologian would be at a loss to express his gratitude for such liberation. Barth has clearly shown that philosophy and theology belong to different spheres. However, he has not been the first to do this—a point to which we will return before the end of the chapter. Let it suffice to note our accord with this first intention of Barth.

A second point with which we ought to stress our agreement is the necessity of a philosophical position in the approach to a scientific study of the testimony of revelation. A man cannot devote himself to the interpretation of the Bible without the intellectual ballast of a certain number of indispensable truths. He cannot, for example, disregard God's existence. Further, he must have clear ideas on the possibility of a special intervention by this God, which can baffle one who sees only fixed laws of nature. His intellect must be well informed on the norms of truth and cognizant of their unity and laws. As a result, he cannot admit formal and irreducible contradictions on the plane of revelation, as he likewise cannot admit them on the natural plane, nor even between these two planes. Finally, he must be assured of the objectivity of his research. His philosophy must convince him that knowing is not an experience in a closed container. In short, he needs a good theory of knowledge and that intellectual equipment which

theology calls the *praeambula fidei*. In this measure and with
these clarifications, we are ready to acknowledge with Barth the
absolute necessity of philosophy for exegesis.

However—and here we resolutely part company with him—we
cannot admit that the adopted philosophical position does violence to the object, that the encounter of object and subject ends
in a conflict.[54] This position of Barth is like an aftertaste of
Kantianism. For Barth, as for the great German philosopher,
knowledge consists in a sort of modelling of the object, so that it
enters the a priori categories of the knowing subject.

We cannot here go into an exposition of the various theories
of knowledge. Let us remark, nevertheless, that this belittling of
philosophy is itself of philosophical origin. Certainly Barth has
a perfect right to put us on our guard against the encroachments
of reason in areas that do not belong to it. Have not the philosophies of the nineteenth and twentieth centuries given us more than
one example of an incursion into the field of revealed religion?
Philosophy must remain in its own domain; but within that domain it is indispensable to us. To belittle philosophy to excess in
comparison with faith is equivalent to renouncing reason. In belittling the human intellect, Barth ends up by discrediting *all theology* without exception. The extreme emphasis on the divine
transcendence and revelation leads finally to calling this transcendence itself into question. Has not Barth yielded to a new temptation of theological angelism?

Are all philosophical systems worthwhile? Does the Word of
God pass the same judgment on each of them? Are they all just
as useful or harmful to the Word? The answer to this question
falls outside the range of our exposition. Let us say simply that
in our opinion such an attitude sets little value on the unity of
truth. What is truth? The conformity of the intellect to the
reality which it knows, in a word, to being. But is not being one?
Can the same being at one and the same time both be and not be
under a given aspect? Is not an assertion to the contrary a viola-
tion of a law of our intellect? If being is one, truth is one, and so
is philosophy.

In an age which has indulgence only for relativism in some

form or other, one must have courage to assert that philosophy is one, that there can be only one final, rational explanation of the world and of man. Such an assertion in no way closes the gate to progress. This postulate of the soundness of the human intellect is, on the contrary, the first principle of all true development. Can one say that philosophy truly progresses in a succession of choices which mutually exclude each other?

The unity of philosophy, nonetheless, bears no prejudice against the existence of many cultural mentalities. The unique truth can be approached from several angles and at different levels. From one culture to another, from one moment of civilization to the other, one meets with new ways of expressing the principal attitudes common to all balanced thought, and even with different fields, studied in more or less fortunate way. The study of Indian thought, for example, has disclosed to us research in an area little examined in the West. Especially where both systems tackle identical problems, the formulation provided by another mentality furnishes us with especially stimulating fresh insight. All this, however, remains and should remain in the field of complementary research and of heteromorphism of expression within the homogeneity of unique philosophical truth.

Although the principles are clear in these matters, their application often remains complex. Nevertheless, we cannot delay a single instant over the proposition that Karl Barth makes—namely, of jumping from one system to another in interpreting the Bible. One would be Aristotelian at one time, Kantian at another, Hegelian at another, according to the needs of one's interest. This would be to destroy the unity of philosophical thought. Certainly all the virtualities of revelation will be in our reach only when they shall have been approached through all the virtualities of a fully developed philosophical system. Thus it is entirely advantageous for the understanding of the Word of God that philosophy develop by confrontation with the different historical syntheses and with the many cultural contributions, and that it enrich itself by intussusception. On the condition, however, that one does not confuse this growth of something living with a superficial eclecticism which would like to reconcile the irreconcilable.

Futhermore, the opposition arises from a profound conflict: that between the natural and supernatural. The two spheres, for Barth, are totally separated from one another; they either disregard or oppose each other. For him there is no *gratia perficiens naturam*. We are obliged, besides, to lower the tone of the assertion we have just made. Barth has clearly separated philosophy and theology, but, instead of making them two successive steps of *the one, same truth,* he makes them *two truths* which collide and negate each other. The line he traces is not the horizontal one that separates two planes and dissolves in the subordination of philosophy to theology *(philosophia ancilla theologiae)*; rather it is a vertical line indicating the respective victories of two enemies, which confront each other on the same field of battle. Philosophy, according to Barth, is a closed, walled-in system which avers that it is complete and open to no higher order. Such is not the case with a philosophy aware of its limits, whose sublimest act will be precisely an admission of powerlessness and an appeal.[55]

The only legitimate exegesis which will enable us to approach the Word of God, according to Karl Barth, is the one that fulfills these three conditions:

1. *It must be objective;* that is to say, it must seek by an effort at penetration to meet with the inner thought of the sacred authors, in order to convey this thought in terms comprehensible to the contemporary world. It is to be regretted, however, that Barth did not, on this point, abide by the rules he himself set up.

2. *It should be theological;* that is to say, it should take into consideration the Christian decision imposed by the *fiducia* of the exegete. This is what obliges him to reject the literary types, daring to affirm the non-reality of such or such an event presented as real in the Bible. There cannot be opposition between critical exegesis and theological exegesis as long as the former is satisfied with acknowledging the historical truth of a passage or its problematical character *(Sage)*. Conflict is inevitable where it has recourse to mythological explanation. As a matter of fact, however, Barthian exegesis degenerates very often into an unbridled allegory. This lapse, moreover, is not *praeter intentionem,* but is based on an exegetical theory establishing an unjustifiable distinction between *Historie* and *Geschichte*.[56]

3. *It should be prudent.* While acknowledging the indispensability of the use of a philosophy for any exegesis whatever, we cannot lose sight of the fact that every rational contribution is necessarily a deformation of the Sacred Word. It is desirable, then, to vary, as much as possible, the philosophical casting of one's interpretation. On this point, Barth adopts a determinedly skeptical attitude.

# notes

## to chapter seven

1 A. von Zahn-Harnack, *Adolf von Harnack,* p. 532.

2 *Ibid.,* p. 534.

3 See for example the *Kurze Grundlinien des Neuprotestantismus,* written by Georg Rost and published in the ChW, 1920, vol. XXXIV, pp. 743–744. Formulated for the *Neuprotestantische Vereinigung Buxtehude,* this "confession" was adhered to far and wide. Among the adherents were included Rudolf Eucken and Ernst Troeltsch.

4 RB (1919), pp. V and VI. We wish to remind the reader that this abbreviation is being used to designate the first edition of *Römerbrief.* RB, without any date, refers to the second edition, of which all subsequent editions are merely a reprinting. Barth, however, added one preface or another. Our citations will be taken from the seventh reprinting (1940).

5 *Ibid.,* p. V.

6 In 1923, Barth observed with amazement: "Das Merkwürdigste, was dem Buch seither (since 1919) widerfahren ist, ist wohl die Tatsache, dass es von Bultmann in der Hauptsache freundlich begrüsst und von Schlatter in der Hauptsache ebenso freundlich abgelehnt worden ist" (RB, p. XIX). But in 1925–26, R. Bultmann diverged from Barthianism and joined M. Heidegger.

7 A. Jülicher, *Ein moderner Paulus-Ausleger, in* ChW, 1920, vol. XXXIV, pp. 453–457 and 466–469.

8 RB, pp. X–XIII.

9 ChW, 1920, vol. XXXIV, p. 454.

10 RB, p. XV.

11 RB, p. XV.

12 O. Cullmann, *Les principes posés par la méthode exégétique de l'école de K. Barth, in* RHPR, 1928 (without volume number), pp. 70–83.

13 O. Cullmann, *art. cit.,* pp. 71 and 73.

14 O. Cullmann, *art. cit.,* p. 78.

15 O. Cullmann, *art. cit.,* p. 81.

15a This is possible, in fact, only within the fold of the Church.

16 P. Althaus, *Die Auferstehung der Toten. Zur Auseinandersetzung mit Karl Barth über die theologische Exegese,* 1925, p. 420, cited from F. Holmström, *Das eschatologische Denken der Gegenwart,* p. 186.

17 ChW, 1920, vol. XXXIV, p. 468.

18 RB (1919), p. 181. Cf. H. Windisch, ThLZ, 1920, vol. XLV, c. 200 and 201.

19 ThLZ, 1922, vol. XLVII, c. 541.

20 RB, p. X.

21 Preface to the work by L. Fendt, *Die alten Perikopen (Handbuch zum Neuen Testament,* 22), 1931, cited by H. Meylan, RTP, 1944, vol. XXXII, pp. 205–206.

22 *Credo,* p. 223.

23 Cf. KD, vol. I, 2, p. 811.

24 Barth is here referring merely to the categories of relations and historical analogy. Cf. *Credo,* p. 233. We are completing his thought which he affirms elsewhere. Cf. especially KD, vol. I, 2, pp. 815–825.

25 Cf. KD, vol. I, 2, p. 813.

26 Cf. KD, vol. III, 1, p. 84.

27 KD, vol. III, 1, p. 63.

28 Cf. KD, vol. III, 1, pp. 63–64.

29 Cf. KD, vol. III, 1, p. 87.

30 Cf. TK, pp. 8–12.

31 Cf. KD, vol. III, 1, pp. 88 and 91.

32 KD, vol. III, 1, p. 88.

33 Cf. KD, vol. III, 1, p. 91.

34 Barth leaves no room for doubt on this subject. He realizes that he is altering the meaning of current language, and he candidly informs the reader of these changes. Cf. KD, vol. III, 1, p. 88.

35 On this subject, cf. Paul Tillich, RGG, vol. IV, col. 363 and 366.

36 Cf. W. Baumgartner, RGG, vol. V, col. 41. "Popular tradition" is the closest English equivalent for the German *"Sage."*

37 Cf. H. Gunkel, RGG, vol. I, col. 219–220.

38 Cf. A. Robert, *Initiation biblique,* pp. 24 and 25.

39 *Credo,* p. 234.

40 "Diversa dicendi genera non possunt nec debent excludi a sacris Libris; ea compossibilia esse cum notione Inspirationis nullus est qui neget, si excipiatur illud dicendi genus, nempe mythicum, quo notiones falsae, aut figmenta absurda exhibentur. Quodnam in peculiari casu sit genus dicendi determinari debet ex criteriis litterariis" (J. Balestri, *Biblicae introductionis generalis elementa,* p. 441).

41 Cf. *Comm. bibl.,* 23 June 1905, *Denz.,* 1980.

42 R. Prenter draws attention to the main lines of Barth's position in his article *Die Einheit von Schöpfung und Erlösung, Theol. Zeitschrift,* 1946, vol. II, pp. 161–182.

43 Cf. R. Grosche, *Zur theologischen Schriftauslegung,* in *Catholica,* 1935, vol. IV, pp. 174–180.

44 *Rechtfertigung und Versöhnung,* vol. III, p. 25, cited in KD, vol. I, 2, p. 816. It is in this volume, from p. 815 to p. 825, that Barth presents his main treatment of the subject before us. We have thought it unnecessary, therefore, to note repeated references to that section.

45 This sympathy is motivated by the fundamental principles of the Barthian system. Just as the *content* of the Bible cannot be attained through a critical research which would presume to state what lies beyond the text itself, so too exegesis must limit itself to a study of the meaning, without inquiring into the historical facts to which the content bears witness. The *Formgeschichte,* in fact, pursues a similar line of thought, but for entirely different motives. Cf. KD, vol. I, 2, pp. 547–548. We must call attention to the fact, however, that Barth is not steadfastly loyal to the principle he enunciated in 1932. In his commentary on creation, published in 1945, he is obviously striving to "guess" what lies behind the text. If there is an exegesis which does not rest content with arriving at the form, this is certainly it.

46 This philosophical method is called by Husserl: "Die Methode des Einklammerns oder der phänomenologischen und eidetischen Reduktionen." Cf. J. Geyser, *Max Schelers Phänomenologie der Religion,* p. 18.

47 "Am Anfang war die Predigt. Das ist die Grundthese, auf die alles Weitere aufgebaut wird" (E. Fascher, *Die formgeschichtliche Methode,* p. 54).

48 "Granted all this, what then is the problem of Jesus? One could say roughly that it has been simply declared insoluble. One of the postulates of the school is that the gospel documents can inform us of the primitive community's faith, but we must not ask anything more from mere documents" (F. Braun, *Où en est le problème de Jésus,* pp. 223–224). Cf. also P. Benoit, *Rev. Bibl.,* 1946, vol. LIII, p. 498; O. Cullmann, RHPR, 1925, p. 477.

49 Cf. P. Benoit, *Rev. bibl.,* 1946, vol. LIII, pp. 506–509.

50 In the first volume of his *Kirchliche Dogmatik,* Barth does not hesitate to say: "Theology, through its use of human language, is a philosophy or conglomeration of all sorts of philosophies" (KD, vol. I, 1, p. 171).

51 The same is true of culture. Although it is a desirable quality in the make-up of a theologian who must speak to his contemporaries who have been formed in a particular cultural milieu, nevertheless, it can never set itself up as the criterion of dogmatics. Cf. KD, vol. I, 1, pp. 300–301. See also p. 86.

52 In the brief comparative critique which follows, we will not consider each of the five points, since their respective importance is unequal. We will simply consider, one by one, Barth's fundamental positions on the relations between philosophy and exegesis.

53 *In extremis,* 1943, vol. IX, p. 34.

54 "It is erroneous to believe that, in the *Römerbrief,* I have adopted a consciously critical attitude, deliberately taking my bearings from the thought of modern

man. I have simply attempted, insofar as I am a modern man, to submit to Paul's word. It could not be otherwise. Dogmatics must come into conflict with philosophy, whatever its character be. And practically speaking, theology must protest against every species of realism and idealism" (*Credo,* p. 231).

55 The entire Thomistic doctrine of natural desire inserts itself at this point.

56 This distinction is based on an erroneous concept of history. Prehistoric facts, in the Barthian sense of the word, can be known only through revelation (and not through divination). Nevertheless, *all* examples of divine intervention which are accredited by testimony of any kind (oral tradition, written documentation, eye-witnesses, divine revelation), pertain to the domain of history. Other facts, which lie hidden in the mystery of God, are of no interest to the exegete.

# part three

*The Church's Proclamation:*

*The Matter of Dogmatics*

# the sources of
# karl barth's ecclesiology

$B$ARTH'S CONCEPT of the Church was shaped by the great eccle- siologies of Protestantism. Before evolving his personal syn- thesis, the theologian of Basel made a comparative study of his predecessors. Though he introduced original elements into his construction of a new ecclesiology, it is nonetheless true that he borrows important ideas from the three ecclesiologies of Luther, Calvin, and Schleiermacher. To the last-mentioned he will be in- debted for his concept of collective election.

## A. The Ecclesiology of Luther.

Luther's entire ecclesiology is based on justification by faith. This thesis did not, however, have full and immediate impact on his concept of the Church. It was only gradually, in the measure in which his theory of universal priesthood was developed and ex- plicated as a result of his difficulties with the Holy See, that the fundamental opinion of Lutheranism exerted an influence in ecclesiology.[1] It was in his *Manifesto to the German Nobility,* published in 1520, that the theologian of Wittenberg defined explicitly his doctrine of a universal priesthood.[2] At that time, the new ecclesiology attained definitive form, and two years later, after he had been ordered to appear in Rome, precise formula- tions of it can already be found.[3]

"The just man is not the person who performs many good

works; rather it is he who, without good works, has great faith in Christ. The law says: 'Do that,' and the deed is never accomplished; grace says: 'Believe in Him,' and from that point on, 'all is accomplished.' " [4] These two statements are a lucid summary of what is the very heart of Luther's theology. Elsewhere he goes on to say: "It is not sufficient for the Christian to believe that Christ has become high priest for men in general, but he must believe that he himself is one of those men saved. For even the devils and the godless know that Christ is high priest for mankind, but they do not believe themselves numbered among those for whom Christ is high priest." [5] This strongly marked doctrinal position was immediately reflected throughout Luther's entire theology. If faith is the whole of Christianity, the rest—Roman authority, a separated church body, priesthood—all, in a word, that can center around the idea of apostolic succession, is insignificant. If there is a Church, it will be a Church of faith. In his *Sermon on Excommunication* (1518), Luther stated that excommunication can deprive one of external communion with the Church, but that no one can take away that spiritual communion which unites a person to all true believers.[6]

However, this fellowship of true believers in intimate contact with God is impossible without some kind of mediation. Certainly, the mediation of men is excluded; but there is another: that of the Word of God. Faith does not rise spontaneously in the soul; it is an answer to a summons from the Word of God and from the sacraments that are its seal. The Church, according to Luther, is neither at Rome nor in the Bishops only, but wherever may be found the Word, the sacraments, faith, hope, and charity. Wherever the Word of God is proclaimed, there is the true faith. It is the sole intermediary between God and the believing soul: "Christ rules His Church only through the power of His Word." [7] Divine action knows no other instrument.[8] In a thesis proposed in 1520, the German reformer shows quite clearly how the encounter between the Word and faith is effected: "When the Word of God, which is Trust, re-echoes in time and the heart clings to it through faith, it is filled with that truth contained in the Word. Like a piece of kindling, it bursts into flame on contact with the Word and burns with a holy fervor." [9] The Church is said to be founded on faith and, at the same time, on the Word of God which arouses that faith. Henri Strohl gives a fine summary of Luther's position: "The Church is the real, but the invisible product of the Word acting through its witnesses." [10]

In the essential structure of the Church there are two constitutive elements, which Luther in his *Treatise on the Papacy* (1520) designates as "physical, external Christianity" and as "spiritual, internal Christianity." [11] The Gospel and sacraments comprise the first; faith constitutes the second. Harmony between the two is effected by the Holy Spirit. True faith, as a matter of fact, is a creation of the Holy Spirit, but He acts only through the Word of God and the sacraments. God's action is exercised on men in two ways: from without and from within. From without, God acts on them by the spoken Word of the Gospel and the visible signs of the Word, namely, baptism and the Holy Supper. Within their hearts, God acts through the Holy Spirit, who generates faith and other gifts, but according to the guiding principle that the external features must necessarily precede and the internal follow through the mediation of the external.[12]

Luther's concept of the Church is not that of an invisible Church, which would be larger than the entire visible Church and which would embrace the elect outside the ranks of the visible Church who are known to God alone. For Luther, spiritual Christianity is to be found within the confines of visible Christianity. In other words, he says that there are no true believers *except* among those to whom the Word of God has been addressed and who partake of the sacraments. It is in this sense that we must understand his classic definition of the Church: "An assembly of the holy in which the pure Gospel is taught, and the sacraments properly administered (*Congregatio sanctorum, in qua Evangelium pure docetur, et recte administrantur sacramenta*)." [13] The first part of the definition points to the assembly of believers (the corresponding German text reads: *Versammlung aller Gläubigen*); the second part designates the visible feature of this Church. In defense of the *Confession of Augsburg*, Melanchthon recalls to mind that his second part, containing the "external features," was added to forestall the objection of having made the Church a kind of Platonic city-state.[14]

Nevertheless, in the preface to the Apocalypse (1530), Luther strongly avows that the Church cannot be seen, even if one were to avail himself of all the lenses in the world: it must be the object of our faith.[15] This is a statement that he repeats on several occasions and which is related to his idea of the "spiritual and internal fellowship" of the Church. Since the Church is founded on faith, it cannot be seen. It has nothing in common with the external machinery and visible organization which, to Luther's mind, characterized the Roman Church. Faith is a subjective quality which cannot be judged from without. Since, moreover, the Church is constituted precisely by this "internal fellowship" of which the "external fellowship" is but the physical framework and prerequisite condition, we can say that the Church, according to Luther's mind, is invisible.[16]

If the community of true believers is not evident in any tangible way, it is still true that each believer knows that he has faith and is, therefore, aware of belonging to the Church.[17] This is an essential point in Luther's synthesis. Faith is unqualified trust in Christ who has served us personally, and it carries within itself its own certitude. Man, who can and must be brought to this level, knows by that very fact and without the shadow of a doubt that he is saved and belongs to that spiritual and internal community which constitutes the *congregatio sanctorum.* From external appearances, it is impossible to determine the members of the Church; but each person can decide for himself whether he believes or not, whether he is a Christian or a pagan.[18] So the Church remains invisible only for those who are situated outside it. Each believer has a very clear awareness of the Church's existence, which is identified with the faith that the Holy Spirit has created in his soul.

## B.  Calvin's Ecclesiology.

If the Church, for Luther, was the fellowship of believers, for Calvin it was the society of the predestined. Assuredly, the theologian of Wittenberg, himself, had a well-developed theory of predestination. We find it given clear expression in his *De servo arbitrio.* However, in Luther's system, it was a unit in itself and did not affect certain basic positions, such as that of justifying faith. Luther was keenly aware of this lack of coherence at the very heart of his thought and, since the experience of faith had the place of honor in his system, he had no hesitation in advising his friend Staupitz (who was deeply troubled by the thought of predestination) to cast aside all preoccupation with this matter and to surrender himself purely and simply to the love of God and the wounds of Christ.[19] Orthodox Lutherans—whose precursor was Melanchthon—were preoccupied with a systematic presentation of doctrine, that would readily abandon the Protestant concept of predestination and cling to the idea of faith alone.[20]

Calvin's teaching on the Church was not original; he borrowed it from the reformers of the fourteenth and fifteenth centuries. Wycliff and John Hus had, before his time, defined the Church as the society of the predestined.[21] Calvin was, nonetheless, more logical than Luther. His thesis on predestination will be the foundation of his entire system, and it will extend its consequences to the final conclusions of his theology.[22] Calvinism is, indeed, unthinkable without its double predestination. Clear proof of this can be seen in the efforts expended at the time of the Synod of Dordrecht (1618) and later to mitigate this teaching which some found too severe.[23] The abandonment of predestination brought about the downfall of Calvinism. Without it, reformed theology was a structure without a framework.

God in His eternal and immutable plan, by a perfectly free exercise of His sovereign dominion, has destined some men for salvation, others for damnation. Such is Calvin's teaching on predestination. "Whoever wishes to be considered a god-fearing man simply will not dare to deny predestination, by which God has ordained some to salvation and consigned others to eternal damnation." [24] Predestination is absolute, and neither merit nor lack of merit enters the picture. Furthermore, reprobation is not an effect of Adam's fall; rather it is antecedent to it. To put it in Calvin's own words, let us say that is "supralapsarian" and not "infralapsarian." "The first man fell for the simple reason that God had judged his fall expedient. We know nothing of why He so judged. It is nonetheless certain that He would not have so judged had He not seen that it would redound to the glory of His name." [25] Reprobation as well as predestination, then, find their ultimate explanation in the watchword, *soli Deo gloria.*

For every Christian, there is necessarily a tension between his present and future states. The Catholic, who has weighty reasons for believing he is in the state of grace, cannot rely on the same reasons to presume his eternal salvation, for he has no way of being sure of his final perseverance.[26] The example of Staupitz, mentioned above, is clear proof of a like experience for the conscience of every Lutheran, faithful to the primitive teaching. Is the same true for Calvin? In his system, can the present condition of a Christian be other than what his future state will be? No, replies the theologian of predestination. The chosen one of God has his faith, lives in grace, and could not lose these precious gifts. The reprobate, whatever he may do, could not gain access to faith and grace. "It is certain that Jesus Christ in his prayer for the elect sought for them what he had sought for Peter: that their faith never fail. Wherefore, we conclude that they are immune from the danger of perdition, seeing that the Son of God, having requested that they should stand firm, has never been refused. What could Christ wish to teach us by this, if not the assurance that we shall have eternal salvation, since we have once and for all been made His own?" [27] The utter impossibility of losing faith and grace is bound up inseparably with Calvin's theme of predestination.

The essential point is to know whether one belongs to the group of the elect, and, consequently, is a member of the Church. On this point, Calvin's position is identical with that of Luther. It is through faith alone that a person can have knowledge of his salvation.[28] To look for reasons on God's part can yield no decisive assurance, nor can an objective, external evaluation of one's conduct. On the eve of his death, Calvin wrote to the Duchess of Ferrara that it was quite possible that the Duke of Guise was not numbered among the reprobate. Now this man, stained with the blood of Huguenots at Vassy, had met death at the hands of an assassin.[29] Yet, not every faith is a sure sign of election; faith does not consist solely in the external acceptance of the Gospel message, but implies, in addition, an enlightenment from the Holy Spirit. "Whence it follows that this interior calling is an infallible criterion of salvation." [30] Entertaining doubts regarding one's eternal salvation was for Calvin, as it was for Luther, the most serious temptation of the devil. "The devil has no more serious or dangerous temptation, with which to unnerve the faithful, than when he disturbs them with doubts of their election, and leads them off the true path. I consider it a vain search far from the true path, when a poor human is driven to probe into the unsearchable secrets of divine wisdom." [31]

To have been certain of possessing faith, for however short a time, is sufficient reason for refraining from ever doubting one's eternal election. Oliver Cromwell, on his death-bed, summoned Goodwin, one of his preachers, and asked him if it were really true that the elect could never fall or incur final reprobation. "Nothing is more certain," was the minister's reply. "Then I have no fear," replied the Protector, "for I am certain of having once been in the state of grace." [32] And yet, this certainty does not appear so easy for everyone. It is quite understandable how a person, after he once had the conviction of living in the state of grace, may subsequently experience the equally clear impression of living in sin. In such a case one begins to doubt the objectivity of the first impression and looks for means of reassurance. For this reason, we find in the theology of Zwingli and Calvin, an appeal to the guarantees of faith. Such an appeal, because of which deeds, which were formerly spurned, now assume an important role in Protestant theology, is found nowhere in Luther's theology. On this point the German reformer takes an unequivocal stand. The extraordinary success within the sphere of reformed theology of what was soon designated as "the practical syllogism" is undoubtedly due to the fact that the appeal to the sole experience of faith had already, by Calvin's time, led to numberless excesses.[33]

In Calvin's system, the teaching is barely outlined and has none of the rigidity we shall later find in it. Predestination can only be rooted in God.

Scripture everywhere teaches that the efficient cause of our salvation is the mercy of Our Heavenly Father and the purely gratuitous love He has borne for us. . . . When there is question of grounding and strengthening their faith, the saints did not look to their good works, but fixed their gaze solely on the goodness of God. Not only do they look to that above all else as the beginning of their beatitude, but as its fulfillment as well; and in this they find contentment and peace.

God, then, is the source of our predestination, its cause, and its foundation. However, this does not rule out our ability to discern the results of that choice and to find in them a source of encouragement.

> After one's conscience is so grounded, formed and strengthened, it can draw further strength through the consideration of its good works, namely, in as much as these are testimonials to God's dwelling and reigning within us. . . . We do not object to its being sustained and strengthened by all these indications of God's blessings. For, if all God's gifts, when recalled to mind, are like rays of light from the splendor of His countenance serving to inspire us to contemplate the majestic glory of His goodness, much more so should the good works He has given us serve this purpose, *since these prove that the Spirit of adoption* has been granted to us.[34]

Calvin's teaching is clear: the practice of good works follows upon and is, consequently, the sign of the divine election.

From this principle, thus proposed, later tradition will draw a demonstrable proof of predestination. Three years after the final edition of the *Institution chrétienne,* the *Catechism of Heidelberg* in answer to the question, "Why must one perform good works?" gave the following reply: "So that from its fruits we may be certain of our faith." [35] The argument quickly assumes the attractiveness of systematic thought and becomes the famed practical syllogism we find clearly expressed in the writing of J. Wolleb:

> In the study of our election, we must proceed through a methodical analysis from the means of carrying out the decree to the decree itself, taking as our starting point our sanctification. This method can be expressed in the following syllogism: Whoever experiences within himself the gift of sanctification, through which we are dead to sin and live to justice, is truly justified, called, given over to the true faith and elected. But by God's grace, I am aware of being in this state. Therefore, I am justified, called, and elected.[36]

So the certitude of personal predestination is discovered in a kind of examination of conscience. It is hardly necessary to call attention to the fact that this maneuver shifts the whole weight of primitive Calvinism. But the development was fatal; Calvin had set it in motion, and the obligation of holding fast to a fixed rule of moral conduct had precipitated the movement along these lines. Proof that it was inevitable can be found in the anathema fulminated by J. Wolleb: "It is truly the work of the devil to cling to the following line of reasoning: If I am among the elect, good works are useless; if I am lost, they are injurious." [37]

The foundation of Calvinistic predestination is the impossibility of losing one's faith. The Christian can find the certainty of his election in the experience of faith and confirmation of it in the holiness of his life. And since the concept of the Church is founded on predestination, we know from this very fact that the Christian who enjoys predestination can and ought to be sure of his membership in the Church. From without, despite certain rather vague indications, it remains impossible to determine with certitude those who make up this society.[38] Such, in summary fashion, is the Calvinistic teaching on the invisible Church.

For Calvin, himself, the concept of church is two-fold. Besides that Church, which is exclusively the object of faith, there is another which is plainly visible. On this point, Calvin seems to borrow purely and simply the Lutheran definition of the "physical and external fellowship." "Wherever we see the Word of God preached and heard in all its purity and the sacraments administered according to Christ's institution, there undoubtedly is the Church, insofar as the promise He gave cannot deceive us: 'Wherever two or three shall be gathered together in my name, I shall be in their midst.' " [39] In his teaching on predestination, this two-fold concept is based on the distinction between universal and particular calling:

As for the statement of Christ, that many are called but few are chosen, there will be no ambiguity if we but recall the rather evident truth that there is a double species of calling. For there is the universal calling, which consists in the external preaching of the Gospel, whereby the Lord calls to Himself all men indiscriminately—even those to whom He extends his invitation in the odor of death and as matter for more grievous condemnation. There is another, a particular calling which He directs seemingly only to His faithful followers and only after His teaching has been effectively rooted in their hearts by an interior illumination of His Spirit.[40]

Elsewhere Calvin wrote: "If one asks why the universal election is not always constant or efficacious, the reason is clear: God does not impart the spirit of rebirth to all those to whom He offers His word, in such wise as to unite Himself with them. The result is that, though they have the external call, they do not have the internal strength to persevere unto the end." [41] We should then define the invisible Church with J. Wolleb, as the *"coetus tantum electorum,"* and the visible Church as the *"coetus communiter vocatorum tum electorum tum reproborum."* [42]

What connection is to be established between the visible Church and the invisible? We have just observed that certain members of the visible Church, namely the reprobate, do not belong to the invisible Church. The question is this: Does Calvin restrict himself to Luther's position, according to which the invisible Church exists only within the visible Church? In other words, does Calvin deny the existence of predestined souls outside the Church of the Word and outside the sacraments? His teaching on the sovereign dominion of God forces the Genevan reformer to reply in the negative. Speaking of certain adversaries who objected that, since new-born infants are unable to benefit by predestination or consciously share in the sacraments, they ought not to be baptized, Calvin replies: "They fail to observe that Saint Paul speaks only of the *ordinary way* in which the Lord operates in giving faith to His own; not that He cannot proceed differently, as indeed He has done with many who, without ever having heard the Word, have been moved interiorly by Him and drawn to the knowledge of His name." [43] This particular discussion was the occasion for Calvin's formulating a universal principle: God can, in extraordinary circumstances, communicate faith by other means than those of the visible Church. The Latin text adds a qualification, namely, that the extraordinary communication takes place by the *Spiritus illuminatione.* We can conclude, therefore, that though the visible Church contains, along with the reprobate, the majority of predestined, still, by a special decree of Providence, a portion of the invisible can be vivified outside the confining limits of the visible Church.

## C. The Ecclesiology of Schleiermacher.

Along with an ecclesiology of faith and an ecclesiology of predestination, Protestant theology has retained an ecclesiology of religious experience. Schleiermacher does not use this expression to designate what constitutes the fundamental choice of his system; he prefers to speak of the "feeling" of total dependence.[44] But in point of fact, religious experience is his main concern. The reborn soul, according to Schleiermacher, is the preson who has succeeded in awakening within himself the feeling that makes him dependent, not on the universe, but along with the universe on a being that is beyond this world.[45] Rebirth then is at the basis of religious feeling. Religion is first and foremost feeling. This constitutes the originality of Schleiermacher's religious philosophy as compared with other contemporary systems.[46]

The Church is the assembly of regenerated souls, brought together for the purpose of mutual aid and collaboration.[47] The doctrine becomes clear when we consider his dependence on two other doctrines: that of predestination and that of the Holy Spirit.[48] We cannot delay on a consideration of the latter. It must suffice to say that the "Holy Spirit" is not a person in the sense we accord to this term; rather, it is the common spirit which quickens the lives of the community of believers.[49]

We must treat at greater length the doctrine of predestination. On this point, Schleiermacher's position is a new one, but akin to Origen's teaching on universal restitution. He rejects the positions of the great reformers, both because of their teaching on reprobation and in opposition to the individualism of their viewpoints.[50] To understand his position clearly, we must bear in mind two key ideas, which seem to dominate the thought of the romantic theologian on this subject. The first is the unqualified efficacy of the divine call.[51] The classic distinction between "called" and "chosen," which is based on the text: "Many are called but few are chosen" (Mt. 22:14), can signify only a provisional arrangement. For some, predestination has attained its full flowering; while for others, the work of God is still hidden, but no less real. The second principle depends on the first: God works in orderly and successive stages. This is one of the laws of the divine method of governing the world.[52] On these two principles rests the entire system. The difficulty arises in applying them universally. No one can deny that many people reach the end of life without having fully realized the religious experience that makes the regenerated soul. For them, Schleiermacher makes an exception to the general rule forbidding him to speak of the hereafter. He imagines that their growth is not arrested by death, but that the seed planted in them reaches maturity later.[53] So we find ourselves in the presence of a new kind of *apokatastasis.*

Reprobation then loses all meaning. There is no rejection; there is only an apparent "by-passing." God temporarily leaves in the world a certain number of people whose later reception into the Church He reserves to Himself. Personal predestination itself, that freely chosen decision of God to save a given soul, no longer has a place in the new synthesis. At best, there remains a divine will assigning to each person a time of justification.[54] Schleiermacher can then conclude: "There is a genuinely divine predestination that elects the totality of the new creation in the entirety of the human race." [55]

The mutual relationship between Church and election now appears with clarity. When man has reached the term of his evolution in the eschatological period, the society of regenerated souls will be coterminous with that of the elect. Until that time, the Church will enfold only a part of this group: those who have actually attained the fullest development of their religious experience.

Before concluding this section, we must say a word on the distinction between the visible and the invisible Church. The Church has a double polarity, from which results a state of constant tension. On the one hand, it depends on Christ; on the other, it sustains the pressure of the world. Its relation to Christ imparts to it permanent and changeless qualities; its position in the world marks it with essentially temporal characteristics.[56] The notes of the invisible Church, then, will be perfect unity and infallibility; those of the visible Church, division and error mingled with truth.[57] Consequently, no visible Church can claim for itself the totality of truth; none can boast of having truth in its pure state.[58] We are not unaware of the influence of this theory upon the ecumenical movement at its very beginning. The opposition between the visible and the invisible Church will be suppressed in the eschatological Church, in which the world will no longer be able to exercise its divisive influence.

*

\*     \*

Visibility, the note common to both, has helped us to bridge the gap between the ecclesiology of faith and that of predestination. What Luther calls "physical and external communion" and what Calvin designates as "visible church" are one and the same thing: the Word and the sacraments.

But the precise nature and, especially, the extension of the concept of universality keeps them apart. For the theologian of Wittenberg, a Christian can be aroused to faith only by the Word and the sacraments. Whereas, for the Genevan reformer, the Word and the sacraments are ordinary means of attaining to that interior call of predestination; but God, eminently free, can employ other means, for example, an interior illumination. The ultimate answer is that, for Luther, the true Christian exists only within the Christian establishment, while, for Calvin, he can be found equally well outside this framework.

For Schleiermacher, the Church is the society of souls regenerated by religious experience. This view implies the provisional separation between those who are already living with that profound sense of dependence and those whose lives are still restricted to the level of the world and sin. But there are no individuals who are destined to remain forever outside the fold of the Church. Some day or other, they will be beneficiaries of that universal predestination which envelopes all humanity. Thus the theologian of romanticism, by his concept of the Church's visibility, is set off quite clearly from Luther and Calvin. What constitutes the Church is not the Word and the sacraments, but a state of submission characterized by separation and error.

# notes
## to chapter eight

1 Cf. H. Hohlwein, RGG, vol. III, col. 799–800. A. Jundt points out clearly that Luther's original intention was to preach the Gospel in the Church of Rome. Cf. ONE, p. 113.

2 Among other things, Luther there states: "All Christians truly belong to the ecclesiastical state; there exists among them no difference whatsoever, if there is no distinction of function. . . . Every single one of us has been consecrated a priest through baptism, as St. Peter said (1 Peter 2:9): 'You are a royal priesthood and a priestly royalty'; and the Apocalypse (5:10): 'Thou has made us a royal race of priests through the shedding of thy blood' " (WA, vol. VI, p. 407).

3 Rome had issued an order to the general chapter of the Augustinians, which convened at Heidelberg in April, 1518, to demand a retraction from Luther. No steps were taken. Luther appeared there as a conquering hero. On August 7, 1518, as a consequence of renewed denunciations, the Apostolic See summoned the innovator to Rome; his presence was demanded within sixty days, under pain of excommunication. Nevertheless, Rome effected a compromise and summoned Luther before Cardinal Cajetan at Augsburg. Luther proceeded to Augsburg, but refused to retract. At this moment he began his open revolt.

4 Theses 25 and 26, defended at the Heidelberg chapter in 1518, WA, vol. I, p. 353.

5 "Notandum quod non satis est Christiano credere Christum esse constitutum pro hominibus nisi credat se esse unum ex illorum. Nam et daemones et impii sciunt Christum esse pontificem pro hominibus, sed de seipsis non credunt" (*Luthers Vorlesung über den Hebräerbrief*, ed. E. Hirsch and H. Ruckert, p. 172).

6 "Sicut illa spirituali communione nulla creatura potest animam vel communicare vel excommunicatam reconciliare nisi Deus solus, ita non potest communionem eandem ulla creatura ei excommunicatam reconciliare nisi Deus solus, ita non potest communionem eandem ulla creatura ei auferre seu eam excommunicare, nisi solus ipse homo per peccatum proprium" (WA, vol. VI, pp. 639 ff.).

7 "Nulla alia potestate regit Christus ecclesiam quam Verbo" (*Luthers Vorlesung über den Hebräerbrief*, ed. E. Hirsch and H. Rückert, p. 111).

8 The same holds true for the sacraments, which are absorbed into the theology of the Word. Christ, through the Word—whether it be that of preaching or that of sacramental rites—creates a new life. Cf. H. Strohl, *L'épanouissement de la pensée de Luther*, p. 162.

9 WA, vol. VI, pp. 10 ff.

10 *L'épanouissement de la pensée de Luther,* p. 292.

11 "Eine leibliche, äusserliche Christenheit . . . , eine geistliche, innerliche Christenheit" (WA, vol. VI, p. 297). Cf. H. Strohl, *L'épanouissement de la pensée de Luther,* p. 311.

12 "Constanter tenendum est Deum nemini Spiritum vel gratiam largiri nisi per verbum et cum verbo externo et praecedente" (*Articuli smalcaldici,* art. 8, J. T. Müller, *Die symbolischen Bücher* . . . , p. 321).

13 *Confession d'Augsbourg,* art. 7, CR, vol. XXVII, col. 276.

14 The Catholic theologians charged by the Emperor, Charles V, to refute the *Augsburg Confession,* had written the following with reference to the famous seventh article: "Septimus confessionis articulus, quo affirmatur, ecclesiam esse congregationem sanctorum, non potest citra fidei praejudicium admitti, si per hoc segregentur ab ecclesia mali et peccatores. Nam ille in Constantiensi damnatur concilio inter articulos damnatae memoriae Joh. Hus et plane contradicit evangelio" (*Confutatio confessionis augustanae,* ad art. 7, CR, vol. XXVII, c. 102–103). In the first edition of the *Apologie de la confession d'Augsbourg,* Melanchthon replied: "In septimo articulo conantur nos pergravare mentione Joh. Hus, cum nos aperte paulo post fateamur (art. 8) in Ecclesia multos malos et hypocritas esse. Hos etiam vocant adversarii nostri mortua membra ecclesiae. Quare cum definivimus Ecclesiam, recte complectimur viva membra. *Et ne quis dicat nos platonicam civitatem somniare,* addimus externas notas, quibus Ecclesia agnosci debet, videlicet consensum de Evangelio et usum sacramentorum consentientem Evangelio. Illa congregatio est Ecclesia, in qua exstant haec signa, sed in his qui habent haec signa, quidam sancti sunt, qui recte utuntur his signis, alii sunt hypocritae et mali, qui his signis abutuntur. Quid potuit simplicius dici, aut quis unquam pius aliter locutus est?" (*Apologia prior,* ad art. 7, CR, vol. XXVII, c. 283–284). Lutheran humanism is even more explicit in the second edition of his *Apologie:* "At Ecclesia, non est tantum societas externarum rerum ac rituum, sicut aliae politae, sed principaliter est societas fidei et Spiritus Sancti, in cordibus, quare tamen habet externas notas, ut agnosci possit, videlicet puram Evangelii doctrinam et administrationem sacramentorum consentaneam Evangelio Christi. Et haec Ecclesia dicitur corpus Christi, quod Christus spiritu suo renovat, sanctificat et gubernat" (*Apologia altera,* ad art. 7, CR, vol. XXVII, c. 525).

15 EA, vol. LXIII, p. 168.

16 A. Jundt, in ONE, p. 116, summarizes Luther's ecclesiological doctrine quite clearly: "On the one hand, we have the Word of God, an external principle, effective and normative; on the other hand, faith, an internal element, effected and conformed. These two elements are not merely the essential but the unique elements of the Lutheran doctrine on the Church."

17 Cf. A. Stakemeier, *Das Konzil von Trient über die Heilsgewissheit,* pp. 53–63.

18 Undoubtedly such trust can call for an effort, at times a painful one. It is necessary, in short, to distinguish between faith and the feeling of faith. Consciousness of our faults can render this *fiducia* very difficult. And yet, it is a Christian's duty to transcend this feeling, which is aroused in him by the evil spirit, and to cling to Christ. Cf. A. Stakemeier, pp. 59–62.

19 O. Scheel, RGG, vol. IV, col. 1375.

20 A later development of Lutheranism was quick to adopt the Catholic doctrine on predestination.

21 John Hus' first proposition, condemned at the Council of Constance, was worded as follows: "Unica est sancta universalis Ecclesia, quae est praedestinatorum universitas" (*Denz.*, 627).

22 The Calvinist doctrine of predestination is nothing but a systematization of the ideas scattered throughout Bucer's works. Cf. E. F. K. Müller, PRE, vol. XV, p. 600.

23 The Synod of Dordrecht condemned the Armenians, but, due to the influence of conciliatory elements (among others, certain Anglicans), it refused to define the Calvinist teaching on predestination in its primitive supralapsarianism. The Synod of Dordrecht is clearly infralapsarian.

24 *Inst. chrét.*, III, 21, 5, CR, vol. IV, col. 460.

25 *Inst. chrét.*, III, 23, 8, CR, vol. IV, col. 496.

26 Without a personal revelation, it is impossible, according to St. Thomas, to know with absolute certitude whether a person is in the state of grace. Nevertheless "cognoscitur aliquid conjecturaliter per aliqua signa. Et hoc modo aliquis cognoscere potest se habere gratiam: in quantum scilicet percipit se delectari in Deo, et contemnere res mundanas; et inquantum homo non est conscius sibi alicujus peccati mortalis" (I–II, q. 112, a. 5). Regarding knowledge of personal predestination to glory, only a revelation can give us certitude. Such, in fact, is the teaching of the Council of Trent: "Si quis dixerit, hominem renatum et justificatum teneri ex fide ad credendum, se certo esse in numero praedestinatorum: A.S. Si quis magnum illud usque in finem perseverantiae donum se certo habiturum absoluta et infallibili certitudine dixerit, nisi hoc ex speciali revelatione didicerit: A.S." (*Denz.*, 825 and 826). It is interesting to compare two articles of St. Thomas on this subject: "Utrum praedestinatio ponat aliquid in praedestinato" (I, q. 23, a. 2), and "Utrum gratia ponat aliquid in anima" (I–II, q. 110, a. 1).

27 *Inst. chrét.*, III, 24, 6, CR, vol. IV, col. 514.

28 "It is certainly true that from our point of view faith is confirmed by believing, and that God's plan, which was hitherto hidden, is made clear to us" (*Inst. chrét.*, III, 24, 3, CR, vol. 4, col. 508).

29 Cf. A. Lecerf, in ONE, p. 147.

30 *Inst. chrét.*, III, 24, 2, CR, vol. IV, col. 507.

31 *Inst. chrét.*, III, 24, 4, CR, vol. IV, col. 509. Cf. A. Stakemeier, *Das Konzil von Trient über die Heilsgewissheit*, pp. 66–69.

32 J. Paquier, DTC, vol. IX, vol. 1237.

33 Self-confidence and voluntarism, so characteristic of Calvinist morality, flow from this revalorization of good works. Cf. O. Scheel, RGG, vol. IV, col. 1375.

34 *Inst. chrét.*, III, 14, 17 and 18, CR, vol. IV, col. 289 and 291.

35 "Warum sollen wir gute Werke tun? Darum, dass wir bei uns selbst unseres Glaubens aus seinen Früchten gewiss seine" (q. 86, W. Niesel, *Bekenntnisschriften* . . . , p. 170). The first edition of the *Institution* (in Latin) is dated 1536; the last (in French) which Calvin could have revised was that of Geneva in 1560. The *Catéchisme de Heidelberg* dates from 1563.

36 "In exploranda nostra electione methodo analytica progrediendum (est) a mediis exequutionis ad decretum, facto initio a sanctificatione nostra. Tali syllogismo:

Quicumque in se sentit donum sanctificationis, qua peccato morimur et vivimus justitiae, is justificatus, vocatus seu vera fide donatus et electus est. Atqui per Dei gratiam hoc sentio, ergo justificatus, vocatus et electus sum" (J. Wolleb, *Christianae theologiae compendium,* 1. I, ch. IV, par. 2, can. 15, ed. Bizer, p. 21). The author can hardly be suspected of maintaining on this subject a thesis which was daring and original. He is of interest to us because he is a representative of the opinion common among his contemporaries. "Wolleb war kein schöpferischer Geist; er hat keine neuen Wege gesucht und inhaltlich weicht seine Darstellung nur in verschwindenden Einzelheiten von der damals allgemein üblichen ab. Er ist vielmehr ein Klassischer Vertreter der Zeit, dessen vornehmstes Anliegen die treue Bewahrung und die schulmässige Formulierung des in der Reformation errungenen Gutes war" (E. Bizer, p. iii of the preface).

37 *Loc. cit.,* can. 16.

38 The docility of the faithful in listening to preaching seems to be a probable sign of their election. "Those whom God decrees for damnation and eternal death, in order that they might be instruments of His wrath and examples of His severity, He either deprives of the ability to hear His Word or through the very preaching of the Word He blinds and hardens them still further, in order that they might atttain their predetermined end. . . . We ourselves have daily experience of this, and Scripture provides abundant examples. One hundred men will hear the same sermon: twenty will accept its message in faithful obedience; the others will either take no account of it, or ridicule it, or reject and contemn it" (*Inst. chrét.,* III, 24, 12, CR, vol. IV, col. 521–522). Nevertheless, in this refusal, Calvin is not willing to see the sufficiently vague probability of their reprobation. "We do not know those to pertain to the number and to the company of the elect or not." Elsewhere Calvin invites us to recognize as members of the Church, *through a charitable judgment,* all those who acknowledge God and Christ through a confession of faith, good example, and partaking of the sacraments. Cf. *Inst. chrét.,* IV, 1, 8, CR, vol. IV, col. 576.

39 *Inst. chrét.,* IV, 1, 9, CR, vol. IV, col. 576.

40 *Inst. chrét.,* III, 24, 8, CR, vol. IV, col. 516.

41 *Inst. chrét.,* III, 21, 7, CR, vol. IV, col. 466.

42 *Christianae theologiae compendium,* 1. I, ch. XXV, par. 1, can. 5 and 7, ed. Bizer, p. 92.

43 *Inst. chrét.,* IV, 16, 19, CR, vol. IV, col. 954.

44 "Das Wesen der Frommigkeit ist, dass wir uns unserer selbst als schlechthin abhängig, oder, was dasselbe sagen will, als in Beziehung mit Gott bewusst sind" (*Der christliche Glaube,* 4, vol. I, p. 16). We cite the principal work of Schleiermacher according to the Berlin edition of 1830–1831.

45 Cf. *Christl. Glaube,* 107–109, vol. II, pp. 180–221.

46 "Die Frommigkeit ist rein für sich betrachtet weder ein Wissen noch ein Tun, sondern eine Bestimmtheit des Gefühls oder des unmittelbaren Selbstbewusstseins" (*Christl. Glaube,* 3, vol. I, p. 7).

47 "Die christliche Kirche bildet sich durch das Zusammentreten der einzelnen Wiedergeborenen zu einem geordneten Aufeinanderwirken und Miteinanderwirken" (*Christl. Glaube,* 115).

48 Cf. *Christl. Glaube,* 116, vol. II, p. 266.

49 Cf. *Christl. Glaube,* 123, vol. II, p. 320.

50 "Daher wäre nun die als Auskunftsmittel aufgestellte Formel immer eine Abweichung von den Bekenntnisschriften beider evangelischer Teile. Denn so bestimmt beide in der Ausschliessung eines Teiles des menschlichen Geschlechts übereinstimmen, ebenso auch darin, dass sie den Ausdruck Vorherbestimmung auf den einzelnen Menschen in seiner ganzen Wirklichkeit betrachtet beziehen" (*Christl. Glaube,* 119, 3, vol. II, p. 293).

51 "Wir sind uns der von der Kirche immer ausgehenden Verkündigung Christi als einer lebendigen mithin nicht erfolglosen Wirksamkeit bewusst" (*Christl. Glaube,* 119, 2, vol. II, p. 287).

52 "Dies ist der Ordnung des göttlichen Ratschlusses gemäss, indem es in jeder zeitlichen Entwicklung notwendig ein Nacheinander auch des ursprünglich Gleichzeitigen gibt" (*Christl. Glaube,* 119, 2, vol. II, p. 288).

53 "Der Zustand, in welchem er stirbt, ist dann nur ein Zwischenzustand" (*Christl. Glaube,* 119, 3, vol. II, p. 290).

54 W. B. Selbie gives a clear summary of the German theologian's teaching on election: "As the Incarnation involves the potential regeneration of the whole human race, so the spread of the Gospel is gradual and subject to the conditions which determine all human activity. . . . Schleiermacher reiterates his conviction that the Divine fore-ordination to redemption comes ultimately to embrace the whole human race" (*Schleiermacher,* pp. 216–218).

55 Cf. *Christl. Glaube,* 119, 3, vol. II, p. 292.

56 Cf. *Christl. Glaube,* 148, vol. II, p. 480.

57 Cf. *Christl. Glaube,* 149, vol. II, p. 484.

58 Cf. *Christl. Glaube,* 153 and 154, vol. II, pp. 498 and 501.

# 9

# the ecclesiology of barth

BARTH'S ECCLESIOLOGICAL position is best seen in the light of his stand on traditional predestination. He does not accept Calvin's theology, as it stands. He does intend to retain the German reformer's fidelity to Scripture, and he makes a show of being more Calvinist than ever when he cites biblical texts from the *Institution*. It is of paramount interest for the history of the Church and dogma to reproduce faithfully Calvin's teaching on predestination; but the theologian must push ahead and not be satisfied with restating the interpretation of a sixteenth-century theologian.[1]

## A. Can Faith Be Lost?

Two important points to examine, which are pivotal in Calvin's concept of predestination as it affects his ecclesiology, are the impossibility of losing one's faith and the subjective certitude of that faith. Can a person, according to Barth, *lose* his faith? In the light of our previous remarks, we can formulate a reply.[2] Faith is not of man's doing; it is the action of God drawing a free act, completely independent of any external continuity. Faith, then, is an intermittent thing; it is quite simply the Word of God given or denied this or that man. If this is the case, our answer to the question is simple: Faith could not be continuous; it is constituted of moments, the possession of which eludes man. Of its very nature, it is capable of being lost; never is it the abiding property of man.

Moreover, just as the concept of predestination coincides in

159

this regard with all the concepts of Barth's theology (reconciliation, creation, election, justification, glorification), it combines all with that of faith.[3] The intermittent quality of faith entails as a consequence the intermittency of predestination. Predestination is "the very act of the divine will, not an abstraction, nor a fixed or permanent state of that will." "Divine predestination is a dynamic act." [4] The Catholic theologian will notice certain points of contact between his own position and that of Barth. The theologian of Basle is not as far from Catholicism on this point as Calvin. One does, however, run the risk of being led astray by certain verbal confusions. With some satisfaction, it will be observed that Barth has deserted the idea that grace cannot be lost and considers it an unstable gift that man can well lose.[5] However, one will refuse to follow him when he looks on grace as a plaything of God, Who now bestows it and now withdraws it, alternately elevating man and letting him fall back with no justifying reason other than the exercise of his sovereign dominion.[6]

Another source of confusion and error is what amounts to the identification which Barth creates of faith, grace, and predestination.[7] The fusion blinds him to the clear-cut distinction between the human level and the divine plane of activity. The series of events that constitute the record of human salvation is transported as such into the eternity of God. This is certainly an instance of anthropomorphism, which has as its basis a rather poor notion of time and eternity. Eternity, for Barth, is simply time situated outside our own time, but which is ostensibly composed of successive stages like our own time. The fact that faith may at this moment be given to man and soon afterwards taken from him means only that God has in two successive acts decided to choose, then to reject this man. Such is the Barthian concept of actual predestination; it does not consist in the successive effects of a unique and eternal act of God, but in the present sequence of effects of successive will-acts of God.

We agree with Barth that the effects of predestination do not appear as changeless and definitive in time; we even grant him that there is not one election which takes the form either of a faith given from the very first that cannot be lost or of an irrevocable and helpless reprobation; we admit that grace and sin can give way to one another in a human life. But we deny that there are as many divine acts as corresponding effects and that predestination cannot be eternal because its effects are actuated in time.[8]

## B. Can One Be Certain of His Personal Predestination?

Here again, our observations on Barth's theory of faith provide us with a completely satisfactory answer.[9] Since Calvin, all Protestant theology has linked the certitude (certainty) of faith with awareness of faith; but according to Barth, faith cannot be perceived. It is a divine action that will always elude man's grasp, whether it is called religious experience, intellectual knowledge, or even prophetic inspiration. A wall separates human consciousness from the action of God transpiring within him. For God, in an instantaneous but essentially efficacious gesture—Barth is always opposed to a purely forensic justification—embraces man, makes him his own, chooses, and predestines him in a flash. And all this occurs without man's even knowing it.[10]

It is for this reason that man's attitude can be at best what Barth calls *fiducia:* that profound feeling of expectant hope and abandonment in the face of a torturing anxiety, the despairing cry of a soul persuaded that God perhaps will save him, but of this salvation he will never have the least assurance.[11] If such is the teaching of Barth in the *Kirchliche Dogmatik,* it was not always so. The thesis, advanced in 1927, had not yet reached such a degree of privation.[12] Therein can still be found a doctrine of the *Glaubengewissheit* which fits in better with what Protestant tradition meant by this term. Whereas the Calvinist school looks to the experience of that inner testimony of the spirit for its certitude, Barth finds it in baptism. A Calvinist would never propose this thesis. Doubtless, he states quite clearly that faith is imported by the imperceptible intervention of the Holy Spirit; nonetheless, it is the role of baptism to make possible that intervention. Let us follow his thought carefully. Barth does not mean to say that the Spirit exercises his intervention solely in those who are baptized and not in others—this is a difficulty he does not raise—but he wishes to affirm that this first sacrament is the sign of a personal alliance of myself with grace and the Spirit. This is the irrefutable witness of the fact that God is manifesting Himself to each one of us personally. It suffices for the Christian to look in retrospect on the actual fact of his baptism in order to enjoy the full, total certitude of being personally the recipient of the divine action of faith.[13]

It could be argued that this theory has been inspired by Catholic teaching on the sacraments. Karl Heim, in his letters, says that the Barthian solution *"ist beinahe Römisch sakramental."* [14] How can it be? Actually, the Barthian theory of 1927 agrees with Catholic tradition in the affirmation that the sacrament of baptism is a sign of grace, but it immediately branches off by saying that this sign is not efficacious.[15] It is neither an instrument of grace nor does it produce grace. Although baptism is indisputable proof that grace is imparted to the baptized child, it is not the channel of grace; it is only the ceremonial manifestation of it; it assures us that grace has been conferred directly without its mediation.[16]

We see how far removed this doctrine is from that of *Kirchliche Dogmatik.*[17] Furthermore, it cannot be reconciled with the theory of the intermittent and essentially mysterious character of the intervention of the Word. It dates from a period when existentialism still exerted a determining influence on Barth's thought.[18] Following Karl Heim's change of position, the theologian of Basle retracted and recalled the fact that he had surrounded this teaching with a rampart of corrective qualifications, which he was most anxious to have taken into consideration today.[19] As far as man is concerned, there will never be any personal *Glaubensgewissheit.*[20] This pertains to God's sphere of activity. Undoubtedly, God is true to His promise; but am I personally the object of these promises? In this world I shall always be ignorant of this. Barth does not rescue man from his deep-seated anxiety; for this reason, he stands worlds apart on this subject from the reformers.

In this final and probably definitive formulation of his expression of thought, is he not saying that the Council of Trent exhibits more of the reform than the reformed theologies? [21] With the exception of a special revelation, the Council, in fact, did reject all certitude on the matter of predestination. But we must bear in mind that the predestination envisioned by the Council of

Trent is eternal predestination *ad gloriam* and not the predestination of actuality proposed by Barth. The problem raised by his type of predestination is more closely allied to another question considered by Catholic theology: Can one be certain of actually possessing grace? Saint Thomas gives the clear answer that exclusive of a privileged favor of God, certain knowledge of this fact is for us impossible; but he also states just as clearly that we can surmise, we can perceive likely indications of the state of our soul.[22] This is a far cry from Barth's theory of grace, which declares that nothing in man can afford the slightest probability of the personal justification of such a believer.

We know now what Barth thinks of the practical syllogism and the Calvinist *Selbstvergevisserung* which is its premise. To Barth's way of thinking, the reformed theology contains a dilemma that cannot be resolved: at times predestination requires of man trust and abandonment; then again, certainty and self-scrutiny. In the actual order it is difficult to reconcile these two attitudes. The Christian who focuses his attention on God's free choice in Christ is spontaneously moved to rely on the divine judgment and to abandon himself completely—along with his very anxiety—to *trust* in God and *faith* in Jesus Christ. In such a moment of anxiety, he can only refuse further investigation. Is it the same with the faithful soul who anxiously looks to his good works for a proof of his salvation? Not much remains of abandonment and confidence any longer. He is inclined to replace them by rigorous observance and exacting morality. This dilemma cannot be resolved within the framework of the traditional doctrine of reformed theology on predestination; either one clings to the mercy of God and the witness of Christ in the accomplishment of faith, or he relies on the witness of his deeds. Actually, the majority of Calvinist theologians have committed themselves to the second alternative. The antithesis cannot be resolved except on the higher plane of Christocentric predestination, and we shall speak of this in the following section.[23]

The same principle of the mystery of faith will not admit the possibility of the slightest vision of the interior condition of the soul as reflected in one's external conduct. That a believer hears the proclamation of the Word and seems drawn to it proves absolutely nothing to Barth.[24] Granting the complete objectivity and disinterestedness of our observation and accurate criteria on these points, still the judgment we reach—and which Calvin reached—can only be our personal judgment and in no way God's verdict. The freedom of the Divine Word is thus eliminated. Before he opens his Bible, man has already a fixed opinion. His pastoral experience has already allowed him to make a provisional selection between sheep and goats. He looks to Scripture for confirmation of his personal judgment and an answer to his question. Barth sees in this procedure a new instance of the longing for a synthesis between God and man (traces of which he thinks he finds in the majority of theologians), which attributes the division that the theologian and pastor make between Christians and unbelievers and between good and bad Christians to God and to his eternal choice.

## C. Our Predestination in Christ.

It is impossible for us to conduct a lengthy analysis of a doctrine to which Barth devotes a full six-hundred pages, because it has only an indirect bearing on our study. It suffices for our purpose to isolate certain general lines of argument. Moreover, this will amply provide us with knowledge of the cause of the problem interesting us, namely, the Church. We must note furthermore that Barth, when he presents his theory of predestination, prefers to restrict himself to the term "election" (*Erwählung*).[25] This slight change in terminology is common among those who have abandoned the classic position of Calvin. The traditional term is unsuitable for expressing the new meaning which they wish to introduce into the concept.

Barthian election is Christocentric and collective.[26] Barth holds that only one is predestined: Christ.[27] Christ is at once the subject of predestination and its object.[28] This last point is of importance to us. Let us listen to Barth's own words:

What did God intend by the eternal election of Jesus Christ. . . ? The election, choice and predestination of God above all affects *Himself:* God chose to give and send His own Son. *God determined to speak* (utter) *His Word.* We must look to God Himself to find the first moment in which the Son becomes obedient to His Father. In the very Godhead Itself, there was, as it were, a concretizing of His will as a decision of his whole being. This is the first point we must bear in mind. But there is a second: God has chosen man, this Man; the divine decision and its execution fall on Him. He decided that His own Son would have the life of a son of David. His decision was to *let His Word be heard in the world of men.*[29]

The decisive statement in this passage is that in which Barth shows that, in his theology, election is above all a decision which touches God Himself, a divine decision which brings God to manifest Himself externally in His Word. This point is intimately connected with Barth's teaching on the Trinity.[30] There is not a real trinity of persons, not three really distinct hypostases. Barth's solution is unwittingly one of modalities. The *Logos* is God as He speaks, revealing Himself, God as he goes out of Himself, appearing in a new light.[31]

Briefly, the Barthian election is a statement on God's activity. Man plays no role in this activity on his own except as the object of Christ's redeeming actions. Christ's predestination involves then the predestination of a community of individuals who form a circle around Christ their center.[32] From that center issue forth rays that are ever renewing the peripheral points at which they terminate. "Like the circle of Jesus' friends at Nazareth, the community of the elect affords the stage where the promise of God is revealed in Person: there we listen to Him and believe in Him; there God bears testimony to Himself through and in Him; there the good-tidings of His loving will and saving mission are welcomed and received in faith."[33] This vitalized (dynamic) community is the very presence of God, the activity and revelation of His being. We should be not at all surprised when Barth states, *"Das Sein der Kirche, das heisst aber Jesus-Christus."*[34] This statement must be taken literally.

## D. Karl Barth's Ecclesiological Principles.

The Church for Barth is founded on the Word of God. It is a Church of the Word of God, as the Church for Luther is a Church of faith, and for Calvin a Church of the predestined. We have seen why Barth could not base his ecclesiology on the faith of the Reformers. He could not conceive of faith as an abiding gift of which we could be conscious. Predestination, itself, must be thoroughly reappraised before it can meet with Barth's approval. To his mind, there is but a single reality that constitutes, at one and the same time, predestination and the Church: namely, the Word of God.

This Word of God was not alien to the traditional ecclesiology. The mark of visibility, common to the theologies of Luther and Calvin, was concretized precisely in the Word of God and the sacraments. Barth's position is original in that it makes the Word of God both the constitutive element of the invisible Church and the distinctive characteristic of the visible Church. This is made possible only by assigning to the "Word of God" two obviously different meanings. To the reformers, the Word of God was simply the fixed revelation contained in certain books; there was no distinction between the Word of God and the Bible. To Barth, on the contrary, the distinction is clear-cut. On the one hand, we have the Word of God, a spontaneous and discontinuous, mysterious and imperceptible manifestation. On the other hand, we have the testimony of the Word of God collected and handed down through the Bible. The Church, properly speaking invisible, is founded on the Word of God; the visible society is founded on the testimony of the Word of God, the Bible.

The Church, then, is founded on the Word of God. From all the definitions at his disposal, Barth deliberately selects that formulated by Luther: [35] "The Church is the assembly of believers in which the Gospel is taught in all its purity, and the sacraments rightly administered." [36] The formula in the Heidelberg catechism which assigns a prominent role to the divine initiative in the formation of the Church receives high commendation from Barth: "From the midst of all humanity, the Son of God has chosen for Himself a community (*Gemeinde*) marked for eternal life. From the dawn of creation to the end of the world, He gathers it together, guards and preserves it in the unity of the true faith by means of His Spirit and His Word." [37]

Throughout his courageous struggle to guard the Church against the encroachments of German civil power, Barth has constantly defended this position. On May 20, 1933, the day after the German political-revolution, Karl Barth affixed his signiture to a document known since that time as the *Theses of Dusseldorf.*[38] The first of these theses reproduced verbatim one of the theses of Berne of the year 1528. "The holy Christian Church, whose sole head is Christ, is born of the Word of God; therein it dwells and hears no alien voice." [39] The third thesis further elaborates the definition: "The Word of God spoken to us is Our Lord Jesus Christ." [40]

We know that this document did not end the difficulties or controversies. In a statement, intended to provide an authentic interpretation of the Reformation's profession of faith within the German Evangelical Church, and historically known as the *First Declaration of Barmen,* Karl Barth, as the sole author of the document that became the creed of all reformed groups determined not to allow themselves to be secularized by the new regime, returns to this definition of the Church.[41] First, he rejects the error of believing that "revelation, grace, and God's glory are not the only determinants of the message and structure of the Church. . . . " He then states: "The Church has its origin and existence exclusively from the revelation, authority, mercy, and action of the Word of God, spoken once and for all by the Eternal Father, through His Eternal Son, Jesus Christ, in the form of the Holy Spirit, and in the fulness of time." [42] We must observe, however, that, although these aforesaid texts may be admitted by all Protestants faithful to their own tradition, without adopting fully Barth's ecclesiology, it is nevertheless true that, for Barth himself, the expression *Wort Gottes* must retain the very precise sense which it has in his personal synthesis. Thus, in a work which slightly antecedes this period, Barth states that the Church can be neither constant nor continuous in history, because it only exists in the eventuality itself of the Word and faith.[43] In other words, the Church is an essentially changing reality. The existence it has and maintains is constantly being renewed; the occurrence of faith does not always reach the same individuals.

Furthermore, the Church is invisible. Barth would not admit this, but the fact is evident. If he denies that the Church is invisible, it is because of the damage wrought upon confessional churches by a theology of an invisible Church. The Barthian concept of invisibility differs no doubt from that of the liberal theologies; it is nevertheless real. Barth fears that the expression "invisible Church" may evoke in the minds of believers a vague Platonic state or *Wolkenkukucksheim,* which would dispense them from membership in any visible Church.[44] Such precaution is understandable; the fact remains that the true Church is founded exclusively upon the action of the Word of God, which can be neither controlled nor perceived.[45]

The visible Church is the assembly of those who have taken the Bible seriously and for whom Scripture is normative.[46] If the word "faith" is taken in the Barthian sense as synonymous with "Word of God," and if we recall the meaning which Barth attaches to the word *fiducia,* we can state then that the invisible Church is the Church of faith, while the visible Church is that of *fiducia.*[47] The latter, we recall, is an attitude of complete, unsupported surrender to God, an unqualified acceptance of the Bible as the unique and ultimate norm, though it runs counter to certain appearances. In fact (for Barth), the Bible in its human structure affords no guarantee to fiducial faith. And this we must bear in mind in order to understand that belonging to the visible Church is a leap into the unknown.

But the leap must be made. Countless theologians before Barth had minimized the necessity of belonging to a visible Church. To Paul Tillich, for example, adherence to a religious confession is completely optional.[48] A person can join the invisible community through civil as well as a religious society. Culture, as well as religion properly so-called, can serve as a point of departure for the preaching of revelation. Barth admits that God is not restricted to the visible church, nor does the latter involve any surrender of his freedom, since God can still raise up from "these stones sons to Abraham." [49] There is no doubt, as he said in one of his earliest works, that God can utilize a sunset, a bouquet of flowers, or a dead dog as instruments of his revelation.[50] But it would be a gross deception to attach undue importance to this aspect of his doctrine. Barth considered it necessary to insist on this, particularly at the outset, to show in all probability that he was not falling into a narrow orthodoxy. We must look elsewhere for the heart of his teaching on this matter and consider this early remark as a corollary of secondary importance merely to be noted in passing. Barth never admitted that civil society and the Church could be placed on equal footing. He always insisted that the Church enjoyed a privileged status because of its intimate connection with revelation. And this privileged status is due to the Church as sole custodian of a promise to which Barth attaches considerable importance: "I will be with you until the end of time." No such promise has been made to civil society. "God himself and God alone makes man the recipient of his revelation, but he does so in a determined area. This determined area is the Church." The Church has within its confines, undoubtedly, good and evil; but that in no way calls into question the fact that " . . . in a real and unequivocal way, in a definitive and exclusive sense, the Church is the place where God makes men recipients of His revelation." [51] Barth uses the expression "area" advisedly. He does not wish to make revelation and the visible Church identical. The latter represents the area in which revelation occurs, but revelation does not occur simultaneously everywhere. The invisible Church achieves its existence in the visible society according to God's free interventions.

Though God in his dealings with the Church remains as free as He was in his dealings with the synagogue, the faithful do not enjoy the same freedom. If they wish to present themselves before God and to share in His revelation, they have no choice; a single path lies open to them: membership in the visible church.[52] Barth frequently avails himself of the traditional principle: *Extra ecclesiam nulla salus.* The validity of this principle for the invisible Church is certain; this Church alone effectively guarantees salvation. Barth goes further by applying it purely and simply to the visible and historical Church.[53] Though God remains free, the believer himself can only look to the visible community for salvation. Consequently, in Barthian theology, an extraordinary revalorization of the visible Church is found, which is subject, however, to God's judgment.[54]

Before completing our exposition of Barth's ecclesiology, we must observe that every Church claiming to be Christ's is not necessarily the true, visible Church. For that Church has distinguishing marks, all of which can be summarized in one: conformity with Scripture. According to Barth, we further note that the visible Church is the assembly of those who accept the Bible as the only norm. Wherever this criterion is not verified, we are confronted with a false church.

We can consider a *dissimilar* Church as a 'sister Church'; the same will not be true of a false Church. An example of a *dissimilar* Church would be the Lutheran Church, whose peculiar character is grasped only with difficulty. As I listened to a Lutheran sermon, some disturbing thoughts occurred to me. I did not find the preacher enunciating God's sovereignty with sufficient clarity, on account of a Lutheran tendency to credit the creature with a definite value. I do not find among Lutherans the doctrine of sanctification in its entirety; its concept of 'ministry' strikes me as unsatisfactory and suspect. Yet, despite these few questions which arise in my mind, I can still recognize here the one Church and, consequently, affirm community of faith with the Lutherans, and participate in the Lutheran Holy Supper. A union between Lutherans and Reformed is not excluded on principle.

But the society of churches can be effected in other ways. Then it is the *false Church* which emerges. It is possible to be confronted with churches in which we are no longer able to discern the one true Church; in the presence of these, we are obliged to take a clear-cut position. For example, the Catholic dogma of Papal Infallibility militates against the Kingship of Christ so that it is impossible for me to recognize the Church wherever dogma has the force of law. I could cite other examples. The doctrine of justification, as the Council of Trent defined it, obscures the doctrine of free grace. . . . Confronted with these facts, we can make but one comment: God's ways are not our ways. God recognizes His own in ways we cannot comprehend. . . . To the degree that *the Gospel is taught in its purity and the sacraments properly administered,* we can and ought to believe that *the Church* exists in the *false Church*.[55]

Briefly, the Roman Catholic Church, whose doctrine is not in conformity with that of the Bible, does not belong to the visible Church, which should unite Christians. "Our only attitude towards Catholics," said Barth at the Amsterdam conference, "is one of mission, of evangelization, but not of union." [56] God, however, whose power and liberty suffer no limitations, can therein choose His elect.

## E. The Multiplicity of Churches.

The Word of God, then, establishes the Church and effects its unity. In other words, Jesus Christ Himself constitutes the Church and is its unifying bond. But the problem is not resolved for all that. The Word of God and the action of Christ escape our observation; unity escapes our experience. Barth clearly defines the role of theology: to control the Church's proclamation. Where are we to find this Church whose teaching we verify? The theological problem leads us back to the mutual relationship of the unity and multiplicity of the Church. The division within Christianity is a fact. Before proceeding further, we must determine Barth's attitude on this point.

Did God desire this plurality? Does God wish that churches be in opposition to churches, not merely on minor points of detail or geographical distribution, nor on cultural or ritual questions or other accessory points, but with regard to faith, an essential point? St. Paul gives us the answer: There can be but "the same Lord, the same faith, the same baptism; with the same God, the same Father of all." [57] The unequivocal attitude, which the Apostle took in the community of Corinth, which was torn by factions, proves sufficiently that within the fold of the Church, only a single party can be admitted: that of Christ. We must recognize that although a plurality of churches is excluded, the New Testament admits a plurality of communities, of gifts, and of persons within the same Church.[58] The primitive Church is one in faith, but divided into diverse communities dispersed throughout different centers of population.

Where do we stand today in this respect?

Communities, in fact, a considerable number of communities oppose one another on all the central points of Christianity. What one community calls revelation, another condemns as error; what one shuns as heresy, another extolls as dogma. The organization of one group can appear to another, not only strange or inadmissable, but even intrinsically evil. The adherents of diverse confessions may perhaps find a large area of friendly understanding, but the essential is excluded: they cannot pray together, nor celebrate the Lord's Supper as a community, nor preach the Word of God, nor listen to it.[59]

Present-day Christianity has disobeyed the order of God, such as we can find it enunciated in Scripture. The separation of the Church into churches is a degradation, a *sin*. If there be any possible explanation for the present state of Christianity, it can only be this: a sin, for which we must bear responsibility, but from which we are not able to free ourselves through our own powers. The sin weighs heavily on our shoulders, and we cannot shake off its yoke. God alone, Christ alone, the cause of unity, can give to the world a Church which will be a true witness to the unity of the Word of God.

No theory permits us to attempt, through our own ideas and energies, to escape from the anguish of unity lost by sin. Every attempt to reunite the religious confessions according to a federalist plan is, consequently, in opposition to this primordial statement. There is an ideology of Anglo-Saxon origin which is the source of the ecumenical movement. Among its tenets is the theory that the multiplicity of churches is a normal development, a harmonious and necessarily varied expression of a grace too rich to be limited to one single form. Inasmuch as this ideology accepts the division as something good, it falls under the condemnation of God.[60] According to the divine plan, there cannot be a superior organism gathering together, without absorbing, the Roman Church, the Greek Church, the Lutherans, the Reformed, the Anglicans, and all other confessions. Not only would this be in opposition to the Bible, but it would be a Utopia as well. If we could ever arrive at such a state, we would have to acknowledge " . . . the cult of the Virgin at Einsiedeln, Wittenberg, and Geneva; the Roman Mass and the Protestant supper; Greek iconostasis and episcopal autonomy; the polytheism of 'German Christians' and the Protestant exposition of the First Commandment"—all of these as merely different branches of one and the same tree, which could grow and develop side by side, nourished by the sap of one common trunk.[61] These creations of the philosophy of history and of sociology are mere subterfuges to conceal the central, undeniable fact: sin and the absolute impossibility of extricating ourselves from sin through our own efforts. Every attempt, every prayer which does not spring from this anguished distress is ineffectual; they are performed in the spirit of disobedience and end in failure. "The

Church is the society of those who give up the idea of effecting any solution, but only so that they may place themselves in the hands of One greater than they: their Savior and Master." [62]

If the will of Christ, manifest so clearly in the New Testament, imposes unity on the visible society of Christians, can we be resigned to passive inactivity, to a fatalistic acceptance of a state from which it is impossible to liberate ourselves? Such cannot be the attitude of Christians. In the Word of God they find a command; their response must be an act of obedience. If, then, the churches must strive to reconstruct unity, how will they go about doing so? Should it be along lines already attempted in the past? Or should it be through the extension of an attitude of tolerance which we owe to the eighteenth century? To follow such a procedure would be to lose sight of the fact that this attitude of tolerance was due not to the vigor of the Faith but to its weakness, imposed from without because of political and philosophical preoccupations. Must we have recourse to new alliances of the same variety as those which already exist and have existed for many years throughout the world? No, for here too, one bases unity not on the essential but on mere accidentals. Such courses of action respond to purely secular considerations. Are we not made painfully aware of this by the fact that more often than not in such meetings an intercommunion cannot be established. It must certainly be admitted that, in its present state, the ecumenical movement itself has not attained more success in this matter; it has not touched the heart of the problem. Under such conditions, can it undertake to direct new efforts? [63]

*Unam Sanctam* will not consist solely in mutual respect and support, nor in active collaboration on the temporal level. The effort to promote mutual understanding and to find common points cannot suffice. Intercommunion itself will not effect unity. The decisive criterion will be a common confession of faith.[64] All men who call upon the name of Christ must be able to adhere to the same faith.[65] Without an identical attitude towards the Bible and its content, there can be no hope of unity.[66]

This poses gigantic problems and, before anticipating the possibility of such unity, we must weigh carefully the indispensable conditions it presupposes: 1) A common confession of faith could not at any price be the expression of an indifference in this realm of the weakness of one Church or another. 2) It could not be motivated by a secular preoccupation: the desire to effect unity on a national or international scale cannot be sufficient reason for renouncing disunity on the ecclesiastical level. 3) It cannot demand the renunciation of an iota of what a particular Church believes it must profess in obedience to Scripture. 4) Only the fruit of disobedience to Scripture would be abandoned: all foreign elements which have become intermingled with the faith and corrupted it. Too often have national, racial, philosophical, or historical questions provoked or nurtured disunity.[67]

The exposition of these conditions makes evident that the task of effecting a unity lies beyond human powers. Thus we are brought back to the heart of the matter: Christ alone, who is the unity of the Church, can bring about once more its observable unity. We must recall that the Church, during the interval between the Resurrection and the Parousia, is the constitutive element of God's Kingdom in a period of humanity's history when Christ is not as close to His own as He was during the forty days following the Resurrection and as He will be, above all, in the resplendent glory of His Kingdom. This absence of Christ has as its consequence a lack of cohesion within His Church, as well as sinfulness in its members.[68] Neither the fact of sinful disunity, nor that this disunity can be explained by humanity's *status viae,* nor finally the practical impossibility of man's ever knitting together the splintered fragments of the Church, permits him to neglect his duty to strive in this direction, a duty imposed by the witness of the Word of God. Although success in this enterprise is not promised to man, nevertheless the orientation which his efforts must follow is clearly manifested.

When the theologian, according to his profession, applies himself to the task of verifying the Church's message, he cannot wait for the *Unam Sanctam* to be visibly constituted; nor can he view the problem as if he himself were not linked with one of the Church's splintered fragments. Theology requires faith; consequently, it presupposes actual membership within the visible Church, within *one* Church. Upon the proclamation of *his* Church, then, the theologian must lean. Departing from his own confession of faith and confronting it with the norm of all faith, he will find himself orientated in the direction willed by God. Thus, the divided state of Christianity will not, according to Barth, hinder the theological enterprise; for this enterprise, in its precise and technical sense, is the only conceivable means of orientating oneself towards unity.[69]

## F. The New Structure of the Church.

The visible Church is always faced with the danger of decadence; at every moment it runs the risk of disappearing into nonexistence, into multiplicity and the fragmentation of denominations. It is necessary, says Barth, that the Church pull itself together unceasingly, or rather, that it be pulled together. The Church cannot exist save through a continual reform. Such reform is the exclusive work of Christ, who founded, constituted, and preserves the Church. Man, however, is not a total stranger to this reform; he can remove certain obstacles which hinder the divine activity of constant renovation. Theological reflection on this theme provides Barth with an occasion to discuss the structure of the Church of the future and its ecclesiastical constitution would offer the least resistance to the Word of God.[70]

We have already seen that the invisible Church becomes actually present in the very bosom of the visible community. What conditions must the latter present to fulfill this welcoming role? It must reduce as much as possible whatever separates it from its Lord. It must place itself in a state in which it can receive His intervention without any intermediary. Barth bases his entire doctrine on a single verse of Scripture: "Where two or three are gathered together in my name, I am there in the midst of them" (Matt. 18:20). This cultural cell is the basis of the ecclesiastical constitution which Barth envisages as the salvation of Protestantism.[71]

This cultural cell is above all the local congregation, whose limits correspond with those of a group of dwellings that makes possible participation in one and the same Sunday service.[72] Since cult consists essentially in the proclamation and repetition of the testimony of the Word, it is an appeal to the direct intervention of the accomplishment of the Word of God. Now the Word is the

constitutive element of the one true Church. In itself, the form
of worship alone provides from the human standpoint the necessary prerequisites that the invisible Church become a reality in
the bosom of the visible Church. When a religious group has organized a form of worship and lives within it, it has done the
most it can do for the renovation of the Church: it has straight-
ened out the paths of the Lord.

However, is it not indispensable that someone lend his assistance to this encounter between Christ and the Community? Must
we not provide an intermediary, a pastor or some ecclesiastical
authority? Barth shrinks from such a thought. The community
is a visible whole in which certain services (*Dienste*) can be distinguished, but in which there are neither functions (*Ämter*) nor
authorities or dignitaries. Christ alone and the Bible can claim
real power in the community.[73] The community is composed of
services which are complementary but not subordinated to one
another. Among these services—and it is desirable that all the
members of the community participate in some service or other—
there is one special service: that of the Word. This service, however, provided for the community by the same right and on the
same level as that of the "elders" or the sexton, does not constitute a degree of hierarchy. It is superfluous, then, to distinguish
different classes within the interior of the local community. There
are neither clerics nor laymen, no more a purely teaching Church
and a Church merely taught. Since the services are orientated towards the community and spring from it, every living member
of the community participates in a certain measure in each of the
prerogatives, which one would oppose wrongly.[74]

Such is the organization of the local community, which constitutes a cell within the Church and is an autonomous element.
It is not the final subdivision of a huge unitary organism. The
local community *is* the Church.[75] True, Barth does not ignore
the existence of a larger organism; however, he always conceives
of it as a community of communities, which owes its origin to the
fact that the local communities acknowledge and mutually recognize each other by support and aid to one another. The supra-
communitarian community does not, however, constitute a supra-

communitarian authority; rather, it is an instrument of coordination, itself centered around a form of worship. It will not be a synod
but a synodal community. In this manner, and in this manner
alone, does Barth envisage the unity of the Church. The instruments of coordination can be situated on diverse levels; the final
instrument, at the summit, will be on a world-wide and ecumenical scale, but it can never supplant or limit the authority of the
local, cultural community.

Conceived in this manner, the Church would be conformed to
the Bible. It would be utopian, indeed, to demand of Scripture
a specific text describing the Church's constitution, but the testimony of the Word of God can give us more. Recalling to our
minds the sovereignty of divine liberty and divine intervention,
it invites us to conceive of human institutions in the light of this
data. Whatever places a screen between the local community and
the Lord of that community must be mercilessly rejected. Neither
the Catholic Church, conceived on a monarchical structure, nor
the Episcopal churches, nor the synodical Presbyterian constitutions find favor in Barth's eyes.[76] They all labor under the same
defect: they introduce a foreign element between Christ and His
members. This reproach holds a fortiori for the national constitutions in which political elements occupy a large place.

Barth's Church will be then a Congregationalist Church. Among
the ecclesiastical organizations of the past, only the English Congregationalism of the sixteenth and seventeenth centuries is free
from the defects denounced by Barth.[77] History likewise provided
him with an a posteriori argument in favor of the solidity of these
constitutions. The fragmentation of the Church into tiny local
communities would injure neither the unity of the faith nor its
cohesion. English Congregationalism survived the rationalist
crisis of the eighteenth century with much less damage than the
Episcopal or Presbyterian churches, since the Pilgrim Fathers who
emigrated to America were not lacking in the genius of organization. It is to English Congregationalism that Barth attributes the
political vigor and maturity of the English people.[78] With Fried-
rich Loofs he feels authorized to conclude: "If the day should come
when national churches in the Old World pass away, would not

all of that foreshadow a very promising future for the Congregationalist organization of the Church in our midst? " [79]

\*

\*   \*

Karl Barth brings serious modifications to the ecclesiology of
the Reformers, from whom he derived his inspiration. He cannot
accept a notion of faith which would be acquired and incapable
of being lost, just as he cannot give his adhesion to classical double
predestination. His Christocentricism simply restates under a new
form the two major theses of the system: the mystery and the
intermittence of the Word of God. His entire theory of the invisible Church revolves on these two hinges. On the other hand,
his doctrine of the visible Church depends on a value judgment
of Scripture and a decision taken on this subject through *fiducia*
which has no foundation outside itself. This *fiducia*, moreover,
accepts a priori the idea that the invisible Church does not normally realize itself, except in the framework of the Church as a
visible social reality.

The theologian, whose mission it is to judge the Church's message by comparison with its criterion, cannot place himself on the
level of the invisible Church. There can be no question of this. It
is the message of the visible Church which he must examine. Also,
he cannot remain above confessional divisions. Faith places him
within a Church and he cannot ignore his actual state. He must,
then, devote himself to the message of his confession.

The theological enterprise of confrontation between the preaching of his Church and the unique norm of all preaching is the
most and the only efficacious method of striving towards the unity
of the Church and providing the ecclesiastical organization most
in conformity with the exigencies of the Word of God. As a result the Church is at one and the same time the postulate of
theological reflection and its fruit. The theologian works within
the Church of yesterday and prepares for that of tomorrow.

# notes
## to chapter nine

1 Cf. KD, vol. II, 2, pp. 12 and 37.

2 Cf. ch. V.

3 Cf. KD, vol. II, 2, p. 202. At the Congress of Calvinist Theology of 1936, the thesis of actual predestination was defended by Peter Barth (brother of Karl Barth) and by Pierre Maury. Cf. *De l'élection éternelle de Dieu,* pp. 21–56 and 183–200. See Barth's detailed treatment of the Congress in KD, vol. II, 2, pp. 207–214.

4 KD, vol. II, 2, p. 198.

5 "By centering our attention on faith, we will avoid conceiving salvation as a kind of beatitude mechanically bestowed. . . . The principal problem is knowing whether faith is a possession which a person can turn to his account or a gift of the Holy Spirit which must be requested repeatedly" (P. Maury, *De l'élection éternelle de Dieu,* pp. 196 and 154). The author, of course, chooses the second member of the disjunction. It is interesting to note how often the problem of faith is tinged with an unconscious Pelagianism in the writings of this representative of Barthianism. (Barth would not follow him to this point.) Predestination and reprobation are the two terms of God's ambivalent will. He proposes the choice to us, and what a choice we have! "We can apply this dual decree only to ourselves, because we merit the negative verdict only insofar as we receive the positive grace" (*op. cit.,* p. 194).

6 This runs counter to the universal salvific will of God, who withdraws His grace only from sinners. On the other hand, God is neither directly nor indirectly the cause of man's sin: "Deus non potest esse causa peccati . . . quia omne peccatum est per recessum ab ordine qui est in ipsum sicut in finem. Deus autem omnia inclinat et convertit in seipsum sicut in ultimum finem. Unde impossibile est quod sit sibi vel aliis causa discedendi ab ordine qui est in ipsum" (*S.T.,* I–II, p. 79, a. 1).

7 Faith (a theological virtue rooted in the human intellect), grace (man's formal participation in the divine nature), and predestination (an eternal act of God efficaciously directing every man towards his own special end), have become practically synonymous in Barthian theology. This lack of distinction makes Barth difficult reading for the theologian accustomed to Catholic terminology.

8 Divine knowledge, the cause of existent realities, remains invariably constant despite the constant variability of the effects emanating from it. Cf. St. Thomas, *Summa Theologica,* I, q. 14, a. 15.

9 Cf. ch. V.

10 Cf. ch. IV. The supposition that God's image has been totally destroyed in man compels Barth to conclude with such a radical doctrine.

11 Cf. CD, p. 138; KD, vol. I, 1, pp. 246–249 and 486; vol. II, 1, pp. 6–8.

12 Cf. CD, pp. 297–301.

13 "In meiner Taufe, gerade als Kindertaufe, als Wassertaufe, als einmalige Taufe ist mir gesagt . . . dass die Gnade *mich* angeht, dass sie auch zu mir gekommen ist" (CD, p. 300).

14 Cf. *Glaube und Denken,* first edition, 1931, pp. 417ff. Cf. KD, vol. I, 2, p. 225.

15 "Dieses Zeichen ist nicht die Gnade, es bringt und gibt sie auch nicht, sie wird durch dieses Zeichen weder vermehrt noch vermindert. . . . Die Taufe ist nicht, aber sie bedeutet die Wirklichkeit der Gnade" (CD, p. 299).

16 It is interesting to note how often, at this period, Barth emphasizes the importance of infant baptism. He reverts to it frequently afterwards. On this subject, see the fact related by J. S. Javet in *Verbum Caro,* 1947, vol. I, p. 45. Barth's new attitude is clearly proposed in his short treatise of 1943: *Die kirchliche Lehre von der Taufe.*

17 Barth does not hesitate to say: "Es gibt eine sakramentale Selbsterkenntnis" (CD, p. 301).

18 Consider the conclusion of the text already cited in note 13: "In meiner Taufe . . . ist mir gesagt . . . dass ich Anlass habe, der Stimme meines Existentialbewusstseins, gegen deren Glaubwürdigkeit so vieles einzuwenden wäre, zu vertrauen . . ." (CD, p. 300).

19 Cf. KD, vol. I, 2, p. 225.

20 "Heim hat mir mit jener Kritik doch der grossen Dienst erwiesen, mich noch mehr von seinem eigenen Weg, dem Weg der Reflektion über die Möglichkeit einer Glaubensgewissheit, abzudrängen" (KD, vol. I, 2, p. 225).

21 "War dieser (der Tridentiner Katholizismus) nicht reformierter als jene Reformierten, wenn er auf eine so zu begründende Erwählungsgewissheit lieber verzichten zu wollen erklärte?" (KD, vol. II, 2, p. 370). This reproach is directly intended for more recent Calvinists, but it is equally valid against Calvin himself.

22 *Summa Theologica,* I–II, q. 112, a. 5. See also *De Ver.,* q. 6, a. 5, ad 3. For Barth, as for the majority of Protestants, the concepts of faith and grace are perfectly equivalent. From their point of view, uninformed faith does not deserve the name of faith.

23 "Im Rahmem der klassischen Prädestinationslehre konnte das Eine nur zu Ungunsten des Anderen, im Rahmen der christologisch begründeten Prädestinationslehre kann und muss Beides geschehen" (KD, vol. II, 2, p. 375).

24 Cf. KD, vol. II, 2, p. 40–43.

25 At the Calvinist congress of 1936, Peter Barth distinctly proposed the dilemma: "Die Frage unseres Kongresses geht dahin: Erwählung oder Prädestination—auf der einen Seite die freie Erwählung und Verwerfung von Gott her, oder auf der andern Seite die doppelte Prädestination; entweder-oder, nicht beide gemischt!" (*De l'élection éternelle de Deiu,* p. 176).

26 Classical predestination, caused by the individualism of the Renaissance, would be, according to Barth, the cause of pietistic and rationalistic individualism. Cf. KD, vol. II, 2, pp. 337–339.

27 According to Barth, the treatise on predestination should be separated from the treatise on providence and joined to that on redemption: "(Die Gnadenwahl wird) deutlich von der Lehre von der Vorsehung geschieden und dafür *in besonderen Zusammenhang mit der Lehre von der Versöhnung gebracht,* gewissermassen als deren zuerst und zuletzt und auch in der Mitte zu beachtender Schlüssel verstanden" (KD, vol. II, 2, p. 87).

28 *Jesus Christus der Erwählende und der Erwählte.* Such is the title of a very lengthy paragraph in which Barth states his position. Cf. KD, vol. II, 2, pp. 101–156. "Das Prädestinationsdogma besteht also in seiner einfachsten und umfassendsten Form in dem Satz: die göttliche Prädestination ist die Erwählung Jesu Christi" (KD, vol. II, 2, p. 110).

29 KD, vol. II, 2, p. 176. The reader will note in this passage how often the exegesis of St. John's Prologue has a leading role in developing Barth's teaching on predestination. A lengthy exegesis of the Prologue can be found in KD, vol. II, 2, pp. 102–106.

30 "The Trinity is not construed—as it was in the early Church—in terms of questions arising from biblical texts dealing with the relations between the Father and the Son. . . . The Trinity, moreover, in Barth's opinion is not composed of three persons. This doctrine emphasizes above all the unity of revelation: the Revealer, revelation, and the fact revealed are identical, with the result that we are dealing with God Himself in a threefold manifestation. God is three times over other than God, but in each of His modes of being, He remains personal and free" (J. Rilliet, RTP, 1944, vol. XXXII, pp. 132–133). "Wenn es richtig war, im biblischen Offenbarungszeugnis die drei Momente der Enthüllung, der Verhüllung und der Mitteilung oder: der Gestalt, der Freiheit und der Geschichtlichkeit oder: der Ostern, des Karfreitags und der Pfingsten, oder: des Sohnes, des Vaters und des Geistes hervorzuheben, . . . wenn wir mit diesem Satz wirklich dreimal unauflöslich anders dreimal dasselbe gesagt haben, dann ist jetzt zu schliessen: die Offenbarung muss in der Tat als Wurzel oder Grund der Trinitätslehre verstanden werden" (KD, vol. I, 1, p. 351).

31 KD, vol. I, 1, p. 320.

32 We must not push the similarity between Schleiermacher and Barth too far. The point common to both is the priority which each gives the community over the individual. We must also beware lest we identify Barth's concept of a community's election with certain modern substitutes of that idea: totalitarian authoritarianism and collectivism. Cf. KD, vol. II, 2, pp. 341–344.

33 KD, vol. II, 2, p. 256.

34 KD, vol. I, 1, p. 2.

35 Barth's ecclesiology bears a resemblance to that of Luther.

36 *Conf. Aug.,* art. 7. Cf. KD, vol. I, 1, p. 74.

37 *Cat. Heidelberg,* q. 54, W. Niesel, *Bekenntnisschriften . . . ,* p. 162. Cf. KD, vol I, 2, p. 236.

38 Although this document presents Barth's entire thought, he is not the sole editor of it. Cf. W. Niesel, *Bekenntnisschriften . . . ,* p. 326.

39 "Die heilige christliche Kirche, deren einiges Haupt Christus ist, ist aus dem Wort Gottes geboren; in demselben bleibt sie und hört nicht die Stimme eines Fremden" (W. Niesel, *Bekenntnisschriften* . . . , p. 327).

40 W. Niesel, *Bekenntnisschriften* . . . , p. 327. In the same edition and in the same locus, notice Thesis V: "Die Kirche lebt allein davon, dass sie täglich neu von ihrem Herrn berufen und getragen, getröstet und regiert wird."

41 The first declaration of Barmen dates from January 3 and 4, 1934. A second is dated May 29–31 of the same year. This latter is of lesser importance for the topic under consideration, because it is less explicit. The confessional synod which approved its decisions included Reformed, Lutheran, and "United Brethren." For this reason, a common declaration could not be as precise as the one formulated for the Reformed alone, four months earlier. Cf. J.-L. Leuba, *Verbum Caro*, 1947, vol. I, p. 26.

42 I, 1 and II, 1, W. Niesel, *Bekenntnisschriften* . . . , pp. 329–330, cited in Leuba, *Verbum Caro*, 1947, vol. 1, pp. 27–28.

43 "Also ist auch die Kirche nicht konstant, nicht kontinuierlich die Kirche Jesu Christi, sondern sie ist es je in dem Ereignis, dass das Wort Gottes zu ihr gesprochen und von ihr geglaubt wird" (KD, vol. I, 1, p. 275). "The Church exists in the world as a human assembly and a human community. It is a segment of human reality, consisting of and represented by men as a part of their history; and it has been realized through the act of the glorified Jesus Christ, who gave Himself to His own in communicating to them His Spirit. *It is precisely in the very event which lays the foundation of the Church that Christ governs the Church. This act can not fall into the past*" (Credo, pp. 179–180).

44 Barth here borrows the vocabulary of Melanchthon (*Apol.*, VII, 20, CR, vol. XXVII, col. 283–284 and 525), who, just as Barth, wished to have nothing to do with a Platonic Church-State. Cf. KD, vol. I, 2, p. 241; *Credo*, p. 187; DG, p. 167.

45 This is the very root of Barth's entire theology. Among numerous texts which could be cited, cf. KD, vol. I, 1, p. 74.

46 Cf. ch. V.

47 Cf. ch. V.

48 P. Tillich, *Kirche und Kultur*, 1924, pp. 10ff., 16ff., and 19, cited by Barth in KD, vol. I, 1, p. 48.

49 Cf. KD, vol. I, 1, p. 48; vol. I, 2, p. 230.

50 For example, consider the following text: "What was the event foreseen by this anticipation (of the coming of the Word of God)? In its expectations, what was the meaning of the phrase 'God is present'? Evidently it does not signify exactly the same thing as when we apply the same expression to a cherry tree in blossom or Beethoven's Ninth Symphony . . ." (PD, p. 134). This idea is further developed in KD, vol. I, 1, p. 55. Cf. also L. Malevez, RSR, 1938, vol. XXVIII, p. 416.

51 "Die Ausnahme bestätigt also doch die Regel: Gott selbst und Gott allein macht den Menschen zum Empfänger seiner Offenbarung—aber er tut dies in einem bestimmten Raum, und dieser Raum ist, wie wir nun Altes Testament und Neues Testament zusammenfassend sagen dürfen: der Raum der Kirche. Das alttestamentliche Korrektiv behält seine Gültigkeit gegenüber denen, die in der

Kirche sind. Es weist hin auf die Scheidung der Guten und Bösen, auf das Gericht Gottes, dem auch sie unterworfen sind. Es stellt aber nicht die Frage, dass wirklich und eindeutig, endgültig und ausschliesslich die Kirche der Ort ist, wo Gott Menschen zu Empfängern seiner Offenbarung macht" (KD, vol. I, 2, p. 230).

52 "Ist Gott gewiss an die Kirche so wenig gebunden wie an die Synagoge, so sind es doch die Empfänger seiner Offenbarung: sie sind, was sie sind, indem Kirche ist und indem sie in der Kirche sind, nicht ohne die Kirche und nicht ausser der Kirche. Wobei unter 'Kirche' nicht zu verstehen ist die innere und unsichtbare Zusammengehörigkeit derer, die Gott in Christus die Seinigen nennt, sondern auch die äussere und sichtbare Zusammengehörigkeit derer, die, dass sie in Christus Gottes sind, in der Zeit gehört und sich zu diesem Hören bekannt haben. Das Empfangen der Offenbarung geschieht innerhalb nicht ausserhalb dieser doppelten Zusammengehörigkeit" (KD, vol. I, 2, pp. 230–231).

53 "Wir haben also die Kirche immer auf der Ebene der zeitlichen, sichtbaren, denk- und erfahrbaren Dinge zu suchen. Und das *extra ecclesiam nulla salus* besagt also immer auch: die subjektive Wirklichkeit der Offenbarung vollzieht sich für jeden jederzeit und überall auch in einer zeitlichen, sichtbaren, denk- und erfahrbaren Begegnung und Entscheidung" (KD, vol. I, 2, p. 240).

54 The life of a child of God, therefore, is at one and the same time visible and invisible. "Wenn nun diese seine Offenbarung in geschichtlicher Wirklichkeit nicht umsonst geschehen ist, wenn der Zeit, die er für uns hatte, entspricht eine Zeit, die wir für ihn haben dürfen, dann ist diese Entsprechung seiner Menschwerdung, dann ist also das Leben der Kinder Gottes, die Kirche, auch sichtbar. Gewiss auch unsichtbar: so gewiss es auch in der Menschwerdung unsichtbar bleibt, dass es das ewige Wort ist, das hier Mensch wurde, so gewiss auch hier Anfechtung und Ärgernis möglich sind, so gewiss Gott auch im Fleische nur durch Gott offenbar werden kann" (KD, vol. I, 2, p. 239). Whence it follows that the Church is both visible and invisible: "So ist die Kirche nicht nur unsichtbar kraft der göttlichen Erwählung . . . sondern in dem allem ist sie auch sichtbar. Die Kinder Gottes sind ja sichtbare Menschen; ein sichtbares Geschehen führt sie zusammen, eine sichtbare Einheit hält sie beieinander" (KD, vol. I, 2, pp. 239–240).

55 *Credo*, pp. 241–242.

56 *Foi et Vie*, 1948, vol. XLVI, p. 495.

57 Eph. 4:5.

58 *Dir Kirche und die Kirchen* (= KK), pp. 6 and 11. It is in this fascicule of the collection *Theologische Existenz heute* that Barth presents most explicitly his position on the problem presently engaging our attention. It treats of four conferences given in 1935 at the ecumenical seminar of Geneva.

59 KK, p. 11.

60 Barth has always manifested a critical attitude towards the ecumenical movement. In 1928, he expressed his reasons for refusing any cooperation with the movement in the following terms: "I do not wish to criticize any of those who feel that they are performing a good work, a work full of promise, in organizing an orchestra comprising the most diversified voices of Christianity. Nor do I wish to criticize those who collaborate in such an enterprise. I am well aware of the fact that such meetings are the order of the day, and I willingly admit that their intentions are genuinely earnest. Consequently, the more serious-

minded proponents of these modern methods will also understand how assemblies of this type can evoke or strengthen the following opinions: 1. that the unity of Christians in Christ can be visibly attained through a fusion of the most diverse viewpoints; 2. that Christian truth consists in the sum total or average of Christian convictions and opinions currently in circulation; 3. that the Christian religious consciousness can be realized only in a selection and by a leveling of diverse positions" (*Theologische Blätter*, 1928, p. 208, cited by M. Pribilla, *Um Kirchliche Einheit*, pp. 198–199).—If Barth has participated in ecumenical seminars, the reason has always been to propose his own point of view without any possible concessions. He never seeks a common denominator. Could he recently, since the Ecumenical Conference of Amsterdam (1948), have abandoned a position which we had every reason to believe was definitive? Barth, in fact, not only deigned to participate in that assembly as a delegate, but he went on to assume a major role. Before the meeting, he forwarded to the assembly a statement on the nature of the Church (*The Living Congregation of the Living Lord Jesus Christ*). He even inaugurated the session with a theological dissertation on the theme of the conference: *Man's Disorder and God's Design.* I do not believe that we must recognize in this action a contradiction of his former refusals. Barth went to Amsterdam to express what was in his mind; he did not change his way of thinking. "To be open to the thoughts of others, and to propose questions in terms common to others"—this is the sum and the substance of Barth's ecumenism (*Foi et Vie,* 1948, vol. XLVI, p. 491). Moreover, in his opening address he appeared rather critical of any ecumenical activity: "I am amazed at the sort of melancholy which emanates from everyone of the documents submitted for our perusal . . . , a melancholy which seems to derive from the fact that too many among us labor under the delusion that we, Christians and members of the Church, must bring to a successful issue an undertaking which God alone can and wishes to accomplish Himself" (*Foi et Vie,* 1948, vol. XLVI, p. 424).

61 KK, p. 10.

62 KK, p. 13.

63 KK, pp. 14–16. Barth's severe criticism of the ecumenical movement coincides on numerous points with that of the encyclical *Mortalium animos.* This is evident from the following excerpt: "How can one conceive of a Christian union each of whose adherents would preserve his own particular manner of thinking about and judging the very object of our faith, even though their ideas are in opposition to the theories of others? And how, may we ask, could men who adhere to contradictory opinions constitute one and the same moral union? We do not see how this profound diversity of opinion can pave a way to church unity . . . , but we do assuredly see that such diversity becomes a stage which very easily degenerates into religious negligence, and leads to indifferentism and modernism, whose unfortunate advocates assert that dogmatic truth is not absolute but relative." Cf. Aubert, *Le Saint-siège et l'union des Églises,* pp. 137–139.

64 In 1925, during a conference preparatory to the meetings of the world-wide council of the *Alliance of the Reformed Churches holding the Presbyterian system,* Barth had already dealt with the subject. His observations, however, were restricted to the churches of Calvinist persuasion. His conference, entitled "Une confession de foi commune à tous les réformés," was printed in 1928, in TK, pp. 76–105.

65 This is how Barth interprets the Catholic Church's abstention with respect to the various ecumenical conferences. Cf. KK, p. 16.

66 We must recognize, nonetheless, that Barth's attitude has made no little contribution towards inspiring interesting qualifications in the ecumenical movement. Ecumenism must be doctrinal, not federalist: this is Barth's position. This implies with utmost necessity that the resolutions of the ecumenical committees be formulated, not according to a democratic system based on representation, but by reference to a norm: Scripture. In other words, Barth advocates recourse to a prophetic element. Had he not severely criticized the Ecumenical Council of Geneva for having refused to adopt a definite stand during the German political regime's persecution of the Church? In these circumstances, the German organization had been paralysed by its representative structure; for this precluded the adoption of a definite position without the unanimous mandate of the member churches involved. In a preliminary work at the Amsterdam Conference (1948), the acting General Secretary of the Ecumenical Council, Doctor W. A. Visser 't Hooft, without relinquishing the representative system, which is basic to ecumenism, advocated granting a more important role to the prophetic element. Not only the general assembly, as an elected body, would be able to make a decision reflecting the opinions of the different churches, but the Ecumenical Council itself (a more restricted and permanent body) would have the right of adopting a position spontaneously, without preliminary soundings, as often as a command of God became evident through circumstances. Cf. W. A. Visser 't Hooft, *Le Conseil oecuménique des Églises: sa nature et ses limites,* in *Hommage et reconnaissance à Karl Barth,* pp. 124–125.

67 KK, pp. 17–18.

68 KK, p. 12. Since God simultaneously diffuses light and shadows by means of the Bible, the dogmatic differences and oppositions are ultimately attributable to divine causality. Cf. KD, vol. I, 2, p. 711. On this subject, consult the discerning observations of J. Fehr, *Das Offenbarungsproblem in dialektischer und thomistischer Theologie,* pp. 97–98.

69 KK, p. 24. See further, KD, vol. I, 2, p. 660.

70 "Die Ordnung der Kirche muss auf alle Fälle so beschaffen sein, dass sie der Erneuerung der Gemeinde durch ihren lebendigen Herrn die denkbar geringsten Widerstände bietet, der durch ihn zu vollziehenden Reformation gegenüber auf der menschlichen Seite ein Maximum von Offenheit, Bereitschaft und Freiheit sicherstellt" (SK, p. 36).

71 SK, p. 36.

72 "Unter 'Gemeinde' ist nicht notwendig . . . dir Ortsgemeinde . . . zu verstehen. Aber die einfachste und naheliegendste und insofern die exemplarische und reguläre Form solcher Versammlung ist in der Tat die Ortsgemeinde, deren Grenzen mit denen einer bestimmten Wohngemeinde zusammenfallen: konstituiert durch die Möglichkeit regelmässigen gemeinsamen Gottesdienstes" (SK, pp. 37–38). The translator of Barth's address at Amsterdam has provided an excellent definition of the notion of "Gemeinde" in a footnote: "In this paper Barth uses the word 'Gemeinde' to denote the *worshipping community,* meeting regularly in a given place, entirely dependent on the continually new activity of the Lord Jesus Christ" (*The Universal Church in God's Design,* p. 67).

73 "Es gibt schon in der Gemeinde keine kirchliche 'Obrigkeit' ausser dem Worte Gottes in seiner biblischen Bezeugung. Ihm dient die ganze Gemeinde in allen ihren Diensten" (SK, p. 38).

74 Cf. SK, pp. 38–39.

75 "(Die Ortsgemeinden sind) jede für sich im Vollsinn des Begriffes die Kirche" (SK, p. 39).

76 Cf. SK, pp. 36–37 and 42.

77 Barth is not, however, unaware of the fact that Congregationalism, as it exists today, is not free from all faults. "Not even the *congregationalist* church order is above criticism. Its representatives have not yet been able to offer a satisfactory answer to the problem of the unity of the Church and of the Churches. But the principle of Congregationalism—the free congregation of the free Word of God—is sound enough" (*The Living Congregation of the Living Lord Jesus Christ*, in *The Universal Church in God's Design*, p. 75). The Congregationalists, also called Independents or Brownists, were founded by Robert Browne (1550–1630). Browne separated from the Church of England, due to questions of ceremonies, and soon afterwards, he became an itinerant preacher, revolting against the Church and the bishops everywhere. Since, under the rule of Elizabeth, the situation remained confused on account of the Puritans who were trying to establish cells within the official Church without overtly professing their convictions, Robert Browne had the courage to attack the Puritans openly. In opposition to them, he published his treatise, entitled *Essai sur la réforme sans attendre personne*. After a sojourn in Holland where the quarrels among his disciples disheartened him, he returned to his native country and submitted to the established Church. Since each congregation was completely autonomous, the sect rejected any constitution as externally imposed law.

78 Barth did not rest content with formulating the principles for a new ecclesiastical constitution. His influence is clearly perceptible in a projected constitution drawn up by his son, Pastor Markus Barth. As a consequence of rather astonishing political contingencies, the canton of Basle (together with surrounding areas) still possesses no ecclesiastical constitution, and all official authority is in the hands of the civil authorities. In order to cope with this paradoxical situation which has already lasted over a century, several plans have been proposed, among which was that of Karl Barth. This plan is distinctly Congregationalist, despite the fact that it still bears traces, at certain points, of synodical Presbyterian tendencies. It has been translated and published by J. L. Leuba, in *Verbum Caro*, 1947, vol. IX, pp. 32–43.

79 Fr. Loofs, PRE, vol. X, p. 693. Cf. SK, p. 44.

# the proclamation
# of the church: its
# content and authority

CLOSER SCRUTINY of Barthian ecclesiology will enable us to conclude our exposition of his dogmatic method with a brief study of the material of dogmatics: the proclamation. The proper role of the theologian is, as we have seen, to compare the proclamation of the Church with its norm.[1] We have already seen the meaning of "norm" and "Church" to Barth. There remains only the determination of the exact extension and comprehension of the concept of "proclamation."

## A. Proclamation and Sacrament.

Proclamation (*Verkündigung*) can be defined in its broadest sense as follows: human discourse about God, delivered within the Church, with the claim of giving expression to the very Word of God.[2] Proclamation cannot help but be human discourse, subject to all the relative factors of every human activity. Moreover—and this is its distinguishing note—it is spoken in the hope that God at a given moment will agree to accept it and make it His own Word. The hope that God will do so is based on the fact that proclamation does not boldly take the initiative in this enterprise on its own authority; rather it gives expression to the Word of God only insofar as divinely commanded: "You, therefore, must

go, making disciples of all nations . . . teaching them to observe
all the commandments which I have given you." The divine command, moreover, is not simply a command; it includes a promise:
"And behold I am with you all through the days that are coming,
until the consummation of the world" (Matt. 28:19–20). Command and promise, therefore, justify the preacher's expectation.[3]

This command also limits the scope of the preaching. Has not
human imagination tried to extend it in all directions? Paul Tillich, for example, thinks it is necessary to expand the notion of
"*Verkündigung*"; its content would be greater than mere oral
repetition of the Bible message. In his opinion, a Protestantism
lacking breadth would have failed to distinguish between *Verbum*
and *Oratio*. Although *Oratio* is identified with the scriptural
sermon, *Verbum* is broader in its concept and includes other
symbols, among which must be included the "silent symbols of
art." [4] As is well known, Barth has no difficulty in speaking iron-
ically about a symbolism which loses sight of the transcendental
character of the Bible message, especially when a representative
of such symbolism (Julius Smend) feels no hesitation in calling a
melodious organ a "second throne of truth." The theological
reason that condemns these fantasies, in Barth's eyes, is the distinction between what God can do and what He commands—a
distinction which these fantasies overlook. God *can* speak both
with and without symbols, but the *command* which He gives to
men limits human initiative to scriptural proclamation.[5]

Scriptural proclamation, nevertheless, must necessarily be realized in two forms: one oral, the other visible. Oral proclamation
will be what we call preaching or the sermon. The sacrament will
be visible proclamation.[6] Before we try to assign a reason for the
double form of human activity in the service of the Word of God,
we must recall once more that it is found as such in the divine
command already mentioned: "you, therefore, must go out, making disciples of all nations, and *baptizing them in the name of the
Father, and of the Son, and of the Holy Ghost.*" [7]

Baptism and instruction, sacrament and proclamation by word
of mouth, are, therefore, inseparable in the very command of
Christ by which they were instituted.

Though this command alone is the basis for the activity of the

Church, nevertheless, a posteriori—fides quaerens intellectum—
man is not forbidden to seek reasons for the divine decision. We
must keep in mind that all human activity, which is Christian,
has for its end, according to Barth, the representation of divine
action.[8] It is, properly speaking, neither a prolongation nor an
instrument of the divine action, but parallel imitative activity.[9]
Now what is the role of proclamation in its broadest sense? Is it
not to represent the accomplishment of the Word of God? This
Word, as we know, is not simply discourse; it is also an event. It
is not simply truth but actual reality.[10] Without the sacrament
which intervenes to complete it, the oral repetition of the Bible
message would be only a deficient representation of the Word of
God. It is true, the sacrament adds no further truth to the message, but, like a seal, it conforms by an act what the Word has
revealed: [11] "The sacrament seems to say to preaching: This is
not merely a matter of words; something of great moment is occurring. The sacrament is the sign of that which is occurring,
namely, the birth of a new man, his subsistence and conservation
in the life of the Spirit. To man's word is added an act." [12] Briefly,
the sacrament signifies the basic efficacy of the accomplishment of
the Word of God.

The Barthian theory of the relation proclamation and the sacrament is manifestly an important reassertion of certain principles of the great Lutheran confessions. One might recall, for
example, the articles of Smalkalde:

> In matters pertaining to the external, oral Word, the following prin-
> ciple must be firmly maintained: God gives no man His Spirit or grace
> except by means of, and together with, the external Word which must
> precede it. This principle is our protection against the enlightened
> and spiritualists, who boast of having received the Spirit without, and
> before, the Word. And they, consequently, judge, interpret, and falsify
> Scripture or the oral Word according to their own whim.[13]

However, neither Luther nor Calvin were perfectly consistent in
applying their principles. That each should retain infant baptism
is irreconcilable with a perfectly logical application of the principle enunciated above.[14] This sacrament could not actually be
given cum verbo externo et praecedente to a human being who

has not yet attained the use of reason.[15] In the subsequent history of Protestantism, the tendency towards a certain kind of sacramentalism is more evident among Lutherans than among Calvinists. Concerning the mutual relationship between preaching and the Holy Supper in Sunday worship, the Lutherans manifested a tendency to separate the two into two distinct celebrations, while the Calvinists were inclined more to omit whatever was not properly speaking preaching. At a time when certain Lutherans sought to place the altar and the "sacrament of the altar" at the center of Christian worship, members of the Reformed Church let the Supper fall into disuse and celebrated it only in exceptional circumstances.[16]

Barth vigorously affirms against both Catholicism and a certain species of Lutheranism that the sacrament cannot exist independently of preaching. Against an impoverished Calvinism, he recalls the need for the sacrament in order that the message of the Church be complete: "The Holy Supper, as Calvin required, ought to be celebrated at each gathering of worship. A complete evangelical service ought to begin with baptism, continue with preaching, and end with the Holy Supper." [17] The sacrament, therefore, is an "annex" of preaching, but an indispensable "annex." [18]

Barth defines preaching and sacrament in the following manner:

> Ventured by a member of the Church, who is especially called to this end, preaching is the attempt to express in human words a threefold divine promise: revelation, reconciliation, and vocation. In the form of biblical exegesis, its purpose is to render intelligible to contemporary man the promise of God. . . . The sacrament is a symbolic action, performed within the bosom of the ecclesiastical community according to the prescriptions laid down in the Bible. This action accompanies and confirms oral preaching. It seeks to give witness to the accomplishment of revelation, redemption, and divine calling, which is, at one and the same time, the basis and the full realization of the promise.[19]

Before concluding this section, we must point out once more Barth's insistence upon the contemporaneity of preaching: " . . . its purpose is to render comprehensible to *contemporary* man the promise of God." In other words, Barth repeats that preaching cannot be a simple reiteration, a simple lecture on the Bible message. As contact between the Word of God and the Christian soul is one of direct confrontation, so too, preaching must resemble closely that meeting on the level of representation and sign.[20] But how is such testimony to be rendered contemporary? Barth explains this at length when he speaks of objective exegesis and of the role of philosophy in theology.[21] In our opinion, however, his method does not come up to his ambitions, and the message which the Barthian preacher addresses to us today presents no sufficient guarantee of conformity with a teaching twenty centuries old. Subjectivism plays too large a role in it.

## B. Proclamation and Confession of Faith.

Although the role of the theologian is to examine the preaching of the past, it is impossible for him to examine it in its entirety. It simply eludes his grasp. To begin with, only one part of the heritage is at his disposal; the rest has disappeared with the surge of history. Whatever remains at our disposal is not equally valuable; certain documents do not represent in any authoritative way the message of the Church. One cannot demand that the "dogmatist" present the proclamation of the past in its original form; it must first be stripped of all oratorical embellishment and reduced to its doctrinal skeleton. Since past preaching, except for the relatively recent, has already been *geprüft, kritisiert, korrigiert,* the theologian must study and analyze above all the results of the history of dogmatics.[22] In short, the study of proclamation, for all purposes, means a study of the Church's confessions of faith. For the confession of faith is actually the crystallization of the Church's message at a determined period.[23] The same is true of dogma.[24] Barth makes no distinction between confession of faith and dogma.[25] The latter is not, as it is within the realm of Catholic theology, a truth revealed and defined as such by the infallible magisterium of the Church; rather, it is an essentially provisional result of dogmatic endeavor. It is, for all that, worthy of the greatest regard and most attentive consideration, inasmuch as it is the fruit of the ecclesiastical community itself.[26]

## C. The Authority of the Confession of Faith.

This, therefore, poses the problem of value of the confession of faith. Barth finds himself in the presence of two extreme positions: Liberalism and Catholicism. The idea of the first would be to ride rough-shod over all dogmatic history in order to rediscover Scripture in its freshness and purity. Certain liberals naïvely believe that they have successfully achieved such a goal. Catholicism, on the other hand, has seen clearly that the Church existed before Scripture; that Scripture could not express the life of the Church in its plenitude nor contain all revealed truth; and that, consequently, "some unwritten traditions . . . handed down, as it were, from hand to hand . . . coming from the very mouth of Christ or inspired by the Holy Spirit and preserved in the Catholic Church through an uninterrupted succession" [27] must be admitted as a complement to the canonical writings and the very condition necessary to assure their existence. These unwritten traditions are held in veneration by the Catholic Church with the same sense of loyalty and reverence which she accords Holy Scripture.[28] Since, along with the written books, they are the source of the Church's teaching authority, we can say that, contrary to liberalism which refuses to accord any authoritative value to the confessions of faith, the Catholic Church acknowledges in them divine authority.[29] In the matter of faith or morals an ecumenical conciliar canon or a dogmatic definition of the Sovereign Pontiff has exactly the same authority as a biblical text. The statement contained in the Gospel according to Saint John: " . . . the Word was made flesh," and the dogma of the Immaculate Conception require the same adherence of faith from the members of the Church. Obviously, in the total synthesis of dogma, these two truths do not occupy the same rank: the Immaculate Conception is only a consequence of the redemptive Incarnation. The true believer, nevertheless, does not give to the second an adherence which is less firm than the one given to the first, nor is his assent inspired by a less elevated motive. Such is the Catholic doctrine.

Barth pursues a middle course: the confession of faith has a real authoritative value, but it is purely ecclesiastical. It is, as a matter of fact, the voice of our fathers and brothers in the faith and constitutes the very continuity of the visible Church.[30] Wherever the Church of the past or the faith of our contemporary co-religionists does not make its voice heard, the visible Church does not exist as a community.

In my opinion, the entire question of tradition is dominated by the Fifth Commandment: Honor thy father and thy mother. This authority is assuredly limited; we ought to obey God more than our father and mother. I would like to say to all those who feel repulsion upon hearing the word "orthodoxy," "council," "catechism": My dear friends, retrain your emotions! There is no question of bonds nor of slavery; it is simply a matter of obeying the Church's past, the "elders" in the Church. This is simply a matter of order. We cannot begin everything anew in 1935 and bring about a *creatio ex nihilo*. In obedience to the Church's past, we always remain free theologians. Yet we ought to know that, as members of the Church, belonging to the *congregatio fidelium,* we are not permitted to speak without having first listened. The Reformers were aware of this. In their confessions of faith, they expressly turned to the councils of the ancient Church, and with respect to the content of their message, there can be no doubt that reference was made to the already existing dogmatic knowledge of the Church.[31]

The confession of faith is imposed upon us like a master; we must pass under its demanding rod. It is not one of those numerous texts which one can say that he has read; it must have been read, reread, and studied. It seeks to serve as our principal commentary on Holy Scripture [32]—a commentary whose only role is to lead us to Scripture so that we receive an immediate knowledge of it. We can no longer term it the unique commentary which would free us of the responsibility of adopting definite positions ourselves; rather, it is the principal pedagogue that God gives us. To imagine that this manner of procedure distorts judgment or that other methods are better suited to give us the true sense of the Bible is mere superstition:

In the eighteenth and nineteenth centuries, time and time again, arose the possibility of rejecting the Nicean Creed, orthodoxy, scholasticism, the Fathers of the Church, the confessions of faith—all with a flourish of trumpet—with a consequent adherence to the Bible. I am thinking of G. Menken, J. T. Back, Hoffman of Erlangen, Adolf

Schlatter—all men of genius. It is a strange thing, but this procedure, which appears to be so consistent with the scriptural principles, has always resulted in a very "modern" theology. The reason is that these determined biblicists partook of the philosophy of their times and reflected that philosophy in their study of Scripture; consequently, just as the Fathers of the Church and the Scholastics did before them —and in greater measure—they found in the Bible their own ideas. They had freed themselves of the dogma of the Church, but not of their own dogmas and their own ideas.[33]

To grasp the divine message intended for the world today, one must first give heed to the voice of the Church, which, before us and fully conscious of its responsibility, has adopted in a decision of faith a definite stand consonant with the great truths of Scripture.

The confession of faith has, however, only a provisional authority. It is necessarily fallible and always open to reform. Under definitive and irrevocable guise, it is an eschatological concept, namely, the praise which the glorified Church will render to its Lord.[34] Such, according to Barth, would be the traditional—if not permanent—attitude of Protestantism as a whole, or at least of Calvinism:

Neither antiquity, nor customs, nor the multitude, nor human wisdom, nor judgments, nor arrests, nor edicts, nor decrees, nor councils, nor visions, nor miracles should be in opposition to the Holy Scripture; on the contrary, all things ought to be examined, regulated, and reformed according to it. After the Bible, we acknowledge three Creeds: the Apostles', the Nicean, and the Athanasian, because they are in conformity with the Word of God.[35]

Although such is the opinion of the *Confession de Foy* of 1559 regarding previous councils, it does not seem to admit that *its own* affirmations are likewise reformable; at least it makes no mention to that effect. Upon this point, the *Confessio Scotica* of 1560 is less pretentious and more conscious of the relative and provisional value of its efforts: "If anyone observes that an article or even a phrase (of this Confession) is in opposition to the Word of God . . . let him please bring it to our attention by letter. To one who renders us this service, we promise to correct through the mouth of God, i.e., from Holy Scriptures, the error which is pointed out to us." [36]

This attitude is, moreover, the only one compatible with that of Calvin. Basing his argument upon several examples, he declares:

Since we have shown that the Church does not have the power to introduce new doctrines, let us speak now of the power which the papists attribute to it in the interpretation of Scripture. Certainly we admit quite willingly that, if dispute arises over some article, there is no better nor more certain remedy than that of assembling a council of true bishops to discuss the matter. For such a decision, arrived at through common consideration and with the agreement of all the shepherds of the Church, under the invocation of the Holy Spirit, will have much more significance than if each one individually drew up a resolution of his own and preached it to his flock. . . . But I deny that it would be perpetual, that is, that every interpretation which meets with the approval of the council would be true and consonant with Scripture for that reason.[37]

Despite the great value he accords conciliar decisions, Calvin does not wish to recognize in them anything more than a purely human authority. A council is an assembly of specialists in theological matters and nothing more. This value-judgment passed on all councils is equally valid for all the confessions of faith born of the Reform.

The Lutheran position, according to several of its representative sources, is perceptibly different. In the introduction to the first part of the *Formula concordiae,* after having cited Scripture as the sole norm of faith, Lutherans recognized a certain authority in other written documents. These are the three *Creeds,* the *Apostles',* the *Nicean,* and the *Athanasian,* the *Confession of Augsburg,* the first edition of the *Apology of the Confession of Augsburg,* the *Articles of Smalkalde* of 1537, and, finally, both the *Little* and the *Large Catechism* of Luther. While they note that these documents cannot be compared to Scripture, the sole rule and judge of faith, the assembled theologians declare that all doctrinal writings must be in conformity with the Bible and these documents, or else be liable to condemnation.[38] Although they recognize the secondary value of the ecclesiastical texts in comparison with the Divine Word consigned to the Scriptures, Lutherans seem to think that the creeds and confessions of faith contain, in an immutably determined form, Christian truth. On this point, the introduction to the second part is more clear. It accepts the *Confession of Augsburg* (in its first edition) " . . . not because it was drawn up by our theologians, but because it was drawn from the very Word of the Lord and solidly established upon the foundation of the sacred writings." [39] Hollaz is in perfect agreement with this view when he affirms that the confessions were drawn up with the help of a "special concursus of God," and that one cannot "without danger" affirm *"sine adjecta declaratione"* that the confessional writings are mere human writings.[40] This is a far cry from Calvin's theory and the invitations of the Scottish theologians.

The confession of faith can only be a stage, Barth tells us.[41] Here again an effort must be made to grasp his meaning. As it stands, this statement could be accepted by a Catholic theologian. A declaration of the *magisterium* is a stage. Since there is a "homogeneous evolution" of Catholic dogma, it in no way excluded the explicitation of a conciliar decision by a later conciliar decree, or concern by the *magisterium* in new areas. But this is not the sense in which Barth uses the term. The preceding stage does not bind the Protestant theologian. Since former ecclesiastical decisions are fallible, the prospect is altogether possible that new decisions prepared by theologians will not be simply a development of preceding positions, but substitutions for out-of-date, obsolete positions.

Since this attitude rests upon the refusal to accept tradition as a norm of faith alongside Scripture, the Catholic historian of Protestantism must express at this point a difficulty that he has in following Protestant logic. Several Protestants are the first to recognize that there are traditions in the heart of Protestantism:

The members of the Reformed Church, like others, are more dependent upon tradition than they care to admit. In the question of Sunday worship, the washing of feet (of which Jesus spoke in words which could be considered a formal institution: " . . . you in turn ought to wash each others' feet"), infant baptism, and the organization of Churches—in all of these, the contribution of tradition is quite clear. When members of a Christian persuasion, such as the Adventists, enter into debate with the Reformed on these various subjects in the name of Holy Scripture, they are, before the debate starts, victorious; the texts by which our Church defends its position, apart from the role of tradition and without invoking the "spirit of revelation," are rare and do not warrant adherence to our position. We prefer to say it straightforwardly and affirm that there is a Protestant tradition.[42]

But John Cadier corrects himself immediately by adding: "At least this tradition does not contradict Scripture, and makes no pretence of adding anything to it." Is not that qualification made rather quickly? It is true that infant baptism is not in contradiction with Scripture; but can it be said that it adds nothing to Scripture? Where in Scripture is there to be found a decisive affirmation favoring the baptism of infants? Is not the interpretation of tradition absolutely indispensable for finding it in Scripture?

There exists a more striking case: that of the first creeds and the Canon. O. Cullmann explains the origin of the first confessions of the Christian faith in terms of the necessity of a résumé of apostolic doctrine. This need, very great inasmuch as the Christian message had been spread abroad in oral form alone, in no way came to an end when the neotestamentary writings appeared. "When the first Christian writings appeared between 50 and 150, with an abundance of which our present day New Testament gives us but a vague idea, a doctrinal résumé remained necessary." [43]

This need remained, according to our author, after the Canon had been determined. "During the formation of this Canon, which under its definitive form would still number twenty-seven works, it was too extensive to assume the role of a rule of faith." [44] And so, from the avowal of one of the best Protestant exegetes, we see that an intervention on the part of the Christian community was necessary, not only to fix the Canon, but also to draw up a résumé of faith; it remained indispensable, even after the number of the inspired books was decided upon. Is not such an avowal an implicit acknowledgment of the existence of an oral tradition, not only antecedent to the Scriptures, but also concomitant and subsequent to them. Is it not an admission that the Scriptures must be interpreted by an external element? Cullmann utilizes this principle elsewhere to determine the "center" of the Christian message. True, he qualifies his stand by adding: " . . . one does not want to place *all* of ecclesiastical tradition above Scripture; it is rather a question of dethroning all *future* tradition in the name of apostolic tradition." [45] I believe that the Catholic theologian would be in full accord even here. The Council of Trent clearly distinguishes between divine traditions and apostolic-divine traditions on the one hand, and purely ecclesiastical traditions (or ecclesiastical-apostolic) on the other hand; and it extends only to the first type validity as a rule of faith.[46] Who, therefore, will be able to *discern* with sufficient certitude the apostolic traditions, if not the Church?

In the name of the obedience which the Church must accord to revelation, Barth condemns all tradition which would be ranked as a rule of faith.[47] The Church must be submissive to the Word of God. If then, in addition to the testimony of the Word of God, it were necessary to acknowledge the existence of unwritten traditions which would be the authentic interpretations of the Word, would not this be an admission that the relationship has been reversed and that the Church has usurped control of revelation? The entire argument rests upon the complete identification of the Church and non-written tradition.[48] It would be correct if the successive decisions of the Church *constituted* those objective truths, which are the traditions by their progressive appearance. But that is not the case: there is a clear-cut distinction between the *magisterium* and the sources of the *magisterium*.[49] The *magisterium* does not create non-written tradition: rather, the tradition precedes it. The Church draws from tradition; it does not invent it. When we admit that tradition has a value equal to that of Scripture, we are maintaining with Barth the absolute principle of submission of the Church to revelation.

The Church, nevertheless, has a privileged position regarding tradition as it does in its relationship to Scripture. Since it is of the utmost importance that the faithful are not left in uncertainty about the norms of faith, Christ has entrusted to the Church the gift of *discovering* the divine, or divino-apostolic tradition, and of infallibly *discerning* in the complex deposits of ecclesiastical history those traditions which are entitled to adherence on the part of the faithful. It is true, Barth will tell us, that this infallibility is precisely the point at which the two concepts clash. This is undoubtedly proof that everything in the last analysis can be reduced to these two clearly divergent views of the Church. In fact, Barth contests the visible existence of a humano-divine Church. In his opinion, the visible Church is simply human and includes all the relationships such visibility entails. The invisible Church, on the contrary, is purely divine. There exists between the two no union whatsoever, not even in those mysterious moments which Barth calls interventions of the Word of God. In brief, the doctrine of the Incarnation prolonged in the Church is not to be found among Barth's teachings.

\*

\*     \*

The role of the theologian is to revise the message of the Church unceasingly. The proper attitude for such a task cannot be dictated by any a priori doctrinal self-complacency. It presupposes at the outset a penetrating study of the proclamation which is considered. Encountering the confession of faith of his own Church, the concrete form of ecclesiastical proclamation at a given moment, the theologian must judge its fidelity with respect to its norm, by confronting it with the Bible, and eventually work out a more faithful expression of that proclamation. The theologian always finds himself poised between yesterday's confession of faith and that of tomorrow.

And yet, he cannot limit his study to the oral or written doctrine of his Church. The Church also expresses itself through the sacraments. It falls within the province of the theologian, therefore, to submit the sacramental practice of his confession to the final tribunal of all Christian activity: Scripture. The critical function of dogmatics extends to that point.

# notes

## to chapter ten

1 Since the Church has a priority over its members (cf. KD, vol. I, 2, p. 230), the theologian is not faced with the task of creating an entirely new message, but of correcting yesterday's message. This correction in turn will be a preparation for tomorrow's message. Cf. KD, vol. I, 1, pp. 79–81. "Dogmatik ist Zurüstung zur kirchlichen Verkündigung, sie formuliert die Sätze, die zu bedenken sind, bevor kirchliche Verkündigung ihre Sätze formuliert" (KD, vol. I, 1, p. 297).

2 Cf. KD, vol. I, 1, p. 52.

3 Cf. KD, vol. I, 1, pp. 58–59.

4 Cf. KD, vol. I, 1, p. 64.

5 "Nötigt die Frage: was kann Gott tun? die Theologie zur Demut und Offenheit, so nötigt sie die Frage: was ist uns geboten? zum konkreten Gehorsam" (KD, vol. I, 1, p. 55). "Verkündigung muss sein als Vollstreckung des göttlichen Befehls an die Kirche" (KD, vol. I, 1, p. 84). This order, joined to a clear consciousness of not being able to *possess* the Word of God, brings it about that the message is a calculated risk in obedience.

6 At times Barth qualifies "sacraments" with the words *verba visibilia*. Cf. KD, vol. I, 1, p. 82. The reformers willingly spoke of *pictura verbi*.

7 Cf. KD, vol. I, 1, p. 58.

8 "Die Repräsentation des göttlichen Rufes selber" (KD, vol. I, 1, p. 78).

9 "Der Mensch tut in der Tat etwas Entsprechendes, Paralleles, Analoges in seiner eigenen, der geschöpflichen Seinssphäre, angesichts dessen, was Gott in der seinen tut, indem er sich ihm offenbart" (CD, p. 138).

10 Cf. KD, vol. I, 1, pp. 60–61.

11 This is the source of Barth's preference for the definition of the sacraments given in the *Heidelberg Catechism*. Among other definitions it gives the following: "Es seind sichtbare heilige Wahrzeichen und Sigill, von Gott darzu eingesetzt, dass er uns durch den Brauch derselben, die Verheissung des Evangeliens desto besser zuverstehen gebe, und versiegele" (Q. 66, ed. W. Niesel, *Bekenntnisschriften* . . . , p. 164).

12 *Credo*, p. 244.

13 Part III, art. 8, ed. J. T. Müller, *Die symbolischen Bücher* . . . , p. 321.

14 Barth draws the logical conclusion from the principle set forth when he declared: "Das ist es, was von der Ordnung der Taufe zu sagen ist: Sie ruft nach

Wiederherstellung. Was sie verlangt, ist sehr schlicht: an Stelle der jetzigen Kindertaufe eine auch auf Seiten des Täuflings verantwortliche Taufe" (*Die kirchliche Lehre von der Taufe*, p. 40). Apart from Catholic sacramentology, it is, in fact, impossible to give a satisfactory explanation for infant baptism.

15 In the very act of adopting the Schmalkaldic viewpoint, Harnack clearly perceived the contradiction between its teaching and the doctrine of infant baptism. In 1876, in a letter to Mme. von Anrep, he wrote: "Die Sakramente sind von Christus für seine Gemeinde eingesetzte Handlungen, die für denjenigen, der sie gläubig braucht und hinnimmt, die Gnade Gottes und Vergebung der Sünden versichern sollen, nicht anders, wie das Wort selbst. . . . Zur Verteidigung freilich der Kindertaufe, wenigstens ihrer Notwendigkeit und Heilsamkeit schon für das nicht denkende und nicht glaubende Kind, verfüge ich über keine Theorien" (Letter cited by A. von Zahn-Harnack, *Adolf von Harnack*, p. 97).

16 Cf. KD, vol. I, 1, p. 72.

17 *Credo*, p. 244.

18 In the following passage Barth summarizes his stand: "Also nicht das Sakrament allein, und wenn man exakt reden will, auch nicht einfach zweispurig: die Predigt und das Sakrament, sondern: die Predigt mit dem Sakrament, mit dem ihre menschliche Rede als göttliches Werk bestätigenden sichtbaren Handeln ist das konstitutive Element, die anschauliche Mitte des Lebens der Kirche" (KD, vol. I, 1, p. 71).

19 KD, vol. I, 1, pp. 56–57.

20 KD, vol. I, 1, pp. 59–60.

21 Chapter VII in its entirety was devoted to this question.

22 Cf. KD, vol. I, 1, pp. 79–80. This will necessarily bestow on dogmatics an academic character.

23 "Eine kirchliche Konfession ist eine auf Grund gemeinsamer Beratung und Entschliessung zustande gekommene Formulierung und Proklamation der der Kirche in bestimmtem Umkreise gegebenen Einsicht in die von der Schrift bezeugten Offenbarung" (KD, vol. I, 2, p. 693).

24 "Was die Konfession formuliert und proklamiert, das erhebt den Anspruch kirchliches Dogma zu sein" (KD, vol. I, 2, p. 699).

25 "Das konkrete Dogma (ist) nichts anderes als durch die Kirche geprüftes, vorläufig bereinigtes, auf eine bestimmte 'rechte' Formal gebrachtes *Kerygma*" (KD, vol. I, 1, p. 84).

26 Cf. KD, vol. I, 1, p. 15.

27 Council of Trent, session IV, April 8, 1546, *Denzinger*, 783.

28 "Pari pietatis affectu ac reverentia" (*ibid.*).

29 Since we are considering solely the case of truths defined *as revealed*, there is no need for us to adopt a position on the possible existence of an ecclesiastical faith distinct from divine faith. The object of such a faith would be truths irrevocably defined, but not, however, defined as revealed: "infallible truths" and "dogmatic facts." A number of competent theologians refuse to make a distinction between ecclesiastical faith and divine faith. Cf. Ch. Journet, *L'Église du Verbe incarné*, p. 412 (English trans., *The Church of the Incarnate Word*).

30 Cf. KD, vol. I, 2, p. 725.

31 *Credo,* p. 227.

32 Cf. KD, vol. I, 2, pp. 727–728.

33 *Credo,* p. 226.

34 KD, vol. I, 2, p. 737.

35 *Confession de foy,* art. 5, ed. W. Niesel, *Bekenntnisschriften* . . . , p. 67.

36 *Confessio scotica,* introduction, ed. W. Niesel, *Bekenntnisschriften* . . . , p. 85.

37 *Inst. chrét.,* IV, 9, 13, CR, vol. 4, col. 754 and 756.

38 "Ad has rationes paulo ante monstratas omnis doctrina in religionis negotio conformanda est, et, si quid iis contrarium esse deprehenditur, id rejiciendum atque damnandum est, quippe quod cum unanimi fidei nostrae declaratione pugnet" (*Formula Concordiae,* I pars, introd., ed. J. T. Müller, *Die symbolischen Bücher* . . . , p. 518).

39 Cf. J. T. Müller, *Die symbolischen Bücher* . . . , p. 569.

40 Cf. KD, vol. I, 2, p. 738.

41 Cf. KD, vol. I, 2, p. 739.

42 *Les grandes conférences œcuméniques,* pp. 210–211.

43 *Les premières confessions de foi chrétiennes,* p. 7.

44 *Op. cit.,* p. 8.

45 *Op. cit.,* p. 9, note 9.

46 Cf. A. Michel, DTC, vol. XV, col. 1315.

47 Cf. KD, vol. I, 2, pp. 606–637.

48 Barth gave a definition of Catholic tradition: "Als göttliche Offenbarung qualifiziertes Moment des kirchlichen Lebens" (KD, vol. I, 2, p. 607).

49 The reader will have noticed that we are using the word "tradition" in its objective sense (the meaning which it has in the Council of Trent), and not in its active sense. One of Cardinal Franzelin's major contributions to theology has been the introduction of this distinction. Revelation, the sole norm of faith, has been handed down in two ways: through the written word and the living voice. In a less proper sense, we can speak then of two sources of faith: Scripture and tradition. (Cf. the remarks of the Vatican Council on this subject, in *Denzinger,* 1792.) This tradition, composed of teachings transmitted in an oral manner, the theologians refer to as *objective tradition* or *tradition.*—The word "tradition" can also be considered in its *active* sense; then it designates the transmission of truths or precepts. In this sense it becomes formally identical with the actual teaching of the Church and consequently, with its infallible teaching authority. This active tradition is the "sole immediate norm" of faith. Objective tradition, therefore, is the object of active tradition; it is a remote rule of faith, whereas active tradition is the immediate norm. Cf. A. Michel, DTC, vol. XV, col. 1347.

# part four

*The Value of Barth's Principles*

*and Their Immediate Origin*

# 11

# barth's principles
# and their consequences

A$^{\text{T}}$ THE end of this exposition we must give a résumé of its conclusions. The following pages are intended simply to highlight the results which we believe we have reached in as brief a summary as possible.

## A. The Three Principles of Barthism and Their Logical Consequences.

1. *The actual and discontinuous character of the manifestation of the Word.* The Divine Word—an expression which groups together all the redemptive actions of God: revelation, grace, justification, election, predestination, and the Church—is not distinct from God Himself. It is God Who speaks. The Divine Word is God speaking to humanity, an expression identical with the Divine Substance, which never results in an effect that is separate from it. Similar to grace, revelation is also composed of contacts with the divine which appear as often and as long as God takes an interest in us.

Yet an important though implied point is that an anthropomorphic viewpoint allows the supposition that the liberty of God does not manifest itself, as in Thomistic theology, by effects which were decreed *ab aeterno,* but by successive will-acts which are directed to such and such an object or to such and such a person. When God is interested in a human being, it is not in order to continually sustain him by God's own uncreated action, but rather to raise him today and allow him to fall back again tomorrow. The sovereign divine liberty, as Barth conceives it, seems to demand this effect.

The personalism of the Word, therefore, leads to an actualism that is opposed by that very fact to all continuity. No gift is given to man or to humanity. God does not conserve revelation and grace; he always recreates them. It follows that Barth is unable to give a satisfactory explanation of God's created work. He is obliged to deny it proper consistency and to make of it a symbol and sign of the only authentic realities, namely, the intermittent accomplishments of the Word of God.

2. *The essentially mysterious character of the Word of God.* Can these sudden intrusions, such as the first principle has called to mind, be seen by intelligence or by human experience in certain momentary illuminations? Not at all. Sin has destroyed the last hope of entering into conscious contact with God. Sin, without lessening human nature, has totally secularized it. Man has lost the faculty for hearing the Word of God. The will is incapable of doing good; furthermore, intelligence and human experience are faced with the *radical* impossibility of understanding the Word of God. Human nature is nothing before the advent of the Word.

From these two first principles we can deduce the absolute negation of all direct knowledge of the Word of God or of revelation. Without a faculty for understanding revelation before the advent of the Word, human nature remains just as impoverished after its advent. Revelation does not bring it any possibility of hearing it. All direct knowledge, whether conceptual and clear (faith and reason in Catholic theology) or experimental and ineffable (Schleiermacher and the adherents of Protestant mysticism), is, consequently, excluded.

Barth, therefore, eliminates *analogical knowledge*. According to his theory, this knowledge would be reducible to direct knowledge and founded on the potentialities left in human nature by God, both in theodicy and in the apprehension of revelation properly so-called. The Bible, itself, no longer expresses the Word of God, because, first of all, it is situated in continuity while the Word of God is intermittent, and secondly, especially because the

Word of God is absolutely mysterious to human understanding. The Bible is a human word, necessary, fallible, and practically speaking, vitiated by errors.

3. *Credo quia absurdum.* The true coming of faith is not an act which we place, but is rather that divine, unexpected and mysterious touch, which the first two principles have described. Faith is not an act of man who knows God, but an act of God Who knows man, without man's awareness that he is or has been the object of Divine Knowledge.[1] It is like an ultra-sonic sound which really reaches us, but which our ear cannot hear.

Man, hence, is incapable of positing the act of faith. At this point, fideism enters. Man chooses to believe; he decides to believe. While the appearances may perhaps militate against faith and the Bible presents itself as a purely human document about a tribal religion of the Near East, and while Christ appears as a rabbi of a rather ordinary kind, man runs the risk of believing. This moment of trust (*fiducia*) is essentially a leap into an absolute void. Man entrusts himself to a God whose existence nothing can prove and about whom no document of revelation presents the slightest intrinsic guarantee of truthfulness.[2] It is a gesture of pure despair without any counterpart, which never terminates in an interior certitude or in the testimony of the Spirit. The risk remains pure risk; the despair remains despair. *Credo quia absurdum.*

This trust (*fiducia*) is at the root of *indirect knowldege.* Man turns himself anew to the Bible and decides to see there evidence of the Word of God. But the evidence does not unveil itself. In this gesture of trust, the believer runs the risk of recognizing the veil which hides the reality. The study of the Bible, whose opacity cannot be pierced even for an instant, is the indirect knowledge on which Barth's theology is based.

Dogma ought to be a continuous fidelity to this indirect knowledge. Preaching has but one function: to repeat in today's idiom what is contained in the Bible, the provisional criterion of all Christian activity. Transposition is not possible, however, save insofar as the preacher uses a key, which will be a philosophy or a more or less coherent set of principles borrowed from several philosophies. Certainly, by so doing the preacher falsifies the evangelical message, but it is impossible to do otherwise in this necessary transposition. Here the theologian should intervene. His role is to reduce to a minimum the human contribution needed to express the Word of God in contemporary language. His constant care should be a ceaseless correction of the preaching of the Word and preparation thereby for a more pure and faithful expression.

## B. Theological Methodology.

Barthism is based, therefore, on an option and on a postulate which is not only indemonstrable but irrational as well. To what is this opinion bound? What is the content of the postulate? Through trust (*fiducia*) the Christian picks up again the Bible which his reason has rejected. He gives it a decisive value and attributes to it the prerogative of being the normal place for the sudden and mysterious advent of the Word of God. *Fiducia* persuades the Christian that, among all institutions and human documents, the Bible enjoys a certain preference in the eyes of God. Thus, the Church, from the faithful to the theologian, should restrict itself to studying and repeating this message, which will not, however, enlighten the understanding. The Bible is no longer a means of knowledge, a way that permits the understanding to perceive in human terms a little of the divine reality; it is only a place, an *occasion*. Consequently, it seems that one could define Barthian methodology as the theory of that privileged stage where a believer has a right to hope for the free and sovereign intervention of the Word of God.

## C. The Two Planes.

In the last analysis everything is situated on two planes: that of divine action and that of human action. God in his sovereign liberty can by "vertical interventions" play a real, but hidden, role on the human plane; but man cannot even raise his head; he is caught in the grips of a horizontal continuity. God is found in the order of truth; He makes truth. Man is found in the order of obedience. Within the limits of trust, he has discerned the order to conform himself to a Scripture which does not contain the truth but which could become truth.

Everything "supernatural" is carried out on two levels: there is the Word of God and the testimony of this Word in the Bible; there is the true criterion of dogmatics and the human criterion; there is the true Church and the apparent Church; there is true faith and *fiducia,* the human risk; there is the direct knowledge by which God knows man and the indirect knowledge by which man works hard to know the veil that separates him from God.

## D. Agnosticism and Fideism.

Are we faced here with an impasse? This theory of "knowledge" replaces the object with a screen and substitutes obedience for truth. The whole New Testament concept of the knowledge of God, so well summed up in the verse of St. John: "Eternal life is knowing thee, who art the only true God, and Jesus Christ, whom thou hast sent" (John 17:3)—this whole concept is compromised here. Is the revelation of Barth different from "non-revelation"? Is theology in the traditional sense still possible under such conditions? In brief, we are forced to summarize the results of our investigation in the following fashion: the methodology of Barth is founded on an agnosticism which he tries vainly to escape by fideism.[3]

## E. The Sources of Barth's Thought.

What were the sources of Barth's thought? He will reply: the Bible. A thinker in the Reformation tradition, the theologian of Basel does not wish to recognize any but a single foundation for his theology: the inspired text. This is the sole possible norm of all human action in the actual state of affairs. To be sure, the Bible does tell us of the antithesis between God and creature, Divine Holiness and sin. This essential distinction, however, is not the exclusive dualism of Barth; it is not a rupture.

By stressing this fundamental dualism, has not Barth dangerously exposed his very theological methodology? By a paradoxical reversal, ought we not to say that his violent dualism caused the existence of this? An agnosticism which frees itself from the Barthian antithesis would be founded on the Bible. But does the Bible escape agnosticism? Is it an absolutely indubitable and certain norm on which to build despite any methodology, even that of Barth? Not at all. Scripture, the work of man, is ambiguous and thus is itself condemned; it is not a rule of truth. Such is the judgment passed by Barth. Where are we consequently? Has not the entire ensemble of value-judgments been compromised by the absence of solid foundations? [4]

The Bible presents matters quite otherwise. Barth has hardened its positions. On this point he was influenced more than he would have no doubt desired by non-biblical thought. An entire philosophical attitude orients and modifies his theological vision of the universe and God; Barth has not escaped his times. From what philosophical basis did Barth derive his dualism? This last point remains to be clarified.

# notes
## to chapter eleven

1 To illustrate these conclusions, we would like to cite several passages from contemporary philosophers who, though they took as their point of departure principles often quite different from ours, were compelled to admit the same conclusions. Consider the view of Maurice Blondel regarding Barth's *Analogia fidei*: "Can a faith which makes itself known without being known call upon, as a witness for its defense—be it ever so slight a call—a tradition which from its very origin has extolled and followed the Light which enlightens every man who comes into the world?" (*Bull. de la soc. franç. de phil.*, 1933, vol. XXXIII, p. 220).

2 Is it worth noting that Barth's system can include not even the least apologetic? Apologetic and fideism are irreconcilable contraries.

3 "I feel the same impression that G. Marcel described for us recently: you think you can settle down on the fifth floor of a building whose first four floors have disappeared" (Léon Brunschvicg, *Bull. de la soc. franç. de phil.*, 1933, vol. XXXIII, p. 207).

4 "It seems to me that this idea of Barth's is guilty of a kind of semi-conscious usurpation . . . ; for in some way it arrogates to itself as Barthian thought, some of the privileges which it attributes to the Word of God. In other words, it sets itself up as an absolute. On this point, nevertheless, we have a right to register a firm protest . . ." (Gabriel Marcel, *ibid.*, p. 200).

# 12

# the principal source of barth's thought: sören kierkegaard

THE QUESTION of the sources of an author's thought is always a complex problem. So many influences determine the progressive formation of a system that it is impossible to highlight them all. The task is probably just as difficult for the author himself. Hence, in this study of the sources of Barth's thought, we shall restrict ourselves to its fundamental position and principles underlying his system. The fundamental postulate, which we summarized in the preceding chapter in three principles, is a dualism which places God, transcendence, and absolute liberty in opposition to the creature, man, and sin. To whom does Barth owe this dualism?

## A. The Problem of Citations in the Recent Work of Barth.

Until 1927, Barth did not hesitate to admit all that he owed to Sören Kierkegaard, the Danish theologian, philosopher, and poet. At the beginning of the second edition of the *Römerbrief*, he says quite plainly: "If I have a system, it consists in having kept continually before my eyes what Kierkegaard calls the infinitely qualitative difference between time and eternity, with its full positive and negative significance. God is in heaven and you are on earth. The relationship of *this* God to *this* man and, conversely,

215

of *this* man to *this* God is for me the theme of the Bible and the summary of all philosophy." [1] In the preface to his *Christliche Dogmatik,* Barth recognizes that Kierkegaard is to be numbered among the theologians with whom he feels himself in agreement on a number of important points.[2]

Since then, the silence is complete; one no longer finds such avowals. In the four thousand pages of the *Kirchliche Dogmatik,* which have actually appeared, the name of Kierkegaard appears only six times. He is cited four times as a reference for a point of detail or within the scope of thought of another author. In only two instances does Barth adopt a definite position on his subject on important points, and each time it is to criticize him mercilessly.[3] Still more surprising is his attitude in a short autobiography, which appeared in 1945.[4] Barth carefully enumerates there those who have played a role in his own doctrinal formation. He does not cite Kierkegaard, while he does tell us about others of lesser importance. On this point he seems to have forgotten his past.

How can this change be explained? Barth realized eventually that his thought had taken a wrong turn. A penetrating study by Th. Siegfried, which appeared in 1930, greatly aided him no doubt in seeing this clearly. In a summary of various texts from the *Christliche Dogmatik,* the author concludes: "We know now in every case the decisive response of Barth to the question of the nature of theological thought: it is an existential thought. . . . It is on this foundation that Barth endeavors to construct his dogmatics." [5] Barth becomes aware of what he has done and subjects himself to a *Selbstkritik* in the first half-volume of his *Kirchliche Dogmatik.*[6] He sees that it is difficult to exonerate himself; his language accuses him, since it apparently favors the notion that we can base a theology of the Word on the study of the concrete circumstances of the preacher or of the believer, briefly on anthropology. He takes great pains thus to demonstrate that such was not his intention and that no one can in any way conceive of the Word of God as a "predicate" of man.[7]

Has Barth, then, abandoned Kierkegaard since 1932? No, that would have been impossible. In his *Römerbrief,* Karl Barth accepted the individualism of Kierkegaard along with his dualism. He could not rid himself of the latter notion. But he would in great measure throw individualism overboard. Any suggestion that it was possible to derive the Word of God from the study of the human drama would be abandoned. Barth would consider, moreover, this individualism as residue of pietism and, characterizing it as secular individualism, would not hesitate to put Kierkegaard on the same footing as other individualists such as J. J. Rousseau, the young Schleiermacher, Max Stirner, Ibsen, and Nietzsche.[8]

Barth was inevitably led to this choice. Individualism and dualism are contradictions in Kierkegaard's thought.[9] All followers of the Danish thinker were driven sooner or later to the same choice. Although he retains the dualism of Kierkegaard—to abandon it would be equivalent to abandoning his own theology—the theologian of Basle prefers to pass over in silence its doctrinal parent and not risk the accusation of placing philosophy at the basis of his theology. For, as we shall show, Kierkegaard's dualism, exaggerating biblical dualism, is clearly of philosophical origin.

## B. Karl Barth before Barthism.

One will not understand Barth's reaction, unless some account is taken of the doctrine which he believed himself obliged to oppose. Karl Barth does not owe his stand to influences on him during his university formation. While he has retained much, it was not his decisive impression. The first work that gives evidence of his revolutionary evolution is a conference given in 1916. At that time Barth was thirty years old and had been in the pastoral ministry for seven years. He was pastor at Safenwil (Argovie, Switzerland) where he was destined to remain until 1921. Before his appointment, he had resided for two years in Geneva as suffragan pastor of the German-speaking community of the National Church.[10]

What was Barth before the advent of Barthism? "I belonged to liberalism and I knew its attractions." [11] Thus, he himself sums up this period of his life. After he completed his university studies at Berne, Barth returned to Berlin, where he became in his own words, "an enthusiastic disciple of Harnack." At Tübingen, where he went next, he was unable to discover any point of contact with A. Schlatter, the orthodox theologian,[12] although he conceived a passion for F. Kleiner's course in ecclesiastical law. He finally ended his cycle at Marbourg under W. Herrmann, W. Heitmüller,[13] and A. Jülicher. By the time he finished his studies, therefore, Barth had broken with the orthodoxy still represented by his father and grandfather, both of whom were pastors.

He had become a determined disciple of the modern school for whom Christianity was, "according to the orientation given it by Schleiermacher and Ritschl, a phenomenon to be studied by critical methods and a matter of personal experience with pronounced moral tendencies." [14] A sign of the conviction which Barth at that time felt in the service of liberalism was his nomination as consulting editor of the *Christliche Welt,* the official organ of liberalism, edited by Martin Rade, an intimate friend of Harnack. Appointed in the autumn of 1908, Barth was destined to fulfil this role for several years until his appointment to Geneva.

During the first years of his pastoral ministry, Barth recklessly devoted himself to the theory and practice of socialism. The impotence of German social-democracy in 1914 must have deceived him and caused him steadily to abandon this activity. He describes the causes of direct influence in his doctrinal evolution which was to result in the *Römerbrief* of 1918. Socialism and liberalism had both led him to an impasse. The latter theory particularly seemed incompatible with the charge he had accepted of preaching the Word of God. Could he sincerely retain his liberalism and explain the Bible as was necessary according to the expectations of the faithful? In a conference given in 1922, Barth explains his position on this point:

Independent of my theological formation, I have always been impelled quite forcefully by all sorts of circumstances to occupy myself with the primary pastoral problem: preaching. I was always seeking . . . to open a path between the problems of human life and the content of the Bible. As a pastor, I had to speak to men at grips with the unparalleled contradictions of life, while I preached the not less unparalleled message of the Bible, which presented itself as a new enigma in the face of life's own contradictions. . . . Can theology do anything more than express the insoluble situation and the unanswered question of the pastor? Can it do anything but describe as truthfully as possible the embarrassment in which a person places himself who dares to approach this task? Can theology be anything more than a cry springing out of a great distress, a hope of salvation? [15]

The curve—brought about by the failure of both liberalism and socialism—which Barth's thought traced at this time was termed by him a return "without prejudice" to the Bible. Contact with the thought of the two Christophers Blumhardt (father and son, to whom Edward Thurneysen introduced him) and his personal relations with Herrmann Kutter, pastor of Zurich, led him to turn his mind in this direction. Not a word is said here of Sören Kierkegaard, who played, nonetheless, a decisive role in his evolution. [16]

Before Barthism, therefore, Barth was influenced by the twofold current of liberalism: the historical current represented during his university years by Harnack and Jülicher, and the systematic current of Wilhelm Herrmann. We have already dealt with the first in the chapter on Barth's exegesis. We must now treat of the second and more important influence.

## C. Wilhelm Herrmann, Disciple of Albert Ritschl.

Certain authors are self-explanatory: they elaborate an entire, homogeneous system. Others are content to develop or modify the thought organized by a predecessor. Wilhelm Herrmann belongs to this second category. He took over the thought of Ritschl and corrected it wherever he thought it to be defective. We must, therefore, speak first of Ritschl before we treat of his commentator, who was the immediate master of Karl Barth at Marbourg. [17]

Better than anyone else, Albert Ritschl discerned the danger of Schleiermacher's thought, exposed as it was to the arbitrariness of an unbridled subjectivism. Thus the central principle of his system consists in the negation of every possibility of immediate contact with God. The only real knowledge of God must lie in positive religions; the only revelation consists in the history of a definite religion. A. Ritschl excludes consequently, once and for all, all supposed, immediate relations with God. Neither rational knowledge nor experimental knowledge find favor in his eyes. The sole source of religious knowledge is historical revelation.[18]

If this assertion be true, it equivalently states that, in the case of Christianity, the sole source of religious knowledge is Christ. Ritschl's system is clearly Christocentric. Christ is the Revealer above all; He is in Himself the revelation of God. Since the personality and life of Christ have exerted a decisive influence on Christian life, it is of primary importance to know who Christ is.

In Ritschl's eyes, Christ appears as the *sittlich-religiöse Persönlichkeit,* a personality at once moral and religious. Without scorning it, Ritschl does not interest himself in the "marvelous" side of Christ's life: the virgin birth, the miracles, the resurrection —these do not interest him. The emphasis, moreover, should not be placed on Christ's death, but rather on his whole life, which was spent in God's service for the establishment of the kingdom on earth. Divinity, thus, no longer consists in a metaphysically divine personality, but in the moral and religious activity by which Christ proves his complete communion with God and his sovereign liberty with respect to natural life. The metaphysical divinity of God is hence transformed into an ethical divinity. Christ appears to men as the acme of religious and moral activity.

His person thus becomes the norm of Christian life. Christian perfection, like the perfection of Jesus, is at one and the same time, both religious and moral. It is religious because the Christian gains a consciousness of his liberty, despite the trials and obstacles of natural life, through the interior conviction of being a child of God and under the care of His Providence. It is likewise moral because the Christian permits himself in each of his actions towards his neighbor to be guided by a free and spontaneous love, which he deems an effect of the very grace of God. And in this way he realizes the reign of God.

One of the most sympathetic characteristics of Ritschl's conception of Christianity is surely its personalism. The Christian only comes in contact with happiness when he has achieved a resolution of the tension within himself between consciousness of his individuality and of his situation in the heart of nature. On the one hand, he feels and knows himself independent and separated from nature; yet, on the other hand, he sees himself an element of that very nature and subject to it in its entirety. The religious instinct, the satisfaction which alone can bring happiness, waits for a solution to the conflict. The certitude of having a God Who keeps watch over him and directs him results in the suppression of the fear, which tests the Christian, of being absorbed into the life of nature.[19]

At a time when the development of the experimental sciences tended to integrate man into their determinism, Ritschl's theology could restore to man a confidence in himself and an awareness of his superiority. This theory, nonetheless, exposes its flank to serious attack. Religion, since its supernatural content is not considered, does not fit such a system. It becomes an instrument of self-value and consciousness of self. It is but the intensification of a value immanent in this world.[20] One can see already how these theories are vulnerable to the attacks of dialectical theology and to those of its own dualism.

The weakest point of Ritschl's synthesis is the relation he constructed or rather failed to construct—between faith and history. Faith, let us admit, ought henceforth to concern itself with historical revelation, principally New Testament writings. In the orthodox view, these writings obtained an absolute value thanks to the nowadays-abandoned dogma of inspiration. The writings on which faith ought to concentrate its attention are no longer divine documents but purely human ones, which escape none of the relativisms of history. Christ Himself, the subject of these documents, is swept away in the same stream. At the heart of the Protestant tradition, the idea of faith is indissolubly linked with that of subjective certitude, with absolute confidence, *Glaubensgewissheit.* The notion of history, as the rationalism of the end of the last century conceived it, is linked to research, to provisional results, to hypotheses always subject to possible revision. A faith, essentially certain, makes use, then, of an instrument which is essentially uncertain: the fact that faith is founded on history and does not transcend it led Ritschl into contradiction. Faith flounders in relativism.

This last point of his master Wilhelm Herrmann particularly intends to correct. While he accepts the Christian life as personalism seeking escape from the determinism of nature, and while he adopts the historical Christocentrism of Ritschl, Herrmann clearly detected the deficiences of the system with respect to faith and revelation.[21] According to Herrmann, revelation does not simply consist in the facts of revelation; these facts count for nothing, insofar as they are not accepted by faith.[22] The commentator on Ritschl thus re-introduces an element of experience into theology. He does not, however, go back to Schleiermacher's position. This experiential element is not a direct nor mystical communication with God; its awakening depends on the presentation of the facts of revelation. The history of the events of the New Testament, then, is not revelation; neither again is the personal experience; it is only their conjunction that constitutes revelation properly so-called. On this question Herrmann maintains a middle position between Schleiermacher and Ritschl. From the former, he revives the experimental character of the religious fact; from the latter, he retains the mediation of history. God reaches us only in the likeness of Christ.

How does this doctrine differ from historical relativism? How will this experience of faith escape the provisional character of history? Herrmann lets go of everything that history discusses:

> Learning to perceive Christ is the way of salvation for a Christian. It is useless to proceed in this direction, if we merely follow the account of the New Testament and teach them that Jesus was born of a virgin, that he taught this or that, that he worked miracles and raised the dead to life, and that, finally, he himself arose from the dead and after his ascension to his Father, reigns all powerfully. Such a tale, though presented to make an impression, is not the Gospel . . . , for such a teaching is an obstacle to our age: the majority of men, in effect, can no longer accept these things with the guilelessness of children.[23]

But aside from those facts which are left to the study of historians, two traits of Christ's personality escape relativism: the personal conviction of God's goodness (*Messiasbewusstein*) and moral perfection. This latter trait consists in a synthesis of moral strictness linked to gentleness and unbounded goodness. These two traits constitute the interior Christ (*das innere Leben Jesu*) and escape from all "historicism" because they are supratemporal and suprahistorical. When in our distress and our desire for a truly personal life we commune with ourselves before the image of Christ, Jesus becomes so immediately present and tangible to us that religious conviction is released within us and all doubt about the historicity of His person vanishes,[24] like a causality emanating from Christ which is translated within us into an intense religious experience.[25]

*Theoretically,* the advantage of this position over the preceding one of Ritschl is quite clear. By disengaging the two traits in the personality of Christ which elude history, Christ is contemporaneous with us, and certitude is restored to faith. But is not this theory arbitrary? Is there truly a way of isolating just two traits without considering the others? Can the Messianic consciousness of Christ and His moral perfection be separated from the mass of other facts and teachings that Herrmann has disposed of by omission and which, moreover, pertain to the very thread of the evangelical history. And what is more, while one apparently escapes relativism, it is only to plunge the more into psychologism. Revelation becomes revelation only when it encounters a consciousness which is alert. Is there not a risk that this consciousness will become the measure of revelation? [26] In fact, is not this the result of Herrmann's theory? Revelation is not thrust upon an obedient mind from without. Rather the contrary takes place: revelation must be sifted by the mind which allows passage only to what it judges good.[27]

## D. The Anti-Hegelianism of Kierkegaard.

If Barth directly adopts the attitude of Kierkegaard, it is because he finds an echo of a resentment akin to his own. Save for a century separating them, the Danish thinker and the Swiss theologian are in accord because they are both *anti*. The anti-Hegelianism of the former fits in so neatly with the anti-liberalism of the latter that these two representatives of pronounced transcendentalism find themselves before long one in thought. Barth will turn against the tendency of Schleiermacher, Ritschl, and Herrmann the weapon of war forged by Kierkegaard against the monism of Hegel.

In Kierkegaard's time, Hegel was the outstanding thinker. The

young Dane was eighteen when he began his university studies
in 1831, the year in which the German philosopher died. At that
period, Hegelianism was at the peak of its glory. One could say
that it dominated philosophical thought in Germany and in the
countries under German cultural influence from 1820 to 1840.
Kierkegaard could not avoid Hegel. He had to meet his system
and either adopt or contest it. His own, very personalistic thought
chose the latter.

Hegel is not well understood save in his historical context. He
came after Kant and undertook to exploit and elaborate quite
thoroughly his fundamental tendencies.[28] He retains particularly
the "autocracy of thought" of the philosopher of Königsberg. For
Kant thought was a kind of absolute.[29] Its authority cannot be
submissive to any foreign element, i.e., to that of the object; all
authority comes from the exercise of intelligence. Thus thought
attains clear independence with respect to whatever is outside
of it. Autonomy of thought, however—and this now is Hegel's
criticism—can easily degenerate into subjectivism. The life of
thought is extremely limited in those perspectives to individual
certitude. For thought is not everything; there is always something more than itself. At the basis of the Kantian system we find
a duality of thought and matter, of thought and object, of thought
and being. Hegel will attempt to reduce this dualism, the cause of
subjectivism, to a common denominator. Hegel's preoccupation
was to guarantee the autonomy of thought, which notion he
owes to Kant, by supporting it and setting it on solid foundations. It is necessary first to overcome the duality of thought and
being. Aristotelianism resolved the problem by submitting
thought to being. Hegel will, on the contrary, absorb being into
thought. "The last end and whole interest of philosophy consists in the reconciliation of thought and concept with reality." [30]
This reconciliation is possible because thought penetrates the
whole of reality. After identifying the two poles that constitute
the Kantian dualism, Hegel then proposes the fundamental postulate of his own system: unity. Philosophy in his mind has no
other role than the study of the question of unity.

Everything is mind: God, nature, reason, will, history, art,
philosophy—all are mind. And, on the other hand, everything is

one. "The absolute is mind; such is the most perfect definition of the absolute." [31] The theme of Hegelian thought will be, therefore, the development of the Absolute Mind (*die Selbstentfaltung des absoluten Geistes*). Unity, which is at once the unity of reality and the unity of thought, is called by Hegel the *system*. It is the complete whole that takes in everything that is. This unity must be understood in a very homogeneous manner. The system is not a sum of disparate unities which would form a unity of aggregation by their collection; it is not a unity such as the inhabitants of a city form by their community. No, it is a unity which remains within itself, which is through itself. Only the whole is reality; only the whole is truth.[32]

This homogeneous whole is not, however, a solidified and dead block. On the contrary, it is all in motion. There is no static state of being. Reality is motion and becoming.[33] But how is one to conceive motion? As the linear movement of a rectilinear progression? No, for that conception would not be compatible with the notion of a *closed* whole. Hegel's system has nothing in common with the idea of an expanding universe. It is a question of circular movement, where what is last is also first, where what is first is also last.[34] The whole is not, moreover, only the outer shell containing the motion; it is the motion itself whose rhythm is distinguished by three periods: thesis, antithesis, and synthesis. The movement which is always present in this triadic form Hegel calls the dialectical movement. The motive force of this dialectic is the opposition between thesis and antithesis.

To suppose that contradiction does not merit the label of a determination of being is a prejudice. If one were forced to choose one of these concepts, it would be necessary, Hegel says, to decide in favor of the first. Identity is the form of dead being; contradiction is the condition of living being and the source of all movement and life.[35] Contradiction, however, is not an end in itself; rather it sets in motion the movement towards unity. From the contradiction of thesis–antithesis, there follows a progression towards synthesis. A good example of this dialectical movement is found in the problem of being. It is impossible to conceive of pure being without immediately thinking of the idea of total indetermination and void. The thought of being is thus com-

pletely bound up with that of non-being. I cannot think of one
without the other. Despite this relationship, being is not non-
being, but their unity is realized on a higher plane where being
passes into non-being.[36] The synthesis, then, is realized in becoming.

In order to designate at one and the same time the suppression
of duality and its assumption into a higher unity, Hegel makes
use of the verb *aufheben*. This verb in Hegel's vocabulary has
two meanings which seem contradictory. It signifies at the same
time to destroy and to conserve: *tollere* and *sustinere*. Being and
non-being are, in effect, both suppressed and conserved in becoming.[37] This synthesis contains the preceding stages but in a
state of mediation and not in their duality of thesis and antithesis.
The final end of reality and of philosophy is precisely this unity,
this monism of Mind.

The notion of an ideal and rational whole dominates, therefore,
Hegel's thought. The whole is the final unity, the only reality;
this whole is a whole of the spirit. The real movement, which
leads to it, is identified with the logical movement of mind. The
concept in its most formal aspect has become the content of
reality.[38] Being is only thought. What is rational is real; what is
real is rational. Ruttenbeck very well sums up the position of
Hegel by saying: "Rationality is the criterion of reality. That
only is real which lets itself be caught in the nets of thought,
and which is known as rational by reason." [39] In Hegel's system,
there is a perfect identity between rationality, reality, and ideal-
ity. A true philosophy can only be an idealistic one.[40]

In this rational whole and ideal monism the particular and
individual find no place. Thought denies the forms of the particular and produces only the general. If it stops to consider the
former, it does so after it has disengaged the particular from its
particular form and reduced it to the general. The singular is
not true except as multiplicity of the particular. This same judgment applies to the *self*. "The particular individual is the incomplete mind."[41] The only thing that interests the philosopher
is the individual as he is found in other individuals, that is, the
general individual, the common self. From that point, Hegel
sets out on a campaign against all forms of subjectivism. Com-

posed, as it is, of private opinions and personal convictions, it is fruitless.[42] It is necessary to pass beyond it and to raise one's self to a higher plane of objectivity. This objective point of view alone is philosophically defensible.

These principles of Hegelian philosophy allow us now to pass to his philosophy of religion. It is really only another aspect of the same philosophy. Hegel's philosophy is, in reality, a *Religionsphilosophie,* since its unique theme is the *Selbstentfaltung des absoluten Geistes*. Rosenkranz, one of Hegel's disciples, properly defined the philosophy of his master as a "continuous definition of God." [43]

Religion in its highest form is identical with philosophy. Faith and knowledge are one and the same thing. Hegel thus is unalterably opposed to Schleiermacher's idea which made sentiment the faculty of religious experience. If religion were only sentiment, it would fall back to the level of subjectivity and particularity, while Hegel wishes to stay on the level of rationality and generality. All believers, however, do not know how to raise themselves to this plane; they remain in an inferior form of religion which has not yet evolved into philosophy. Must one say then that these believers do not possess the truth? No, they do have it but in a pre-philosophical state. Religion and philosophy possess the same truth but in different forms: the first under the form of imagination, the second under the form of thought. [44] The religion of the imagination is thus presupposed by the religion of thought and is historically anterior to it. The progression moves from images to concepts; the religion of the imagination is *aufgehoben* (destroyed and conserved) in philosophy.

The identification of the idea of religion with philosophy leads to the pantheism of Hegel. The finite is but a stage of the infinite; so true is this that, when the finite person thinks of the religious problem, it is the infinite that thinks of it through him. One knows the celebrated definition of religion: *"Das Selbstbewusstein des absoluten Geistes."* It is God who is thinking in our minds. We are right in the middle of pantheistic monism. God is not separated from the world; He exists only insofar as He is in the world. Mind exists only insofar as it manifests and gives evidence of itself. The finite which we would wish to consider opposed to

the infinite is not the true finite. The finite is penetrated throughout by the infinite.[45] Under these conditions—need it be said?—
there is no place in Hegel's religious philosophy for the personality
of God.[46] God is not distinct from the whole.

The various Christian terms have in consequence been emptied
of their traditional meaning and filled with purely philosophical
notions. The historical person of Christ is of no interest to Hegel;
he is but the *idea* of the unity of finite and infinite. He shows us
that the finite and infinite are not incompatible.[47] All of Hegel's
philosophy becomes equally a philosophy of reconciliation (*Versöhnung*). Sin has no role to play in it. Christian reconciliation, as
Hegel conceives it, is accomplished by a conscious grasp of the
"superability" of the opposition which apparently separates the finite and the infinite. Salvation is consequently simply the development of a concept, a rational movement that owes nothing to a
superhuman intervention, a *Selbsterlösung:* man saves himself.
Christ does not intervene save as a *clause de style.* Hegel does
speak of a certain role for Christ, but without conviction. Human
reason would not have arrived at the idea of identity, without having before its eyes the sensible form of the synthesis realized in
Christ. But this point is of such little importance in Hegel's views
that one is obliged to consider it only an accommodation to the
received doctrine, a polite gesture to the thought of the Church.[48]

The *general* character of Hegel's philosophy appears most clearly
in his ethics. Hegel distinguishes *Moralität* and *Sittlichkeit*. *Moralität* belongs to that stage in which "what is demanded by the
categorical imperative is the morally good. Duty for duty's sake—
that is moral goodness." [49] But this Kantian morality, based on the
individual conscience, leads to subjectivism and cannot be the
ultimate norm of human activity. Individual conscience is re-
placed by the collective conscience, expressed in the *Sittlichkeit,*
whose content rests on the spirit of the society and which will find
its supreme realization in the State.

The norm of human activity is thus finally found in the State,
the incarnation of the "general." The State

will enjoy absolute autonomy. It recognizes nothing above its self in its
own sphere. Every dependence that would subject the State to individuals would destroy its very essence. For it is an end in itself, and indi-

viduals are but means to that end. Individuals develop in the moral order to the extent to which they are permeated by the spirit of the State, to the extent in which they become one with this spirit. It would be a serious error, thus, to look for the origin and establishment of the State in a contract among individuals, as liberalism supposes. To make the State arise from a social contract would be equivalent to making the universal come from the individual, which is a gross misunderstanding. According to Hegel, the universal does not come from the individual; to the contrary, the individual comes from the universal. No conflict of individual conscience, of opposition by the individual to the State, can thus arise. He must bow before the collective conscience, the public conscience and submerge himself in the State with all his being and activity as an individual. The moral life of the individual (*das moralische Leben*) is thus linked to the moral life of the State (*das sittliche Leben*), which is dependent on the objective spirit.[50]

Assuredly the crushing of the individual by the "general" is most clearly seen in this Hegelian concept of ethics.[51] One can consequently understand without difficulty the vigor of Kierkegaard's reaction against the Hegelian ethic.

Kierkegaard will reproach Hegel, not on certain secondary points, but on his fundamental position. He will have none of this pantheistic monism which dissolved God in the creature, nor this notion of the whole, of system, of the general, which has only contempt for the individual. "The work of Hegel," says Jean Wahl, "is the most powerful attempt ever made to give us a global philosophy, in which everything is explained by idea. Philosophical reflexion, through this essential dialectic, has been put by Kierkegaard in a way that extends beyond the global to rediscover the particular." [52] To the unilateralism of the whole, Kierkegaard will oppose the unilateralism of the singular and the self.

## E. Man before God, according to Kierkegaard.

Contrary to Hegel, the essence of Kierkegaard's thought can be summed up in the proposition: man is before God. The two members must be distinguished. There is no question of a synthesis, no monism of man and God. Far from it: man and God appear as two contraries without any possible mediation. Kierkegaard's thought is situated within the limits of a deep-seated dualism, irreducible to any synthesis. After we have thus rapidly described this opposition, we can go on to each of the extremes: man and God.

1. God is not on the same level as man. He is not even a summit towards which man can progressively raise himself. "If God were immediately related, even as an ideal, to humanity, it would be correct to desire to express this immediate resemblance. When a remarkable man is related to me as an ideal, it is normal on my part to desire to express this immediate resemblance. For from the fact that we are both men, we both live within the same sphere. But between God and a man . . . there is an absolute difference; the absolute relation of God to man should express this absolute difference, and direct resemblance becomes self-conceit, rudeness, and presumption." [53]

One can, as does Torsten Bohlin, explain this fundamental dualism by saying that the natural man ought to be considered as totally corrupt, and that everything which comes from God ought to appear paradoxical. Man in himself is non-truth; he is not merely indifferent to the truth; he is at war with truth. Everything which comes from above—revelation for example—thus runs counter to what already exists and forms with it that total opposition which Kierkegaard calls the paradox.[54] By this conflict, dualism is placed at the very center of Kierkegaard's thought; its elimination would cause its collapse: "One has reached his haven when, as the *alcedo ispida* (ice bird), one can build his nest on the sea." [55]

2. Man, who finds himself both close to and far away from God, is not the general individual of Hegel; on the contrary, it is the individual in that which is most personal, most inalienable, most incommunicable: "If I could wish for an inscription on my tomb, I would wish none other than: 'This individual.' " [56] It is an individualism to the extent that all Christianity is conceived as dependent on it: "Why do I make so much of this category of individuality? Simply because all of Christianity is embraced by it, and in it Christianity has still such a sway over men that, as soon as man is subjected to the eternal responsibility of individuality, he becomes a Christian. All the rest is merely medicine destined to prolong his sickness." [57] We can sum up this assertion by saying

that the Christian is essentially the exception. He cannot be reduced to a universal category.[58]

The individual, therefore, is not an element subordinated to the community. Kierkegaard puts the individual in opposition to everything which is mass, number, aggregation, public—"Among animals, the individual is never more important than the species. . . . Among men, the individual is created in the image of God. The individual is more important than the race." [59] If Kierkegaard is so opposed to what could bring man to the level of a universal, it is because the idea of community destroys the essential element of individuality: responsibility before God. The individual is indeed responsible before God. Thus, by reason of this enlistment which introduces him into life, the individual is not a static, metaphysical category, but a dynamic, ethical one. "Ethics exerts its pressure on the individual immediately, by demanding that he exist ethically. It does not debate with millions of men or generations; it does not take humanity as a heap, any more than the police arrest humanity at large. The ethical is concerned with particular human beings, and—note this well—with each as an individual by himself." [60]

After having defined the individual negatively, in terms of what he is not, and having outlined his essential dynamism, we must describe, insofar as it can be done, the content of this mysterious individuality. Kierkegaard sums it up in one word: existence, which is, itself, defined as "interior silence before God." [61] "The misfortune of our age is that it has too much knowledge and has forgotten what it means to exist, and what inwardness signifies."[62] Existential inwardness is a profound study of one's self—Kierkegaard returns frequently to the Socratic catchword: "Know Thyself"—and a constant rebuilding of one's superstructure. "Through reflection, man descends into the almost fathomless sea of his soul. The more this investigation is prolonged to fathom the mystery of one's own intimate life . . . the better this becomes, because the soul becomes all the more profound." [63]

Kierkegaard's entire epistemology is based on existential inwardness. It can be summed up in the phrase: "Subjectivity is truth." [64] One can imagine how discreditable such an assertion would be to the Hegelian tradition. Hegel had rejected subjectivity as a shameful thing; he relegated it to the stage of pre-philosophy. For Hegel, thought is objective and cannot be otherwise. Kierkegaard reverses these categories and places subjectivity at the summit of epistemology. Subjective knowledge is a knowledge in which the individual has committed himself. The subject thinks himself by thinking of the object: "To understand what one is saying is one thing; to understand one's self in what one is saying is another thing." [65] Existential reflection, then, is inseparable from a *persönliche Interessiertheit*.

Kierkegaard explains his meaning at length in the *Postscriptum:*

The way of objective reflexion leads to abstract thought, to mathematics, to historical knowledge of every kind; it never ceases leading away from the subject, whose existence or non-existence from the objective viewpoint quite rightly becomes infinitely indifferent; quite rightly, I say, because existence and non-existence have, as Hamlet observes, only subjective significance.[66]

Objective thought, therefore, seems to Kierkegaard to lead only to pure forms, to some sort of detached essences of the real, because the entire question of existence and non-existence depends on subjectivity.

Subjective reflexion turns its attention inwardly towards the subject and wishes in this intensification of inwardness, to realize the truth; it proceeds in such a way that, just as in the proceeding objective reflection subjectivity disappeared to the advantage of objectivity, now on the contrary, subjectivity becomes the final stage, and objectivity disappears as a vanishing factor. In this case, a person does not forget for a single moment that the subject is an existing one.[67]

All right. But will not subjectivity dissolve into pure subjectivism? One must admit that certain passages expose their flank to such accusations:

On which side is there more truth . . . : on the side of one who seeks only objectively the true God and pursues the approximate truth of the God-idea, or from the side of one who, driven by the unlimited passion of his need of God, feels an infinite concern for his own relationship to God in truth? The reply cannot be in doubt for anyone who has not been demoralized with the aid of science. If one man, living in the midst of Christendom, enters the house of God, the house of the true God, with a true conception of God in his mind, and then prays, but not be in truth; and another man, living in an idolatrous community, prays with all the passion of the infinite, although his eye rest on the image of an idol—in which case is there more truth? One prays to God in truth, even though he worships an idol; the other prays to the true God, but not in truth, and hence he truly worships an idol.[68]

We have no intention of endeavoring to discover whether, through Kierkegaard's process of subjective thought, one can arrive at a true realism. The attempt seems to us, at the very least, quite doubtful. Let it suffice to point out that, for Kierkegaard, existentialism and realism are on an equal footing. The Danish thinker takes strict account of the judgment which might be passed on his manner of conceiving the problem of knowledge: "In a merely subjective determination of the truth, in the last analysis, madness and truth become indistinguishable since both of them may possess inwardness." [69] We must be careful in taking the author of the *Postscriptum* at his word. It is a question, above all, of a one-sided reaction against Hegelian intellectualism. For Kierkegaard, " . . . there is no question of a dilemma between the subjective or the objective in the apprehension of religious content of revealed truth. This is the question: should *emphasis* be placed on the doctrinal content as such, or on the personal assimilation of religious truth? What our age needs, without the shadow of a doubt, is a subjective thinker in this sense of the word." [70] In 1835, in a passage of his journal, he expresses himself in a more guarded manner: "It is a question of understanding my destination; I must find a truth which is true *for me.* . . . Most certainly, I do not wish to deny that I shall acknowledge an imperative in knowledge, and that in virtue of such an imperative men can be acted upon; *but it is necessary then that I imbibe it as a living being,* and that is now essential." [71] What Kierkegaard seeks is a truth which will be related to the most profound root of his existence. Truth cannot reside in some distant *aseitas;* it must have an intimate relation with the subject.

The knowing, existential ego is then a living individual. Now that which gives impetus to life is passion: "It is impossible to exist without passion, unless we understand the word 'exist' in the loose sense of a so-called existence." [72] Passion for an existing individual is precisely the very culmination of existence." [73] It is in the very tension of passion that existence and the ego become conscious.

In his description of existence, we must pass from the idea of passion to that of decision. When truth exercises its hold on an individual and elevates him to a state of impassioned enthusiasm, he must commit himself to an active enterprise. There must be an expression within him, an expression which will take the form of a decision: "It is said that when he went aboard the ship that carried the expedition to overthrow the tyrant, Dionysius was heard to comment that, even if he were to die enroute, he would still have performed a glorious deed." [74] But it would be wrong to suppose that an exterior decision would have greater value than an interior one. Such a proposition is ". . . worthy of contempt, worthy of a degenerate people, faint-hearted, and crafty and ignorant of the highest ideal. To suppose that the external action and not the interior decision could determine something for all eternity and make it irrevocable, while the internal decision is not thus decisive is to entertain a contempt for what is sacred." [75]

Kierkegaard's insistence on the importance of decision is a new manner of defending himself against frigid intellectualism and the universal: "To bestow on thought a supremacy over all else is characteristic of gnosticism." [76] Elsewhere Kierkegaard commented further: "Existence is a protest against pure thought." [77]

3. God's thought is revealed to the individual only in complete isolation. It is through subjectivity that a person finally attains the person of God: "Inwardness at its apex, giving further proof of the realistic *intention* of its thought, is again objectivity. And this is a presentation of the principle of subjectivity, of which I know no antecedent example." [78]

In the concept of God, he wishes to highlight one element: absolute divine transcendence. Here more than elsewhere, dialectical thought is dominated by dualism. God is above all sovereign, majestic, omniscient. He has the attributes which render Him "totally other." "God is not the kind heavenly Father, passing His time by listening to the wishes of His obedient children." [79] Kierkegaard goes further: he is of the opinion that God is so elevated above men that He becomes morally different from them. So much so that men are always wrong in relation to Him. God, so different from men, cannot help but direct to them an imperative language: *Thou must.*[80] Man is obliged to obey this order without any why or wherefore. There is no common standard of measure between divine wisdom and human sagacity; the infinitely qualitative difference finds its most satisfactory expression in silent adoration.

God cannot become the object of an intellectual certitude. His transcendence is opposed to it:

This is a result of the viewpoint adopted by Kierkegaard in his theory of knowledge. For example, if we consider nature to discover God, he remarks, we will find many things which bear witness to divine wisdom and omnipotence; but we will also discover much in nature which troubles and disconcerts us. We cannot, through this way, pass beyond probability.[81]

The attempt to prove God's existence, then, is a superfluous enterprise. Kierkegaard will go even further and designate it as sacrilege:

To prove the existence of one who is present is the most shameless affront, since it is an attempt to make him ridiculous. But the misfortune is that people have no inkling of this, and even seriously consider their undertaking a pious one. But how could it occur to anyone to prove that another exists, unless one has permitted himself to ignore his existence, and now to make matters worse, by an attempt to prove his existence before his very nose. The existence or presence of a king is commonly acknowledged by an appropriate expression of submission and subjection. What would one say if an attempt to prove his existence were to be made in the very presence of a king? Is that the way to prove it? That would be making a fool of him, for his existence is demonstrated by the expression of subjection and submission. . . . In the same way the existence of God is proved by worship —not by proof.[82]

According to Kierkegaard, we do not establish the truth of God's existence. We enter into immediate contact with Him: "If I am capable of grasping God objectively, I do not believe; but precisely because I cannot do so, I must believe. And if I wish to dwell in faith, I must always be vigilant in maintaining an objective uncertainty, in such a way that I find myself more than 70,000 leagues under the sea, still staunch in my faith." [83]

The aspect of the Christian God's transcendence is especially emphasized by Kierkegaard; but he is not alone in doing so. God is still love: "If, on some point or another, I have been mistaken, it remains nontheless true that God is love. I believe this, and one who believes it is not mistaken. If I am mistaken, this will certainly become evident to me, I am sorry to say . . . but God is love. We can say that He is love, He has been love, but not that He will be love; no, because the future would be too long for me to wait; He *is love*." [84] It is a very striking paradox that the thought of God's love sustained the Danish thinker during an entire lifetime devoted to accentuating the distance which separates God from man. "Love of God is the only form of contented love." [85] "The fact that God is love is, in the last analysis, the essential fact." [86] In spite of all the interest which Kierkegaard manifests in this benevolent aspect of the divine physiognomy, we must not forget that God is above all *erhaben*—transcendent and distant. Yet, one consideration does not abolish the other; God is at one and the same time a transcendent God and the God of love. Such is the paradox which no Hegelian dialectic can resolve.

## F. Kierkegaard's Major Themes.

The characteristics which we have disclosed in Kierkegaard's fundamental position reappear in each of the major themes of his thought. We must now dwell for a moment on a brief consideration of those principal themes which have influenced Barth's thought.

Thus we shall examine Kierkegaard's theological attitude towards each of the following problems: the *Moment,* revelation in Christ, contemporaneity, Sacred Scripture, and faith. Lest we falsify a system of thought extremely complex and full of nuances, we will present Kierkegaard's own words as much as possible, as we did in the preceding section and be content to present the texts in a logical order and to draw from them the conclusions which impose themselves.

1. The question of revelation is intimately linked with the theme of the *Moment*.[87] To what extent can the truth be learned? This is Kierkegaard's point of departure. We are dealing here with truth properly so-called, with the only truth of importance: divine and supernatural truth. Kierkegaard considers two possible replies to the question: the first is the Socratic hypothesis; the second, the Christian.

For Socrates, man possesses truth, but in a hidden manner. Revelation is nothing but the rediscovery of a treasure which for all practical purposes was unknown. All study, every inquiry is but a recall, "in such a manner that one who is ignorant needs only a reminder to help him become aware, through his own efforts, of what he knows. Truth is not conveyed to him; it was in him." [88] The role of the teacher in this *processus* of the discovery of truth consists in aiding his disciple to rediscover, through his own efforts, his own wealth. Thus Socrates compared himself to a mid-wife, whose role is not that of bearing the child, but of aiding others in their travail.

The teacher must not place himself above his disciple. If he has been of any use at the moment of the truth's delivery, he becomes superfluous thereafter. Our possession of truth does not depend on a continual transfusion coming from the teacher: "Whether the doctrine of Socrates or Prodicus was of this nature or that interests me only from an historical viewpoint; for the truth in which I rest was within me and came to light through myself; Socrates was no more capable of giving it to me than a coachman is of hauling the load for his horse, though he may help them haul it through a judicious application of his whip."[89]

The dualism which is at the base of all of Kierkegaard's thought forbids us from stopping at this first hypothesis. Confronted by transcendent truth, man is essentially in a state of error. In no sense is he the possessor of truth. The teacher cannot awaken the recollection of truth within him. The only thing that he can do is to awaken in the mind of the seeker a recollection that he is in error. A teacher who would wish to put his disciple in possession of the truth would have to be able not only to give the truth, but also to provide him with the condition necessary for understanding it. Truth and the instrument of understanding truth are complementary, and thus inseparable. Condition and the one conditioned are reciprocally related. It goes without saying, then, that more than a teacher is necessary for the communication of truth.

But what has caused the disciple to be deprived of the condition necessary for comprehending the truth? Did God create him with this deficiency? Impossible: man would have previously been nothing but an animal, and would have become a man only at the moment when he acquired truth. No, God endowed him with the condition essentially related to the gift of truth, and God's gifts are given without regret. If then man is today in a state of error, he alone is responsible. He has placed himself outside the realm of truth; he has battled against truth. "This state (of being in error by reason of one's own guilt), how shall we designate it? Let us call it *sin*.[90]

A teacher who will come and give truth will be more than a maieutic teacher. What shall we call him? He will deliver us from error, a bondage from which we cannot deliver ourselves; above all, then, he is a deliverer, a savior. Then too, since man's error is due to his own guilt, the teacher who will bestow truth on him will be a reconciliator, taking away the wrath impending upon that of which the learner has made himself guilty.

The disciple in turn will be interiorly transformed: "He will become another man; not in the frivolous sense of becoming another individual of the same quality as before; but in the sense of becoming a man of a different quality, or as we might call him a new creature." [91] The gift of truth is, therefore, a *new birth*. But it is also a *conversion*, since one who up to the present has been departing from truth, now resumes the course of his life in the opposite direction. Moreover, since man is conscious of the fact that he was in error by reason of his own guilt, he cannot help but be stricken with remorse in retrospect. His rebirth and conversion is, therefore, as well a *repentance*.

As yet we have not mentioned the word *Moment*. As a matter

of fact, up to this point we have been dealing with it exclusively. The decisive contact with truth, formerly not possessed, is the Moment:

> In the Moment, a man becomes conscious that he is born; for his antecedent state (to which he may not cling) was one of non-being. In the Moment man also becomes conscious of the new birth. . . . Had his preceding state in either instance been one of being, the Moment would not have received a decisive significance for him, as has been shown above. Whereas all the pathos of the Greek consciousness concentrates upon recollection, the pathos of our endeavor concentrates on the Moment.[92]

In another text, Kierkegaard sums up other characteristic traits of the Moment: "Such a Moment has a peculiar character. It is brief and temporal indeed, like every other moment, elapsing as every moment does with the advent of its successor; yet, it is decisive and filled with the eternal. Such a moment ought to have a distinctive name: let us call it the *Fullness of Time*." [93]

If we wish to sum up the nature of the Moment, we would say that it is a moment in which two heterogeneous splendors are united. In the passage of the *Fragments,* which we have just quoted, Kierkegaard describes it as essentially theocentric; it is *von Gott her.* It is from God that we must await the truth and its essential condition. We must not, however, lose sight of the fact that theocentricity is in no way opposed to the theory of existence, of inwardness, and of subjectivity. Through a new paradox, subjectivity and theocentricity overlap. There is a second point of interest to be noted in retrospect: the Moment is a conscious moment. According to Kierkegaard, the disciple experiences—and this is certainly in the pietistic tradition—the Moment which causes him to be reborn. Finally, we must make one further observation on a subject which Kierkegaard passes over quickly: the Moment is nothing but a moment, that is, it does not persist. It is decisive, but brief and transitory. This final point is of importance because of the influence of Kierkegaard's thought on Barth. We will return to it later in our exposition.

2. Revelation is realized in the person of Christ. It finds in Him its concrete form. Kierkegaard accepts here the dogma of

Chalcedon: Christ is, at one and the same time, God and man. In the writings of the Danish thinker, there is no attempt to reduce this opposition of two natures into an Hegelian synthesis. The two natures, one as true as the other, clash in the person of Christ. For this reason, Jesus is the *paradox* par excellence:

> For His contemporaries, the paradox consisted in the fact that this particular, definite man, who appeared to be like all others, who spoke with them and observed their customs, was the Son of God. For subsequent ages, the paradox was different; since we do not see Christ with our bodily eyes, it is easier for us to represent Him to ourselves as the Son of God; but another stumbling block arises: he delivered His message in the thought-pattern of a determined period.[94]

In Kierkegaard's thought, the idea of paradox is inseparably associated with the closely related concept of *incognito*. God disguised His divinity because He wished to become man. This *incognito* was imposed upon Him by His love for man.

> God had to reveal Himself under the form of a *servant*. But this servant-form is no mere outer garment, like the king's beggar-cloak which for that reason flutters loosely about him and betrays him. . . . It was His true form and figure. For this is the unfathomable nature of love: that it desires equality with the beloved, not in jest, but in earnest truth. The omnipotence of this love is so resolved that it is able to accomplish its purpose, which neither the king nor Socrates could do, because their assumed figures constituted after all a kind of deceit. . . . The servant-form was no mere outer garment, and therefore, God must suffer and endure all things—hunger in the desert, thirst in torment, abandonment in death—in every detail like the least of men.[95]

If the *incognito* were absolute, revelation would certainly be entirely suppressed. Kierkegaard notes this fact and expresses himself in more guarded language than his disciple, Karl Barth:

> The absolute paradox would be that the Son of God became man, came into the world, went hither and yon, without anyone's having become aware of the fact; that He was in the strictest sense of the word an ordinary man with a wife, a trade, etc. If such had been the case, God would have been the greatest of ironists; He would not have been God nor the Father of men. Herein lies the divine paradox: the

Son of God did not go unperceived, at least on the Cross; He performed miracles, etc., in which He was at least recognizable through His divine authority, even though faith was necessary to resolve the paradox.[96]

The divine paradox, then, allows the divine nature of Christ to appear through the human nature to which it is joined. Such is the law of revelation.[97]

3. Because Christ is not only man but also God, the distance which normally separates a being of the past from a being of the present disappears: Christ becomes *contemporaneous* with us. The Christian finds himself in the immediate presence of Christ, before the absolute in Christ. There is no difference between the historical contemporaries of Jesus and His present-day contemporaries. The historical mediation becomes secondary and accessory:

Men of subsequent generations certainly believe by virtue of what (Christ's) contemporaries relate of Him; but they believe in the same sense as His contemporaries, by virtue of their perception and immediate knowledge.[98]

The man who truly believes that Christ was and is God, prays each day, and finds his joy in the intimacy of converse with Him—such a man will surely know how to relegate the historical to its proper place. What nonsense to claim that he would be deeply disturbed if one Evangelist were to say this and another that; he can, in fact, address Christ in prayer and say to Him: "This discrepancy disturbs me, but is it not true that You are and dwell in me." It is foolish to claim that historical detail could have decisive importance, affecting a faith which one has in a person who is present within him, and with whom he converses intimately each day. . . . A simple historical figure, a man, has only an historical existence; thus each detail will assume great significance. It would certainly be useless for me to speak to a marble bust of Socrates in order to learn what I ought to know about him. I must seek out the facts from history, or draw from the well of my own mind. But the life of Christ must be understood in an entirely different sense. At this point, it becomes evident how much strict orthodoxy disparages Christ. For, in spite of the paradox involved, it is nevertheless true and in conformity with Christianity that, for Christ, historical details are nowhere near as important as for Socrates and other like personages. This is so precisely because Christ is Christ, an eternally present Being, since He is the true God.[99]

The theme of contemporaneity is thus one of the principal motifs in Kierkegaardian thought: it assures a transcendence of historical relativism. The "being before God," which is Kierkegaard's fundamental position, reveals itself as a "being before Christ." Herein lies a certain similarity between the thought of Kierkegaard and W. Herrmann. Both strive to transcend relativism through recourse to the immediate. Each of them, however, conceives of the immediate in an entirely different manner. In Kierkegaard's system it is linked to the dogma of the divinity of Christ, who is still existing and present today. Thus He is immediate to an existing person, and His restoring action can now be felt. For Herrmann, on the contrary, the immediate consists in direct recourse to a fact of the past, without the deforming mediation of history. Christ is our contemporary only in terms of His message and example. The ethical divinity of Jesus does not at all imply a supratemporal divinity of nature.

4. This presents the problem of the value and usage of Sacred Scripture. If the historical is truly an accessory in the matter of faith, does the Bible still have a role to play? In studying this aspect of Kierkegaard's thought, one point must be noted immediately: all objective, historical research which has the Bible as its object is absolutely superfluous. The only problem of interest to the Christian is his eternal happiness. To attain this he must have absolute certitude. Now what can historical research contribute on this subject? "Even with the most amazing perseverance and erudition, and even if the heads of all the critics were affixed to a single neck, one would still go no further than an approximation." [100]

We will bring all the resources of our mind into play in order to arrive at a decisive result, and we will never attain that goal. The least objection will disturb all:

A number of topics come up for consideration: the canonicity of the individual books, their authenticity, integrity, the trustworthiness of their author; this is sealed with a dogmatic guarantee: inspiration. When we reflect on the work which the English have devoted to digging under the Thames,[101] on the immense expenditure of energy involved, and how a little accident was able to disrupt the entire enterprise for such a length of time, we can form some idea of the enterprise of the art of criticism. What an outlay of time, of magnificent industry, of admirable minds must be devoted to this marvelous enterprise by each succeeding generation in order to bring this miracle to pass. And for all that, the least dialectical doubt bearing on its presuppositions can disrupt all by its very shadow for a prolonged period of time, closing the subterranean way to Christianity, which men have attempted to construct objectively and scientifically, instead of allowing the problem to come to birth in its true light: the subjective.[102]

Undoubtedly at times we attain partial results, but this merely transplants the difficulty; we block up one hole by opening another.

Objectively, the contemplative inquirer expresses himself in the following farewell words, as he faces the final end of his life: When I was a young man, books were in doubt; but today their genuineness has been demonstrated. It is true, recently doubts have been raised about books which up to the present had fallen under no shadow of suspicion. But surely some scholar will soon arise among us, who will . . . and so forth.[103]

Must faith, then, hang in suspense? If Christianity is an historical document, if faith depends on a quest ever approximating but never converging upon its goal, there is no faith. Kierkegaard is bent on demonstrating that faith is absolutely independent of all historical research. Let us follow the Danish thinker in his examination of the alternative view which sums up all the hypotheses:

I assume, accordingly, that the critics have succeeded in proving about the Bible everything that any learned theologian, in his happiest moment, has ever wished to prove. These books, and no others, belong to the canon; they are authentic; they are integral; their authors are trustworthy. . . . Furthermore, not a trace of contradiction can be found in the sacred writings. . . . Let us assume that all that concerns the Scriptures is in perfect order.—What follows? Has anyone who previously did not have faith been brought a step closer to its acquisition? Not a single step. For faith is not simply the consequence of a direct scientific inquiry; it does not come directly at all. On the contrary, in such objectivity one tends to lose the infinitely personal and passionate interestedness which is the condition of faith. . . . How about the man who previously had faith? Has his faith grown in force and vigor? No, not in the very least; rather is it the case that in this voluminous knowledge, this realm of certitude which lurks at the door of faith and threatens to devour it, he is in so dangerous a situation that he will need to put forth much effort in great fear and trembling, lest he fall a victim to the temptation to confuse knowledge with faith.[104]

The heterogeneity of faith is more clearly evident in the other point of the disjunction:

Now let us assume the opposite, that the enemy has succeeded in proving whatever they wish to establish about the Scripture, and this to a degree of certitude that it surpasses the most ardent desire of their most passionate hostility—what then? Have the opponents thereby abolished Christianity? By no manner or means. Has the opponent acquired the right to be relieved of the responsibility of not being a believer? Not at all. In fact, if these books are not the work of the alleged authors, if they are not authentic, not in an integral condition . . . , it does not follow that those authors have not existed; nor does it follow above all, that Christ has not existed. Thus the believer still remains free in his decision, and entirely so. We should take careful note of this fact.[105]

Faith then forms a separate, totally transcendent category. The revolutionary status of any other category whatsoever, be it even that of reason, cannot shake this impregnable fortress.

For whose benefit does one seek proof? Faith has no need of it; in fact, faith must even consider the proof as its enemy. When, on the other hand, faith begins to feel embarrassed and ashamed of itself, like a young woman for whom her love is no longer satisfactory, who secretly blushes because of her lover and feels the need of having some proof there is something extraordinary in him; when faith thus begins to lose its passion, when it begins to cease to be faith, then a proof becomes necessary to command respect from the side of unbelief. As for the effects, which such a confusion of categories has brought about on this subject, the rhetorical stupidities perpetrated by clergymen, alas, let us pass over them in silence.[106]

A faith without the support of proof, then, is more solid than one buttressed by reason.

Faith is a category apart because of anti-objectivism in existence and of subjectivity:

Christianity is a spirit; a spirit is inwardness; inwardness is subjectivity; subjectivity is essentially passion, and in its highest form an infinite, personal, passionate interest in one's eternal happiness. As soon as the subjectivity is eliminated, and from subjectivity passion, and from passion infinite interest, there is no decision, neither in this problem, nor in any other. All essential decisiveness is rooted in subjectivity. . . . From the objective viewpoint, there are results everywhere, but nowhere a decisive result. This is a perfectly logical position, precisely because decisiveness inheres in subjectivity alone, essentially in its passion, *maxime* in personal passion, which is infinitely interested in its own eternal happiness.[107]

This brings us to the second point. If historical research is vain, if it can contribute nothing to faith, must the Christian retain any interest whatsoever in a document of the past? Has the Bible any value for him? Certainly, replies Kierkegaard. The Bible retains its value. It is merely necessary to know how to appreciate it. The Bible has no objective value for faith, but it has an immense subjective value. A person who wishes to approach the Bible objectively does violence to it: "Above all, read the New Testament without any commentary. Every commentary deflects you from your course. He who reads the Sacred Scriptures with ten commentaries open before him will perhaps write an eleventh, but he will be treating Scripture *contra naturam*." [108] The true Christian will enter into personal contact with the Bible and consider it a means of engaging in dialogue:

Will a person have the true mind of a lover if he reads the correspondence of his beloved with a commentary in hand? Will the letter of my beloved be written in a language I do not comprehend? In such a case, I will learn the language, but not on any terms will I read the letter in the light of the commentaries of others. If the thought of my beloved is truly close to my heart, just as the resolution of identifying my will with her desires and wishes, I will read this letter and understand it quite well.[109]

The Bible has value in terms of our subjectivity.

The third point of our exposition on the value and use of the

Bible depends on the first two. If faith must remain a category apart, Sacred Scripture must not enter into dangerous competition with it by contributing deceptive flashes of light. Sacred Scripture would then appear to us *in forma servi:*

> It is said at times, "If there is a Sacred Scripture, there must be a perfect agreement to the least detail." What an absurdity! No, Sacred Scripture presupposes faith. It is for this reason that disagreement is necessary. Thus, faith will have an opportunity to make a choice; faith can remain a choice; and the possibility of scandal can stretch faith. . . . What holds true for the concept "God-Man" can also be said of "Sacred Scripture." [110]

This idea of a parallelism between the person of Christ and the Bible is dear to Kierkegaard. As Christ is a paradox and a scandal, so too will Scripture be a paradox and a scandal. Barth, who obviously draws his inspiration from Kierkegaard on this precise point, goes even farther than his forerunner. For the Danish thinker, the Bible is undoubtedly a paradox, but not an absolute paradox. The divine paradox of Christ is distinguished from the ethical paradox in the fact that he does not totally conceal His divinity. This is quite evident in the passage in which Kierkegaard claims for the Bible a decisive authority because it is truly the Word of God. The divine splendor of the Bible is dimmed by the paradox, but it remains clearly perceptible.

5. Not much more remains to be said about *faith*. "Being before God," "existence," "inwardness," "contemporaneity," are merely different expressions to signify one unique reality: faith. We must not lose sight of the fact that Kiekegaard is concerned solely with questions which are properly religious. Unlike his disciples, Karl Jaspers and Martin Heidegger, he is far from an attempt to apply a religious epistemology to the sphere of the profane. Kierkegaard's entire theology of faith is centered around two principal ideas: separation and contact. Faith is at odds with all else, because it is a separate category. Thus it is a daring undertaking: "Without risk, there is no faith." [111] The image of a *leap* is commonly employed by Kierkegaard to express this idea. "Christianity is a radical cure, which men are reluctant to take . . . ; Christians lack the strength for this desperate *leap*." [112]

Faith, then, is at odds with all that represents the universal, the objective, but especially with Hegelian intellectualism: "The realm of faith is not a class for *minus habentes,* an asylum for the feeble-minded. But faith is a sphere in itself, and every error concerning Christianity is recognizable by the fact that it transforms it into a doctrine and elevates it into the sphere of intellectualism." [113] The object of faith does not consist in realities situated beyond the possibilities of reason, but realities entirely *opposed to reason:* "The absurd is precisely by its objective repulsion the measure of the intensity of faith in inwardness. . . . The absurd is the proper object of faith and the only object that can be believed." [114] The desire to utilize reason in order to arrive at faith is equivalent to putting the cart before the horse; and the preaching of the faith to pagans has no need to seek points of contact.

It now remains for me to outline the effect which the man outside of Christianity ought to have upon Christians. For this purpose it will suffice to recall how Christians considered pagans and their gods as the work of the devil, their virtues as dazzling vices; how one of their own leaders declared man to be a log, a stone before Christ; how they in no way grafted their teaching of the Gospel to man as he was, but always began with "Change your hearts!" burdening their Gospel with what was foolishness to the pagans and a scandal to the Jews.[115]

This completes our treatment of Kierkegaard's absolute rejection of historical and critical apologetics. He goes further and rejects all psychological apologetics just as unconditionally. Attacking those pastors who did their utmost to dispel doubt with the aid of apologetics, Kierkegaard wrote:

They try to defend Christianity. It was never a question of authority; they never did avail themselves of it; never did they let the phrase "you must" pass their lips for fear of provoking laughter. They defended Christianity and said: "Do not look down upon Christianity; it is a gentle doctrine, containing sweet consolations, of which every man, sometime in his life, might very well need. Heavens! Life will not always smile on us; we have need of a friend, and Christ is a true friend; do not disregard Him. He is so concerned for your welfare." And they succeeded. People listened to these sermons attentively and lent ready ear to this beggar (for though He Himself was not a beggar, His representatives begged in His name). There seemed to be an element of truth in this doctrine; it flattered the pride of a Christianity greedy for domination. It seemed to imply that they were entitled to cast a vote. Fine! On these conditions, we will accept Christianity. God of Justice! . . . and this scene occurred in the very heart of Christendom, where all are Christians! And Christianity was accepted on those conditions—by these Christians.[116]

Morality is another form of the universal to which faith is opposed: "The ethical as such is universal, and on that score is applicable to each person." [117] In contrast with morality, faith will be a critical moment which places the individual above the level of generality and in immediate relation with the absolute. Completely at odds with the mediation of morality, faith appears as a paradox. "It is now my intention to draw out from the story of Abraham the dialectical consequences inherent in it, expressing them in the form of *problemata* so that we may see what a tremendous paradox faith is—a paradox capable of transforming murder into a holy act, pleasing to God; a paradox which gives Isaac back to Abraham; a paradox which no amount of reasoning can master because faith begins precisely there where reason leaves off." [118] "Faith is precisely this paradox that the individual as the particular is above the universal, a norm justified against the universal since the particular stands in an absolute relation to the absolute. This position cannot be mediated, for all mediation comes about precisely by virtue of the universal." [119]

If we forget the element of contact and consider only this aspect of separation, we impoverish Kierkegaard's thought considerably. We must recall what was said earlier about opportunity. The dualism which is at the basis of the idea of schism does not prevent an immediate encounter with God. God is present to us. "Contemporaneity . . . is faith." [120]

Kierkegaard's faith acquires, consequently, a truly mystical character: it involves an immediate intuition, an apprehension, non-conceptual and non-rational, of God's reality. Such "mystical knowledge," has nothing in common with the experience designated by the same term in Protestant theology. Kierkegaard is vigorously opposed to certain forms of mysticism, namely, romantic subjectivism and pantheism: "The object of faith is the reality of another. . . . The object of faith is God's reality. . . ." [121] "Knowledge does its utmost precisely to enable the ego to dissolve into its object; faith makes every effort to conserve the ego with and within its object." [122] Kierkegaard is determinedly opposed to Schleiermacher on these diverse points.

## G. The Ambivalence of Kierkegaard's Thought.

In opposition to the monism and objectivism of Hegel, Kierkegaard proposes dualism and subjectivity. His one-sided antagonism is thus expressed in an ambivalent formula: *the qualitative difference of the infinite,* and *existential inwardness.* All the authors who have studied Kierkegaard's thought recognize the existence of these two lines of thought, which can be designated, in a rather simplified vocabulary, the *line of paradox* and the *line of mysticism.* "Paradox is pathos proper to the intellectual life." [123] This statement reflects a facet of Kierkegaard's thought; but, to be a true reflection, it must be supplemented by another in which the Danish thinker describes the "little cell in which every person truly prays in wholehearted sincerity." [124] For Kierkegaard is, in his own way, a religious and mystical soul. His *Journal* bears witness to his propensities towards this sphere. Among his favorite authors, one can find the names of Hugh of St. Victor, Tauler, Thomas à Kempis, Fénelon, Tersteegen, the author of the *Deutsche Theologie,* and many others.[125] These two lines are complementary and mutually corrective: the paradox prevents Kierkegaard's religious intuition from becoming an experience of the Schleiermacher variety, as well as safeguarding the divine transcendence; while the mystical contact prevents paradox from leading to agnosticism, pure and simple.[126] The two lines are complementary precisely because Kierkegaard does not extend them to their limits: the Kierkegaardian paradox is not an absolute paradox, nor is his subjectivity a total subjectivity. Between these two elements lies a hidden synthesis, of which, perhaps, Kierkegaard was not fully aware. His disciples who wished to be perfectly logical have found themselves compelled at a certain point in their reasoning to choose one line at the expense of the other.

In the *mystical line,* experience plays a major role. Nevertheless, we must not lose sight of the fact that existence for Kierkegaard is an existential *thought*. Torsten Bohlin has a tendency to reduce inwardness to *Erfahrung*; [127] consequently, the Swedish theologian overlooks one of the elements which separates Kierkegaard from Schleiermacher. In Kierkegaard's epistemology, intuition plays a role which is by no means negligible; for this reason, subjectivity expressly enters into relation with objectivity. Kierkegaardian thought is obedient response to the object. Every human being bows down before the object of its thought and submits to it.[128] Did Kierkegaard come to an authentic realism? We must leave this question unanswered, since its investigation would lead us too far astray from our subject.

More important is the origin of the line of paradox. Bohlin, on this point, has several opinions which seem to us rather sound. Dualism, which leads to a *"Kreuz der Spekulation"* thwarting all reflection, is in his eyes a philosophical postulate which can lead only to absolute meaninglessness. Without hesitation he defines it as an "absurd *complexio oppositorum*." [129] Such criticism, undoubtedly, is exaggerated to the extent that it does not take sufficient account of the "corrective" character of dualism: as we stated above, there is in Kierkegaard's thought a real, but hidden, synthesis. In our opinion, Bohlin does not accord a sufficiently important place to the passage of the *Journal* (cited above) in which Kierkegaard shows that the divine paradox is neither an absolute nor an ethical paradox.[130] A single, tiny escape hatch remains open, which Bohlin seems to want to close at all costs. Nevertheless, it is perfectly true that in Kierkegaard's system dualism is hypertrophied, and that, by overrunning the entire rational conceptual sphere, he compromises the equilibrium of the whole. To make faith a separate category is legitimate, but to cut it off from every connection with other categories is to do violence to the human mind. Kierkegaard's dualism is not Christian. Hardened as it is, its philosophical origin can no longer be doubted.

How did Kierkegaard ever come to put a philosophical option at the center of his thought, and what was its origin? In claiming that Kierkegaard's dualism is of Hegelian origin—or more exactly, that it is an Hegelian antihegelianism—we ourselves may appear to be the victim of paradox. Yet it is perfectly true. At first glance the assertion that Kierkegaard is dependent upon Hegel seems absurd. The main point of Hegel's thought is summed up in the *Aufhebung,* whereas Kierkegaard regards the dilemma and paradox as the center of his message. Hegel wishes to rationalize; Kierkegaard wishes to irrationalize.[131] Wherein lies the common element?

Kierkegaard is Hegelian to the extent that he agrees to formulate the problem in Hegelian fashion. Hegel stated that if one had to choose between identity and contradiction as the law of all reality, he would have to choose without hesitation contradiction.[132] Hegel was not obliged to make such a choice, since in his synthesis he united identity and contradiction. Kierkegaard, on the contrary, chose contradiction. Kierkegaard's Hegelianism is an incomplete Hegelianism without mediation. In his thought there is no dialectic of being, but simply a dialectic of mind. For Hegel unity is realized in a synthesis of being which is identified with the synthesis of mind; for Kierkegaard, on the contrary, all dialectic consists in the successive affirmation of "yes" and "no," without ever passing into "entitative" synthesis of "yes" and "no." The dialectic of mind, because it is not based on a mediation of being, is composed of "heterogeneous moments and qualitative leaps, of conversions." [133] Bound to a continual movement of balance, it never comes to rest in stability.

The Hegelian dialectic is essentially dynamic, since it is ever in motion towards an entitative synthesis; Kierkegaard's, on the contrary, is static. It does not rest at affirmation or negation, nor does it surmount this dichotomy. Instead of a triadic movement, Kierkegaard's paradox is diadic motionlessness.[134] Kierkegaard's dependence regarding Hegel's thought is thus ambiguous, because he accepted the Hegelian manner of formulating the problem. Once on this level, no other alternative remains for him save acceptance of a monistic and pantheistic synthesis, or hopeless involvement in a contradiction. There is a third solution, which it is impossible to find while one still makes use of the Hegelian postulate as a point of departure.

## H. The Univalence of Karl Barth's Theology.

In opposition to Hegel, Kierkegaard thus adopts two principles: one he draws from the very philosophy of his adversary: the paradox; for the other he is indebted to the pietist tradition: mystical intuition. Although Barth likewise is opposed to a pantheism, which has numerous traits in common with Hegel, he sees in liberalism not an objective but a subjective pantheism. Whereas Kierkegaard, in his polemic, emphasizes his pietistic antecedents, Barth's first theological reaction is to oppose the philosophico-religious pietism of Schleiermacher, whose influence can be perceived in a large part of the liberal school (in the writings of W. Herrmann, among others). In his battle against liberalism, Barth can make use of only one of the weapons placed at his disposal by Kierkegaard. He must construct his entire system on one idea: the paradox. On no other score will he be a dualist.

The rejection of mystical knowledge is found in Barth's thought from the very beginning of his personal work. It suffices to recall his violent attacks against Schleiermacher and unconditional endorsement of Emil Brunner's book, *Die Mystik und das Wort*.[135] Nevertheless, he does not seem to have immediately noted the fact that a type of mystical knowledge is included in Kierkegaardian individualism. Consequently, as a still inexperienced disciple of the Danish thinker, he is seen to juggle for some time the fluid words of Kierkegaard's existential vocabulary. But as soon as he perceived that such individualism would lead to a type of religious and intuitive noetic, he abandoned this equivocal manner of speaking, which might be prejudicial to the fundamental and essentially polemical idea of his work.[136] If then he accepted the vocabulary of subjectivism for a time, he did so in a very superficial manner, without committing himself to the Kierkegaardian noetic properly so-called. Barth's thought, then, from the very beginning was resolutely univalent.

It now remains for us to show how this univalence of dualism influenced the elaboration of the three Barthian principles.[137] First of all, it is evident that dualism led him to formulate his *second principle:* the total mystery of the Word of God as far as human perception is concerned. Since dualism has been followed inexorably to its final logical conclusions, it is evident that the Divine Word could never, in any manner whatsoever, be approached through human psychology, at least in man's present state.

In his elaboration of the *third principle,* dualism has a twofold role: first, the separation of all human activity from the activity of God. Thus, *fiducia* becomes totally heterogeneous from faith, since it is man's decision, whereas faith is an act of God. These two movements have nothing in common. Secondly, dualism intervenes once more to isolate *fiducia* within the sphere of human activity. The *credo quia absurdum* presupposes that *fiducia* is an autonomous sphere, free from any connection with reason. *Fiducia* is not only suprarational, but, perhaps, diametrically opposed to reason. Dualism, therefore, isolates three grandeurs: reason, *fiducia* (the act of man), and faith (the act of God).

Barth's *first principle* is a renewal of the Kierkegaardian theme of the *Moment.* In that theme, theocentrism was clearly evident. But its brief and transitory character was explained solely because the moment is synonymous with the momentary crisis of existence and inwardness. Man can raise himself to the level of supernatural intuition only for a few brief moments. "Then the leap stands revealed in the only way possible: either that it is inevitable, or that it has occurred." [138] The abandonment of Kierkegaard's subjectivism compelled Barth to invert the entire doctrine of the problematic of the Moment. How can the instantaneousness of the Moment be explained, since all explanations derived from the weakness of human psychology must be abandoned? Barth transposes the cause of instantaneity into the freedom of God: the acts of God's will are moments. Consequently, to justify the discontinous character of the accomplishments of the Word of God, Barth must assume that there are successive volitional acts in God, and thus conclude with an anthropomorphic concept of God. Barth was led to this stop-gap solution, once again, because of his dualism.

*<br>*　　*

We find ourselves in the presence of a strange paradox: the indirect dependence of Barth's thought on that of Hegel. Dualism dominates the entire problematic of Barth. This dualism has the dualism of Kierkegaard as a progenitor, but it has been exacerbated by the abandonment of subjectivity. Now Kierkegaard's dualism was clearly of philosophical origin, which his thought sought to combat: Hegelianism. We must acknowledge the fact, then, that the element which is properly original in Barth's thought was borrowed, paradoxically enough, from the thought of the man who had elaborated the *System,* G. W. F. Hegel. Certainly, Hegelian thought could not exercise any direct influence on that of Barth. The theologian of Basel did not draw from it a single one of his solutions. Must we be reminded that the philosopher of mediation could not be the father of Barth's dualism. But Kierkegaard and Barth, in the very act of rejecting Hegel's solutions, accepted his method of presenting the fundamental problem of philosophy and religion. Barth's dualism, a hardening of biblical categories, is somewhat akin to the Hegelian opposition between thesis and antithesis.

# notes
## to chapter twelve

**1** RB, p. XIII.

**2** Cf. CD, p. VI. *Christliche Dogmatik* appeared in 1927. We must not confuse it with *Kirchliche Dogmatik* whose publication did not occur until 1932. In the same work (pp. 71 and 72) Barth seems to adopt, without hesitation or qualification, Kierkegaard's existentialism. He writes: "Wir stehen hier vor dem Punkt, wo einst Kierkegaard gegen Hegel die Interessen des Christentums und der Philosophie meinte wahrnehmen zu müssen." The context is also interesting for its understanding of Kierkegaard's thought; for it points out clearly that existence must be an enlistment in an enterprise. We cannot rest content with the attitude of a spectator (*Zuschauer*); we must boldly take part in the action (*Tat*).

**3** Cf. KD, vol. I, 1, p. 19; vol. II, 2, p. 338.

**4** Cf. *Schweizerköpfe der Gegenwart*, pp. 117–121.

**5** Th. Siegfried, *Das Wort und die Existenz*, p. 35.

**6** Cf. KD, vol. I, 1, pp. 128–130.

**7** In *Christliche Dogmatik*, Barth obviously wished to treat the problem of the Word of God under two distinct aspects: the phenomenological aspect and the existential aspect. Cf. p. 49. Th. Siegfried has called attention to the philosophical difficulties which this method entails. Barth acknowledges the criticism: "Der Einwand, den ich mir selbst seither gemacht habe, ist eben der, dass diese Begriffe, welches auch ihr Inhalt und ihr Verhältnis untereinander sein möge, entscheidende Einschnitte auf dem Weg des dogmatischen Denkens, wie es dort vorausgesetzt schien, überhaupt nicht machen oder bezeichnen können" (KD, vol. I, 1, p. 129). But later he notes that his intention was misunderstood: "Eine solche Aufnahme eines philosophischen Themas war nun auch in der ersten Auflage nicht meine Absicht. . . . Ich hätte aber über die bessere Meinung hinaus einsehen müssen, dass die Heranziehung jener Begriffe gerade an jener Stelle ein im Verhältnis zu dem, was ich schon damals sagen wollte, überflüssiges und gefährliches Spiel bedeutete" (p. 129). Barth had described his existential method in the following manner: "Setzen wir aber den Menschen als einen Faktor in unsere bisherige Rechnung . . . , dann müssen wir alles bisherige verstehen als eine konkrete Situation, als eine Handlung, in die wir selbst verflochten sind. Denn nur dann setzen wir hier den Menschen ein, wenn wir auf allen Punkten uns selbst einsetzen. Nur der denkt ja wirklich den Menschen, der sich selbst denkt, seine Existenz; und nur der denkt Sachverhalte und Beziehungen, an denen der Mensch beteiligt ist, der sie denkt als konkrete

Situation, als Handlungen, in die er selbst *existentiell* verwickelt ist, nicht als Zahl, nicht als Ding, auch nicht als Schauspieler, in keinem Sinne in der Lage, sich selbst objektiv als Unbeteiligten zu betrachten. Wo es wirklich um den Menschen geht, da ist das Subjektive das Objektive" (CD, p. 48). This manner of viewing the question made it evident that a knowledge of the Word of God could be attained through a study of the human situation. In 1932 Karl Barth withdrew this position: "Ich habe damals doch den falschen Göttern Reverenz erwiesen. Wenn das Wort Gottes etwas sicher nicht ist, dann nicht ein Prädikat des Menschen" (KD, vol. I, 1, p. 130).

8 Cf. KD, vol. I, 1, p. 19; vol. II, 2, p. 338.

9 It is interesting to note that the rejection of the epistemology of existential individualism coincides with the censure of analogy. Certainly these two modes of knowledge have nothing in common, but it would have been difficult for Barth to denounce analogy in the name of an inconsequential dualism. It would have been illogical to condemn analogy as a "synthesis" of God and man, at a time when he himself seemed to allow a "synthesis" in existential experience. Once this last link was severed, Barth could present himself as the defender of a radical dualism which admits no compromise.

10 Most of the information has been taken from the autobiography published in *Schweizerköpfe der Gegenwart*, pp. 117–121. The citations with no accompanying references are taken from this autobiography.

11 *Credo*, p. 228.

12 Adolf Schlatter (born in 1852) was appointed at Berlin in 1893 to act as a counterbalance to the tendency of Harnack, whom the controversy on the Apostles' Creed had discredited with the official Church. He was appointed at Tübingen in 1898. Cf. A. von Zahn-Harnack, *Adolf von Harnack*, p. 209.

13 Wilhelm Heitmüller, who died in 1926, was an exegete attached to the *religionsgeschichtlich* school.

14 Karl Barth's father (Fritz B.) had been not only a pastor, but in 1889 he was appointed "privat-docent" and later professor of theology at Berne. Karl Barth had been his father's disciple before leaving Berne for Berlin. He also had as teachers at Berne: Steck, Lüdemann, and Marti.

15 PD, pp. 128–129.

16 Nor is any mention made of Franz Overbeck, to whom Barth was deeply indebted. Cf. *Die Theologie und die Kirche*, pp. 1–25.

17 Cf. T. Bohlin, *Glaube und Offenbarung*, pp. 18–27.

18 "Jeder Glaube an einen unmittelbaren, konkreten, übernatürlichen Verkehr mit Gott—das ist der stillschweigend vorausgesetzte Ausgangspunkt, ein Hauptpunkt aller Theologie. . . . So wird die Geschichte der Religion zur einzigen Offenbarung Gottes" (G. Hök, *Die elliptische Theologie Albrecht Ritschls*, pp. 47–48).

19 "Alle Religion entspringt aus dem Contrast, in welchen sich die Menschen ursprünglich hineingestellt sehen, dass sie gemäss ihrer natürlichen Ausstattung unselbständige Theile der Welt sind, abhängig und gehemmt von anderen Wesen, welche auch nur Theile der Welt sind, und dass sie gemäss ihrer geistigen Kraftausstattung sich von aller Natur unterscheiden, und sich zu einer übernatürlichen Bestimmung angelegt fühlen. . . . Denn eben die Gottesidee

und die nach ihr bemessene Weltanschauung hat überall die Bedeutung, dem Menschen über den Contrast zwischen seiner natürlichen Lage und seinem geistigen Selbstgefühl hinweg zu helfen, und ihm eine Erhabenheit oder Freiheit über der Welt und dem gewöhnlichen Verkehr mit ihr zu sichern. Da etwas, was uberall unter denselben Umständen eintritt, auf ein Gesetz hinweist, so ist die Religion als das geistige Organ des Menschen, sich mit der Hülfe Gottes von der gewöhnlichen natürlichen Bedingtheit seines Lebens frei zu machen, ein praktisches Gesetz des menschlichen Geistes" (*Rechtfertigung und Versöhnung*, vol. III, pp. 173–174, cited by G. Hök, *op. cit.*, p. 143. Whenever there is no indication to the contrary, *Recht. u. Vers.* has always been cited according to its first edition).

20 Religion simply completes (*ergänzen, Ergänzung*) the selfconsciousness man possesses. Cf. *Recht. u. Vers.*, vol. III, pp. 173–174; 439–440. These passages are cited in their entirety in the work of G. Hök, p. 143.

21 T. Bohlin, *Glaube und Offenbarung*, pp. 30–31.

22 "The individual subjective experience of passing from darkness into God's marvellous light, together with its objective historical cause, but not that cause itself, is called revelation" (A. E. Garvie, *The Ritschlian Theology*, p. 197).

23 *Verkehr des Christen mit Gott*, pp. 63–64, cited by A. E. Garvie, *op. cit.*, p. 204.

24 T. Bohlin, *Glaube und Offenbarung*, pp. 33–35.

25 According to Barth, Herrmann's intermediate position is especially apparent on the question of Christ's interior life: "Sie ist darum zum Schibboleth der herrmannschen Theologie geworden, weil man an ihr am deutlichsten Herrmanns Stellung in der Geschichte der neuen Dogmatik, seine Abgrenzung gegen Orthodoxie und Liberalismus, seine Korrektur Schleiermachers durch Ritschl und Ritschls durch Schleiermacher erkennen zu können glaubte" (TK, p. 274).

26 "In Herrmann's treatment of the Subject there is a tendency to limit revelation by individual experience, and so make every man a measure of revelation" A. E. Garvi, *The Ritschlian Theology*, p. 203).

27 In speaking of this "unauflösliche Korrelation von Offenbarung und Glaube," Barth states: "Sie wirkt wie ein Rudiment des pietistisch-rationalistischen Versuchs, dem Ärgernis der auf alle Fälle unvermeidlichen Glaubens- und Gehorsamsforderung auszuweichen, wie ein letzter Versuch, von dem aus, was *menschliche* Wahrhaftigkeit Wirklichkeit nennt, eine Brücke zu schlagen zu dem, was nur durch *göttliche* Wahrhaftigkeit, durch *veracitas Dei*, Wirklichkeit ist" (TK, p. 277). The scandal of Herrmann's theology consists in his desire to eliminate the scandal of revelation.

28 In our recourse to texts to illustrate Hegel's thought, we have followed rather closely the presentation made by Walter Ruttenbeck in his *Sören Kierkegaard*, pp. 42–57, as well as that of Torsten Bohlin in *Kierkegaards dogmatische Anschauung*, pp. 429–534. Among the works which have been particularly helpful, have been Jean Wahl's *Études kierkegaardiennes* (ch. IV is devoted to Kierkegaard's anti-Hegelianism) and an article of A. Rohner, *La conception hégélienne de l'état*, in *Nova et Vetera*, 1946–47, vol. XXII, pp. 331–337. Our presentation is limited to those elements in the German philosopher's thought which are particularly important for the understanding of the Danish thinker.

29 "Der Standpunkt der kantischen Philosophie ist, dass das Denken durch sein Raisonnement dahin kam, sich nicht als zufällig, sondern vielmehr in sich selbst

als absolut letztes aufzufassen" (*Vorlesungen über die Geschichte der Philosophie*, in *Werke*, vol. XV, p. 500). We cite Hegel's works according to their first edition, which has not yet been incorporated into Georg Lasson's critical edition (*Sämtliche Werke*—SW).

30 *Werke*, vol. XV, p. 617. In the same citation note further: "Im Begreifen durchdringen sich geistiges und natürliches Universum als ein harmonierendes Universum."

31 "Das Absolute ist der Geist: dies ist die höchste Definition des Absoluten.— Diese Definition zu finden und ihren Sinn und Inhalt zu begreifen, dies war die absolute Tendenz aller Bildung und Philosophie" (*Encyclopädie*, 384, SW, vol. V, p. 335).

32 "Truth is the whole. But the whole is merely the essential nature fulfilling and completing itself through the process of its development" (*Phénoménologie de l'esprit*, trans. by Jean Hyppolite, pp. 18–19, SW, vol. II, p. 21).

33 "Der ausgeführte Zweck oder das daseiende Wirkliche ist Bewegung und entfaltendes Werden" (*Phänomenologie*, SW, vol. II, p. 22). Jean Hyppolite translates this passage in a manner which sheds little light on it. Cf. pp. 20–21.

34 "The outcome is what is the beginning, because the beginning is the final stage" (*Phenomenologie*, trans. by Hyppolite, p. 20, SW, vol. II, p. 22).

35 Cf. *Logik*, II, SW, vol. IV, p. 58.

36 "Das reine Sein und das reine Nichts ist also dasselbe. Was die Wahrheit ist, ist weder das Sein, noch das Nichts, sondern dass das Sein in Nichts, und das Nichts in Sein—nicht übergeht—sondern übergegangen ist" (*Logik*, I, SW, p. 67).

37 Kierkegaard expresses himself on this subject in an amusing manner: "There exists in popular language a simple expression by which the impossible is expressed humorously: 'whistling while your mouth is filled with hot mush.' When speculation uses a word which indicates its precise contrary, it is attempting a similar feat" (*Post-scriptum*, trans. by P. Petit, p. 147, Iena, vol. VI, p. 275).

38 "Der Begriff ist hiermit die Wahrheit des Seins und des Wesens" (*Encyclopädie*, 159, SW, vol. V, p. 154).

39 W. Ruttenbeck, *op. cit.*, p. 49.

40 "Diese Idealität des Endlichen ist der Hauptsatz der Philosophie, und jede wahrhafte Philosophie ist deswegen Idealismus" (*Encyclopädie*, 95, SW, vol. V, p. 118).

41 Hegel continues: "A concrete form in the total being (*Dasein*), of which only one determinable element is predominant, while all others are present only as subdued lineaments" (*Phenomenologie*, trans. by Hyppolite, pp. 25–26, SW, vol. VI, pp. 8–9).

42 "This platitude (Hegel is speaking of a discourse by Fries) consists essentially in making science repose not on the development of ideas and concepts, but on immediate sensation and dependent imagination, which dissolves into the formless sentimentalism of friendship and enthusiasm, this rich, intimate articulation of the moral world which is the State; this rational architecture which by a very fine distinction of the spheres of public life and their respective

legitimacy and by the rigidity of the measure which supports each pillar, each arc, each buttress, gives rise to the strength of the unified whole, the strength of the harmony of the members. As Epicurus did with the world in general, this conception delivers, or rather should deliver, the moral world to the subjective contingence of opinion and arbitrariness" (*Principes de la philosophie du droit,* preface, ed. Jean Hyppolite, pp. 25–26, SW, vol. VI, pp. 8–9).

43 "So hat also die Religion einen gemeinschaftlichen Inhalt mit der Philosophie, und nur die Formen sind verschieden" (*Vorl. ü. d. Gesch. d. Phil.,* in *Werke,* vol. XIII, p. 95).

44 Cf. *Encyclopädie,* 94–95, SW, vol. V, pp. 115–118.

45 "Wir sollen Gott *im Geist und in der Wahrheit* erkennen; Gott ist der allgemeine, der absolute, wesentliche Geist" (*Vorl. u. d. Gesch. d. Phil.,* in *Werke,* vol. XIII, p. 88).

46 Cf. *Religionsphilosophie,* III, SW, vol. XIV, p. 142.

47 Georg Lasson gives an excellent introduction to Hegel's religious philosophy in volume XII of his edition, pp. 1–148. He insists on the objectivity of religion: "Das was bei Hegel der modernen Denkweise befremdlich erscheint, ist der Umstand, dass er auf die Objektivität der Religion das grösste Gewicht legt. Man ist heute durchaus daran gewöhnt, zwischen Religion und Religiosität überhaupt keinen Unterschied zu machen" (p. 12).

48 Cf. *Religionsphilosophie,* III, SW, vol. xiv, pp. 145–148.

49 A. Rohner, *La conception hégélienne de l'État,* in *Nova et Vetera,* 1946–47, vol. XXII, p. 332.

50 A. Rohner, *op. cit.,* p. 333.

51 Moral philosophy becomes identified with philosophy of law, and all subjectivity is eliminated: "The state cannot recognize moral certitude in its particular form, that is to say, as subjective knowledge, no more than in science an appeal to a sincere subjective opinion can have any value" (*Principes de la philosophie du droit,* 137, ed. Jean Hyppolite, p. 118, SW, vol. VI, p. 115).

52 Jean Wahl, *Études kierkegaardiennes,* p. 158.

53 PS, p. 278, Iena, vol. VII, p. 98.

*Method followed for references to the works of Kierkegaard.*

## I. Works properly so-called.

We cite in the first place the French translation, followed, whenever possible, by the corresponding reference in the German translation of Iéna (N.B. PS = *Post scriptum,* trans. Petit). Wherever we could not cite the French translation, we refer directly to the Iéna edition. Since we had at our constant disposal only volumes VI and VII of this translation (in the second edition: 1925), citations drawn from other volumes (in their first edition) will be indicated and their source noted (N.B. R = Ruttenbeck, *Sören Kierkegaard*).

II. Journal.

The classical abbreviations, Pap. and E.P., refer to the two Danish editions of the *Journal: Sören Kierkegaards Papirer* and *Efterladte Papirer*. These abbreviations are followed by a reference either to a French translation *Christ. Fragments extraits du journal*, trans. Tisseau; *Journal. Extraits*, trans. Ferlov and Gateau), or to a work which cites the passages (R; Wahl = Jean Wahl, *Études kierkegaardiennes*). When a passage from Kierkegaard is taken from an author who cites him, we give the reference in full (cf. note 59 for an example). Thus, when Jean Wahl cites the *Journal* according to Ulrich or Haecker, after noting the Danish edition, we give the reference to the German text before giving that to the *Etudes kierkegaardiennes*.

54 Cf. T. Bohlin, *Sören Kierkegaard*, pp. 109–110.

55 II, A, 6, 12, Ulrich, p. 220, Wahl, p. 617.

56 Pap., VIII1, A, 482, R, p. 133.

57 Pap., VIII1, A, 125, R, p. 134.

58 Cf. T. Bohlin, *Glaube und Offenbarung*, pp. 105–106.

59 X2, 426, Haecker, p. 138, Wahl, p. 654.

60 PS, p. 214, Iena, vol. VII, p. 18.

61 Iena, vol. IX, p. 62, R, p. 136.

62 PS, p. 179, Iena, vol. VI, p. 316.

63 Pap., VII, B, 235, p. 59, R, p. 138.

64 PS, p. 230, Iena, vol. VII, p. 39.

65 Iena, vol. V, p. 341, R, p. 136.

66 PS, p. 128, Iena, vol. VI, p. 251.

67 PS, p. 130, Iena, vol. VI, p. 253.

68 PS, p. 133, Iena, vol. VI, pp. 257–258.

69 PS, p. 128, Iena, vol. VI, p. 251.

70 T. Bohlin, *Sören Kierkegaard*, p. 166.

71 Pap., I, A, 75, *Journal*, pp. 31–32.

72 PS, p. 208, Iena, vol. VII, p. 10.

73 PS, p. 130, Iena, vol. VI, p. 254.

74 PS, p. 130, Iena, vol. VI, p. 374.

75 *Ibid.*

76 *Ibid.*

77 Pap., VI, B, 56, R, p. 139.

78 X2, A, 299, R, p. 141.

79 Iena, vol. IV, p. 340, R, p. 141.

80 Iena, vol. VIII, p. 112, R, p. 142.

81 T. Bohlin, *Sören Kierkegaard*, p. 168.

82 PS, pp. 368–369, Iena, vol. VII, p. 209.

83 Text is cited without reference by T. Bohlin, *Sören Kierkegaard*, p. 169.

84 Pap., VIII¹, A, 219, R, p. 143.

85 Pap., VIII¹, A, 55, R, p. 144.

86 Pap., VIII¹, A, 25, R, p. 144.

87 Kierkegaard treats of this theme *ex professo* in his *Miettes philosophiques*, pp. 45–66, Iena, vol. VI, pp. 8–20.

88 *Miettes* . . . , p. 46.

89 *Miettes* . . . , p. 50.

90 *Miettes* . . . , pp. 55–56.

91 *Miettes* . . . , p. 60.

92 *Miettes* . . . , p. 64.

93 *Miettes* . . . , p. 60.

94 Pap., IV, A, 47, *Christ*, p. 11.

95 *Miettes* . . . , pp. 84–85.

96 Pap., IV, A, 103, *Christ*, pp. 13–14.

97 Excellent insights concerning the relations of Kierkegaard's Christology with that of Barth are found in an article of Jean Rilliet, *Le rôle de Jésus dans la Römerbrief de K. Barth et la christologie de S. Kierkegaard*, RTP, 1942, vol. 30, pp. 228–239.

98 *Miettes* . . . , p. 178, Iena, vol. VI, p. 78.

99 Pap., VIII¹, A, 565, *Christ*, pp. 29–30.

100 Kierkegaard treats the historical and objective study of the Bible most explicitly in the *Post-scriptum*, pp. 14–21 (Iena, vol. VI, pp. 118–126).

101 "The Thames tunnel, began in 1825, was not completed until 1845, due to accidents" (note of Paul Petit).

102 PS, p. 15.

103 PS, p. 20.

104 PS, pp. 17–18.

105 PS, pp. 18–19.

106 PS, p. 19.

107 PS, pp. 20–21.

108 Pap., X², A, 555, R, p. 213.

109 Pap., X², A, 555, R, p. 214.

110 E.P., 1851, 3, R, p. 214.

111 PS, p. 135, Iena, vol. VI, p. 260.

112 Pap., I, 99, *Journal*, p. 40.

113 PS, pp. 218–219, Iena, vol. VII, p. 24.

114 PS, p. 139, Iena, vol. VI, p. 266.

115 Pap., I, 99, *Journal*, pp. 39–40.

116 Iena, vol. IX, p. 210. This text is cited by Geismar in RHPR, 1926, pp. 55–56.

117 *Crainte et tremblement*, p. 82.

118 *Ibid.*, p. 81.

119 *Ibid.*, pp. 85–86.

120 Iena, vol. IX, p. 3, R, p. 218.

121 PS, p. 218, Iena, vol. VII, pp. 23–24.

122 Pap., III, A, 216, R, 218.

123 Pap., II, A, 755, R, p. 271.

124 Pap., IX, A, 115, R, p. 274.

125 Cf. Ruttenbeck, *Sören Kierkegaard*, p. 274.

126 "My activity as an author, can be considered as a correction of what already exists. The word *correction* is a determination of my own thought, such as: here, there; on the right, on the left. A person who wishes to make a correction must study thoroughly and precisely the weak aspects of existing opinions and then propose their contraries, forcefully and without qualification. The correction consists in this very proposal; so, too, does the resignation of the person who feels obliged to make the correction. The correction, of course, is made to a certain degree at the expense of what is corrected. If such is the case, a seemingly incisive mind can in turn make the charge that the correction views only one side of the situation; moreover, it can easily persuade the public that such is actually the case. Well, nothing is easier than for the person who first made the correction to add to it the complementary aspect. But in that case the correction ceases to be a correction and becomes itself something to be corrected. Such a criticism can issue only from a person who lacks the resignation indispensable for making a correction; moreover, he even lacks the patience necessary to notice that such resignation is wanting" (Pap., X1, A, 640, R, pp. 358–359).

127 T. Bohlin, *Glaube und Offenbarung*, pp. 132–134.

128 Ruttenbeck, *Sören Kierkegaard*, pp. 359–360.

129 T. Bohlin, *Glaube und Offenbarung*, p. 112.

130 Cf. note 96 of the present chapter.

131 Cf. Jean Wahl, *Études kierkegaardiennes*, p. 133.

132 Cf. note 35 of the present chapter.

133 Jean Wahl, *Études kierkegaardiennes,* p. 144.

134 "It is not less true that many of the features of the Hegelian dialectic are retained in the idea of a dialectical development, bound to the idea of nothingness, and characterized by a constant inversion of the negative by the positive, of sorrow by happiness, of non-being by being, . . . . In short, we have contrasted paradox with synthesis; nothing remains but to admit that the two ideas are closely related" (Jean Wahl, *Études kierkegaardiennes,* pp. 165–166).

135 *Die Mystik und das Wort* appeared in 1924. Barth had been attacking Schleiermacher since his first conferences, published in *Parole de Dieu et parole humaine* (conferences delivered from 1916 until 1923).

136 Cf. section *A* of the present chapter.

137 Cf. section *A* of chapter XI.

138 PS, p. 230, Iena, vol. VII, p. 38.

# 13

# General outline
## of the catholic position

WITH THE conclusion of the preceding chapter, our study is complete. In Chapter XI the summary of our historical and critical explanation reduced Barth's system to a fundamental position; in Chapter XII we linked up this basic line of argumentation to its doctrinal sources. We should like, however, as a final step, to briefly explain the Catholic positions that oppose these principles of Barth. This should not be misunderstood; our intent is not to begin a new discussion of Barth's theories. Our lengthy explanations were intended to present the weaknesses as well as the merits of his system of thought. Now we simply want to indicate the solutions which Catholic theology brings to the questions to which Barth gives debatable answers. This last chapter—intended especially for Protestants who may read this work—will present in broad outline the official position of Catholic theology and adhere as closely as possible to the normative decisions of the Church.

Let us recall once more the three principles of Barthianism which, singled out in Chapter XI, we expressed as: 1) the contemporary and discontinuous character of the advent of the Word of God; 2) the essentially mysterious character of the Word of God; 3) the *credo quia absurdum*.

## A. Immediate or Mediate Revelation?

It is Kierkegaard's idea of contemporaneity joined with his problematic of the *Moment,* which dominates Barth's thought on the question of the intermittent communication of the Word of God. Since man is contemporaneous with God and since God's liberty is thought to resemble man's liberty, Barthian revelation occurs in the form of successive moments.[1] Man is immediately face to face with God. A problem, therefore, is implied in Barth's first principle: is revelation mediate or immediate, a fact of the past or a contemporary, present-day communication? Does God speak to us directly or through intermediaries? To this question we must give two replies which are complementary to each other.

1) As a rule, revelation can be immediate or mediate without effecting the nature of faith. The antiquity of the revelation or its contemporaneity, as a matter of fact, changes nothing of the *nature* of faith. As we shall later explain, the motive of faith is the authority of God who makes the revelation. The main point is that God's testimony about Himself be communicated. Whether it is done directly or indirectly does not change in any way the essence of faith.

Catholic theology, under penalty of denying the evidence, does not, therefore, exclude in any way immediate revelation. Such revelation existed among the patriarchs, the prophets, and the apostles. The message which they have passed down to us binds the whole Church.[2] Immediate revelation is thus at the origin of mediate revelation. The point, however, which Catholic theology cannot insist on enough is the adequacy of mediate revelation for the faith of believers. That is one of the bastions of the Catholic position against the encroachments of illuminism. Recall that among the Anabaptists, prophetic illuminism was substituted for scriptural revelation.[3] Their Anglo-Saxon disciples, the Quakers, sought for a compromise by the admission of the existence of two revelations: one exterior, that of the Bible; the other interior, that of the Holy Spirit. At the beginning of the century, this immediate contact became a vague religious emotion in which a certain type of liberal Protestant faith is summed up:

Do not believe, my brother, that the prophets and reformers have passed on their experiences to you in order to excuse you from having your own. . . . The revelations of the past become efficacious and real only if they render you capable of receiving the personal revelation which God reserves for you. . . . Thus the divine revelation which

is not realized in us and does not become immediate does not exist at
all as far as we are concerned.[4]

Although Barth denies it, his thought is, nevertheless, a tribu-
tary of this spiritualistic stream. If we are to understand his
system in the light of its first principle, his thought takes on the
aspect of a prophetic illuminism, quite similar to that of the
Quakers.

Mediate revelation suffices. Saint John records this saying of
Christ for us: "For if you believed Moses you would believe me
also, for he wrote of me. If you do not believe his writings, how
will you believe my words?" (John 5:46–47). Speaking in this
way, Jesus appeals to mediate revelation entrusted to Scripture
and transmitted through it. So it is with Saint Paul, who makes
preaching a normal condition of faith: "But how are they to
believe him whom they have not heard? And how are they to
hear, if no one preaches?" (Romans 10:14). Preaching is an intermediary which necessarily renders revelation mediate.

2) Since we have firmly established the sufficiency of mediate
revelation, we must further recall that the faith of modern believers is based upon it alone. We must distinguish, at this point,
the types of immediate revelations. They are not all private revelations; some have enriched the deposit of faith. Those made to
Moses and Abraham can be called public. Private revelation is
communication without an intermediary to a particular individual, but *for* him alone. Such relevations are still possible today,
since the Council of Trent admits that God *could* give someone
the assurance of his final perseverance by special revelation.[5]
However, they do not belong to the patrimony of the Christian
faith.

If private revelations are still possible today, how can they
be distinguished from those which involve the faith of the
Church? Of course, one could study their contents and judge
them in that way. But such a criterion is obviously insufficient.
Also, by her infallible authority the Church has settled the case
once and for all by declaring at the Council of Trent that supernatural revelation . . . "is contained in the Scriptures and in unwritten traditions received by the apostles from the mouth of
Christ or dictated to the apostles by the Holy Spirit." [6] This

teaching has been restated precisely in the condemnation of the
modernist proposition that "the revelation which constitutes the
object of the Catholic faith did not end with the apostles." [7]
Hence the situation is clear: after the death of the last apostle,
there was no further immediate revelation involving the faith of
the Church.[8]

Some modernists did not hesitate to designate the notion of
closed revelation as puerile. By what right does the Church decide
that revelation was closed at this moment rather than that? Is
not such a decision purely arbitrary? Not at all: the decision of
the Church is conditioned by the history of human salvation. The
history of the world, from the Christian point of view, is not an
indefinite succession of disparate events of equal importance. It
is the history of a primordial creation, of the sin of man, of the
promised salvation, at first longingly awaited and finally realized
in Christ. When salvation was accomplished, a summit was
reached, a plenitude was achieved. As one eminent Protestant
exegete says so well: "The new element brought by Christ to the
faith of primitive Christianity is that, since Easter, the center for
the believer is no longer located in the future but in the past." [9]
The mid-point of history was attained with the death and resurrection of Christ. The rest of human history is simply the extension of the fruits of this decisive victory over sin and death to all
men. The resurrection of Christ has already introduced us into
the final age.

Revelation followed a parallel development. In the preparatory
stages of the decisive event, revelations which became more explicit and urgent helped mankind in his longing and desire for
salvation. Thus the Old Testament, right up to the last prophet,
John the Baptist, is directed towards Christ. Once Christ was given,
revelation no longer has any other role but to make the gift of
salvation known and appreciated. That is why the deposit of faith
was definitely closed with the death of the last direct witness to an
event unique in time: the victorious redemption. Since, with the
coming of Christ, we no longer need await a new redeemer, a
continual revelation would lose all its meaning: it is enough if
it is guarded faithfully and preached unremittingly. There is then
nothing puerile or arbitrary in the limit set on revelation by the

Council of Trent and the Decree *Lamentabili*. On the contrary, those who speak of a revelation constantly increased by new divine communications would be hard put to justify their position by authentically Christian arguments.

Catholic doctrine, therefore, presents two very clear principles in opposition to Barth's immediate revelation: 1) the adequacy of mediate revelation for Christian faith; 2) the absolute exclusion, in man's present state, of new revelations involving the faith of the Church. In this way, Catholic theology, infinitely better than the Barthian position, defends that *Einmaligkeit* of redemption in Christ to which the theologian of Basle seems to attach decisive importance. There is no continual revelation because Christ died once and for all. He can die no more.

## B. The State of the Intellect in a Fallen Nature.

When Karl Barth asserts that it is impossible for man in his present condition to acquire any knowledge whatever of the Word of God, he destroys the idea of revelation. To maintain that revelation cannot be perceived by man is meaningless, for this would presuppose that God is incapable of adopting His teaching to the concrete state of human nature. We cannot undertake again a general discussion of this position which we amply investigated in the body of this study; we simply wish to explain the Catholic position regarding the state of the intellect in fallen nature. We shall not treat of the revelation of supernatural truths: on that point, it stands to reason that, if God reveals them to a nature wounded by sin, then that nature is able to receive them. Of more interest for our purpose is the study of the efforts of human reason to know the truths which concern natural religion. In the following pages, we shall discuss the problem of the relative necessity of supernatural revelation for a knowledge of these natural truths. The Church has taken a determined stand on this question at the Vatican Council. We shall therefore examine the problem in the twofold light of the official teaching of the Church and of theology.

1. Before we approach the question of the usefulness of revelation to the acquisition of a knowledge of natural truths, we must

determine the *strength* of the human intellect independently of revelation. The Vatican Council, in the second chapter of the *Constitutio de fide* and in the canon which corresponds to it, gives us a clear teaching on the subject: "The same Holy Church, our Mother, holds and teaches that, by the natural light of human reason, God, the Beginning and End of all things, can be known with certitude by means of created things. . . . Let him be anathema who says that the one true God, our Creator and Lord, cannot be known with certitude by the natural light of human reason by means of created beings." [10]

What is the precise meaning of this text? [11] First we must note that, according to the conciliar discussions, the Fathers deliberately put the question of fact to one side. The purpose of the Council is only to settle a question of general significance with regard to the *power* of reason. Its intention is to show that "the objective manifestation of God through creatures adapts itself to the structure of human reason, and that the latter possesses the resources by which it can know God in virtue of that manifestation." [12] All changes which sought to reduce this question to particular instances were rejected, and questions referring to the present condition of man were pushed to one side. The *Schema* was even corrected on one point for fear of giving the impression that the Council sought to define as a dogma of faith the impossibility of finding an adult invincibly ignorant of God.

In short, the Council simply wished to define clearly that the natural light of reason is sufficient to enable man in a definite way to know God through creatures. The *certo* has been written into the *Constitutio* to check those who consider reason incapable of arriving at more than probable knowledge in this area. Msgr. Gasser, chairman of the delegation on faith, clearly points out the errors which the Council seeks to combat: "You know the view which the Encyclopedists of France and the first advocates of critical philosophy in Germany have propagated in the minds of many souls. This widespread view holds that the existence of God cannot be proved with full certitude and that the arguments, which have been highly valued in all ages, are not beyond all discussion." [13] Although it affirms certitude in the natural knowledge of God and apparently favors the Thomistic thesis (demonstration), nevertheless, the Council has not condemned those who, in following Descartes, considered this knowledge innate in man.[14] Such toleration, however, is not extended to the ontologists. Without reaching the point of explicit condemnation, the council, nevertheless, indirectly condemned the contrary position by allusion to "created things." Thus it rejects an innate knowledge which would not be mediate, in which recourse to creation would not play any role and which would, in the long run, resolve itself into a sort of philosophical vision of God.[15]

The Council deliberately refrained from a treatment of particular cases. Yet these are of chief interest to us. We must, therefore, look for some complementary teaching in theology. The Council was concerned only with the power of human reason and not with the capabilities of a particular human being. Is it possible—and here is our difficulty—that there are individuals in good faith who do not know God? We are not speaking of the great body of men whose very belief in the existence of God constitutes proof by universal consent. We are dealing here with particular cases, exceptional situations. Is it possible that a man whose reason has reached maturity (therefore neither child nor insane), after he has made a sincere investigation (which is required in order to be in good faith), could still remain an atheist? Theologians reply almost unanimously in the negative. What are their reasons? Theological as well as philosophical arguments are numerous. It is enough to point out that atheism in good faith seems absolutely incompatible with the text of St. Paul in his Epistle to the Romans (I, 20–21): "For since the creation of the world his invisible attributes are clearly seen—his everlasting power also and divinity—being understood through the things that are made. And so they are without excuse, seeing that, although they knew God, they did not glorify him as God. . . ." The culpability of the pagans is based on the fact that, capable of knowing God (and knowing Him in fact to a certain extent), they did not want to recognize Him, and silencing the voice of conscience, they turned to the worship of idols.[16] If this argument is valid for pagans, a fortiori it is valid for all men. Saint Paul does no more than base his argument on the natural order. We live in the midst of creatures, and our mind is spontaneously prompted to look for the cause of everything that falls beneath our gaze. Is it possible under these conditions to avoid the notion of God's existence over a long period of time? Sooner or later the idea will force itself upon us.[17]

Our summary of the defined dogma and the teaching of theology can be thus expressed:

a) the natural light of human reason is sufficient to arrive at a certain knowledge of God;

b) it is impossible for a man who is in good faith and has the use of reason to be ignorant of God.

2. In the dogmatic definition proper, the Council contented itself with the assertion that human reason can know God. Vacant shows, as a matter of fact, that the terms which qualify the word "God" in the first *canon* do not belong to the defined dogma.[18] For example, it is not part of the Council's purpose—this follows clearly from a statement by Msgr. Gasser—to define that God can be known as the Creator from the natural light of reason. The *chapter,* then, must be considered as more explicit on this point: God is therein defined as the beginning and end of all things. This doctrinal supplement, therefore, contains an official teaching of the Church, irrevocably defined and infallible, yet without being a dogma, since it is not repeated as such in the canon.

Philosophy permits us to go further. Reason can know all truths *"ex sensibilibus cognoscibiles"* since they belong to its own domain. From "sensible" natures reason reaches their first cause, God. This knowledge of God, which is analogical in character, extends not only to his existence but his essence and his attributes, insofar as they can be known *"ex creaturis."* Therefore, we can say that human reason is capable of knowing all the truths —both about man and about God—which belong to the domain of natural religion.

In the face of this *maximum* capacity of the human intelligence to attain those relations which unite man with God, theologians acknowledge that no one can actually be ignorant of God if he is living under normal conditions. Invincible ignorance of God is impossible. To be sure, the *minimum* which theologians admit in the most ignorant of men is only a summary knowledge, not explicit and quite imperfect; nevertheless it is enough to exclude atheism.

If a minimum knowledge, reduced to a few essential truths, is acquired by all men, can the maximum be achieved? There is no doubt it could have been in that state of human nature which preceded original sin. At that moment in human history, nature was adorned with such gifts that the exercise of the intellect and will meet with no obstacle. But since then, that sin occurred which has considerably enfeebled human nature. The Vatican Council made the following decision on this point: "We must . . . attribute to this divine revelation the fact that ideas, which in divine matters are not inaccessible of themselves to human reason, could *also* be known *in our present state* by all without difficulty and with firm certitude and the exclusion of all error. However, it is not for this reason that revelation must be called necessary." The canon determines what must be held as dogma in this official doctrine: "Let him be anathema who says that it is impossible or inexpedient for man to be taught by divine revelation about God and the worship due him." [19]

Thus the Council affirms the usefulness of revelation for a knowledge of the truths of natural religion; and it develops the doctrine in three steps:

a) men who have received Christian revelation have an easy and perfect knowledge of these truths;

b) this knowledge must be attributed to Christian revelation;

c) revelation is not absolutely necessary for the knowledge of the truths of natural religion. On this last point, Msgr. Gasser, in his commentary on the text proposed (of which not a single word has been changed), gives the following explanation:

The text teaches that revelation is of moral necessity, that is to say, a necessity which does not flow from the object, since the object is that which, in divine affairs, is not inaccessible to human reason; this necessity flows from the subject, that is, from man in the present condition of the human race. Moreover, it is a matter, not of the power (active) of knowing God, but of an actual knowledge on the part of our understanding—a knowledge which all men attain without difficulty, that is, without a long delay and long research, with firm certitude, even on the part of those who are scarcely capable of grasping proofs furnished by reason; and lastly, of a knowledge without admixture of error. In order to arrive at this actual knowledge and fulfill these conditions by purely natural means, man, such as he is at present, meets with so many great obstacles that supernatural revelation can be regarded as morally necessary.[20]

Therefore, we in no way deny the active capacity of the human intelligence for attaining knowledge of its proper object, even in the present state of human nature. The precise point of the preceding paragraph was to deny the contrary proposition. Furthermore, he has not excluded the possibility that some particularly hardy and gifted individuals could surmount all obstacles and, after much effort and toil, attain to a pure, integral knowledge of the truths of natural religion. The necessity of revelation for an easy, perfect and universal knowledge was the fact confirmed by the members of the Council.

On this point, the Council was merely presenting a summary of the theology of Saint Thomas. The latter deals with the question in very clear terms on several occasions. Here is the final expression of his thought in an article in the *Secunda secundae:* [21]

For man it is necessary to receive as from faith, not only things beyond reason but also certain things known by reason. This is so for three reasons. First, that he might arrive more quickly at a knowledge of divine truth. For the science, whose function it is to prove the existence of God and other truths of the same kind relating to God, comes last of all among those sciences which are given to men for their instruction, since much else is presupposed by it. Thus, only after a long time would men attain to the knowledge of God. Secondly, in order that the knowledge of God might be more widely known. Many indeed cannot make progress in the pursuit of knowledge, either because they have dull minds, or they have other occupations and are busied with temporal necessities, or also because they are apathetic to learning. People of this type would be utterly frustrated in acquiring knowledge of God, if divine truths were not proposed to them by means of faith. The third reason is to have certitude. Human reason is indeed weak in the presence of divine realities: an indication of this feebleness is the fact that men of learning who have carefully investigated human realities have fallen into numerous errors and have contradicted themselves on many points when they examined their opinion on these lofty matters. In order that a certain and indubitable knowledge of God should exist among human beings, the divine realities had to be conveyed to them by God, Who cannot lie.[22]

At first sight, one might think that Saint Thomas is stressing the necessity of revelation too far, by his admission that certain individuals could be deprived of that elementary knowledge of God, conceded by theologians to every man who is in good faith and is capable of reasoning. If we read more carefully, we will see that this is not so. The knowledge of God of which Saint Thomas speaks—clearly apparent in parallel texts—is a perfect knowledge with all the scientific apparatus requisite in these matters. "These people would be utterly deprived" of this kind of knowledge, and not at all of that kind which makes atheism in good faith impossible.

We can see the more delicately developed Catholic position in comparison with the Barthian position. The former takes into account sin, but does not lose sight of the fact that mankind in his fallen nature is descended from the mankind of the primeval creation. To Barth's assertion: "All natural knowledge of God is impossible in mankind's present state," Catholic theology replies that, while man is man, the object of his intellect and his intellect, in itself, have not changed; nevertheless, the normal and harmonious exercise of reason is rendered difficult by sin and hence supernatural revelation is very useful for obtaining a knowledge of the natural truths about God. If the exercise of the human intellect meets with obstacles today, these obstacles, after serious study, using all the resources of a normally developed intelligence, would never justify ignorance of certain elementary and essential truths about God.

## C. Harmony between Faith and Reason.

When Karl Barth, following Kierkegaard, claims that *fiducia* is so independent of reason that it can contradict it, he is not adopting a new position in the history of thought. On more than one occasion, thinkers believed they had solved the problem of the relation between reason and faith by having recourse to the doctrine of the double truth. In the sixteenth century an official

276 The Value of Barth's Principles

intervention by the Church was deemed necessary. At that time Pierre Pomponazzi, an Italian philosopher, distinguished between the philosophically true and the theologically true. Thus he thought that reason could not help but prove the mortality of the soul apodictically, whereas its immortality is taught by revelation.[23] The human intellect found itself, as it were, in the presence of two contradictory truths about one and the same object. The Fifth Ecumenical Council of the Lateran, in 1513, condemned not only Pomponazzi's position on the immortality of the soul, but likewise the principle of the double truth which was at the origin of this assertion: "Since truth does not contradict itself in any way, we declare that any assertion contrary to a truth attested to by an enlightened faith is absolutely false." [24]

1. In the nineteenth century two diametrically opposite errors necessitated a general condemnation. For the rationalists, it was evident that reason could contradict revelation. In this case, dogmatic declarations would be false and opposed to right reason. Pius IX sums up their position in a passage of his encyclical of November 9, 1846: "These relentless enemies of the Christian name do not even blush to teach openly and publicly that the sacred mysteries of our religion are the inventions of man's imagination." [25] Traditionalism, at the other extreme, claims that reason, left to itself, is powerless; hence immediate revelation or tradition, bearing witness to a primitive revelation, is absolutely necessary, not only—as is obvious—for the knowledge of supernatural mysteries, but also for the truths of natural religion.[26]

Between these two extremes, Anton Günther tried to find a harmonization of faith and reason. He did not in any way deny the necessity of revelation nor the inability of natural reason to arrive at a knowledge of mysteries, properly so-called; but he claims that, once in possession of formulas of faith, the human intellect can demonstrate their content. Thus revelation is necessary in a very relative way: it should intervene only to set the mechanism of autonomous philosophical research in motion. With such principles as a starting point, the semi-rationalism of Günther was destined soon to come into conflict with dogmatic formulas, which do not easily admit of accommodation to the manipulations of a philosophical system descended from Kant and Hegel.[27]

Rationalism and Traditionalism have this in common: both acknowledge the existence of two groups of absolutely irreconcilable propositions: those of faith and those of reason. These systems differ only in the value they place on each of the two groups. For the rationalists the propositions of faith have no value; for the traditionalists the conclusions of natural reason yield no certitude. The reconciliation attempted by Günther was not a reconciliation at all, since it finally yielded to pure and simple rationalism. The debate was becoming a danger to souls; the Church had to settle it once and for all. On this question the Vatican Council declared:

Although faith is superior to reason, there can be no real disagreement whatsoever between faith and reason, since God, Who reveals mysteries and gives us faith, is the very same God Who has endowed the soul of man with reason; therefore, it is impossible for God Himself to disavow His own actions, or for one truth to be contrary to another truth. The impression of an apparent contradiction arises especially from the fact that the dogmas of faith have not been understood and explained in accordance with the thought of the Church, or because false opinions are taken for conclusions of reason. We declare, therefore, that any assertion, contrary to a truth, accepted through an enlightened faith, is absolutely false.[28]

The Council clearly affirms the impossibility of discord between reason and faith, and it bases this affirmation on two arguments: the first, from the nature of God; the other, from the nature of truth itself. Only the first argument is developed in the conciliar text: since the same God is the source of revelation and reason, real dissension cannot possibly arise. Faith ascends to God in two ways: first, by means of its object which is a revealed truth; next, by means of the virtue of faith, which is a *habitus* infused into our intellectual faculty which enables us to know revealed truths. Human knowledge also comes from God but through the mediation of the natural light of human reason. This kind of knowledge does not penetrate the secrets of God but the sensible *quiddities* made evident to us by the natural light of our

intellect. Since God is the first cause of all creation, this natural
light finds its origin in Him. Since it would be absurd to imagine
that God could contradict Himself, it must certainly be admitted
that the truths which issue from one and the same source cannot
contradict each other.

The second argument is based on the nature of truth. While
the Council's first argument develops St. Thomas' proof to some
extent, the second, drawn from the same source, is only briefly
outlined.[29] We can explain it in the following way: truth cannot be opposed to truth. Now it is evident that the first principles
of reason, like the articles of faith, are absolutely true; therefore,
we cannot admit one single instance when they could be opposed
to each other. To prove his major premise, St. Thomas recalls the
definition of truth itself: *adaequatio rei et intellectus*. The intellect is true whenever the concept it affirms is conformed to reality.
Moreover, since reality is one because being is one, its intellectual
expression is likewise one. One cannot, as a matter of fact, conceive two different "equations" relating to the same real value. If,
then, two irreconcilable truths are expressed about the same
object, a careful examination will reveal that at least one of these
propositions is not conformed to reality. The absolute unity of
being demands the absolute unity of truth.

With good reason, then, does the Vatican Council request those
who believe they see an opposition between faith and reason to
make a more diligent investigation.[30] This apparent contradiction
can result either from an inexact interpretation of the dogmas of
faith, or from an abuse of reason by which one imagines he can
propose as certain a conclusion what is only a false opinion. "If
therefore," says St. Thomas, "we find something contrary to faith
in the writings of the philosophers, it is no longer a question of
genuine philosophy, but an abuse of a philosophy no longer
obedient to the laws of reason." [31]

2. While it entirely rejects a false transcendence of faith, the
Vatican Council does not lose sight of its true transcendence.
Faith and reason cannot contradict each other; nevertheless, it
remains true that faith far surpasses reason. It is the intention of
the Fathers of the Council to recall this fact when treating of the
formal motive of faith. Rationalism and semi-rationalism had, in

fact, totally neglected the distinction between faith and science. The rationalists doubtless still speak of "religious faith," but they mean by that only "the natural science of that which relates to God and religion." [32] For the semi-rationalists, "all firm belief in God and divine truths constitutes faith, properly so-called, which produces believers; this faith exists even though the motive of assent is not the authority of God but the intrinsic connection between ideas." [33] The disciples of Hermes were the special target of the Council. As documentary evidence, the Acts of the Council have retained the following text of the German theologian: "If . . . we wish to define faith, we must say that faith is a state of certitude or of persuasion in relation to the truth of the thing known, a state to which we are led by the necessary assent of speculative reason or by the assent of the practical reason. This rational faith is the supreme goal of all philosophy." [34] Obviously this point of view is next-door neighbor to Hegel's religious philosophy.[35]

There had to be a clarification. The Council accomplished this by a long definition of faith, the elements of which are taken in large part from the Council of Trent.[36] Among the additions made by the Vatican Council to the Tridentine definition, there appears in clear terms the motive why our intellect decides to adhere to the truths we believe in: "The Church . . . professes that (faith) is a supernatural virtue, by which we believe those things which God has revealed to be true, not because of their intrinsic truth perceived by the natural light of reason, but *because of the authority of God Himself,* Who is revealing them and Who can neither deceive nor be deceived." [37]

The distinction between science and faith is thus clearly delineated. Science, in its highest achievements, attains to the "how" and the "why" of things and perceives the bonds which link one truth with another. In other words, when it formulates a proposition, it sees how the predicate agrees with the subject. Faith misses this intrinsic connection, since it does not have a direct view of the truth it affirms. If, therefore, faith accepts it as true, it does so by reason of an authority which offers all the guarantees of knowledge and truthfulness. Thus "God Who makes the revelation and Who can neither be deceived nor mistaken" is the formal motive of faith.

The Council condemns as heretics those who say " . . . that divine faith does not differ from natural knowledge of God and moral truths; and, consequently, to have divine faith a truth need not be believed on God's authority when He reveals it." [38] To fall under the conciliar condemnation, then, one would have to deny, at one and the same time, the distinction between faith and science and the authority of the revealing God as the motive of faith. Certainly, then, the denial of the transcendence of faith, such as the rationalists and semi-rationalists profess, comes under this anathema.

3. The assistance reason can render in the adherence to revealed truths springs simultaneously from the transcendent nature of this adherence and the deep-seated accord between reason and faith. We will treat here only of the apologetic role of reason. Without demonstrating faith, reason can lead to its threshold. On at least two occasions, the Vatican Council insists on this point. At the beginning of the third paragraph of the third chapter, the Fathers make the affirmation that " . . . the assent of faith (is) in no way a blind movement of the mind." [39] The Council excludes completely the idea of faith as a leap into the absurd in paragraph two of the same chapter, by recalling that God has put very definite signs at our disposal: "in order that the homage of our faith be in accord with reason, God has given us external proofs (*externa argumenta*) of His revelation. . . ." [40]

What is needed so that the homage of our faith may be in accord with our reason? The rest of the text tells us: the fact of revelation must be established with certitude (*divinae revelationis signa certissima . . . externa revelationis suae argumenta . . .*). As Vacant puts it: "If the fact of revelation is doubtful, the assent given to the assertions which claim to be revealed will be equally doubtful." [41] The Council, moreover, does not intend to introduce innovations in this matter; it has simply confirmed a traditional doctrine. A decree of the Holy Office on March 2, 1679, promulgated by Innocent XI against the Laxists, condemned the following proposition: "The assent of supernatural, salutary faith can be reconciled with a merely probable knowledge of revelation and even with the fear that God has not spoken at all." [42] Pius IX in 1846, in the encyclical already cited, recalled the necessity of arriving at the conviction that God has spoken: *"Divinae revelationis factum diligenter inquirat oportet, ut certo sibi constet Deum esse locutum."* [43] Thus the certitude of faith is incompatible with any uncertainty whatsoever about the fact of revelation.[44]

In order to permit reason to establish this fact beyond a doubt, God has put external proofs at its disposal, "namely human acts, especially miracles and prophecies, which, by amply demonstrating the omnipotence and infinite knowledge of God, make known the divine revelation, of which they are the infallible signs, adapted to everyone's intelligence." [45] The *rationabile obsequium,* which we have spoken of in the two preceding paragraphs, requires, then, a preliminary judgment for the act of faith "in which the human intellect recognizes that it can and must believe in such and such a truth." [46] In other words, the act of faith demands a motive of credibility. The text alludes only to the external motives of credibility. Does it mean by that that *externa argumenta* are required for each act of faith? Not at all. It does not, as a matter of fact, exclude the possibility that some purely interior motives could *sometimes* be sufficient. In this case, God places the indisputable proof in the depths of the soul that He is the author of revelation. The question which the Council seeks to answer is this: Are these interior motives given to all believers and are external motives useless because they are powerless to demonstrate the fact of revelation? The Council wishes to combat the tendency to seek refuge in an uncontrolled subjectivism by denying the propedeutic role of reason with regard to faith. For this purpose it recalls that the external proofs are most certain signs of revelation, adapted to everyone's intelligence; it intends to defend itself against a pietism of Protestant origin which threatens to infiltrate Catholicism. A note added to the first *Schema* emphasizes that "among Protestants who acknowledge the Christian revelation there is a great number who reject the criteria by which the fact of revelation is demonstrated and who appeal only to *interior experience,* to *religious feeling,* to the *testimony of the Holy Ghost,* or to an *immediate certainty of faith.* Thus they completely reject the value or necessity of motives of credibility drawn from miracles, from the fulfillment of prophecies, etc.; or, if they do not reject them entirely, they admit them only as aids which come to the assistance of faith

and presuppose it. . . . " [47] The most authoritative representative
of this trend is unquestionably F. Schleiermacher. In one of his
texts he rejects all apologetic proof: "We absolutely reject the idea
of any demonstration of the truth or necessity of the Christian
religion; but we suppose that before any investigation each Christian feels certain that no form of religion other than the Christian
one corresponds to the aspirations of his piety." [48] In an approach
of this kind to the religious problem, reason no longer plays a role.
Everything is reduced to a mysterious meeting between subjective
aspirations and Christianity.[49]

It is understood that the Council vigorously condemned those
who say: "Divine revelation cannot be made credible by external
signs, and hence man must be led to faith only by an interior, personal experience or by private inspiration." [50] By this anathema,
the Church officially defends the rights and duties of reason in approaching the mystery of faith.

In the history of dogmas, the Church has always shown distrust
toward all forms of illuminism. Reason and faith, both of which
come from God, cannot conflict with one another but ought to
give mutual assistance. Consequently, the doctrines of Kierkegaard
and Barth, which admit of compatibility between affirmation and
denial on the same point of doctrine, are unacceptable to both
faith and reason. In no way does it follow that Catholicism reduces faith to reason. On the contrary, it has always fought rationalism with vigor; no religious institution has maintained as constant and relentless a battle with the enemy of the supernatural.
Faith transcends reason. This transcendence, however, does not resolve itself into a conflict. The most obvious proof is that reason,
though incapable of raising itself to the level of faith, can nevertheless lead the inquiring soul towards faith. The world created
by God is not a chaos but a perfectly harmonious, hierarchical
whole.

*
*       *

In the course of its recent history, the Catholic Church has been
confronted with various systems which Kierkegaard and Barth
rightly oppose. Since the Vatican Council, the Church has had to
combat numerous forms of Hegelian rationalism and Schleier-

macher's theology of religious sentiment. Later, at the height of the modernist crisis, the Church was forced to oppose doctrines related to Liberal Protestantism. To each of these errors she put up a vigorous resistance. However, this absolute denial did not destroy the equilibrium of the Christian synthesis. The Church did not combat one excess with another but was able to point out a middle path guaranteeing to reason and faith their respective rights.

# notes

## to chapter thirteen

1 Barth's first principle is based on a twofold confusion: the confusion of revelation with grace, and of grace with the substantial activity of God. This confusion leads not only to a negation of divine immutability, but also to an unconscious adoption of a species of supernatural pantheism.

This first principle implies that revelation and grace affect man only in a purely intermittent manner. We have seen how Barth, by inverting the Kierkegaardian problematic of the *Instant*, felt obliged to situate the cause of this discontinuity in the very liberty of God. This is due to the fact that God "changes his mind"; He decides to let us sink once more into the shadows, after having drawn us to His light for an instant, since revelation reaches us only momentarily. For Barth, the intermittency of revelation is absolutely irreconcilable with a doctrine of divine immutability.

The allegedly discontinuous character of revelation, however, could be explained without recourse to this extremity, just as a series of different effects can be explained without recourse to a series of distinct divine acts. "Aliud est mutare voluntatem; et aliud est velle aliquarum rerum mutationem. Potest enim aliquis, eadem voluntate immobiliter permanente, velle quod nunc fiat hoc, et postea fiat contrarium" (I, q. 19, a. 7). "Deus cuncta mutabilia immutabili voluntate disponit" (Saint Augustine, *Ad Simplic.*, Bk. II, q. 2, n. 4, PL, vol. XL, col., 141).

The very foundation of Barthianism precludes an appeal to this explanation. For to admit this explanation would be equivalent to accepting the possibility of created supernatural effects, that is to say, effects substantially separate from God. It would mean the introduction into reformed theology of the concept of a divine gift which would be the divinization of the Christian. In a word, it would imply the acceptance of the theological category of *gratia creata*. But Barth, following Protestant tradition, rejects this category. If then, the theologian of Basle feels obliged to maintain that revelation is intermittent in man, he cannot explain it by a unique divine act which would be the origin *ab aeterno* of a chain of distinct created effects. He feels compelled to attribute these effects to momentary contacts of God's substantial action. Man's reception of revelation is nothing more than the fact that for a moment he becomes the object of a divine favor. Grace is not a gift of God; it is simply His hand alighting on man's soul momentarily. If then there exists a sequence of acts within man, there must be a corresponding sequence within the divine will. The divine will, therefore, is not immutable.

This identification of grace with the very activity of God leads to pantheism. Barth in fact rejects "forensic justification." God's action is not a purely external imputation; it really, though only momentarily, transforms the person whom it affects. Man is transformed by divine action. Now, at no moment is this transformation of man distinct from the substantial act of God. From this line of reasoning, we must conclude that God Himself is man's justification. Thus we are face to face with a subtle pantheism which, without further ado, identifies redeemed man (in so far as redeemed) with the very substance of God.

If Barth had distinguished between grace and revelation, he would have noted that grace, which is liable to be lost, can be said to be discontinuous (provided this word is properly understood), whereas revelation is given once and for all. If he had distinguished created grace from divine act itself, he would have been able to conceive of a divinization of the Christian, without transporting him beyond his condition of creaturehood.

2 "Abraham put his faith in God, and it was reckoned virtue in him" (Rom. 4:3). Now the revelation in question in Araham's case was an immediate revelation. Such a revelation, therefore, is perfectly compatible with the act of faith.

3 Cf. chapter II.

4 Auguste Sabatier, *Esquisse*, pp. 58–59, cited by S. Harent, in DTC, vol. VI, col. 143.

5 Cf. *Denzinger*, 826.

6 *Denzinger*, 783. This definition was adopted by the Vatican Council. Cf. *Denzinger*, 1787.

7 Decree, *Lamentabili*, July 3, 1907, proposition 21, *Denzinger*, 2021.

8 If certain persons are the recipients of private revelations, they are obliged to believe in them. Indeed, if God speaks to a soul directly, He is pledging His truth. Others are in no way bound to take an interest in a revelation which is in no way addressed to them. They are not even bound to inquire into the subject, since they have a right to disregard it. Since the death of the last Apostle, private revelation no longer binds anyone but the person to whom it is directed. (Cf. S. Harent, DTC, vol. VI, col. 148.)

9 O. Cullmann, *Christus und die Zeit*, p. 70.

10 *Denzinger*, 1785 and 1806.

11 In the interpretation of texts from the Vatican Council, the classical work of J. M. A. Vacant, *Études théologiques sur les constitutions du concile du Vatican*, has served as a valuable guide. We have also referred to Père Th. Granderath's two works: *Constitutiones dogmaticae œcumenici Concilii Vaticani* and *Geschichte des Vatikanischen Konzils*.

12 "Id de quo agitur, et quod Scripturae immediate affirmant, est potentia rationis: quod nimirum objectiva Dei per creaturas manifestatio ordinatur ad hominum rationem, et huic insunt vires, ut possit ex illa manifestatione Deum cognoscere" (*Schema de doctrina catholica*, adn. 6, *Acta et decreta Concilii Vaticani*, col. 520).

13 *Relatio de emendationibus capitis secundi const. de fide*, ad emend. 3, *Acta et decreta . . .* , col. 130.

14 Cf. M. Chossat, DTC, vol. IV, col. 874.

15 The demonstrability of God's existence is a common doctrine of the Church. Demonstration as the *unique* way of coming to a knowledge of God's existence is defended by St. Thomas, in his *Summa Theol.*, I, q. 2, a. 1 and 2.

16 Cf. M. J. Lagrange, *Épître aux Romains*, pp. 24–25.

17 Vacant, *Études* . . . , vol. I, pp. 327–329.

18 Vacant, *Études* . . . , vol. I, pp. 306–311.

19 *Denzinger,* 1786 and 1807.

20 *Relatio de emendationibus capitis secundi const. de fide,* ad. par. 2, *Acta et decreta* . . . , col. 135.

21 Q. 2, a. 4. Although in this text St. Thomas does not explicitly attribute the debility of man's intellect to his present condition due to sin, a comparison of the whole article cited with articles dealing with original justice is sufficient to guarantee that such is certainly his intention. For example, consider the following text: "A consideratione autem plena et lucida intelligibilium effectuum impeditur homo *in statu praesenti,* per hoc quod distrahitur a sensibilibus, et circa ea occupatur. Sed sicut dicitur Eccles. VII: Deus fecit hominem rectum. Haec autem fuit rectitudo hominis divinitus instituti, ut inferiora superioribus subderentur, et superiora ab inferioribus non impedirentur. Unde homo primus non impediebatur per res exteriores a clara et firma contemplatione intelligibilium effectuum, quos ex irradiatione primae veritatis percipiebat. . . . Sic igitur per hujusmodi intelligibiles effectus Dei, Deum clarius cognoscebat quam modo cognoscamus" (I, q. 94, a. 1).

22 We have summarized six texts in which St. Thomas develops this idea. We note them in chronological order: III *Sent.* dist. 24, a. 3 qc. 1; *De ver.,* q. 14, a. 10; *In Boeth. De Trin.,* q. 3, a. 2; *Contra Gentes,* I, ch. 4; *Summa theol.,* I, q. 1, a. 1; II–II, q. 2, a. 4. In his exposition, St. Thomas is directly dependent on Maimonides, whose *quinque rationes* he simply repeats in the first three texts cited above. Beginning with his *Contra Gentes,* he adapts Maimonides' presentation. Thereafter we have a tripartite division, the third part of which we have cited in our text. The most complete treatment of this docrine is in *Contra Gentes,* where the tripartite division is expanded into eight reasons. But here again his dependence on Maimonides is obvious: five of the eight reasons are borrowed from the Jewish philosopher; one is drawn from Aristotle (VII *Phys.*); only two are proper to St. Thomas.

23 Cf. F. Bonnard, DTC, vol. XII, col. 2545.

24 *Denzinger,* 738.

25 *Denzinger,* 1634.

26 Cf. Vacant, *Études* . . . , vol. I, 141–145.

27 Cf. P. Godet, DTC, vol. VI, col. 1992–1993.

28 *Denzinger,* 1797.

29 The two arguments of the Council can be found in *Contra Gentes,* I, chap. 7.

30 When the doctrinal difficulties provoked by Modernism cropped up the Church once again had to contend against a position closely related to the one condemned by the Vatican Council. For this reason the Holy See inserted the following profession in the Oath against Modernism: "Reprobo errorem affirmantium propositam ab ecclesia fidem posse historiae repugnare" (*Denzinger,* 2146).

31 *In Boeth. De Trin.,* q. 2, a. 3.

32 *Schema de doctrina catholica,* adn. 14, *Acta et decreta* . . . , col. 527.

33 *Ibid.*

34 *Ibid.* The text refers to p. 259 of *Introd. philos. à la théologie.*

35 Cf. ch. XII, sec. d of our treatment.

36 Cf. *Denzinger,* 798.

37 *Denzinger,* 1789.

38 *Denzinger,* 1811.

39 *Denzinger,* 1791.

40 *Denzinger,* 1790.

41 *Études* . . . , vol. II, p. 35.

42 *Denzinger,* 1171.

43 *Denzinger,* 1637.

44 Following an analysis well documented with texts from the Council, R. Aubert expresses the opinion that, in paragraph II, Chapter III of the *Constitutio de fide,* the fathers of the Council are making no allusion to "the fact that every Christian, in order that his faith be reasonable, must be convinced that God has truly spoken. (The Council) was not even interested in the judgment of credibility by which a person can on occasion ascertain that the conviction 'God has spoken' is itself reasonable" (*Le problème de l'acte de foi,* p. 166). In assuming this position, R. Aubert is in definite disagreement with Vacant, who maintains that "*every act of faith* supposes a previous judgment in which the intellect recognizes that it can and must believe in a certain truth" (*Études* . . . , vol. II, p. 37). R. Aubert's opinion seems to us too far-fetched, and we feel compelled to agree with Th. Deman's judgment: "This opinion makes all possible use of what the texts do not say. Even if we admit that the judgment of credibility is not necessarily prior to the act of faith, must we not maintain that Christian faith includes the conviction that God has spoken?" (*Divus Thomas,* 1946, vol. 24, p. 219).

45 *Denzinger,* 1790.

46 Vacant, *Études* . . . , vol. II, p. 37.

47 *Schema de doctrina catholica,* adn. 16, *Acta et decreta* . . . , col. 528. Alluding to one of Schleiermacher's disciples, Twesten, the passage continues: "Recentiores vero eadem methodo retenta, huic testimonio Spiritus Sancti plerumque substituunt naturalem *sensum religiosum* vel *indigentiam animi religiosi* . . ." (*ibid*).

48 *Der christliche Glaube,* II, 5 (Berlin edition, 1830–31, vol. I, p. 84).

49 Cf. Oath against Modernism, *Denzinger,* 2145.

50 *Denzinger,* 1812.

# conclusion

KARL BARTH'S work has far-reaching historical significance: it opens up a new period for Protestant theology. Barth was the thinker awaited by his age. He arrived at a moment when exhausted liberalism had given its utmost and could wait for him no longer. Furthermore, liberal theology was not successful in satisfying truly religious souls, who were driven to attempt a new endeavour with new foundations.

In history, however, few things are conclusive. The more up-to-date a theory is, the more easily it can be abandoned. This is equally true of a system so new and revolutionary as Barth's— more true perhaps than for other systems. The theologian of dialectic has not founded a school properly speaking. There is Kantianism and Hegelianism. Can we say there is a Barthianism?

To answer this question, it seems to me that we must distinguish two things: Barth's fundamental purpose and his theological intuition. Barth wanted to give divine transcendence a place which liberalism had bitterly disputed. It was a legitimate intention and much needed. However, are we not forced to acknowledge that the theologian of Basle compromises his original purpose in making the transition into theological formulation? Has he not gone to the other extreme by inseparably associating the transcendence of the Divine Holiness with incommunicability? Thus Barthian theology rests entirely on a deformed truth, a philosophical distortion of a great scriptural theme. A transcendence which does not communicate itself nor surrender itself, which is not incarnated continuously in time—is this the transcendence of a God

Who loves the world and wants to save it? The God of the Bible
was not afraid to sanction a revelation received and handed down
by men and guarded by a Church. Hence contemporary Protestant
theology, insofar as it is under Barth's influence, depends more on
his original *intent* than on his theological elaboration. Barth will
outlive what he *intended* to accomplish.

This is not to minimize the importance of the Barthian reaction.
Let us follow the road which Protestant theology has travelled for
thirty-five years. In this period liberalism alone had any authority;
it alone represented, in Germany at least, Protestant *science*. Of
course, here and there chairs of theology were occupied by representatives of a more confessional, more positive Christianity. These
courses did not attract the students. They crowded into the lecture halls of Harnack and Jülicher, while Schlatter had little success. Any theological science which drew its inspiration from other
principles was scorned as a relic of a dead epoch.

Barth brought about a radical change. His criticism of liberalism remains the most powerful part of his work. He has literally
discredited it. He has shown that the science of a Harnack and a
Herrmann is not theology but a presumptuous "humanism."
These "theologians" did not take the Bible seriously. The Bible
did not command recognition from them, nor did they see God
behind the words of the sacred texts. No doubt liberalism is not
dead. Even Barth had to admit that at the conference at Amsterdam: "I have often had the impression that the line of separation
within the Ecumenical Council is not a denominational one, but
one that crosses through all the confessions. Is not the real division in the 'Churches' that between a biblical system of thought
and a non-biblical humanistic system?" [1] This liberalism, however,
no longer brings the response afforded it in previous decades. A
new movement, oriented towards biblical theology, is taking shape
in a large number of Protestant faculties. They proposed a return
by this to the Holy Scripture, which is accepted as an exterior
norm for the mind of man, as God's order to humanity and not as
a prolongation of a psychological experience.

A Christian can only rejoice over this development. What kind
of dealings, what interchange of ideas could one imagine having

1 *Foi et Vie*, 1948, vol. 46, p. 494.

with liberalism? From the outset we feel ourselves to be strangers. Obviously, it is futile to try to cover up all the divisions that still exist between Protestantism and Catholicism. A profound cleavage still remains. Nevertheless, we are happy to say that, insofar as it has responded to Barth's *purpose,* Protestant theology is closer to our faith. The future will reveal if we are to consider the present-day trend as a permanent attainment, an elementary stage in an ascending purifying movement, or on the contrary, merely the high-point of a descending curve.

# index

Aarau, Barth's lecture at, xxvi; Barth and Harnack at, 107

Abelard, on dialectic methods in theology, xxxvi–xxxvii

Absolute Mind, development of as theme of Hegelian thought, 225

Activity, Barth on human, 50

Actualism, Barthian, 34–35, 208

Agnosticism, as root of Barthian methodology, 211

Allegory, Barthian *Sage* as, 121–122; Catholic theology on, 123

Althaus, Paul, on traits of reform, 112; on true faith, 77

Ambivalence, Kierkegaard's, 249–251

Anabaptists, 19, thesis of, 20–21

*Analogia entis,* xv; Barth on, xx–xxi; Barthian meaning of, 69–70; Barth's rejection of, 69; Barth's use of, xvi; as method, 69; relation of, to knowledge of God, 71

*Analogia fidei,* xv; Barth on, xxi; Barth's use of term, 70–71; relation of, to knowledge of God, 71

Analogy, Barthian definition of, 70–71; as means of attaining knowledge of God, 69; von Balthasar on Barthian, xiii–xvii

Angelism, theological, 128

*Anknüpfungspunkt,* 45; Barth on, 50; Catholic theology on, 50–51

Anthropology, Barth's rejection of philosophical, 65–66

Anti-Hegelianism, Kierkegaard's, 223–229

*Apocatastase,* Origenist, xix

Apologetic proof, Schleiermacher's rejection of, 282

Apologetics, Kierkegaard's rejection of, 247–248

Aristotelianism, on relation between thought and being, 224

Articles of Smalkald, on relation between Spirit and Word of God, 22

*Aseitas,* 31

Atheism, culpability of, 271–272

*Aufheben,* Hegelian use of term, 226

*Aufklärung,* 41, 124–125

*Augsburg Confession,* on relation between Spirit and Word of God, 22

Baptism, Barthian theory on, 161–162

Barth, Fritz B., 218

Barth, Karl, on Christ's humanity, 42–44; evolution of thought of, xxvi–xxxi; pre-Anselmian Augustinianism of, xxxv; principles of, 207–210; on relation of Spirit to Scriptures, 88–90; on relation between Spirit and Word of God, 24; on Schleiermacher's position, 65; and use of term canon, 100

Bartman, B., on Catholic theory of canonicity, 98–99

Baur, F. C., Tübingen school of, 125

Being, Hegelian concept of, 226; philosophical relation of, to thought, 224

Benoit, on influence of Hegelian rationalism, 125

Bible, as an occasion, 210; authority of, 95–102; Barth on character of, 208–209; Barthian theory on, 101–102; Kierkegaard's parallelism of, with Christ, 246; Kierkegaard on value of, 242–244, 245; new movement toward, 290–291; relation of Church to, 96–101; role of, in Modernism, 101. *See also* Scriptures

Blumhardt, Christopher (father and son), 219

293

Grace, Barthian identification of, with faith and predestination, 160; Barth's theory of, 163; relation of nature to, xvi–xvii; St. Thomas on possession of, 163
Groot, J. C., v
Günther, Anton, semi-rationalism of, 276
Guohier, Henri, xviii

Harnack, Adolph von, xxvi, 217, 218, 290; on Barth, 107; on Luther's use of verbal inspiration, 19
Hegel, G. W. F., on concept of Jesus, 41; influence of, upon Barth, 254
Hegelianism, 224–229
Heidegger, Martin, 246
Heidelberg catechism, on role of *fiducia*, 74
*Heilsgeschichte*, and *geschichte*, 118
Heim, Karl, on Barthian baptismal theory, 162
Heitmüller, Wilhelm, 218
Hermeneutics, relation of to theological exegesis, 117
Herrmann, W., 218; as disciple of Ritschl, 219–223; and Kierkegaard, 242
*Historiae notitia*, role of in faith, 75
Historical fact, limitations of, 32
*Historie*, and *geschichte*, 117
History, Catholic viewpoint of, 268; Ritschl on relation of, to faith, 221
Hollaz, on Lutheran confessions of faith, 196
Hugh of St. Victor, 249
Humanism, Barth's reaction to, 290
Humanity, of Christ, 40–44; Barthian concept of God's, xxx–xxxi; role of, in act of faith, xxxvii–xxxviii
Hus, John, influence of upon Calvin, 143
Husserl, phenomenology of, 125
Hypostatic union, and humanity of Christ, 43

Ibsen, Henrik, as individualist, 217
Identity, Hegelian concept of, 225
Illumination, role of, in understanding Scriptures, 88
Illuminism, Catholic distrust of, 282; prophetic, 267
Incarnation, end of and humanity of Christ, 43
Individual; Kierkegaard's concept of, 231
Individualism, Barthian rejection of, 216–217; Barthian rejection of Kierkegaard's, 252

Infallibility, Barthian Concept of Church's, 198-199
Inspiration, Barthian concept of, 94, 95; Barthian theory of, 90–95; Catholic concept of, 94–95; limitation of, 94; relation of faith to, 95; role of, 95; signs of, 95–101; Thomistic concept of, 94–95
*Institution chrétienne* (Calvin), on canonicity, 97, 99
*Institution of Christian Religion, the*, 8–9
Instrumental causality, theory of, 89
Intellect, Barth on profanity of, 51; Schleiermacher on role of, 64; state of, in fallen nature, 269–275
Intelligence, Barth's concept of human, 48–49
Intuition, Kierkegaard on role of, 250; mystical, 252; theological, 289–290
Interventions, vertical, 210
Inwardness, existential, Kierkegaard's concept of, 231–232

Jaspers, Karl, 246
*Journal* (Kierkegaard), 249
Jülicher, Adolph, 109, 218, 290; on Barthian interpretation of St. Paul, 114; on Barth's *Römerbrief*, 113
Justice, disappearance of original, 46–47
Justification, Barthian doctrine of and Catholic theology, xxiv–xxvi; principle of, 96; Protestant reaction to doctrine of, 73
Justification by faith, as source of Luther's ecclesiology, 139–140

Kant, Emmanuel, influence of, upon Hegel, 224; on knowledge, 128
*Karl Barth, Genesis and Evolution of Dialectical Theology* (Bouillard), xviii
*Karl Barth. Word of God and Human Existence* (Bouillard), xviii
Kierkegaard, Sören, essence of thought of, 229; and Herrmann, 242; influence of, upon Barth, 215–254; philosophy of, 125
*Kirchliche Dogmatik* (Barth), xiii, xxviii, 161, 216; exegetical theory in, 115–124
Kleiner, F., 218
Knowledge, Barthian concept of, 60 ff.; Barth's elimination of analogical, 208; *Fiducia* as root of indirect, 209; relation of faith to theological, 87–88; Ritschl on source of religious, 220; role of faith in exegetical, 123

Vatican Council, on canonicity, 99; on relation between faith and reason, 277–282; on state of intellect, 270–274

Verbal inspiration, Luther's concept of, 18–19

*Verbum,* 188

*Verkündigung,* Tillich on, 188

*Verstehen und Erklären,* Barth's explanation of, 109

Vignaux, Paul, xviii; on *Monologion,* xxxiv

*Vollgestalt der Analogie* (Barth), xiii

von Balthasar, Père H. U., v ff.; on Barthian analogy, xii; presentation and interpretation of theology of Barth by, xi, xii–xvii

Wahl, Jean, xviii; on Hegelian value, 229

*Welthaftigkeit,* doctrine of, 39–40

Will, Barth on profanity of, 51

Will-acts, place of, in Barthian principles, 207

Wisdom, St. Paul on, 92, 93

Wobbermin, George, on use of empirical science in theology, 7

Wolleb, J., on the Church, 148; on predestination, 146; on role of good works, 147

Word, personalism of, 208

Word of God, as act, 29; as Almighty, 28–30; Barth's concept of, 207; Barth's identification of, with Being of God, 28; Barth on nature of, 27–35; contact with, in faith, 59–78; as Contemporary, 33–35; as Creative, 28–30; as criterion of dogmatics, 9–10; as decision, 32; as foundation of Barth's "Church," 165–166; as Free, 30–33; Luther on, 140; mysterious character of Barth's, 208–209; mystery of dualism in Barthian concept of, 252; relationship of, to Scripture, 17–24; role of, in Barthian "Church," 165–170

Works, Luther on good, 74; relation of good, to predestination, 146

Wyclif, John, influence of, upon Calvin, 143

"Zeitgeschichtlich bedingt," 111

Zwingli, H., 19; and guarantee of faith, 145; as pantheist, 124

A NOTE ON THE TYPE

IN WHICH THIS BOOK IS SET

*This book is set in Baskerville, a Linotype face, created from the original types used by John Baskerville, the eighteenth-century typefounder and printer. This type has long been considered one of the finest book types ever developed. The letters are wide and open and have a businesslike approach. The finer hairlines give exquisite delicacy. The heavier strokes give color and strength. The relation of the two in combination gives a brilliant effect and makes for easy reading. The book was composed and printed by the Wickersham Printing Company of Lancaster, Pa., and bound by Moore and Company of Baltimore. The typography and design are by Howard N. King.*